Third World Health

Hostage to first world wealth

Théodore H MacDonald LMus BSc, MA BTh, PhD, MD

Professor (emeritus), formerly Director of Postgraduate Studies in Health, Brunel University; Member of the Institute of Human Rights and Social Justice, Metropolitan University of London; Fellow Royal Society of Medicine

D0556114

Foreword by

Desmond M Tutu

Radcliffe Publishing
Oxford • Seattle

Radcliffe Publishing Ltd
18 Marcham Road
Abingdon
Oxon OX14 1AA
United Kingdom

www.radcliffe-oxford.com
Electronic catalogue and worldwide online ordering facility.

British Library Cataloguing in Publication Data

A catalogue record for this book is available from the British Library.

ISBN 1 85775 769 6

Typeset by Advance Typesetting Ltd, Oxford
Printed and bound by T J International, Padstow, Cornwall

Contents

Appendices

Foreword

My country was until the end of apartheid rule regarded by many as a 'third world' country because of the way in which the great majority of its citizens were compelled to live. Of course, it was not a third world nation for the white minority, most of whom enjoyed enviable health and educational facilities and a high economic standard of life. South Africa is still, in many respects, a third world nation, ravaged by HIV/AIDS (Human Immunodeficiency Virus/Acquired Immune Deficiency Syndrome), and we are progressing only slowly in overcoming many of the deficits of our once-divided society. I therefore identify with many of the issues raised in this book. The author's thorough analysis of the HIV/AIDS pandemic in Africa and elsewhere is not only statistically sound but intimately reflects his concern with the need for international equity.

Théodore MacDonald writes with passion, as well as with sense. Much of what he has to say is drawn from his own experience working as a medical doctor and a mathematician in a broad range of the world's poorest nations. But overarching that is a powerful insight into social and economic issues, along with well-honed skills as a communicator. His thorough knowledge of history and politics has enabled him to contextualise what he has witnessed and laboured to remedy. His writing style is astonishingly accessible, informing and inspiring the lay reader as much as the professional. The analyses underpinning both his exposition and his arguments are penetratingly accurate and embrace a wide readership. Where he feels that lay readers may be disadvantaged, he convincingly explains such technical matters as compound interest on loans, relevant statistical arguments, etc. It is regrettable but true that many books which address the issues herein from a position committed to equity are under-powered with respect to evidence and analytical rigour. Such certainly does not characterise the present volume.

The author deals in an admirably balanced style with vexatious issues which, in less experienced hands, could easily lead to shrill political rhetoric and narrow sectarian argument. But MacDonald clearly feels that the issues are far too important for ideological point-scoring. To him, the crucial thing is to equip the reader, lay or professional, not only with the facts but also with an insight into how they came about. Readers are often made aware of some particularly outrageous violation of human rights with respect to international trade – and the enormous health and social deficits which ensue – but this book allows us to see beyond these particulars to the consequences of sitting back and doing nothing. MacDonald persuades us of our power to influence local events, to develop an informed community stance on environmental issues, etc.

In discussing solutions, the author strongly makes the point that it is too easy to allow one's commitment to global justice to be siphoned off into something completely negative, like anti-Americanism. As he points out, the United States is the most powerful nation on earth and has a history of sustained commitment to the values of democracy, accountability and justice. He argues that we need to delve behind the actions of some of its large corporations: the globalisation of finance under terms favourable to corporate greed and exploitation. As a nation, the United States has contributed, and continues to do so, massively to human culture and civilisation. It is a repository of so many positive values, achievements and of so much creativity. The problem, argues the author, is not the dominance of one particular country in global economic affairs, but is our failure so far to truly transcend national interests in response to global needs. It was for that very purpose that the United Nations was established. But that organisation is often powerless under present rules governing it. It cannot intervene effectively without real transnational authority in areas such as health, education and other human rights.

I am pleased to recommend this splendid book enthusiastically.

Desmond M Tutu
Archbishop Emeritus
Capetown, South Africa
February 2005

Acknowledgements

In reality, and truly illustrative of the point made in this book itself, that individuals can only be effective in the context of community action, the present work came to fruition through the efforts of many people other than the author. Not all can be named – dozens of people in various countries whose work-related comments informed the research immensely, patients who shared confidences with me, etc. For direct field information I am especially indebted to Drs Govinda Dahal and Padam Simkhada, both recently senior health specialists in their own country, Nepal, but now active as researchers in Britain. Dr Tennyson Mgutshini, originally of Zimbabwe but now a specialist in mental health in England, was of enormous help in providing me with current data on HIV/AIDS incidence in that nation. Ray Adeyemi of Nigeria and now a nurse in London was also most helpful in this regard.

The actual word-processing of the text was a gargantuan task and one that I could not perform because of deteriorating vision. My very close friend, Dr Hannah Caller, a hospital doctor, and a number of our mutual comrades organised and carried all of that. They are: Dr Caroline Hodd, David Howarth, Scott Plimpton, Richard Roques and Cat Wiener. This involved not only hours of typing, but all of the high-tech production of the many complex charts and diagrams.

The publishers have provided outstanding support and editorial expertise in bringing this book to fruition and to them I offer deeply felt thanks. Especially due for mention are Gillian Nineham, Editorial Director; Susan Rabson, Promotions Manager; Paula Moran, Editorial Project Manager and Lisa Abbott, Editorial Assistant. Their skilfully coordinated efforts assured an exceptionally rapid transition from raw manuscript to the volume now in the hands of the reader.

Finally let me say that without the love and encouragement of my wife, Chris, and our son, Matthew, I would never have had the inner strength to have even started.

Théodore H MacDonald
February 2005

Needless to say, any errors or imperfections in this book are the author's own and he would welcome correspondence with his readers at theo@macdonaldbn17.fsnet. co.uk

This book is gratefully dedicated to the memory of

Bob Hunter
(13 October 1941–2 May 2005)

Greenpeace co-founder, whose direct action in initiating the Rainbow Warrior
was matched by his vision of ethical revolution – a great Canadian and
a true internationalist

Introduction

Why health?

About one quarter of the world's people live on one US dollar or less per day! Nearly 80% of our fellow inhabitants do not have reasonable access to clean water! Of course, such issues can be described as 'economic' or 'politic' – or both – but they quickly manifest themselves as health issues. Health, then, is a good barometer of equity/inequity worldwide. If a sizeable proportion of the world's people are in significantly worse health than the rest of us, then something must be wrong with the system. There are many causes, but the most obvious has to do with international trade and the globalisation of the US dollar. I argue that the huge discrepancies in health status between 'wealthy' and 'poor' nations are the cause of what I call 'trade-related illnesses'.

We, in the United Kingdom (UK), the United States (US), the European Union (EU), Japan, Canada, Australia, etc., have become so deeply accustomed to the theme of 'progress' since the nineteenth century that we tend to think it is universal. We, in the wealthier nations, are living longer and have better quality lives. Our sense of human dignity, our creativity in science and the arts, our advances in popular education, etc., have all been tremendously enhanced. Maybe that is why, in the 1970s, we stopped speaking of 'poor' countries or 'underdeveloped' countries, and started to use the phrase 'developing' nations. But that phrase really is a euphemism, a mistake, caused in good measure by our feeling that the 'progress' we were experiencing was 'universal', a 'given'. But it isn't.

My experience in working in many of these so-called 'developing' nations was that most of them were not 'developing' at all. They were going backwards, becoming more deprived. All of the relevant statistics garnered by UN agencies, such as the World Health Organization (WHO), and other international bodies, show the gap is widening. If this trend should be allowed to continue, the only outlook is an increase in preventable suffering and mortality, terrorism, war, famine, etc. It is not sustainable and the very survival of human civilisation is at stake.

This book shows that the analysis of international trading relations indicates that its present organisation and administration is grossly iniquitous. We have, since the 1930s, evolved a system of 'financial imperialism' that is much more devastating, and less costly to those profiting by it, than British imperialism in its heyday. We, in the wealthy nations, feel we have 'progressed' because we have foreign aid programmes which did not exist at government level before. Most of us are proud and willing to pay taxes to support it.

But something has gone wrong here, somehow.

In the late 1990s Ghana – which had previously taken out a World Bank (WB)/ International Monetary Fund (IMF) loan – found itself paying off the accumulating compound interest on it at such a rate that these annual disbursements were eight times higher than its spending on health and education combined. Effectively, the lending banks in the UK and US were making a profit out of aid to Ghana – and they still are.

Ghana is not an exception. Most of the poor nations on earth are supporting bank stockholders in a few rich ones. As will be explained in subsequent chapters, the poor nations have to trade in a global currency (US dollars). It is those trading relations which largely account for their appalling standards of domestic health. Their health is forfeit to the wealth of our banks and corporations. Moreover, their continued decline in health can be directly accounted for by the huge adjustments they have to make to domestic programmes to sustain foreign aid. As I show in succeeding chapters, such distortions lead to: massive deforestation, pollution of rivers and water sources, wars, abrogation of workers' rights, etc.

Throughout the book I will be raising the question 'But what can we do about it?' and will be exploring possible solutions. As they used to say during the Second World War, 'War is too important to be run by generals.' Or in this case, 'Peace, justice and the survival of civilisation are too important to leave up to bankers.'

Chapter I

Health and poverty

Life and death in Cambodia

All seemed normal when Sath, a 27-year-old Cambodian woman pregnant for the first time with twins, felt the onset of labour. Then she began to bleed profusely. No doctor was on duty at the nearby clinic – doctors in rural Cambodia made so little money that they often supported themselves by practising on the side – and no one in her village, Phum Dok Po, had a phone, so a relative bicycled to the nearest town to secure transport to the hospital. A taxi driver in the town agreed to take Sath the 30 miles to the hospital for US$37 – more than one third of Sath's husband's yearly income. Desperate, her husband borrowed the money from fellow farmers and sent Sath on her way. After a slow and jolting journey, along a muddy, difficult road, Sath reached the hospital but she had lost too much blood. Her first child was born dead, the second survived but Sath did not. A physician consulted after about her case concluded that the bleeding likely was caused by a tear in the birth tract made worse by anaemia, a lack of vitamin A and other uncomplicated conditions that ought not be fatal in the twenty-first century. 'People get sick because they are poor,' said Dr Nicole Seguy, medical coordinator in Cambodia for Doctors Without Borders (Médecins Sans Frontières). 'And also they get poor because they are sick.' A study by the relief agency Oxfam reports that 45% of Cambodian peasants who become landless have been forced to sell their acreage because of illness, making disease the largest single factor in the loss of agrarian livelihood. The first four most frequently reported diseases of those who lost land are malaria, Dengue fever, tuberculosis and typhoid – all preventable or curable diseases.

'The ill health ensures that a country will not be able to break the shackles of poverty,' says Jim Tullock, country representative for the Geneva-based World Health Organization (WHO), 'sickly children don't grow into productive workers. Money consumed fighting rearguard action against disease is money that won't be spent on economic development. A country whose population is chronically ill is a country which is condemned to remain forever on the edge of the abyss' (Nickerson, 2003).

Even in the wealthiest countries of the world, there is a measurable correlation between one's income and one's health. Taken worldwide, however, the relationship between the two is so strongly marked that a regression line[1] almost exactly lines up the countries according to wealth/health status, so that, as one moves from poorer to richer, one also moves from unhealthiest to healthiest (*see* Figure 1.1).

In Figure 1.1, the relationship between the gross national product (GNP) in US dollars (2002) and the number of children surviving up to five years of age per 1000 live births is shown for territories of population in excess of 250 000 (Rosling, 2004).

One can see at a glance that there is a strongly positive correlation suggested. The regression line would have a slope of about +5/9 and its regression equation would be (very roughly):

$$9y = 5x + 25$$

Overwhelmingly the data suggest that strong relationship. But, of course, there are exceptions. Take, for instance, Gabon – a wealthier nation, but low on child health. Again, the US (by far the wealthiest) has a level of child health considerably lower than that of many poorer communities. The reader can easily visualise a regression line drawn through this graph, even by eye, and can see that countries like the US and Gabon would fall below it – that is, considering their wealth level, other factors are depressing their child health levels. On the other hand, one tiny country is way off the regression line, far above it, according to its GNP. It is Cuba, and further away from the regression line than many other communities.

If we are to address the matter of health inequalities, we are going to have to look more closely at prevailing conditions in these 'aberrant' communities because they may easily give clues as to solutions. Obviously, prevailing social policy must be a factor. Nations can be extraordinarily rich (such as the Democratic Republic of Congo, Sierra Leone, etc.), by virtue of the fact that they are sitting on top of diamonds, copper or gold, but have a poor infrastructure socially. These are just some of the issues with which this book will deal. But before these matters can be addressed, a few basic definitions and usages are required.

Comparative wealth of nations

Early in its history (1945), the United Nations (UN) set about the difficult task of defining the relative wealth of nations. They came up with the categories: first world, second world, third world and fourth world (MacDonald, 2000). These were defined in terms of GNP (measured in US dollars), but along with some other socio-political factors. The first consisted of the large industrialised, democratic – free elections, etc. – countries. These now include the US, Canada, Britain, Australia, New Zealand, Japan, etc. The second world likewise consisted of modern, wealthy, industrialised countries, but under communist control. It obviously included the old USSR (Union of Soviet Socialist Republics) and Eastern European fraternal socialist countries. It did not include China because at that time China was not communist. In fact, China belonged to the third, to which the majority of the world belonged (and still do). As the Cold War developed, the first was sometimes referred to as the 'Free World' and the third as the 'Non-Aligned Nations'. The fourth world consisted of the really desperately poor nations – people living on less than US$100 annually – and included such states as Chad, Upper Volta (Burkina Faso), etc. Today more than one billion people still live on less than US$1 a day (Carr, 2004).

Such uncertain definitions became of less and less value for rational policy-making or analysis. The phrase 'third world' was particularly objected to as

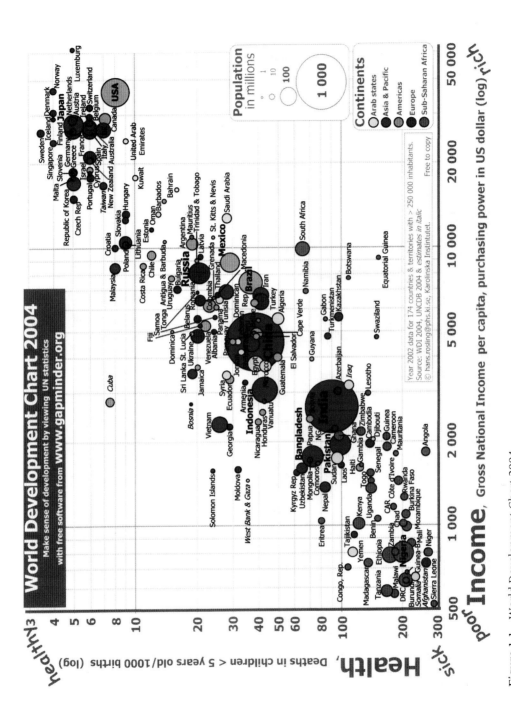

Figure 1.1   World Development Chart 2004.

Sources: WDI 2004, UNCDB 2004

politically incorrect and was replaced with such euphemisms as 'the developing nations'. This author has always resisted using such euphemisms, though, as they are manifestly misleading. Many of the nations concerned are not developing at all, but are going backward in the face of the globalisation of trade.

The latest (2004) UN classification designates five categories, as follows in descending order of GNP:

1 High Income Nations
2 Upper Middle Income Nations
3 Lower Middle Income Nations
4 Other Low Income Nations
5 Least Developed Nations.

The situation on the ground, so to speak, is that Category 1 nations, through the globalisation of the US dollar, are in a dominant fiscal relationship over Categories 2–5. For the sake of convenience – and in keeping with current general usage – Category 1 will be designated as the 'first' and all of the others as 'third'. Over 80% of the world's population is in Categories 3–5.

The link between health and wealth is unambiguously shown in Figure 1.2.

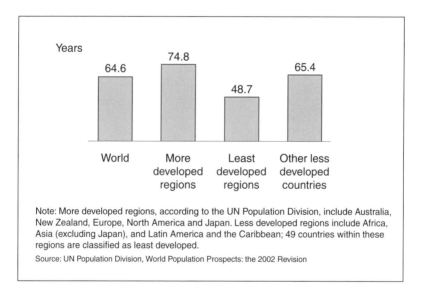

Figure 1.2: Life expectancy at birth (UN, 2003).

When citing charts, etc., from published sources, the author will quote the categories as cited in the original.

Let us look at another breakdown, which exhibits the connection even more strongly (*see* Table 1.1).

Table 1.1: Health spending per capita by country income level 1998

Income group	*Total spending on health per person US$*
Least developed countries	11
Other low income countries (per capita GNP < US$760 in 1998)	23
Lower middle income countries (per capita GNP between US$761 and US$3030 in 1998)	93
Upper middle income countries (per capita GNP between US$3031 and US$9360 in 1998)	241
High income countries (per capita GNP > US$9360 in 1998)	1907

The proportion of a community's money that can be devoted to healthcare obviously depends on the amount available to that community altogether. But only 11% of health spending globally is made available to the 80% of the world's population living in the third. These same countries account for 90% of world disease in total (WHO, 2000).

The WHO report cited above goes on to point out that in third world nations spending on healthcare is only about US$11 per *year*. This falls far below the US$35 or so stated by WHO as the minimum level of spending required if it is also to cover a minimal level of healthcare. Compare that with the US$2000 used yearly per person for healthcare in the first.

It is also a fact that the common diseases that almost exclusively afflict the poorest countries attract much less research funding and professional interest than do high-profile diseases in the first. The levels of spending in each case are largely determined by market forces, especially with regard to pharmaceuticals. Anderson *et al.* (1996) have shown that annual global research spending on malaria in 1990 was only US$65 per fatality due to the disease, opposed to US$789 per fatality due to asthma. In the four years 1975–1979, only 13 of the 1233 drugs that were available to the global market were directed at tropical infectious diseases of greatest concern to the poverty-stricken third world, according to the Global Forum for Health Research (2002).

During the last five years, such initiatives as the Global Alliance for Vaccines and Immunisation have been active in trying to counter this imbalance. They have been successful in stimulating more research and even development in the field, on diseases affecting the very poor nations. Notwithstanding such successes, the

Global Forum for Health Research asserts that only a small part of research and development spending is directed at diseases accounting for 90% of the world's health problems.

It goes without saying that people living in the third world must have significantly less access to modern medical technology than those in the first. Just in passing, consider the impact of HIV/AIDS (Human Immunodeficiency Virus/Acquired Immune Deficiency Syndrome). In the first, antiretroviral drugs are easily accessible. These are produced by the prominent pharmaceutical corporations at a cost far in excess of what the citizens of other countries can routinely be expected to pay. As we know, some of the larger poorer countries, such as South Africa, India and Brazil, have developed generic copies of these antiretrovirals. For some years these have been regarded as medically less efficacious than the commercial brands, but in June 1994, *The Lancet* published an article to the effect that there was no significant difference in efficacy between generic and commercial antiretrovirals (Asamoah-Odei, 2004). But, as a result of this legacy of inequity, AIDS-related mortality rates are soaring in Africa. At the July 2004 meeting in Bangkok of the 15th International AIDS Conference, Kofi Annan commented that HIV/AIDS has now gained a strong foothold also in Asia, although not yet nearly as acute as in some African nations. Particular attention is focused on this condition in Chapter 11. Suffice to say at this point, the impact of HIV/AIDS has already been such that average life expectancy is falling in a number of third world nations (Lamptey *et al.*, 2002). In the seven African countries of Angola, Botswana, Malawi, Mozambique, Rwanda, Zambia and Zimbabwe, the average life expectancy has declined to 40 years and less.

With respect to the Asamoah-Odei research cited above, it is interesting to note that, only a few weeks earlier, the *British Medical Journal* carried an article by Fiona Fleck on 26 June 2004, to the effect that nearly a year earlier, WHO had withdrawn two such generic AIDS drugs from their approval list. In September 2003, Fleck had revealed that the World Trade Organization (WTO) had – after eight months of stalling by the US delegation – finally agreed to give poor nations access to these drugs.

TRIPS

An acronym that occurs often in such discussions is TRIPS – standing for 'Trade-Related Intellectual Property Rights'. The above account of the generic AIDS drugs exemplifies the concept. The expensive pharmaceutical antiretrovirals are, of course, patented. Attempts by desperate third world scientists to create cheaper, domestically produced replacements would constitute a criminal offence if they attempted to sell the drugs in the first. But can the poor in the third world be held to ransom by such legislation? The argument continues but the WTO tries to impose it through its own regulations. Similar examples of this rapacious application of TRIPS against the third world poor, to the advantage of the rich in the first, have become legion since 2002.

Take genetically modified (GM) crops, for example. People tend to get caught up in concerns about their safety. But that is not the urgent issue. Since humankind has been growing crops, they have been genetically modifying food. Would Sir Walter Raleigh (1552–1618) even recognise a potato today as being just a series of genetic modifications of the tiny things he first brought to Europe? To produce GM foods, resistant to various pests, in the third world could represent a breakthrough for equity and health.

But if a particular GM crop is patented – as most are – and this is used (through TRIPS) as a means of preventing the third world routine access to them, that is a question of justice – a political rather than a scientific question. Even worse is the moral problem raised by large US corporations – e.g. Monsanto – patenting crops that are seedless. The third world farmer can use these to produce a magnificent yield of disease-free crops. But without being able to collect seeds for the next year's crop, he is stopped in his tracks. The seeds are only available by purchase from the patent holder – once more rendering third world health hostage to first wealth.

WHO and TRIPS

At the 56th World Health Assembly organised by WHO at Geneva in May 2003, TRIPS centred pivotally in the debate, as delegates argued about the appropriate response to the 'Report by the Secretariat on intellectual property rights, innovation and public health'.

Developed countries, and particularly the US, did not want WHO to take an aggressive approach to international property rights issues. In contrast, developing countries pushed for the delineation of a clearer role for WHO in evaluating the public health implications of increasing intellectual property rights protection in accordance with the Agreement on Trade-Related Aspects of Intellectual Property Rights (TRIPS), as well as under regional and bilateral trade agreements.

Furthermore, while the US focused on prevention and health promotion, many developing countries such as China, Brazil and Cuba wanted WHO to prioritise treatment and provide assistance to countries as necessary to ensure access for all to essential medicines. Brazil emphasised the significance of human rights in the fight against HIV/AIDS.

The US submitted a proposal that exclusively focused on the expression of intellectual property rights as the vehicle by which to spur innovation, and failed to make reference to the Doha Declaration on the TRIPS Agreement and Public Health. A coalition of non-governmental organisations (NGOs) – including Médecins Sans Frontières (MSF), Treatment Action Campaign, OXFAM and Canadian HIV/AIDS Legal Network – responded to the US's proposal, disputing the link between intellectual property protection and research and development, particularly into diseases that primarily affect developing countries, while at the same time pointing out the obvious role that intellectual property protection plays in creating access barriers to existing medicines through higher drug prices and weakened generic competition. A strong pro-health resolution that incorporated developing country concerns was brought to the table by Brazil and later co-sponsored by Bolivia, Ecuador, Indonesia, Peru, Venezuela and South Africa, on behalf of the members of the WHO African Region. The resolution advocated a clear mandate for WHO to monitor the impact of TRIPS, as well as bilateral and regional agreements, on public health and innovation, and also called for the creation of an independent commission similar to the United Kingdom Commission on Intellectual Property Rights. Extensive consultations between Brazil, the US and a number of African delegations led to the adoption of a compromise text in the final resolution on 'Intellectual Property Rights, Innovation and Public Health'. Included is a request for the establishment of a time-limited body to investigate appropriate funding and incentive methods for the development of new medicines for 'neglected diseases' as well as a request for WHO cooperation at the invitation of a member state to develop 'pharmaceutical and health policies and regulatory measures' to 'mitigate the negative impacts' of international trade agreements. NGOs expressed some disappointment with the final text of the resolution, as well as the exclusion of the text proposed by China, which would have reaffirmed the primacy of health over trade concerns and acknowledged the difficulties developing countries face in making use of compulsory licensing as provided for in the Doha Declaration.

Is this a case of, once again, trade rights having priority over health rights? Is this yet another example of a new and more efficient continuation of first world imperialism over the third?

At this point, and before returning to the main argument, it is important to consider the context within which really effective health can best be mediated. I refer to health promotion.

Healthcare and health promotion

The cluster of disciplines which have been coming together since the mid-1970s under the umbrella of 'health promotion' have produced a stable and respected area of expertise to the extent that there are now recognised journals of health promotion, university degree programmes in it and numerous books about it. Although the term 'health promotion' has only featured in the literature since the 1970s, it has been shown that the phenomenon of 'health promotion', as distinct from medicalisation, say, has been around since the dawn of European civilisation, if not before (MacDonald, 1998).

The major advance that we have made in the last 30 years or so is to appreciate just how valuable health promotion is in sustaining community health. When first discussed in the years from 1974 to 1980, while health promotion was recognised as a legitimate focus for study, it was seen almost as an extension of the 'normal' medicalisation of health. Over the intervening years, it is safe to say these two emphases have changed places. In modern first world societies medical advances have so greatly reduced the incidence and seriousness of clinical disease that only a small proportion of people now see medical care as their primary means of maintaining health. Education has guaranteed an increasing understanding of how to personally control lifestyle choices so as to enhance one's own experience of health.

But this is not the case, generally, in the third world. There are many reasons for this. For one thing, 'health promotion', as we have experienced it, is largely a Eurocentric phenomenon. This is true with respect to its origins and its development as dialectic. Thus it is not the sort of thing which can easily be exported to third world societies, in which too many of the contextual factors which render it effective and meaningful in the first are missing. This represents a serious problem because, in the broadest possible terms, health promotion must be global if it is to be of any use anywhere. It is obviously nonsense to speak of, say, 'national' health promotion policies while we know that the really crucial variables – such as environmental pollution, or poisoning of the food chain – are transnational concerns requiring transnational means of control.

In trying to resolve this problem, some people see the matter in terms of cultural differences. Cultural factors – family structures, moral values, food production and distribution systems, etc. – vary from society to society. Would a complete insight into these cultural differences solve the problem? This book takes a different approach. While recognising that any increase in insights into one another's cultures must help, it takes the view that these factors are fairly minor compared to one overriding factor. It is this author's considered belief that the most important factor by far in inhibiting effective health promotion in the third world is the relationship between first and third worlds, and most especially the trading relations which have been developed between them throughout the history of European colonialism. Indeed, it is only these very trading relationships which make sense of the terms 'first world' and 'third world'.

More specifically, the author argues that our attempts to address the problems of gross economic inequity between nations since the end of the Second World War, principally the formation and activities of the International Monetary Fund and the World Bank, have themselves rendered the problem even more intractable. It is argued that if health promotion is to become global, we need to change totally the economic structures which sustain these two agencies. Therefore, while the focus of this book will be on health and health promotion, it will be argued extensively in economic terms. For that reason, the discourse has been structured as follows.

The rest of this chapter will begin to address the nest of problems that besets first health. These include attempts to impose Eurocentric solutions to problems arising in non-Eurocentric contexts, how 'third worldism' is defined, the role of political ideologies and the phenomenon of international debt. Subsequent chapters then deal with the rebound effects of the debt crisis on health promotion globally. Crucial to understanding of this is some insight into first 'belief models' about the third world, and this issue is dealt with in a chapter challenging the logical validity of many of these beliefs. Before those chapters embodying case studies of a number of third world countries, an overview analysis is given of aetiological and epidemiological differences between community health in third world and first world societies.

Having thus set an agenda of identifying problematic issues and having established their relevance to global health promotion, we consider the particulars of how these factors impact on particular health initiatives in the third. This then allows us to close the book with a discussion of possible solutions. The guiding leitmotif throughout is that, as the dictates of humanity transcend cultural and national values, health promotion itself must ultimately be conceived globally to be effective locally.

In July 2000, a new and highly relevant UN document from that body's Economic and Social Council, and for which Professor Eibe Riedel was Rapporteur, appeared on the Treaty Bodies Database of the United Nations Human Rights website. As Professor of German and Foreign Public Law, International Law and European Law in the Faculty of Law, the Pro-Vice-Chancellor for Research at the University of Mannheim, Professor Riedel is one of the world's leading jurists in his fields of expertise. Those who collaborated with him in producing this document are also academics and practitioners of the highest international distinction. 'General Comment No. 14 (2000)' is entitled: 'Substantive Issues Arising in the Implementation of the International Covenant on Economic, Social and Cultural Rights: The Right to the Highest Attainable Standard of Health'.

This brilliant piece of work clearly counterpoints many of the themes of the present book. It raises issues of immense relevance. For instance, if this signal work of Professor Riedel and his colleagues ever becomes regarded, as is clearly intended, as a customary measure of international justice, expressive and protective of fundamental international human rights, then certain structural adjustment policies (SAPs) imposed on developing nations as a condition for IMF support, and which call for a diminution of the public sector in health in favour of private sector enhancement, might well become legally as well as morally problematic. At the very least, we must expect governments and agencies such as the IMF and World Bank to comply with the letter and spirit of this new code.

The relevance of every part of this document (included in this book as Appendix F) is such that this author can only recommend that the reader refer to it freely while considering the ideas raised in my text. In my view, this document will prove to represent a major contribution to international equity in the arena of human rights with respect to health.

Within-community variation and between-community variation

As we know, even *within* such first countries as Great Britain and the United States, there are variations in health. These are particularly acute in the US, where about 32% of the population is unable to afford health insurance and where 'Medicare' and 'Medicaid'[2] provision varies from state to state. Even in such first world nations as Holland, Finland and the UK, the poor die about seven or eight years before the rich. And that is in countries in which all citizens have access to healthcare. Such apparent anomalies can, to a great extent, be accounted for by the fact that poorer people are more likely to seek out pre-cooked meals because they lack the income for good kitchen facilities. They are likely to smoke more and to drink more. They also live in less safe areas of large cities, etc. For instance, in the London Borough of Newham (one of the poorest boroughs in Britain), a primary schoolchild is six times more likely to be run over than is the case in the London Borough of Richmond-upon-Thames. In the latter borough, of course, there are far more parks and play areas safe from road traffic (NHS, 1999/2000).

Likewise, obviously, there is within-country health access variation within the poorest countries of the world. But if we look at the actual diseases that contribute most to the between-community discrepancies in health, we find that the most common are various tropical parasitic diseases such as malaria, and diseases like HIV/AIDS, which depend on widespread lack of education and human rights and lack of access to pharmaceutical prophylactics for their spread and their impact.

In the third world, and especially among the poorest, many of the standard measures of wealth or poverty are not applicable.

The Demographic and Health Survey program (DHS), set up originally in Latin America in the early 1990s, is now proving to be one of the most powerful measures of health status in the third world ever devised. It is a survey research project that is being carried out in Africa, Asia and Latin America. Arising from its initial pilot studies, it is based on measures such as the ownership of (or access to) a refrigerator, television and radio; possession of a car, motorcycle or bicycle; how the household dwelling is constructed and with what materials; the dwelling's source of drinking water; how toilet facilities are mediated; as well as the employment of domestic staff. Obviously, some of the index criteria, such as access to drinking water, are criteria also for health status directly (DHS, 2003).

The household wealth index, in use in the study of the DHS criteria mentioned above, allows researchers to determine a 'country specific' or 'relative' definition of economic status, rather than an 'absolute' definition. They divided the population of each country into five income groups or quintiles, calculated on the bases of their relative standing on the household wealth index within each country involved. For example, the economic status of the lowest quintile in Haiti would not be at all similar to that of the poorest quintile in Argentina (World Bank, 2003).

Economists engaged in such studies of global research often use an 'absolute' or 'universal' measure of poverty. Such an approach tries to define poverty in terms of a minimal level of income or of consumption that is universally applicable and fixed in time. The reader can appreciate the difficulties involved. It would work somewhat as follows. Researchers would estimate the minimal amount of money required for food and other essentials across the countries concerned. Consideration of what level of nutrition is to be taken as basic or of what constitutes 'other essentials' are the subject of much analysis and argumentation.

In 2001–2002, the World Bank calculated that the 'international' or 'absolute' poverty line was approximately US$1 per day average income, but even this had to be statistically adjusted for variations in purchasing power between countries. In the author's experience, while working in communities where such discussions are not academic, the sheer obscenity of real people living out their lives like this is overwhelming.

The World Bank estimated, in 2002, that 1.2 billion people were living (surviving!) on less than US$1 a day. They point out that this represents progress because it is down from 1.3 billion people (a difference of 100 million) in 1990. However, the author calculated – using the same sources – that over the same period there was an *increase* in the number of people living below US$2 per day. That is, money was being transferred from the already desperately poor to those who were even more desperately poor! Any kind of equitable global wealth aid system would shift the money easily from the first to the third to remove *both* obscenities. It would make negligible impact on citizens in the first, while having an enormous impact on the health of people in the third.

Measures such as levels of education, existing health status, languages used and foreign languages known,[3] and living conditions, can be used as crude estimates for determining economic well-being. Such measures can draw attention to aspects of poverty that would otherwise escape notice. In other words, we need to become far more conscious of 'types' of poverty in preparing to address these issues. This will involve the need to go further than standard measures of income and consumption allow us to do in ascertaining levels of poverty and their impact on health.

'The World Bank once viewed poverty as largely income-based, but now we see it as multidimensional' (Quesada, 2003). Much of this change in emphasis is due to the germinal insights of Amartya Sen, who in 1998 won the Nobel Prize in Economics. Specifically, he objected to the conventional ways of measuring poverty, based on working out the share of people whose incomes fell below some 'poverty line'. He is quoted as saying: 'You cannot draw a poverty line and then apply it across the board to everyone in the same way, without taking into account personal characteristics and circumstances.' What Sen advocated was that poverty analysis needs to focus on a person's access to opportunities (profoundly affected by native language, in this author's view) in health and education as well as his/her social capabilities (Mach, 2003).

Within-poor-community variation

The author has already referred to the 'within' community variations in health in such wealthy countries as the UK and the US. Lessons to be learned from this include the sobering realisation that domestic health legislation cannot alone level the playing field, much to the chagrin of social democratic thinkers. For instance, the inception of the National Health Service (NHS) in Britain was hailed as a brilliant triumph for socialist (Labour Party) health legislation in 1948. The author recalls it being referred to by a Marxist-Leninist lecturer in Czechoslovakia at the time as 'so good it will be even as good as the Soviet Union', as he excitedly translated from an editorial in the English-language *Manchester Guardian*. As we know from the Black Report (DHSS, 1980) and other findings, huge (and increasing) gaps in health status within the population prevail, despite an NHS which confers treatment without cost to the patient. In the US there is no equivalent to the NHS, so the same situation is less unexpected.

But what happens in the third, in which government healthcare is patchy or – more commonly – non-existent? Let us look at a number of dimensions of health status as discussed earlier. Care-seeking behaviour, diagnosis and actual treatment, along with disease, incidence and mortality rates, are all measures that are inextricably wealth-dependent. DHS data provided the basis for a huge multicountry study covering the 12-year period from 1990 to 2002. It showed poor/non-poor differences in health status and in use made of existing health services across a whole gamut of reproductive health indicators. *See* Table 1.2 for country-by-country results. As well as that, other multicountry studies have demonstrated statistically significant relationships between health and economic status.

Notes

1 The reader who is unsure as to what a regression line is will be helped by Appendix A.
2 Medicaid: in the US, a publicly funded scheme provides medical aid to people below a certain income level. Medicare is a similar scheme for the elderly.
3 One only needs to work in the third world to realise that people whose native tongue embraces millions – as opposed to, say, one of the 300 languages spoken in Vanuatu – confers enormous health advantage by virtue of increased access to information. To be even partially fluent in a foreign language such as English has an enormous impact on health and opportunities generally.

References

Anderson J (1996) *Malaria Research: an audit of international activity.* PRISM report 7, The Wellcome Trust, Unit for Policy Research in Science and Medicine, London, p.29.

Asamoah-Odei E (2004) HIV prevalence trends in sub-Saharan Africa – no decline and large sub-regional differences. *The Lancet.* 3 July. **364**: 35–40.

Carr D (2004) Improving the health of the world's poorest people. *Health Bulletin 1.* Population Reference Bureau, Washington, DC.

Demographic and Health Survey (DHS) (2003) *Demographic and Health Survey Progress Dimensions No. 4. Fall 2002.* HMSO, London.

Department of Health and Social Security (DHSS) (1980) *Inequalities in Health: The Black Report.* HMSO, London.

Global Forum for Health Research (2002) *Report on Health Research 2001–2002.* International Cochrane Collection, Oxford. www.globalforumhealth.com

Gwatkin D and Davidson R (2003) Initial Country-Level Information About Socio-Economic Differences in Health, Nutrition and Population. November. Karolinska Institutet, Stockholm, Sweden.

Lamptey P, Wigley M, Carr D and Collymore Y (2002) *Facing the HIV/AIDS Pandemic.* Population Reference Bureau, p.1.

MacDonald T (1998) *Rethinking Health Promotion; a global approach.* Routledge, London.

MacDonald T (2000) *Third World Health Promotion and its Dependence on First Health.* Edwin Mellon Press, Lewiston, NY.

Mach A (2003) Amartya Sen on development and health. *To Our Health.* Accessed online at www.who.int/infwha52/to-our-health/amartya.html.

National Health Service (NHS) (1999/2000) *Newham Health Improvement Programme.* p.15. HMSO, London.

Nickerson C (2003) Lives lost in Cambodia. *The Boston Globe*. 4 January.

Quesada C (2003) Amartya Sen and the thousand faces of poverty. IDB America. Accessed online at www.ladb.org.

Rosling H (2004) *Global Health Chart of 174 Communities with 250,000+ Inhabitants*. Division of International Health, Department of Public Health Sciences, Karolinska University, Stockholm.

Sen A (1999) *Health in Development*. Bulletin of the World Health Organization. No. 77 pp 619–23.

UN (2003) *UN Population Division, World Population Prospects: the 2002 Revisions*. United Nations, NY.

World Health Organization (WHO) (2000) *Special Theme: Inequalities in Health*. Bulletin of the World Health Organization, Geneva, No. 78 p.216.

World Bank (2003) *World Development Indicators*. World Bank, Washington, DC, p.193.

Table 1.2: Poor non-poor inequalities in health – selected indicators

Country	Under-5 mortality rate (deaths of children under 5 per 1000 live births)		Malnutrition among women/mothers (% with Body Mass Index* < 18.6 kg/m²)*		Children aged 12 months to 23 months who were fully vaccinated (%)		Women receiving delivery assistance from a doctor or nurse/ midwife (%)	
	Poorest quintile	Richest quintile	Poorest quintile	Richest quintile	Poorest quintile	Richest quintile	Poorest quintile	Richest quintile
East Asia, Pacific								
Cambodia, 2000	155	64	24	17	29	68	15	81
Indonesia, 1997	109	29	–	–	43	72	21	89
Philippines, 1998	80	29	–	–	60	87	21	92
Vietnam, 1997	63	23	–	–	42	60	49	99
Vietnam, 2000	53	16	–	–	44	92	58	100
Europe, Central Asia								
Armenia, 2000	61	30	3	4	66	(68)	93	100
Kazakhstan, 1995	48	40	11	7	21	(34)	99	100
Kazakhstan, 1999	82	45	7	9	69	(62)	99	99
Kyrgyz Republic, 1997	96	49	7	7	69	73	96	100
Turkey, 1993	125	27	3	3	41	82	43	99
Turkey, 1998	85	33	2	2	28	70	53	98
Turkmenistan, 2000	106	70	11	10	86	89	97	98
Uzbekistan, 1996	70	50	12	8	81	78	92	100
Latin America and the Caribbean								
Bolivia, 1998	147	32	0.5	2	22	31	20	98
Brazil, 1996	99	33	9	5	57	74	72	99
Colombia, 1995	52	24	6	1	58	77	61	98
Colombia, 2000	39	20	3	3	50	65	64	99
Dominican Republic, 1996	90	27	10	6	34	47	89	98
Guatemala, 1995	89	38	4	2	49	46	9	92
Guatemala, 1998	78	39	4	0.5	66	56	9	92
Haiti, 1994–1995	163	106	25	9	19	44	2	65
Haiti, 2000	164	109	17	8	25	42	4	70
Nicaragua, 1997–1998	69	30	4	4	61	73	33	92
Nicaragua, 2001	64	19	3	4	64	71	78	99
Paraguay, 1990	57	20	–	–	20	53	41	98
Peru, 1996	110	22	1	1	55	66	14	97
Peru, 2000	93	18	1	2	58	81	13	88
Middle East/North Africa								
Egypt, 1995	147	39	–	–	65	93	21	86
Egypt, 2000	98	34	1	0.1	91	92	31	94
Jordan, 1997	42	25	3	2	21	17	91	99
Morocco, 1992	112	39	6	2	54	95	5	78
Yemen, 1997	163	73	39	13	8	56	7	50
South Asia								
Bangladesh, 1996–1997	141	76	65	33	47	67	2	30
Bangladesh, 1999–2000	140	72	–	–	50	75	4	42
India, 1992–1993	155	54	–	–	17	65	12	79
India, 1998–1999	141	46	50	15	21	64	16	84
Nepal, 1996	156	83	26	21	32	71	3	34
Nepal, 2001	130	68	27	15	54	82	4	45
Pakistan, 1990–1991	125	74	–	–	23	55	5	55

Table 1.2:   Continued

Sub-Saharan Africa								
Benin, 1996	208	110	21	7	38	74	34	98
Benin, 2001	198	93	16	6	49	73	50	99
Burkina Faso, 1998–1999	239	155	16	9	21	52	18	75
Cameroon, 1991	201	82	–	–	27	64	32	95
Cameroon, 1998	199	87	12	4	24	57	28	89
Central African Republic, 1994–1995	193	98	16	11	18	64	14	82
Chad, 1996–1997	171	172	28	21	4	23	3	47
Comoros, 1996	129	(87)	7	9	40	82	26	85
Cote d'Ivoire, 1994	194	97	11	6	16	64	17	84
Eritrea, 1995	152	104	45	21	25	84	5	74
Ethiopia, 2000	159	147	32	25	7	34	0.9	25
Gabon, 2000	93	55	9	4	6	24	67	97
Ghana, 1993	156	75	12	7	38	79	25	85
Ghana, 1998	139	52	18	5	50	79	18	86
Guinea, 1999	230	133	17	9	17	52	12	82
Kenya, 1998	136	61	18	6	48	60	23	80
Madagascar, 1997	195	101	24	15	22	66	30	89
Malawi, 1992	253	172	14	6	73	89	45	78
Malawi, 2000	231	149	10	6	65	81	43	83
Mali, 1995–1996	298	169	16	12	16	56	11	81
Mali, 2001	248	148	13	10	20	56	8	82
Mauritania, 2000–2001	98	79	17	9	16	45	15	93
Mozambique, 1997	278	145	17	4	20	85	18	82
Namibia, 1992	110	76	19	5	54	63	51	91
Namibia, 2000	55	31	–	–	60	68	55	97
Niger, 1998	282	184	27	13	5	51	4	63
Nigeria, 1990	240	120	–	–	14	58	12	70
Rwanda, 2000	246	154	12	7	71	79	17	60
Senegal, 1997	181	70	–	–	–	–	20	86
South Africa, 1998	87	22	–	–	51	70	68	98
Tanzania, 1996	140	98	12	7	57	83	27	81
Tanzania, 1999	160	135	–	–	53	78	29	83
Togo, 1998	168	97	13	8	22	52	25	91
Uganda, 1995	192	113	13	6	34	63	23	70
Uganda, 2000–2001	192	106	15	5	27	43	20	77
Zambia, 1996	212	136	10	8	71	86	19	91
Zambia, 2001–2002	192	92	21	10	64	80	20	91
Zimbabwe, 1994	85	56	6	1	72	86	55	93
Zimbabwe, 1999	100	. 62	9	4	64	64	57	94

Note: Figures have been rounded.
* Body Mass Index is based on weight in kilograms divided by square of height in meters. In some countries, surveys measured malnutrition among women ages 15 to 49 or 15 to 44; in other countries, the surveys measured malnutrition among women with children under 5 years of age.
( ) Parentheses indicate that the figure is based on a relatively small number of cases and may not be reliable.
Source: Gwatkin *et al*, 2003
dash = data not available

Chapter 2

Problems caused by inequities in wealth and by environmental damage

The Christmas 2004 earthquake and tsunamis

In late December of 2004, as we all know, an earthquake with epicentre beneath the ocean floor about 10 km off the coast of Indonesia occurred. It announced the fact that at the touching line between two tectonic plates, one plate overlapped the other under great pressure. The forces released beneath the upper plate pushed the ocean floor up at least 10 metres and it then dropped back again. The earthquake was highly destructive on its own account, but what followed was much worse. The upward and downward movement of the plate sent shock waves running along the ocean floor in several directions. As these vibrations along the ocean floor approached land masses – Indonesia being the closest and first affected, then India, Sri Lanka, the Maldives, etc., even Kenya and Somalia – they were forced to the water surface, creating enormous tsunamis. These raced ashore at speeds of up to 450+ km/hour. This meant that the water carried inland for considerable distances (depending on the contour of whatever land surfaces it struck) causing massive destruction and loss of life in its wake. Such tsunami events – and the horrific impacts on health and economies they can cause – are dealt with in greater detail further on in this chapter.

The scientific community has known for more than 50 years where the tectonic plates lie and where the boundaries between them are. One such boundary is the San Andreas Fault, underlying about 600 miles of California and the western US. Major constructions – buildings, power stations, etc. – have been built on land overlying the fault. These are not stable areas in that along the fault the two plates are slowly moving past one another. At irregular intervals in the past the plates have collided, momentarily overlapping then falling back into place. These events have caused earthquakes of varying severity. The devastating San Francisco earthquake of 1906 was one such example. Obviously means of predicting these events are a global and not merely a regional concern.

As the catastrophe of the Indonesian earthquake and its aftermath made abundantly clear, mechanisms for detecting and reporting tsunami activity cannot remain entirely a matter of whether or not a region can afford the technology. It has to be a globally organised and monitored responsibility, non-contingent on variations in local financial resources. Even as I pen these words in January 2005, only rough estimates of the numbers of people killed or injured are available. We do know that it is already the largest single disaster with which the UN has been confronted. The health consequences following on, as survivors huddle in temporary encampments without access to unpolluted water supplies or medical intervention, have been predicted to kill as many people as did the initial impacts.

This author now would like to draw the reader's attention to the media reportage. The way in which the media has handled the story is crucial for the impact it had on appealing to the levels of altruism and generosity of ordinary people all over the world. The media have also conveyed the feeling that the events themselves were entirely a 'natural' disaster – unconnected with politics and other controllable human activity. But to accept such an interpretation is immensely disempowering. As the rest of this chapter makes clear, our water resources, offshore facilities and beaches are being exploited prodigiously – not so much for the benefit of local inhabitants as for the profitable enterprises and banks financing them from wealthy nations.

The wonderful and immediate displays of selfless generosity by millions of people have once again illustrated the sublime heights of social conduct of which the human spirit is capable. The need is prodigious and will always be because many catastrophes are happening which the media do not feature. To own and operate any of the media, especially television, requires immense financial resources. People and agencies having access to such wealth have their own agendas to consider. Basic human needs and rights do not necessarily rank high on these agendas. Under rational conditions, of course, response to local disasters should not have to depend on pop stars and others manipulating the honest emotions of millions to give. What is required is a transnational agency that can instantly collate resources as required on the basis of impartial access to information. The UN was set up ostensibly to be such an agency, but it is so constituted that its activities can be curtailed at will by local interest groups and governments. For instance, on 8 January 2005, Kofi Annan visited Sri Lanka as part of the coordination of the UN's relief work. The government of Sri Lanka prevented him from visiting Tamil areas (particularly badly affected) thus forcing local political interests to dominate over global ones. As the UN is presently constituted, Kofi Annan could do nothing about it. For some reason, the ongoing conflicts in the Congo, Sierra Leone, the Solomon Islands, Sudan, etc., have not attracted much media pleading for urgent aid. Ongoing disasters such as what is happening in Israel and the Palestinian territories are heavily distorted by the media in different countries for different financial interests.

At the same time, many powerful figures in media ownership have a vested interest in undermining the UN. These same interests have been successful in persuading large numbers of people that the UN is ineffective and even corrupt. To take just one current example, in the Republic of Congo, certain UN peacekeepers have been accused of serious crimes, such as rape, etc. This has been widely used by the media to show that the UN is failing. But the UN itself does not have final control over who is selected and how to serve as its peacekeepers in various trouble spots. Again other interests decide and the UN has to make do with what it is given. If one goes behind media reports of the so-called 'Oil for Food' scandal in Iraq, one finds a similar pattern.

But if not the UN, what? It is obvious that we need to make sure that the UN does have the power to act over and above national interests to mediate peace and conditions for equity and justice. Let us look at the financial question again. Just how much money is available? At the last three G8 meetings, as of January 2005, specific financial promises were made by first world governments to third world governments, but most of these remain unfulfilled. Thus, there is a great difference between international aid pledged by first world governments and the amount that actually is delivered. We are told so far that, between them, the US and the UK governments have *pledged* £500 million (US$690 million) for tsunami disaster relief. But they have so far actually *spent* US$12 *billion* for 660 days of military involvement in Iraq. What this means is that the total US pledge for assistance to disaster relief is only worth 1.5 (approximately) days (or 1/200th) of what they have already spent on the war! The UK government pledge comes to about 5.5 days of money already spent promoting Britain's military intervention in Iraq.

The great majority of people, in both the UK and the US – moved by sense and empathy – have pledged enormous sums of their own money and goods. It seems most unlikely that they would have volunteered so much to promote and prosecute the war, largely on the grounds that there had to be a less destructive alternative. If the UN really were empowered as a transnational organisation, about 10% of that money could have been called upon to create conditions that rendered war and the deaths, injuries, destruction of centres of international historical and cultural significance and spoliation of the civic fabric much less likely. Indeed, it could have been demanded of governments (the war has proved that the money is there!) and would not have to rely on the media deciding on which catastrophes to call upon people to contribute to. Media coverage plays a huge role in determining how much of their own money people give and to which disasters.

The solutions to these issues are not simple. But we cannot dodge the question because it is awkward. In democracies we do have some opportunity to influence government thinking on transnational issues. I deal with these to some extent in Chapter 14.

The broad picture

In this book the author aims to consider the crucial question of how the health of at least 80% of the world's people is adversely affected by distorted trading relations. But these trading relations themselves have a convoluted lineage and it will be necessary to identify useful historical elements that provide a rational basis for understanding what is happening, as well as suggesting avenues for solutions. On top of all that, we are facing rapid ecological and climate changes. Global warming springs to mind. But global warming has been governing ecological and climate change on Earth for as much as 50 million years (*The Observer*, 2004). The entry of humanity into the equation has been exacerbating the situation for millennia and our various civilisations, as well as their rise and fall, have both been governed by climate change as well as accelerating it.

Therefore, we must realise that our present predicament is not a novelty but merely part of a long continuum. It is not enough to identify modern villains – international corporate greed, imperial interests, capitalist industrial corporations – as the cause of all the problems, so that the solutions lie entirely in eliminating them. Rather, we must examine an entire matrix of issues and approach solutions in terms of other types of globalisation. The solutions cannot be local. We can only *act* locally – often at the tiniest community level – but must always *think* globally.

Existing inequities in wealth represent as good a starting point as any. It will be argued in this chapter that these discrepancies foster: exploitation, ecological destruction, diseases and war. Moreover, these in turn often promote short-term solutions disadvantageous to all but a few.

War as a solution?

War is an obvious example. It has accompanied human history from as far back as we are able to know. But do wars work or have they ever worked? A better way to phrase the question is: have they ever solved long-term the problems which led to the war in the first place? The author would now – for most wars – argue in the negative: one war seems always to lay the groundwork for the next one because the problems leading to the preceding one re-emerge. Also, when one thinks about it, it is often difficult to pinpoint the real 'winners' after a war. The soldiers on either side rarely gain enough personally out of it to justify the danger, terror, uncertainty and family break-ups that they had to undergo. Non-combatant civilians – especially in the war zone itself – are usually obvious losers as well.

There are winners, but on the whole they are people who never took any chances. They were generally outside of the war zone, possibly financing or equipping the war, but in no danger of personal harm. As has been shown in modern times, such people would often be winners whichever side declared itself the victor. As many of my friends, who had fought in Korea, used to say: 'The only participants who were completely safe at the time were the bankers and businessmen sitting comfortably in boardrooms in New York. And, you know, they were the only ones who stood to make a profit out of it!' No doubt the same could have been said about bankers in boardrooms all over the world and on both sides of the conflict.

War seems to be so ingrained in human thinking and expression that some have described it as an instinct. Other animals fight members of their own species, but comparatively rarely to the kill. The issues – be it disputes over a mate or food – are usually resolved by the loser leaving. So far as we know, those other animal types are not governed by overarching principles, such as morality, justice, truth, etc. We may have inherited the instinct to fight, but have retained it as other 'higher' faculties have continued to evolve. This has produced a dreadful cocktail, if that is so!

What we do know – as rational beings – is that things cannot continue as they are at the moment. The financial discrepancies between the first and third world nations are becoming more acute. This alone means that the latter harbour diseases from which we can only momentarily remain protected, but from which they routinely suffer and die. Clearly the threat of pandemics thus hangs over all of us because of the ease of frequent international travel. However, the problems go much deeper. In the rest of this chapter the author will briefly outline them.

Global finance

International trade, even if transacted fairly, requires money and the matter is facilitated if the currency used is transnational. The US dollar is now the currency of international trade, but there are currently serious barriers to the transactions being fair. If the US dollar is the international finance medium, then the nations outside of the first world have to develop their produce so as to attract US dollars in export to such an extent that their entire domestic economies are compromised. It is a common characteristic of small, non-industrialised countries that they are only able to produce one or two crops – such as sugar or coffee – that will attract US dollars as exports. This imposes a raft of follow-ons on the economies of such nations.

For instance, the export crop suddenly becomes so crucial that food production for routine domestic consumption gets drastically cut back. Cultivation of maize is required to sustain the local people, but it is useless as a dollar export. A sudden increase in the production of a crop like coffee results in food loss domestically, and hence in increased susceptibility to malnourishment and disease. Then, as well, the export crop has to be brought to ports. This involves a large-scale destruction of forests, etc., to create reliable roads. Routinely, machinery has to be produced and run at commercial levels, leading to a huge increase in the demand for oil – which is paid for in US dollars. Deforestation is one major assault on the local ecology but it very quickly produces a range of pollutants which degrade the ecosystem even more and brings a host of new diseases in its wake.

The intensification of specialised agriculture – to increase the yields of the export crops – requires fertilisers, which in turn pollute the rivers and streams, killing off many local enterprises such as fishing for domestic use. At the trade level, these poorer communities often are forced to compete with one another to produce one commodity. Cane sugar is a very common one. The price it can attract from the buyers is determined by the latter's needs. The producers are often thus pushed to the wall and – having become dependent on that one product – find themselves no longer able to feed themselves.

Water, water everywhere – but not to drink

The reader is no doubt aware that fresh water is not a commodity to be taken for granted worldwide. Very few humans have it on tap, and many of those who do have no guarantee of its potability and freedom from infection. In most of the places in which the author has been privileged to be of service, all except the very wealthy people have to carry water long distances for domestic necessities. Diarrhoea, because of infected water, kills large numbers of infants and frail old people. These deaths – and the inconsolable suffering attendant on them – are largely prevent-able, but not under the present inbuilt inequities between the wealthy and the poor nations.

Even in countries such as the Dominican Republic, a major tourist spot for wealthy people from the first world, tap water is routinely unsafe. The wealthy buy safe water in large bottles, regularly delivered to hotels and to their homes, but the great bulk of the population routinely experience typhoid and other water-borne diseases. Death by such causes is so common and yet within hailing distance of thoughtless pleasure-seekers, who know nothing about it. The ostentatious displays of wealth in that country have to be seen to be believed.

While working over there in medicine in 1985–1987, I constantly met up with tourists and the local wealthy expatriate community, who resolutely did not want to know what was happening so close at hand. They were 'enjoying themselves' and found such information 'unsettling'. They would return to the US and the UK and elsewhere and rave about how lovely the Dominican Republic was. The degraded lives of the dispossessed had nothing to do with them. In a fair world, of course, such attitudes can have no place. Let us take a brief historical look at the development of our relationship with the planet's water supply.

Before the European 'industrial revolution' of the eighteenth and nineteenth centuries, people all over had a somewhat similar association with water. They relied almost exclusively on water available at, or near, the surface of the earth. Rivers, lakes and springs constituted the most commonly used sources. Indeed, it was widely assumed that these sources were inexhaustible, due to the evaporation–rain cycle.

However, in Europe and North America, rapid industrialisation quickly changed all that. Large quantities of the easily accessible water were needed to run generators and other machinery. River sources – and more recently ocean coastlines – became polluted and unfit for use. Sewerage systems became necessary as larger concentrations of people grew up around ports and factories. In the first world, we began our long-term exploitation of underground water resources (aquifers) and even the elaboration of huge desalination enterprises. Aquifers refer to water-bearing rocks, or rock complexes, underground.

As Nares Craig (2002) points out in his book, the first world and some of the third are now exploiting the aquifers at a prodigious rate. Without some kind of international mediation and control, it is difficult to see how this can continue. Aquifers contain about 97% of the planet's water supply. Increasingly these very sources face the danger of pollution, but simply their rate of use must cause alarm. Water tables are now dropping at the rate of three metres annually, according to some estimates.

In the prairie states of the US and the prairie provinces of Canada, up to 15 metres of water are being extracted yearly, while the natural replacement rate of 1 cm is only $^1/_{1500}$ of that!

It is anticipated that aquifer sources of water in North America and Australia will be exhausted by about 2030. Of course, the impact of all this will not be felt first or most adversely in the first world, but in the nations of the third world. As Craig (2002) points out, Beijing's water table has dropped 59 metres in only 40 years! Out of 2.6 million wells in Beijing province, and in two neighbouring provinces, over 100 000 had run dry by 2000.

Even more obscenely, the use on an industrial scale of this non-renewable source strictly for profit in the first world is increasing year by year. It has to be curbed and soon. Even some first world people themselves are now imminently threatened by it – but, of course, it is the poor who bear the greatest brunt.

How about a game of golf?

Golf course maintenance requires extraordinary quantities of fresh water and some lavish clubs, built in poorer countries for the use of wealthy tourists, threaten local people as far apart as Fiji, North, South and Central Africa, Jamaica and the Philippines. The matter has recently become serious even in some first world countries. The US and Canada, and even the UK in the past two years have expressed concerns about it. Giles Trimlett (2004), a reporter from the *The Guardian* newspaper, commented on the situation in the Mediterranean resorts.

These places attract millions of tourists set on improving their golf. Each of an estimated 200 golf courses situated around the southern Mediterranean consumes the same amount of fresh water as a town of 1200 people, according to a report released on 7 July 2004, by the World Wide Fund for Nature (WWF). In the southeast of Spain – already an arid region – it is planned to build 89 more golf courses. Greece is planning 40 more and Cyprus eight. Responsible individuals and agencies are seriously calling on people not to patronise such establishments.

The report's author, Lucia de Stefano, describes the region as wilting under the pressure of 135 million tourists to beaches stretching from northern Morocco and Spain to Greece, Turkey, Cyprus and Tunisia. It is further anticipated that this figure will at least double by 2024.

'The tourist industry depends on water, but it is at the moment destroying the very resource it needs,' asserted Holger Schmidt, a WWF spokesman. He also pointed out that the vast expanse of land being taken out of use by being concreted over for leisure centres is adding greatly to the level of ecological damage. It is understood that the exploitation of the entire coastline for the tourist trade will push urban boundaries further inland, displacing subsistence farmers and destroying the few remaining coastal wetlands and lagoons. Another EU study, reports the same article, states that over 50% of the wetlands (vital for waterfowl breeding and conservation) of France, Greece, Italy and Spain have already disappeared.

In the poor countries of North Africa, steps are already underway to imitate the tourism of the northern Mediterranean. Water demand increase over the next 20 years will have such an impact that even underground (aquifer) water supplies may well be exhausted by about the year 2050.

Morocco's Moulouya Estuary currently embraces about 400 hectares of marshlands, but looks likely to be destroyed in the rush for dollars from the first world's tourists. Threatened with extinction will be the monk seal and such rare birds as the slender-billed curlew and Andalusian hemipode.

At present, tourism accounts for 7% of all pollution in the Mediterranean Sea. Already this has caused major upsurges in ear, nose and throat infections among indigenous people of the area concerned. Hepatitis and dysentery are also on the increase. The negative ecological impact is now rapidly accelerating. Building is proceeding at levels that are not ecologically sustainable. For instance, Tunisia is planning to double the 85 km already built over for tourists and hence remove this land from food production.

France has built 335 000 second homes – largely for big spenders from the other first world nations – in only 20 years. Spain is said to be building 180 000 a year – 40% of them for UK residents. In 27 towns along the Alicante coast in Spain, a stable domestic population of 150 000 is pushed up to 1.1 million (almost sevenfold) every August. Water consumption in the Balearic Islands has increased to 35 times the 1980 levels.

What about climate change?

In *The Guardian* (3 November 2004), we read that the melting of the polar ice-caps, due to global warming, is now proceeding at such a rate that some of our largest cities (e.g. London, New York) face imminent inundation. Some third world countries (e.g. Bangladesh) have been suffering this effect for years, due largely to carbon dioxide (CO_2) emissions from the industrialised first world, and this has barely made the news. But now we are seeing that, in effect, the way we live our lives in the first world is directly threatening its own citizens.

Obviously many of our largest and most advanced cities were built in, or near, sea-coasts for access to ports for trading. But, as the cited *Evening Standard* article pointed out, CO_2 levels are now causing an accelerating diminution of the polar ice-caps. Within only a matter of 20 years or so, the water levels around London could rise by five to ten metres. Three metres would be enough to wipe London off the map. New York is likewise threatened.

The British government's chief scientist, Sir David King, was reported as saying that right now (2004) there is enough CO_2 in the atmosphere to melt both ice-caps, even if we stop at present levels. Of course, it is a comparatively slow process, which accounts for the predicted time-gap. He commented:

> *Climate change is the biggest problem that human civilisation has faced for 5000 years. When the Greenland ice cap goes, the sea levels will rise six to seven metres, but when Antarctica melts, it will rise another 100 metres.*

He made these comments just after returning as the UK government's chief adviser from Moscow, where he had been trying to persuade the Russian government to ratify the Kyoto Agreement to fight climate change. The reader is no doubt aware that the United States was the first major CO_2 producer to refuse to ratify it. As will be discussed later in this chapter, such abstentions render the Kyoto Accord almost useless. Suffice it to say, it underlines the point (*see* Chapter 14) that any effective solution must be internationally mediated to be effective. We cannot be held to ransom by the short-term political and economic interest of individual nations or of their corporations.

Sir David King went on to point out that recent scientific studies have confirmed the worst predictions about global warming. Records from the three kilometre-deep Antarctic snow core show that, during 'ice ages', the CO_2 in the atmosphere remained almost static – at about 200 parts per million (ppm), which rose to about 270 ppm during very warm periods. But human intervention, especially with the onset of industrialisation, has pushed CO_2 levels so high that they have effectively broken the cycle. In the 1990s, CO_2 levels reached 360 ppm and are now at 379 ppm. They are increasing at a rate of 3 ppm a year. That means that they are now at levels not experienced on Earth for 55 million years – when there was no ice at all on the planet. Of course, CO_2 is not the only global warming gas. Methane is another, although much of it is produced in the third world. We commonly come across methane as marsh gas in boggy areas and it is also encountered (and rightly feared for its flammable qualities) in some mines. But a major source of it is due to nothing more than farting. In this way, termites release significant quantities into the atmosphere.

A major source, however, over which control could be exercised, is from cattle. Raising cattle for meat is a very inefficient means of gaining protein. Grazing alone uses up more calories than is gained from the meat produced. The issue has become much worse with the sudden – and apparently global – demand for hamburgers. McDonald's, and many other purveyors of this 'delicacy', routinely convert areas of Brazilian (and other) rainforest to create pasturelands on which to raise their cattle. The flatulation produced by cattle, in the process of metabolising grass, is one of the most important sources of methane.

Implications

This all means, for example, that global warming is an even greater threat than global terrorism. It therefore behoves us to coolly enumerate (and then analyse) the causes – both 'proximal' and 'distal'. By proximal causes, I refer to those that we can control locally, such as car use and ownership. The worst offenders by far are aircraft, so we must seriously address the issue of flying off on holidays abroad, etc. Modern methods of network conferencing could greatly cut back on the need to travel on business or for international conferences. It used to be said in the 1970s, when the Boeing 747s became widely used as passenger carriers, that one flight of a B747 from London to New York used up so much ozone that it would take a hectare of virgin Canadian forest over a century to restore it by photosynthesis (*Toronto Globe & Mail*, 1974). Of course, since then the Canadians (and others) have been busy chopping down their forests to compete in the woodchip trade with Japan!

As mentioned already, this catastrophic rise in CO_2 in the atmosphere has been bolstered enormously by increased trade, by multinational corporations based in the first world. Some reference has already been made in this connection to passenger flights. But consider also global shipping by air and sea. This increased tenfold from 1950 to 2000. It already burns 140 tons of fuel annually (Goldsmith and Mander, 2001). As Derek Wilson and Steele Roberts point out in their book, also published in 2001, air cargo is forecast to treble by 2015. Speaking roughly, the number of grams of CO_2 emitted per passenger seat per km come to 30 for a train, 80 for a car, but 650 for a jet airliner. Should air traffic continue to expand at present rates, by 2015 it will cause half of all ozone layer destruction. Solutions to at least some of these problems lie in the hands of community activists and other protest groups.

The scale of environmental degradation is staggering beyond imagination. This is partly concealed by what are laughingly referred to as the 'costs' of air travel. It is now possible to fly to many destinations in the UK – and to many other European destinations – for a ticket cost much lower than surface transport can offer. But how is the 'air fare' calculated? The company has to make enough to meet certain overheads – payment of the crew, various airport charges, wear and tear on the aircraft, etc. – and then clear a profit. But what many of the flying public do not realise is that the enormous amount of high-octane fuel used (which produces huge CO_2 emissions) is *not taxed*! Likewise, the social costs incurred – noise pollution, environmental degradation caused by the infrastructure of airports, impact on the health of people even living some distance from the airport, etc., has not even been accurately calculated, let alone charged to the airline companies. None of that is included in the airfare. If the price of an air ticket had to cover all of these costs, a return flight from London to Glasgow could well cost in excess of £1000, rather than the £36 one sometimes sees advertised.

All of those can be regarded as 'proximal' issues. The 'distal' ones include such issues as those transcending local control. Individuals can decide that air travel is not ecologically sustainable and therefore refuse to use it. But they cannot so easily control the ravages of international flight associated with large-scale trade between nations. National economic interests are involved. As will be argued more fully in Chapter 14, this would require some sort of international body, independent of national interests, to call the shots in the interests of humanity as a whole.

Attendant consequences of lack of global control

One does not need to look far to see how national economic interests currently create environmental problems for all of us. US President George W Bush was 'elected' on an incomplete ballot-count in 2000. His campaign was very much supported by his country's oil interests, which had felt restricted by some of the attitudes of the previous Democrat administration – for instance, the latter's favourable disposition towards the Kyoto Agreement.

One of President Bush's first actions on taking office was to withdraw US pledges to reduce CO_2 emissions, calling it a 'mistake' (Brown, 2001). He also abrogated legislation intended to control sulphur dioxide (SO_2) emissions from US petroleum refineries. SO_2 not only produces acid rain when it combines with atmospheric water, but within a short radius around the plants concerned has a deleterious impact on the health of residents. Who, one might ask, would be living that close to something as unattractive as a petroleum refinery? It would largely be people far down the economic ladder in the US – black people, Mexican migrants (legal and illegal), etc. George W Bush finally got that legislation passed at the height of the panic and outrage over the two terrorist attacks on the World Trade Center, referred to widely as 9/11 due to the American system for recording dates. In that horror, somewhat over 3000 lives were lost – many of them nameless illegal migrants who cannot even be traced – while the legislation cutting limits on SO_2 may well have killed many more than that of poor American citizens in the first year of its enactment!

Without some sort of worldwide control over such issues, we are surely doomed. Consider, for example, the Bhopal disaster in India, from which many thousands still suffer ruined lives and health, to say nothing of the multitudes who died in the event itself. Bhopal is the capital city of Madhya Pradesh state in central India. In December 1984, Bhopal was the site of the worst industrial accident in history, when about 45 tons of the dangerous gas methyl isocyanate escaped from an insecticide plant in Bhopal that was owned by the Indian subsidiary of the US firm Union Carbide Corp. The gas drifted over the densely populated neighbourhoods around the plant, killing many of their inhabitants immediately and creating a panic as tens of thousands of others attempted to flee the city. The final death toll was estimated at as high as 2500 lives, and local medical facilities were over-whelmed by about 50 000 other people who were disabled by respiratory problems and eye irritation resulting from exposure to the toxic gas. Investigations later established that substandard operating and safety procedures at the understaffed plant had led to the catastrophe.

Needless to say, that plant, which was producing insecticides for the profit of US interests and was selling most of its insecticide to customers in the first world, was situated in a third world country for sound business reasons. In the US there are labour laws protecting workers and a reasonably vigorous trade union system to see that they are applied. However, in the third world and especially in the poorest nations, such legislation either does not exist or is not enforced if it is going to interfere with trade. Health and safety provisions, which are accepted as required in a first world society, are often regarded as dispensable luxuries elsewhere.

Under impartial global control, in which the welfare of people is a dominant criterion, such exploitation would be far less likely to occur. For instance, govern-ments or other agencies within a given economic interest cannot even be allowed to be the sole arbiters of what happens to the natural resources of its own country.

Not long after President Bush (Junior) came to power, considerable discussion arose – and is still being considered – about the possibility of extracting oil from huge reserves recently discovered in Alaska. This would be a godsend for American oil corporations and probably a great relief to the fuel-hungry American people generally. At present, great uncertainty attends US continued access to oil from overseas and especially from the Middle East. As the OPEC (Organization of the Petroleum Exporting Countries) nations did in the 1970s, they are in a position to hold the US (the world's greatest user of oil, by far) to ransom. What could be better for the US than to have the security of an increase in its own supply?

But extracting oil from Alaska would probably destroy, or seriously compromise, the National Park there. Many species unique to the area would face the possibility of extinction. The local rivers and wetlands, as well as coastal fishing interests, would face pollution on a large scale. The use of that much extra oil would greatly exacerbate global warming.

Siberia faces the same problem. In both places – and in a number of similar regions – the permafrost is weakening quickly under the impact of global warming. This is actually now undermining the foundations of buildings and of huge stretches of highways. Bridges and other large structures such as railway lines are threatened, as are port facilities. In the Rocky Mountain regions in both the US and Canada, thawing is resulting in massively destructive rock falls, mudslides and even the collapse of whole mountainsides (Craig, 2002). Much of the approach to global warming used here by this author has been informed by Craig's brilliant little book. Although only 52 pages long and wallet-size in page area, it is an absolute gem of effective exposition and argument. This author would recommend it to any reader interested in setting up community action groups, and frequently uses it himself.

These events often result in the formation of temporary dams, which either divert water flow – jeopardising housing and/or agriculture – or form huge lakes which can suddenly break free of the blockage, wiping out communities in massive deluges. The impact of such 'flash floods' on electrification, water supplies, railways, roads and telephone communications is already common in some parts of Central America, where governments have often sacrificed conservation policies and health and safety for international trade. Much of the latter, indeed, has stemmed from the need to repay International Monetary Fund loans (*see* Chapter 3).

Financial consequences

Many third world countries are hard put to recover from the after-effects of such disasters because of the vast costs of reconstruction entailed. It has been estimated by Dinyar Godrej (2001) that such reconstruction costs will, by 2050, supersede the value of the entire world economy at that time. Insurance payouts alone stemming from climate-related claims have been doubling every decade since the 1960s. In 1964 they stood at $30 billion, due to 16 major disasters, but in 1991 the figure stood at $250 billion, as a result of 70 major disasters. These sums leave out the many secondary costs – many of them not even financially measurable. The Red Cross forecasts that indirect and secondary impacts of disasters like these may well be twice the cost of the direct losses (Godrej, 2001). In fact, climate-related insurance payouts, as opposed to claims, are anticipated to increase from today's $30 billion per year to $300 billion by 2050 (Glugolecki, 2000).

Big tidal waves and tsunamis

These two phenomena are often confused and, since both are important to the concerns of this book, the author will discriminate between them. A tsunami is caused by an eruption (generally volcanic) on the ocean floor. If it is big enough, it can create one or several large waves, which then travel outwards along the floor of the sea. A tidal wave, on the other hand, is a rapid rise of sea level above predicted tidal levels, when water piles up with great force against a coast by powerful offshore winds. 'Storm surge' is regarded as a more correct expression than 'tidal wave'.

The Guardian (29 August 2001) carried an article on tsunamis. Perusal of that article gave some indication that the writer was referring mainly to storm surges, but the content is most emphatically of great relevance. There are, it points out, many notoriously unstable land masses on the planet, but one of the most note-worthy is the Canary Islands, which bears ample evidence of previous tremendous earthquakes. Cumbre Vieja is the name of their major volcano and is regarded by earth scientists as exceptionally dangerous. In one of its eruptions in 1949, a huge fissure opened in its west flank. At some future date it is expected that the resulting enormous and unstable mass of rock – twice the volume of the Isle of Man – will break free and slide into the sea, triggering the largest underwater wave recorded.

It is likewise considered inevitable by scientists that this will generate further giant waves moving westward, still under the surface. Once they have passed at high speed through the depths of the Atlantic, they will strike the shallows of the eastern seaboard of North America. By then, these waves will be several thousand kilometres in length and up to 50 metres high. One does not have to have a particularly profound imagination to realise what such a phenomenon could entail. Waves of that size and force would certainly wipe out life and settlement for several kilometres inland. They would not only affect the US and Canada, but many other areas as well. Maybe all we are waiting for is the eruption of Cumbre Vieja, or a nuclear war!

Less dramatically, the rock could fall due to much more mundane human activities, such as man-induced torrential rains penetrating and weakening the fault line already exposed on the west flank of the volcano. Rock and mudslides like this are now not uncommon. Consider the collapse of the Las Casitas volcano in Nicaragua after a week of torrential rain, resulting from Hurricane Mitch in 1999. In that case, approximately 1400 people were killed but, fortunately, no storm surge took place – only because the mountain concerned was not on the coast.

Especially in the US, there tends to be a cavalier attitude towards the issues raised at the Kyoto talks. Survey after survey carried out by US pollsters shows that, overwhelmingly, Americans would not consider giving up their unnecessarily large, petrol-guzzling cars. Their entire lifestyle is strongly consumer-driven, with the average American gobbling up non-renewable fuels and minerals at a rate of up to 80 times the average European and much more than the average person from the third world. Indeed, as Nares Craig (2002) so ably points out, 'unless greenhouse gases are reduced significantly, today's decision makers in the first world risk being guilty of inflicting on their own populations possibly the most appalling and sudden holocaust in human history'.

How much time do we have left for remedial action to have any chance of being successful? This is not easy to calculate. Even some of the less pessimistic earth scientists assert that, by 2050, about 75% of the world's people could be at serious risk, unless we act now.

To do justice to such issues as to how the global financial control exercised by the first world can, specifically, lead to such health-threatening phenomena as pollution, the trade in illegal drugs, deforestation, war, etc., we must deal with some of the history behind that global financial control. That is the major concern of Chapter 3.

References

Brown L (2001) *Bio-economy*. Earthscan, London.

Craig N (2002) *World Rescue – climate facts/demand for action*. Housmans Bookshop Publications, London, p.7.

Dlugolecki G (2002) *Climate Change and the Financial Services Industry*. www.solstice.crest.org/renewables/gasification-list-archive/msg03619.html

Godrej D (2001) *No-nonsense Climate Change*. Verso Press, London, p.13.

Goldsmith E and Mander J (2001) *The Case Against the Global Economy*. Earthscan, London.

King D (2004) As quoted in: London 'among first to go' as sea level rises. *London Evening Standard*. 18 July, p.16.

Radford T (2001) Wave of disaster warning: scientists conjure up possibility of volcano triggering world's worst natural calamity. *The Guardian* G2 section. 29 August, p.3.

Stefano L de (2004) *The Coming Water Crisis*. Pamphlet issued by the World Wide Fund for Nature, Godalming, Surrey.

The Observer (2004) Global warming – it started 50 million years ago. 11 July, p.2.

Toronto Globe & Mail (1974) Letters. 3 March, p.31.

Trimlett G (2004) Save the planet – don't play golf. *The Guardian*. 16 July, p.3.

Wilson D and Roberts S (2001) *Five Holocausts*. Wellington Press, Wellington, New Zealand.

Wilson J (2004) Global warming will leave the ice free. *The Guardian*. 3 November, p.18.

Chapter 3

Mortgaging the third world

Holding health hostage

As will be shown in this chapter, the whole mechanics for financing development of trade in the third world imposes almost impossible strains on the debtor nation domestic economies. These impact most heavily in health, both directly and indirectly. Imposition, for instance, of policies required by the lender nations force such governments to direct cash from previously public funded services to private. Since, for almost any country, the two largest publicly funded areas tend to be education and health, those sectors are hit most drastically. As we shall see in Chapter 4, such negative consequences are also often indirect, through the impacts of environment, which themselves lead to increase in the incidence of disease. A necessary basis for good health – especially with respect to personal hygiene, diet and sexual activity – is education itself. If there are cutbacks to schooling, health is soon the loser.

The case of Njuma (Holmes, 2000) illustrates the point at the personal level. Njuma is a childless widow, about 70 years of age, who lives in a remote mountainous area of Uganda. She has lived alone since her husband died, largely dependent on food from relatives and neighbours. They are themselves almost as poor as she and cannot provide more than enough to sustain minimal nutrition. She gets no support from her government, nor from NGOs. When she becomes ill, she can only wait until she recovers because she has no access to healthcare.

However, she remains economically active, despite feeling depressed and exhausted and despite having no access to land or productive assets. Her main work is gleaning coffee from neighbours' bushes once they have been harvested. Such work is prodigiously difficult because the bushes themselves are poorly maintained and already picked over by more agile harvesters. As well, these bushes characteristically grow on steep slopes. Through this work, she earns the equivalent of US$0.02–0.03 (2 to 3 cents!) per hour.

Economic surveys and the official census would, if they listed her at all, classify her as poor and unemployed. But, of course, the reality is that she is employed – but at some of the lowest paid work in the world.

What must be appreciated is that many of the attributes of third world status can be expressed in terms of health statistics and not only in economic terms (*see* Figure 1.1). For instance, there is considerable diversity between third world nations, using standard economic criteria, with GNP (gross national product) per head ranging from $120 in Ethiopia to $2970 in Gabon (1991 figures (Hartwig and Patterson, 1998)). If we look at epidemiological data, we still see considerable variation, but there is universal agreement on what is reasonable. Infant mortality is a commonly used statistic in discussing a nation's health status: we know that it is sensitive to such 'non-clinical' factors as maternal education, economic infrastructure, etc., and that we expect – in any country – there to be some discrepancy between urban and rural figures. But in a third world country, this gap will characteristically be much larger. In Mozambique, for example, the infant mortality rate (IMR) in Maputo (the capital) is 92 per 1000 live births (Potter, 1999). Not only is the urban–rural gap enormous, but in the first world, the average IMR is about 9 per 1000 live births.

In the same way, it has been well established that – even in the first world – discrepancies in health status will be observed between urban poor and urban rich, but these are rarely so great as to be measurable in integral ratios. Compare that with, say, the situation in Manila, Philippines, where the IMR in its slums is up to three times what it is in the wealthy areas (Zwi and Ugalde, 1991)! Again, population sizes in third world nations vary greatly but tend to be large by first world standards.

Squeezed between 'upstream' and 'downstream' forces

It is typical of third world agricultural workers that they find themselves increasingly squeezed by avaricious (often corrupt) first world markets lowering their prices for exports and by their own governments (often corrupt) rigidly applying IMF structural adjustment policies (SAPs). In the *Chronic Poverty Report* (2004–2005, p.39), the situation in the Ceres region of South Africa is described in a paper by A Du Toit.

Fruit picked at Ceres in South Africa regularly appears on the supermarket shelves in developed countries. Workers there depend on the seasonal labour generated by the global fruit market. Although race (as well as gender) remains a central component of the South African political-economy of poverty, the dynamics that keep fruit workers poor are not just about exclusion, but to adverse incorporation into the global labour market.

The fruit workers and the globalised fruit industry are interdependent but, for the workers, this is on unfavourable terms. They are trapped in a situation that forces them to rely on poorly paid, scarce and insecure jobs.

As a result of the casualisation of labour, more than half the farms that used to provide on-site housing have ceased to do so. For landless workers, relying on seasonal and temporary demand for labour, dependence on a paternalistic farmer for employment has been replaced by dependence on a contractor who acts as a labour broker.

Due to low incomes and weak access to economic and natural resources for basic household food production, people often have to buy food on credit, in small amounts and at higher prices. Networks of mutual aid and support enable basic survival, but provide only limited protection against shocks. Limited social safety nets and few alternative livelihood options have given rise to a burgeoning underground economy. Rising criminality, violence and exploitative relationships effectively increase the vulnerability of poor fruit workers.

Chronic poverty is maintained among fruit workers in Ceres by both 'downstream' factors (the ways in which products are processed, shipped, marketed and consumed) and 'upstream' factors (the relationships that are involved on the input side of agricultural production). People in chronic poverty are linked to the fruit consumers of Europe via the economies and politics of the export chain.

If you wander into, say, your high street café – how much does a cup of coffee cost? For an answer in global terms, we consult again an article by Thomas Lines and Sofia Tickell (2003).

Over the past five years, massive coffee overproduction has led to a collapse in prices, contributing to chronic poverty at both the micro and macro level.

There are some 20–25 million small farmers dependent on the global coffee market, living in about 50 countries of Latin America, Asia-Pacific and Africa. In Ethiopia, more than 700 000 smallholders are involved in coffee production, and the livelihoods of a further 15 million rely in part on the coffee economy. For these small farmers, the collapse in coffee prices – sometimes to a fraction of the production cost – has meant the collapse of livelihoods, increased food insecurity, asset depletion, resource degradation and a decimated ability to cope with shocks. For many children, it has meant leaving school, as coffee production was the only way their families could earn cash for fees.

Diversification and entry into niche markets are risky, long-term strategies. With few livelihood alternatives, the most vulnerable farmers stay in the coffee market. Others, along with underemployed and unemployed coffee plantation labourers, migrate in search of a new livelihood.

At the macro level, the countries hit hardest by the price collapse are mostly Least Developed Countries, many desperately poor. Over the last five years, Uganda lost about half the amount it has received as debt relief under HIPC (Heavily Indebted Poor Countries initiative). Ethiopia lost half its annual export earnings over a two-year period. Of the 36 countries facing food emergencies identified by the FAO (Food and Agriculture Organization) in June 2003, four are Central American countries experiencing food insecurity because of the international coffee crisis, and six are African countries heavily dependent on coffee exports. The economies of some of the poorest countries in the world – including much of Eastern Africa and Central America – are highly dependent on exports of coffee from small farms (*see* Table 3.1).

While a range of factors has contributed to the coffee crisis, the main problem is a lack of governance since the International Coffee Agreement broke down in 1989. The global coffee market is extraordinarily unequal: an average farmer has about 15 bags of coffee to sell each year, while each of the biggest coffee roasters buys about 15 million. In the context of commodity market speculation, of International Financial Initiatives (IFI) production support to particular coffee-producing countries, and of the pressures for hard currency that encourage indebted countries to increase exports, the absence of governance has undermined the livelihoods of millions of people (*see* Table 3.1).

The IMF and the World Bank

The International Monetary Fund (IMF) and the World Bank were planned by the United States Senate Committee for Foreign Relations (CFR), as far back as 1930. As the Second World War drew to a close, an international conference was convened at Bretton Woods, New Hampshire, in 1944. The basic idea could be seen as almost purely altruistic, with a bit of American self-interest thrown in. The postwar world was dominated by the two great power blocs of the United States (representing free-enterprise capitalism) and the USSR (representing communism and the planned economies). Destitute nations could easily fall prey to overtures from the former USSR, if not to join them directly, at least to act as agents for Soviet international interests. This would clearly not be to the advantage of the United States, or of the

Table 3.1: Declining coffee markets

Selected countries	Share of world production (%)*	Dependence on coffee exports (%)**
Americas	65	
Brazil	33	
Colombia	12	17
Guatemala	4	21
Honduras	3	25
Mexico	3	
El Salvador	2	26
Nicaragua	1	30
Others	6	
Asia-Pacific	22	
Vietnam	13	
Indonesia	5	
India	3	
Others	2	
Africa	13	
Uganda	4	55
Côte d'Ivoire	3	
Ethiopia	2	67
Kenya	< 1	14
Tanzania	< 1	16
Burundi	< 1	80
Rwanda	< 1	43
Others	2	

*June 2002–May 2003; www.ico.org.
**1998; FAO/ILO in Oxfam 2001.

Sources: Charveriat, 2001; Lines and Tickell, 2003; FAO/GIEWS, 2003

Christopher Barret, Thomas Lines and Sofia Tickell reported originally for the Food and Agriculture Organization (FAO) and the International Labour Organization (ILO).

capitalist interests of any of the victorious powers. Put simply, hard-headed senators in the US were persuaded that it would be worth parting with large sums of money from the US treasury to make loans to small struggling economies, if doing so kept them on their side in the Cold War. The rationale was that:

- the money was only to be loaned and thus would be paid back
- the US Treasury would not be the only source of capital, but donations would be extracted from all the other major free-enterprise countries.

Indeed, initially the World Bank and the International Monetary Fund did not anticipate lending all of the money themselves. The idea was that private banks in the US and Britain and elsewhere would be encouraged to make short-term loans to impoverished countries. Repayment costs (interest, etc.) would be high enough for the stockholders of these banks to find the transaction very much to their benefit, while scheduling of the repayments would appear to be within the feasible grasp of the desperate borrowers.

Historically, such fiscal considerations take on a political aspect and become subject to biased interpretation. But it is fair to say that the former ruling elites in many of these war-torn countries were not keen to see populist governments, led by domestic communists who were ideologically answerable to the USSR (and/or to China, after 1949), take their power and privilege from them. They were therefore glad to negotiate with the private banks. If the debt 'went bad', i.e. if a borrowing country could not even maintain payments on the interest, the private bank's shareholders would be protected since once the debt moved into the public sector, taxpayers in the nation whose bank it was would be paying for it.

At this stage we need to be a little more precise about the provenance of the IMF and the World Bank, and about how they work. In theory, and as originally specified by its charter, the World Bank is purely a repository of money. It is a financial institution, not a social service or a political agency (Moises, 1993). Of course, it is difficult to see how an organisation with control over the flow of such large amounts of money could remain neutral. Obviously, the World Bank's directors know what they want and are in a very strong position to make sure it happens! In some ways, the World Bank is a model of 'transparency' in that it publishes volumes of material each year about its philosophy, aims, successes and failures and this material is widely available. But the fact that it even has a philosophy allows its activities to be questioned at the ideological and ethical levels as well as at the fiscal level. By the end of the 1960s critical comments about the World Bank easily outnumbered favourable comments and this differential has increased monumentally since. Within the last 20 years most of this criticism has been directed at what are called 'structural adjustment policies'.

Origins of the IMF and the World Bank

An understanding of structural adjustment is pivotal to any critique of its impact on health promotion in the third world. But before any sense can be made of that, some comment is necessary on the difference between, and the relationship between, the World Bank and the IMF. The two can be regarded as twins – for they came into being simultaneously, as a result of initiatives dating back to the 1930s designed to promote free trade but in such a way that the United States played a dominant role.

By the beginning of the Second World War, the US economy was the most productive in the world, but it was hampered by special relations and preferential tariffs designed to protect the interests of Britain. The countries of the British Empire could trade advantageously between themselves, but US markets were artificially restricted in these same areas of the world. When President Roosevelt met with Prime Minister Winston Churchill in August 1941, he made it clear that one of the conditions for the US entering the war was that Britain would not obstruct free trade worldwide after the war. The British Empire would have to annul the special trading agreements it had with its colonies and dominions (Shoup, in Minter, 1977). What this meant in practice was made perfectly clear by Dean Acheson, US Assistant Secretary of State in 1944, who observed that there was no way that, when peace came, the high levels of wartime productivity in the US could be absorbed by the domestic market alone. He said: 'We need markets overseas for the output of the US and without them we cannot have full employment and prosperity at home' (Nissan, 1974).

From 1942 onwards, the United States and Britain collaborated, through a series of meetings at Bretton Woods, to draw up plans for financing international free trade. The key British delegate in this was none other than John Maynard Keynes. By 1944 the idea of two separate agencies had gelled: the International Bank for Reconstruction and Development (widely called the 'World Bank') and the International Monetary Fund. Moreover, they were both made specialised agencies of the United Nations, which officially removed the controlling interest of the US Senate Committee for Foreign Relations. Both organisations had virtually the same membership (all countries except the communist bloc and excluding Switzerland), but with different functions.

The IMF agrees on broad lines of policy in such matters as establishing and maintaining currency convertibility and avoidance of competitive exchange depreciation. Thus, unlike the World Bank, it was set up as a think-tank and not only as a financial institution. Its basic financial policy was initially to adhere strictly to the gold standard in adjudicating loans to member countries. The United States came off the gold standard in the early 1960s. Thus it was restrained from high-risk lending. Indeed, it only lends to treasuries and central banks of member countries and generally over only five years. It sees its function as to help its members in the short term should they run into balance-of-payments problems (Rachman and Bloch, 1974).

The World Bank has virtually the same membership as the IMF but much more financial flexibility. For instance, it can make long-term loans over periods like 20 years and can now lend to private projects in third world countries. In this way it can directly influence the running of those countries. It makes wide use of private banks in the first and third world, as principal and intermediary lenders. It can also sell outstanding debts on the financial markets. Indeed, it is this capacity of first world bankers to 'sell outstanding debts' that keeps them safe, while mortgaging the third world still further.

Structural adjustment

The most visual impact that the IMF and World Bank policies have had on third world health promotion relates to what the World Bank called 'structural adjustment' and which it began to demand of borrower nations in the late 1970s. In fact, there is a considerable body of opinion that it was this imposition that played a major role in precipitating the so-called 'debt crisis' of the 1980s.

In order to try to reduce the risks involved in lending money to third world countries, the World Bank began to consider the possibility of making their loans conditional on the government of the debtor nation implementing certain changes to its current spending policies. Generally these 'structural adjustments' involved having to move money away from the public sector to the private. They also involved a switch in healthcare and education policy, from 'horizontal planning' to 'vertical' planning.

'Horizontal' planning referred to a nation's attempt to ensure that advances in healthcare affected as wide a range of the population as possible. 'Vertical' strategies, on the other hand, argue that money should be concentrated on high-profile projects in the urban areas that would generate quick financial returns. Don't forget – the purpose of structural adjustment policies is not related to what might enhance the borrower nation's long-term good, but relates only to factors that enable the debtor nation to avoid becoming a bad debt for the World Bank. Sometimes this does not even work in the short term. For instance, in 1973 a number of WHO reports were written, trying to account for why malaria, which had responded well to control programmes in Zambia, was making such a strong comeback. It was found that the main reason was that Zambia had instituted a vertical healthcare priority policy in order to secure an IMF loan and part of this involved increasing the amount of money for malaria control in certain urban areas while withdrawing it from some rural areas which had been almost malaria-free. The results were, of course, predictable (WHO, 1973).

Unfortunately, not all such negative consequences of the change from 'horizontal' to 'vertical' healthcare planning are so obvious.

When one considers its impact on schooling and on literacy programmes as well, it is easy to see that structural adjustment is an important factor in rendering a country's involvement with either the IMF or the World Bank problematic in terms of public health.

The 'debt crisis' of the early 1980s is easily seen to link with structural adjustment policies as well. Very briefly, the debt crisis arose suddenly, and in roughly the following manner. In the late 1970s, the oil-producing nations agreed to raise their prices dramatically. Industrialised nations of the first world cannot do without oil and gasoline, so they had little choice but to accept the consequences. But for poorer nations importing oil-based fuels, such a price rise was catastrophic. They had to keep their factories running to produce and sell in order to obtain dollar currency to pay off their debt bills. The increasing fuel prices meant that they had to renegotiate existing debts and sometimes borrow even more. In 1982 the Mexican economy virtually collapsed under the burden. They, and many other third world debtor nations, had to abide by even more draconian structural adjustment policies dictated by the IMF before the World Bank could lend them more (George, 1992). A brilliantly articulated overview of the precise stages of development of the debt crisis was published by Christian Aid (1998) and the following account is loosely based on that.

Sequence of events behind the debt crisis

During the 1960s the United States found itself more and more deeply involved in the Vietnamese civil war. Initially, during the 1950s, the situation in that country looked as though it could be straightened out and the communists deposed by a combination of US military aid to the anti-communist elements with only a few American advisers sent in to coordinate things. It was never envisaged that the US would get involved in a major war. But, as we know, successive administrations became involved in a major war and found themselves more and more deeply committed to win and get out. The increasingly frantic search for that victory to save American honour, and which they had eventually to forsake in 1975, had cost the US billions of dollars and the lives of hundreds of thousands of their own young men killed in futile action. Even during the 1960s, the American government was already into deficit spending to finance the war. It printed more US dollars to compensate. The dollar was taken off the gold standard and decreased in value.

Oil (which is priced in dollars) dropped in value and in 1973 the Organization of Petroleum Exporting Countries (OPEC) increased their oil prices. This caused them to accumulate dollars, which they then deposited in first world banks, principally in America itself. Of course these banks were having to pay interest on such deposits and therefore found themselves with an immense amount of money that had to be lent out quickly and in volume so that – through collecting interest on such loans – they could afford to pay the interest on the deposits. Impoverished third world countries represented an ideal source of borrowers and the banks were not too fussy about whom they lent the money to or for what purpose. We are talking about routine business transactions here, not attempts to referee human dignity and rights. The debtor nation borrowers were generally keen to get their hands on easy loans. Mainly this was to pay for increased oil prices but, in addition, many of them were recently independent countries and were anxious to build up public infrastructures in such areas as healthcare and education. However, as can be easily imagined, some were run by relatively corrupt administrations and/or sought an infusion of money to purchase arms, for instance, or even to reinforce the power of the ruling elite against their own people. The lenders, as already indicated, were not overly careful.

Many of these loans were high-risk for a variety of reasons. For instance, small ruling elites can suddenly be overthrown and often are. But as observed by a former president of New York Citicorp Bank: 'Individual people who borrow and then cannot pay back before they die represent a loss to the bank. But countries don't suddenly fail to exist!' (George, 1992). In other words, bad debts and high-risk loans are not such a problem when the borrower is a country. True, the regime that negotiated the loan may be overthrown but the country still remains, and the country – not the particular government – must pay back! Thus, many revolutionary regimes which have overthrown corrupt government have found themselves unable to afford promised health and educational reform programmes because they are saddled with debts imposed on the country by the previous rulers.

The loans were offered at low (but variable) interest rates, sometimes even below the rate of inflation. The banks usually assured themselves that a particular third world borrower nation could pay back by ascertaining that it could produce some commodity, or commodities, needed in bulk by the first world, e.g. crops like sugar or coffee. Initially such commodities drew high prices, but this changed as more and more countries found themselves in frantic competition with each other, each nation trying to produce far more and at a greater rate then ever before to satisfy the same markets. This brought about a collapse of markets in these commodities, a situation especially drastic for those poor nations tied to a one-crop economy. The worldwide recession appearing simultaneously meant that export quantities dropped. In the meantime, because the United States government had so grossly overspent on defence and had to cut taxes (to stay in power), they had to increase interest rates sharply. This, of course, increased the costs of debt repayment.

In 1979, the OPEC countries united in raising oil prices. This also impacted with particular severity on poor third world countries which had rapidly begun to industrialise as a means of meeting their commitments. These countries therefore increased their borrowings and negotiated extensions on existing loans. Some, indeed, entered into a spiral of unrepayable debt. As reported by Christian Aid (in 1998) Mexico was but one country which found itself in that situation.

In 1982 Mexico said it could not repay its debts and declared itself bankrupt. The International Monetary Fund (IMF) and World Bank stepped in with new loans under strict conditions to help pay the interest. This pattern was repeated over and over in the following years as other countries found themselves in similar situations to Mexico's. But their debts continued to rise, and new loans were eaten up in interest payments.

In 1992 UNICEF (the United Nations Children's Fund) estimated that 500 000 children a week were dying as a direct result of this debt crisis (UNICEF, 1992). This is a perfect example of the mordant logic behind the comments made by the former president of Citicorp Bank about countries not passing out of existence, even if people do. In this case we are talking about people paying with their lives for debts incurred before they were born and for the benefit of others!

Some consequences of the debt crisis

Three principal consequences thus derived from this international monetary adventurism.

Though a given debtor nation may be impoverished, and/or through poor government be unable to maintain an adequate programme in health and education, these aspects of its national life are often rendered even worse through obligations to the IMF and the World Bank. For instance, from 1995 to 1998, the poorest countries of Africa paid US$13 billion annually to their creditors (Christian Aid, 1998). Contrast this with the US$9 billion which UNICEF estimated was needed for health and nutrition in all of Africa! Then again, in Uganda for every dollar the government spends per person on health, they pay eight dollars per person for debt repayment to first world creditors. According to UNICEF (1998), in the five most indebted countries:

- children are 30% less likely to live out their first year
- a pregnant woman is three times more likely to die in childbirth
- illiteracy rates are about 25% higher, and
- access to safe water is about 33% lower than is the case in the five least indebted.

We have the anomalous situation of the poor funding the rich! In 1996, the debtor nations paid US$1.8 billion more in debt service to the IMF than it received in new loans. Since 1987 the IMF has received $2.4 billion more from Africa than it has provided in new finance. Altogether, the poorest nations in Africa had transferred $167 billion into debt service to their creditors in the first world by the end of 2002. It has been said that it is this transfer of resources from the poor to the rich which explains why sub-Saharan Africa cannot prevent recurring famine.

There is no question but that international financial transactions like these, often conducted in secret by non-representative ruling cliques in the borrower nations with creditors in the West, have greatly enhanced the levels of corruption and injustice. For instance, the post-apartheid regime in South Africa under President Nelson Mandela found its capacity for economic planning and management severely constrained by having to honour debts built up under apartheid. This is doubly ironic when one considers that many of these loans were taken out by the apartheid administration to oppress and tyrannise the very people now required to pay them back. Again, the new government in the Democratic Republic of the Congo may not itself be a model of financial responsibility, but its management of health and education resources is not helped by having to pay back the debts incurred over 30 years by the hugely corrupt Mobutu regime, which served Western interests so conveniently.

Jubilee 2000: a Christian Aid initiative

Certainly one of the most important initiatives to address the problem of international debt was the Jubilee 2000 Project. Christian Aid had, through its single-minded promotion of a straightforward solution to the problem, brought the issue to consciousness (if not the consciences) of a much larger proportion of the lay public in the first world than normally concern themselves with issues of social justice. What, then, was the Jubilee 2000 solution?

It was that first world nations cancel the outstanding debts – ideally all of them, but even if not that, at least those of the poorest countries. The question that needs to be asked is: would such a dramatic gesture help? Considering the level of corruption that prevails in many countries, might not the abolition of debt repayments simply give a new lease of life to such corrupt regimes, without any further benefit accruing to poorer sectors of that debtor nation's economy?

When faced with that question, Christian Aid spokesmen took the view that the third world countries had suffered enough from intrusion into their affairs by paternalistic first world powers. To insist that they only be allowed to borrow from the World Bank or the IMF if they subjected themselves to having their domestic allocation of the money supervised by the lenders would, Christian Aid argued, retard even further the development of healthy, democratic governance.

However, it seems to this author that there are ways by which Christian Aid's Jubilee 2000 Project can be mediated without such interference from outside. For instance, one such approach could be for the lenders (say, the World Bank and/or IMF) to insist that the money be administered by local community groups, possibly under the advice of their government, but with their spending monitored through monthly reports to the lenders. This would, in the best health promotion tradition, empower neighbourhood advocacy, and as well compel the recipient nation's government to negotiate with its own people as more of an equal partner than is customary.

The author puts this point forward, not necessarily as advocating the Jubilee 2000 initiative as the immediate or only answer (*see* Chapter 14), but to demonstrate that Christian Aid's plan is not as utopian as its detractors would like us to believe.

All of this suggests that promotion of health in the poor nations depends primarily on the resolution of huge economic and political problems which transcend both the powers and the responsibilities of debtor governments themselves. It becomes a global problem. The dimensions of this problem will be considered in detail in subsequent pages, first in general terms of how issues such as environmental health and child welfare are compromised by debts, and then by analysing the situation in specific countries.

Environmental is international

If it can be shown that the environment – especially the air or the water supply – of any borrower nation is affected adversely by the sort of economic restructuring required to comply with the servicing of an IMF loan, then we immediately have a worldwide problem. The aqueous and atmospheric environments do not recognise national boundaries! Such a relationship, though, is not too difficult to establish, and one can select from several telling examples. The Transnational Institute (TNI), with its headquarters in the Netherlands, has amply demonstrated this case with respect to deforestation. Before detailing this evidence, though, it is useful to consider the provenance of the TNI itself, for it is but an example of the relatively silent but rapid proliferation of NGOs which have come into existence to counter the negative impact of the international debt system.

Established in 1973, the TNI's aim was to research and to suggest means for ameliorating the gross inequities prevailing between the first and third worlds and their people. Although its administrative centre is in Amsterdam, the organisation is not markedly hierarchical and its personnel consists of 'fellows' (all of equal rank) living in a wide range of other countries. These people are individually committed to presenting sound scholarly evidence in support of the ideological stance that they promote, so that they cannot be accused, by right-wing elements, for instance, of being manipulated by any ideology. They therefore present their findings, and argue them, in a range of publicly accessible fora, from newspapers and radio/TV talk shows to academic conferences. They convene regularly at six-monthly intervals in Amsterdam to discuss their individual findings and to coordinate their activities around particularly pressing issues.

The TNI derives its funding (including small stipends paid to the fellows) from an eclectic array of sources, both government and non-government, both local and transnational, both public and private. Much of its funding comes from successful bids for research funds by individual fellows. This reflects the high esteem of non-partisan agents in which the TNI is held.

What, then, has the TNI discovered about the link between deforestation (a global environmental hazard if ever there were one) and international debt? As has already been explained, the borrowing of huge sums of money by a third world nation from a first world nation must usually involve some agreed-upon arrangement whereby it can be repaid and the rate at which interest on the unpaid balance from year to year will be charged. Not only does this impose on the debtor nation the need to come up with some source of income over and above what it has had before and over a long period of time, but the lender (say, the IMF) will itself want to be satisfied that such potential for repayment does exist in the debtor nation. The most obvious source within a poor nation for export of cash is invariably some environmental resource that as yet had not been heavily exploited and rainforest cover has been a primary victim of this logic.

In the short term the massive depletion of rainforests in the third world generated cash for debt repayment. It also had certain other short-term advantages. To get machinery in (to do the cutting and stripping) and to get the logs out required a huge increase in road building. This greatly opened country for peasant farmers and for exploitation by the local landholding oligarchies, which increased local employment. But these 'pluses' have been so short-term that the negative side of it all had become clear long before the debt had been paid off. In addition, the transnational impacts of destroying huge areas of forest at a rate which makes a mockery of any possibility of replacing them are already adversely affecting our own environment in the first world.

The environment – Gaia, if you like – on which health everywhere ultimately depends, is increasingly being sacrificed in the short-term interests of a very few people in the first world and who in turn are not accountable to the rest of their national community either in terms of national health promotion or more generally.

If we now return to a consideration of the relationship between international debt and the exploitation of forests in the third world, a number of factors need to be kept in mind. Generally speaking the desperately poor anywhere cannot be expected to allow a dispassionate concern for environmental issues to take priority over their immediate survival needs. Thus forests have always been subject to exploitation for firewood, and to some extent for farming, in third world countries.

Collective vs individual

Remember that Lebanon, for instance, was known in biblical times as a thickly forested area with cooling streams. The fact that it is now largely a desert is due entirely to 'low-tech' deforestation by generations of subsistence farmers. However, the scale of deforestation and its rate have increased radically and directly with the acquisition and amount of national debt. The need to clear ground quickly has led to massive slash-and-burn approaches which have had a dramatic effect on greenhouse gas emission. In fact, this does not stop with the actual clearing, for if the land is then turned over to cattle grazing (e.g. as in Brazil) there is a substantial increase in methane production, which adds significantly to the total greenhouse gas emissions.

Of course, greenhouse gases can be and always have been produced by non-human activities, but their immense increase during the 1970s and 1980s can easily be traced to human intervention. Indeed, the third world is not even responsible for most of this. It is estimated that 70% of this accumulation is produced by the richest 25% of the world's people – it is a first world phenomenon. But it is the sudden increase in greenhouse gas emission from destruction of forests in the third world – very much linked with the perceived 'needs' of the world's wealthiest people – that is the basic argument being put forward in this instance.

Norman Myers (1989) and Peter Bunyard (1985) have provided us with empir-ical data on the relationship between the greenhouse gas emission and defores-tation rates in the 1980s, but the rate of deforestation has greatly accelerated since then. Leggett (1990) argues that deforestation in the third world accounts for as much as 20% of the global climate change we are now experiencing. Perhaps the link between this and debt is best illustrated by a table derived from Susan George's pivotal 1992 publication. In Table 3.2 the three columns, from left to right, are to be read as follows. In the first column the top 24 third world debtors are listed in descending order of the amount they had been lent. The second column lists those

Table 3.2: Between third world debt and third world relationship rates of deforestation

Rank	Country (debt in US$ millions)	Rank	Deforestation Acc. 1980s World Resources Index/ Myers	Percentage of original forest already destroyed
1	Brazil (112.5)	1	Brazil*	23
2	Mexico (112)	2	Indonesia*	30
3	Argentina (65)	3	Myanmar	51
4	India (60)	4	Mexico*	58
5	Indonesia (53)	5	Colombia*	63
6	China (45)	6	Thailand*	83
7	South Korea (44)	7	Malaysia*	48
8	Nigeria (31)	8	India*	90
9	Venezuela (30)	9	Nigeria*	61
10	Philippines (29)	10	Zaire*	20
11	Algeria (28)	11	Papua New Guinea	15
12	Thailand (24)	12	Vietnam	77
13	Chile (22)	13	Peru*	26
14	Peru (20.7)	14	Central America*	82
15	Morocco (20.5)	15	Ecuador*	42
16	Central America (20)	16	Philippines*	80
17	Malaysia (19.5)	17	Côte d'Ivoire*	90
18	Pakistan (18)	18	Cameroon	25
19	Columbia (16.5)	19	Venezuela*	16
20	Côte d'Ivoire (14.5)	20	Madagascar	61
21	Ecuador (12.5)	21.	Bolivia	22
22	Vietnam (11.6)			
23	Bangladesh (10.7)			
24	Sudan (10)			

*Member of the 'Over $10 Billion' Debtor Club.

countries which were the largest deforesters from 1980 to 1990, again in descending order. The estimates on which these rankings are based are those of Myers (1989). The third column simply indicates the percentage of forest existing in 1980 which had been destroyed by 1989.

From the figures in Table 3.2, a number of things should be evident to the reader. The expression 'short term' was used in my description of the advantages of deforestation. So short term are these advantages that, at the present rate, the forests will cease to provide this income necessary for debt repayment long before the debt can be repaid. Also, the impact of such large-scale deforestation, even in the short term, has wholly negative impacts on health promotion – both in the countries concerned and globally. Locally, forest cover is removed, wildlife destroyed, water supplies polluted (especially by superphosphates required for quick pasture production) and, globally, the ozone layer is assaulted.

Are the drug trade and debt linked?

Susan George (1992) and many others would argue that the sudden increase in the international traffic of narcotics, largely from the third world to the first, is positively correlated with the growth of IMF economic restructuring programmes in the poorer nations. This is such a startling charge, and has so many implications for health everywhere, that the issue needs some scrutiny.

That there has been a dramatic upswing in the volume, variety and rate of drug use across a widening spectrum of the population in the first world since, say, 1980 can hardly be denied. In the mid-1970s, for instance, the picture of drug use was that it was largely an upper-middle-class, late-adolescence fad associated with the use of cannabis and LSD (lysergic acid diethylamide). By the late 1970s, in the US, one became accustomed to references to cocaine and even heroin derivatives and to adults' use of these agents.

The possibility was even investigated that maybe teenage weed-smoking students didn't 'grow out of it', but simply moved onto more sophisticated narcotics as they moved into professional life! No such simple equation has been unambiguously proven, by the way, but to many it must have looked that way.

Now in countries like Britain and the US, the age range has widened enormously – with younger and younger people routinely taking drugs. The impact of this rapid growth in the first world for drugs such as cocaine (and its derivatives) and opium created a better financial return for struggling third world farmers than they could gain from producing maize to meet local food needs. An alternative, of course, was to cultivate some 'legal' product – such as sugar or bananas or coffee – that grew particularly well in a third world country and then export it in large quantities to first world markets. This would work well enough until and unless the 'purchaser' countries started to lower the price of the other commodity in question. The fate of countries tied to a 'one-crop economy' is well understood. For instance, for decades the Cuban economy could be directly controlled by the US by the latter being able to lower the price of cane sugar by finding other sources of it.

Virtually the only products not easily manipulated in this way are narcotics, even as primary materials which can be exported to the first world for processing or as already usable on the street. To produce the latter, the third world nation must have a reasonably developed infrastructure, including high-technology facilities, reliable sources of electricity and water, etc. Many third world nations requiring IMF loans opt for producing primary source material for drug manufacture.

Such a radical change to disposal of land and resources within a third world nation may improve the economy to the extent that debt repayments are enhanced, but access to locally produced food for that nation's poor is very much reduced. The loan allows the import of foreign goods and foods, but these are only available to the wealthy urban-dwelling citizens. Thus, in the third world, involvement (as a supplier) in the drug trade has had generally a negative impact on health.

Indeed, the situation is even worse. The drug trade cannot be carried out as an independent activity without affecting other variables. For instance, Susan George (1992) has clearly demonstrated that, as the highly profitable export of narcotics develops in a third world country, deforestation rapidly accelerates to create more growing space. This, in turn, leads to a prodigious increase in pollution effects, such as poisoning of water supplies with chemicals. This is even more the case if the debtor country also processes the raw goods to produce 'ready to use' narcotics.

How can the first world protect itself?

Any health or social worker confronted with the dreadful effects of drug use in our inner cities must confront the question: what can be done? Clearly there is no single simple solution. One needs to address both local and global conditions. Locally, there is the need to address inequities of educational and social opportunities, psychological problems, urban planning issues, etc. Globally? Well, what about actually stopping the supply from reaching our shores? The sheer physical totality of such a solution has widespread appeal; it suggests the need to conquer an external enemy. Indeed, the military metaphors have entered deeply into our speech about the issue. We speak, for instance, about 'drug czars' (*The Guardian*, 4 June 1998) or about the 'war on drugs'. It also becomes a convenient part of President George Bush's War on Terrorism (2002), as reported in the *New York Times* (24 May 2004).

The 'War on Drugs' – a term first used, I believe by US President George Bush (Senior) in the context of his campaign against General Noriega in Panama (1989) – has distinctly global implications. Newspaper accounts of gunboats intercepting ships carrying drugs to the US and Britain from third world sources (*Readers Digest*, July 1998) reinforced that image, as did numerous news bulletins showing aircraft defoliating acres of marijuana plants, etc., in remote jungle-surrounded 'foreign' places.

But, dramatic as these images might be and even though they give one a sense of doing something tangible against a real evil, the concept of self-defence against the import of drugs from the third world to the first world is rendered illogical by the reality of international debt. If we were ever successful in preventing the import of such money-generating goods, debt repayments could not be sustained. The stockholders in banks in the first world would not get a return on their investments. Can one really expect them to acquiesce in this? In a sense the brave and determined efforts of our customs and excise officials in trying to protect our shores from the landing of drugs are at cross-purposes with the needs of the lending banks. This really is a problem because, as the next section indicates, first world citizens –

through these elected governments – pay taxes to bail their banks (and the stockholders of those banks) out of difficulty.

Upholding the banks

The IMF and the World Bank come to the rescue of other private banks should their lending activities be too rash. Thus, although the adjectives 'international' and 'world' in the names of the IMF and World Bank might convey the impression of some sort of global, international agency, like the UN or WHO, the reality is that IMF and World Bank loans to third world countries often already have – if things go according to plan – generated real and specific profits for stockholders of private banks in the first world. Do these individuals also face a risk of losing money if things do not go according to plan? For instance, private banks sometimes show poor judgement in making, say, a personal loan. If the borrower defaults or in some other way the bank loses the money unwisely invested in that 'poor risk', it is all part of the rough and tumble of business life. Presumably, banks must insure themselves against such disagreeable events, in the same way that the small corner shop has to carry insurance against shoplifting in that the premiums paid on that insurance are part of the 'overhead expenses'.

However, once the loan is taken over by the IMF or the World Bank, the shareholders do not lose. In all first world countries, such loans are protected through the tax system. If you live in a first world society, and are not a bank stockholder, you do not get a return of the profit generated by loan repayments, but you must pay – through tax increases – if there are losses. In reality this situation is even more bizarre than that. While it is possible for an individual borrower to completely disappear and terminate payments by dying, that almost never happens to a nation, even a third world nation. If, for example, a loan to a third world nation goes 'bad', this rarely means that the money is irretrievably lost. What it means is that repayments are delayed – and interest is even charged on the delays – so ultimately the lending bank has to recover much more than it ever lent out. Since the IMF started, few nations have yet paid off their debt to it. But even though the actual debts remain unpaid, in total the first world banks have made back at least three times the amount they paid out (OECD, 2000). Even if the banks immediately 'forgave' all outstanding debts and folded up their tents and went home, they would have made a healthy profit on the project!

If, for any given tax year, the first world bank had not received the full amount of scheduled debt repayment, tax on it is exonerated. They don't really lose, because when the amount is paid up, they don't have to pay 'back tax' on it. But the effect of this is that the loss of tax to the governments is real enough and has to be made up out of everyone else's tax. Not only that, there has been a tendency since 1980 for 'bad debt' from third world borrowers to be moved from private banks to government responsibility, adding to the tax burden of citizens in the first world. This is well shown by OECD figures for 1989, as represented in Table 3.3, in which the initials LDC stand for 'less developed countries' – another euphemism for the third world.

Table 3.3: Bank loans to and returns from LDC debtors

Year	1982	1983	1984	1985	1986	1987	1988	1989
	($US billions)							
Total LDC debt	854	937	961	1078	1194	1329	1313	1322
LDC debt owed to comm. banks	493	516	520	554	584	630	625	629
% of total debt held by banks	57.7	55	54	51	49	47	47	47
LDC debt service to banks	82.2	69.7	77.9	83.6	69.3	66.5	84.5	82
New bank lending to LDCs	37.9	35	17.2	15.2	7	7	5.8	8.5
Service to banks as % debt held by banks in same year	16.7	13.4	15	15	12	10.5	13.5	13

Source: OECD, 1990

All of this may be regarded as bad news for the first world's citizens, and that aspect shall be dealt with, but the topic must not be left without just one more purely fiscal observation about how the citizens of the third world are double-damned by it all. Whatever the nationality of the people of the borrower nation (the third world country in this case), the transaction is always in US dollars. All the private banks in the first world who are in the business of lending money to third world nations therefore store up US dollars. When these are passed over, therefore, the third world is thus investing directly in the United States. Thus, when the US 'invests' later in that country, say, by buying up the telephone system, they are really, in effect, buying that country's assets with its own money! This is only mentioned in passing to show how Byzantine the whole thing is. It would be hugely humorous, even, if so many people's health and welfare in the third world were not being sacrificed to keep the game going. Without attaching any purely political value judgement to it, this process must strike the reader as dreadfully inefficient. It should not be impossible to come up with a less costly system.

Lowering standards in the first world

Scripture tells us of he who casts his bread upon the waters, 'it shall return to him hundredfold' (Ecclesiastes 11:1). This meaning is obvious, as easy to grasp, as WH Auden's poetic corollary to it that 'he to whom evil is done, will do evil in return' (Auden, 1939). In a sense both of these pearls of wisdom – and the folk sayings of every culture abound in them – simply express the truth that we all share one globe and one environment and whatever one does to the advantage or disadvantage of someone else, it will rebound ultimately to one's own advantage or disadvantage. While one can think of any number of situations in which that does not hold up with individual people, because people sometimes die before repercussions have time to manifest themselves, it certainly applies with greater regularity to dealings between nations. This is another reason as to why health promotion must be global to be effective.

We have seen that the third world has – through the international debt – been impoverishing itself further to the financial advantages of some people in the first world. We have even shown that to some extent those of us in the first world who are not involved in the debt transaction business are called upon to help out those who are when they run into short-term problems with collecting repayments. But if we are concerned with global health inequity, there is another more alarming dimension to the issue. It is that the impoverishment of the third world, in the long run, also impoverishes the first world. The brief of this book does not allow a detailed discussion of this proposition, but it is important to illustrate it at least in passing because it does have to be taken into account if we wish to make the pursuit of health a global enterprise.

Basically the argument is as follows. Under present 'rules', our very jobs and our good standard of living in the first world, including our access to time and facilities for cultural and leisure activities, etc., depend first and foremost on our capacity to produce and market goods and services. By exactly the same rules, if a society is poor, the only way it can get richer is to produce something in abundance that some other society wants. If a society is so poor that it has had to borrow enormously, then it has to – as far as possible – stop using the goods it produces naturally for its own people and instead sell them so that the money thus generated can be used to pay back the debt. If the debt is enormous compared with the country's productive capacity, then the debtor country will not be able to pay off the capital, because it will cost so much simply to pay the accumulating interest on the loan. The lending institution, indeed, may never get any of the principal back, but – at compound interest – the interest repayments will in a few years exceed the original sum borrowed.

A simple explanation of compound interest

Even a non-mathematical reader should comprehend the principle of compound interest, using the standard formula for amount (A) accumulated by principal (P) paid off in m years at r% compound annually. For a derivation of that formula, *see* Appendix B.

$$A = P(1 + \frac{r}{100})^m$$

So if you borrow £1000 at 10% interest per annum and pay it off over eight years, you get:

$$A = 1000(1.10)^8 = £2144 (approx)$$

The interest due, then, over the whole-proposed debt (and at the very short debt life of only eight years) comes to £1144 – that is, *more* than the principal itself! If you were able to pay off the whole interest right away, you would not need to borrow the £1000 in the first place. Therefore you pay off on the interest mainly, with only a slight reduction on the principal as you go along. If you cannot meet even those payments, then interest on the unpaid interest starts accumulating. In the first world, we become accustomed to this sort of thing on a small scale. For instance, it is a common enough experience to 'buy' a house (really the bank or building society buys the house and you pay the mortgage) and spend 25 years paying for it. If you sit down and work out the compound interest you have paid over that time, you will see that even the interest alone has cost you several times what the house originally cost! However, you were willing to do it because:

- you did not have the cash to hand when just starting your career
- if you paid off bit by bit over 25 years, it would cost less than monthly rent – and you end up owning the house.

You can sell the loan if you decide to move. In other words, when you want to move you sell the house for the market price and the buyer gets his bank to buy it from your bank and a new mortgage is set up with the new buyer. You even get back some of the money you put in and if you had held onto the property for, say, four years, you could easily get back more than you had paid in. That is, you not only 'made a profit' but you've lived rent-free for four years.

It is important to understand this little analogy because the basic rules are no different in international lending. In fact, banks in the first world regularly do sell third world debts to one another under exactly the same arrangements. But the banks sell the debt, the third world country does not sell it. Thus, unlike you selling your house after living in it for four years, the third world country does not make any profit. Indeed, it might even have to pay a higher interest rate when the debt is rescheduled, because the original lending bank would not have sold the debt had it been 'good' – that is, if the repayments had been coming in on schedule. And, likewise, another bank would not have bought the 'bad' debt unless they thought that they could realise a profit on it before it even got too 'bad' for them to handle.

But how does this affect ordinary citizens in the first world who are not directly involved in the transaction? We have seen that the debtor country has to suddenly find outside markets for goods it used to use up at home. The situation, of course, is much worse when a number of third world countries are engaged in the same exercise. Any two of them exporting the same commodity – say, sugar, or even cocaine for that matter – will be forced into direct competition with each other and will have to try to undercut each other. This reduces their cash returns unless they can produce more, placing more stress on their workers and depleting their (and our) environmental heritage even more.

Meanwhile, the first world nations making the loans are stuck in a paradoxical situation. They can't erect protection tariffs against the goods that the third world nations are producing because, unless the latter can sell, the former don't get their interest repayments. And here is the rub. If those interest repayments are not made, the bank and its stockholders – not the ordinary first world citizen – don't get their returns. In order to keep those returns coming in, the bank has to bring pressure on the government of its first world country to reduce pay for its domestic industrial workers by allowing the cheaper products produced overseas to come in and compete with their own.

It is obvious, if the reader visits a country like Mexico, that the impact of a 'free market' between Mexico and the United States redounds to clear disadvantage of the health of Mexican workers producing goods for export to the US. But it is also not hard to see how this disadvantages US workers who live in states close to the Mexican/US border. They have to work longer hours with less security and fewer safety rights than they would be entitled to elsewhere. Eventually this must impact negatively on their health.

By 2000, the major automobile workers' unions in the US were feeling the pinch as more and more work producing auto parts under non-unionised conditions came back to Detroit from Mexico.

The conclusion, then, is that most of this has come about through the system of debt from first world to third world nations. If we wish to make access to healthcare global, then clearly a more efficient system for the distribution of the benefits of production has to be found.

Various individual third world countries have tried to buck the system, but since they have done so individually, they were – in most cases – easily isolated and picked off one by one by the first world money lenders. Peru, for instance, got rid of its maverick President García – who tried to rule that debt repayments would not be allowed to exceed 10% of export earnings – and now Peru is hopelessly enmeshed in IMF debt. It had less money in 1993 to spend on schools and hospitals than it did in 1989 and yet a greater demand for those two facilities (George and Sabelli, 1994). This is because the debt repayments, which are not touching the principal borrowed, are so great. Fidel Castro in Cuba never defaulted on Cuba's international debt, but wrote a book about the problem (*The International Debt is an Unpayable Debt*) in 1982. It is even arguable that Cuba would have got away with simply not paying, for two reasons: its population was small, only about 10 million back then, and it would have been easier for Citicorp Bank (the New York bank affected) to write it off as a bad debt than for the US to get bogged down in what would have been a protracted war so soon after the unpopular Vietnam War had come to an end.

Suppose that a huge country like Brazil tried this approach. What would happen? The Brazilian debt produces interest payments that constitute about 23% of the profits of Citicorp. Such a loss would seriously compromise the US domestic economy. Would they go to war? Who knows, but it hardly bears thinking about. It is difficult to see how anyone would benefit.

Consider also the case of Zimbabwe, which tried to take a tough line on the IMF. They managed to hold out alone for four or five years but are now deeply in debt. Indeed, Zimbabwe's case illustrates yet another aspect of the sheer disadvantage of this way of running global finance: corruption! Financial institutions, even honest ones, cannot be expected to make rules and conditions relating to the ethical behaviour of their own government or that of their debtor nation. Their professional concern has to be the correct legal protocols in the administration of the money. Since, in many third world nations, the ruling elite are themselves already sharply divided from the great mass of their citizens, the temptation to indulge in corruption once the money comes in must have been well nigh overwhelming.

This is especially so when we recall the rather artificial way that many of the third world nations came into being, especially on large continental land masses such as Africa. There are very few African nations that arose as nations through linguistic and cultural definition. The borders of many African nations were defined on maps in Whitehall or in the boardrooms of colonial trade offices in Britain. These definitions were based not on what appeared to be 'ethnic bonding', but on what was most convenient in terms of access to river ports, deep-sea harbours and the like. The fact that this resulted in several distinct language groups in one 'country' was explained away as tribal differences. But what exactly is the difference between a tribe and a nation? For instance, in Nigeria we had millions of Hausa, millions of Yoruba and millions of Ibo, all supposedly 'Nigerian', with Nigerian banknotes, one Nigerian flag, and one Nigerian national anthem. But 35 million Hausa, say, is a nation, not a tribe. How did they get split up between different countries? The same goes for the Ibo. Only the Yoruba all ended up in Nigeria. But in any kind of ethnic sense, these groups comprise three different nations, each with a long history and folklore distinct from the other two. One of the few African nations whose borders approximate those of the ancient kingdom whose name it still bears is Ghana.

There is very little likelihood, in an area of mixed but separate ethnic groupings, that the people who take control will not all belong to the most dominant of these ethnic groups, and that they will hold onto power by a combination of keeping wealth and power within the extended family, and by discriminating in all sorts of ways against the less powerful ethnic groupings. Therefore, the infusion of massive amounts of IMF funding into such a nation fuels corruption and renders the ruling elite even more secure in its tyranny. Indeed institutions such as the IMF and the World Bank and such concepts as 'third world nations' revolve around the assumption that nationhood is a 'given' and must be accepted as an invariable in the equation. But, as will be suggested later, this is far from the truth.

Consider small islands communities, for instance, such as are found in abundance in the South Pacific. When the author first worked with UNESCO (the United Nations Educational, Scientific and Cultural Organization) in what was then the British Solomon Island Protectorate (BSIP), the name referred to a patch of about 1000 islands, not all close together, and in which about 300 languages were spoken. It eventually all 'became' or was 'made into' one nation, with its own flag and national anthem. Funds for health development programmes at the village level were mediated, though, through UNESCO and WHO and not through the capital city. Thus funds could be allocated reasonably fairly and at the most local level where their disbursement and effects could be directly assessed and reported on. There would be no real reason why the people of Island X of the BSIP would feel any more kinship with people from Island Y 700 miles away in the BSIP than they would for people living geographically closer, in Papua New Guinea, for instance.

Considerations such as these suggested that the enterprise of mediating global health might involve a transnational administration and that the present system of national market forces run on IMF loans might be retrograde. Indeed, in terms of health promotion – and that includes a broad swathe of social enterprises (schools, lifestyles, race relations, employment opportunities, etc.) and not just clinical medical healthcare – a truly global administration would surely be much more efficient than banks in the richer parts of the world lending to the poorer nations at ruinous interest rates that create a few wealthy stockholders but which redounds to the disadvantage of the majority of the first world's people.

First the goods, then the people

We have seen that the third world debt not only undermines the bases for healthy communities in the third world, but also in the first. The third world is forced into pushing its hard-won basic products onto a hostile world market, where their price is determined in competition with similar products from other equally indebted third world nations. Because this leads to reduced return per unit of produce, the producers back in the third world country are driven to even more desperate efforts to produce more – at immediate cost to their health, social integrity and environment, and at ultimate cost to those aspects of life in the first world.

But, of course, there is a limit to how bad things have to get before people simply give up and flee their country. The limit, we know, is quite extreme. People do not usually flee their home and country, their sense of belonging, their language and culture, for fun. Young people may do so more readily, but they usually return to their own community once the adventure wears thin. However, the systematic stripping of living standards in a country will gradually force increasing numbers of more established people to flee for good. We are not talking here about political refugees, but about economic refugees. In Britain, our treatment of – and social attitudes towards – asylum seekers often overlooks our own involvement in their original flight from home.

In real terms one might ask: why is this distinction important? The British Home Office is greatly exercised about the difference to the extent that would-be refugees seeking asylum here must prove that they did not flee their country only because they could no longer make ends meet there. This is especially ironic when it is reasonable to argue that one reason that the supplicant cannot make ends meet back home is because the first world has distorted his country's economy through IMF-imposed economic restructuring to pay back debt!

It is beyond question that there has been a substantial increase in migration of people from third world to first world countries since the end of the Second World War. And it is not unreasonable to attribute at least some of this to international debt. In a sense, we go into a country and take more and more of their goods until eventually, in desperation, its citizens start to follow the goods out!

Impact of emigration on a society's health

The effect on the home country of citizens fleeing it in large numbers is important to consider. While it is true that the very poorest feel the strongest immediate reason to leave, emigration costs money. There is therefore a tendency for a third world society in this kind of predicament to become subdivided as follows. The most wealthy – usually those in government or closely linked to it – are generally doing very well. They would favour IMF and World Bank loans first because they probably benefit directly from them themselves and second because it strengthens their control at the top. A broad band of middle-level citizens have some money but are disadvantaged by the general economic situation. They have enough money to avoid total desperation, but are worried by the prospect of the fragile situation worsening and leaving them stranded. In addition, they are likely to have had secondary education at least and to face with some degree of confidence the fact that, if they do emigrate, they will have to learn English (or one of the other first world languages) to seek employment.

But if large numbers of this middle-level group do take the opportunity to leave, their country is bereft of many of its former middle managers, teachers, healthcare personnel, etc. When this author was in Jamaica in 1987, on a UNESCO contract, the only two children's clinics within a 20-mile radius of where he was living closed down within a week of one another. Both clinics had been progressively deteri-orating for the previous five years due to cutbacks in healthcare services instituted by a government striving to comply with IMF restructuring dictates. Likewise their capacity to hire local cleaners – even at reduced rates – had been reduced so much that basic hygiene was frequently ignored. It was even said among the local people that the clinics were so infected that a child going there for one illness was sure to be treated for another when he returned home! However, the final closure occurred because all of the staff emigrated to Canada. Not one of them was going to a job for which they had been professionally trained, but to do unskilled work for which they could earn much higher pay and guarantee that their children were able to attend school.

In such parlous situations, what tends to happen is that the absolutely poverty-stricken are driven to heroically desperate measures, such as crime (to secure money for a passage), stowing away, etc. They leave because there is literally no alternative. On doing so, they often leave dependants behind. Usually, the inten-tion is that, once the economic refugee has managed to lie his way into a first world country and secure employment, he can start sending money to his family. In the meantime the latter live even more precariously than they did before he left.

The people just above the level of desperate poverty, but still grindingly poor, observe that they had better hold on just a bit longer to see if they can avert disaster. In one third world country after another this author has seen this sort of scenario unfold, and what it does to community empowerment and individual self-esteem hardly bears discussion. These last, of course, are two critical factors in sustaining physical and psychological health.

Impact of immigration on first world social health

Now let us go to the receiving end of our economic migrant's journey. Enough is already known about refugee health and psychological well-being for us to realise that the migrant faces serious obstacles (Hillier, 1991; Stein, 1986). But as well as that, migrants (whatever their status) in large numbers and arriving without adequate preparation by the host community become themselves a source of conflict within the first world country concerned. In the United States every large town provides graphic incidents of this. In 1968 this author left an upper-middle-class area of Stockton in Northern California to take up a post in Jamaica. In 1983, 15 years later, when one of his daughters returned to the area – 'to see the old house' – while on a visit to America, she described radical changes to the area. Now it was largely a Hispanic, predominantly Mexican, community. Economic refugees were promin-ent in large numbers, driven from their homes by structural readjustments to their country's economy.

According to an article in the *New York Times* of 15 January 1991, the change had occurred suddenly in 1981–1982:

> *Well-off California residents suddenly found themselves living much further south than they had imagined. ('South' in that context means 'in the third world'. Commonly the spectrum between the first and third world is described as the North– South axis.) Homeowners complain that the migrants, who line the roadsides seeking jobs and who camp out at night within shouting distance of their homes,*

bring crime, unsanitary conditions and a breath of third world squalor to their carefully tended to communities.

If such a quote, especially from a respectable broadsheet such as the *New York Times*, sounds shrill and xenophobic, the reader should realise that it is a mild reaction. Much more serious reactions are daily reported in the press, from instances of Turkish refugees being burned in their hostels in Germany (1997) to Pakistani students being murdered on the street in London (2004). Tensions of this kind, exacerbated by economic grievances and a growing sense of job insecurity, are easily exploited by racist groups. Refugees interviewed by this author have eloquently described how bad things have to be to make them flee in the first place. Most economic refugees would not have done it if the economy in their own country had been only slightly better.

The relationship of these community-shattering events can be directly traced to the debt problem. In 1981, the United States had experienced a tenfold increase in illegal immigration from Mexico over the figures for 1965. The accumulation of undocumented aliens amounted to a total pool of four to six million people, living physically and socially unprotected on the margins of American society (George, 1992).

The link with debt is graphically illustrated in Table 3.4, which lists the major 'source' countries in rank order of their level of indebtedness to the IMF (in descending order, e.g. the Caribbean at rank 112 is so much more seriously in debt than is Taiwan at rank 10) in 1988 and compares this with the rounded range of the numbers of their migrants to the US during the period 1983–1988 (George, 1992).

But let it not be assumed that the US alone among the nations of the first world is uniquely affected in this way. *Time* magazine (2 August 1998) presents similar figures for Germany, Italy and even Switzerland.

The solution cannot possibly be greater immigration control per se or better-protected frontiers. People had roamed about the earth's surface looking for safety and happiness for centuries before frontiers were even invented. In terms of global health promotion, solutions based on exclusion and coercion have no place. The whole purpose of the argument put forward in this book is to make it clear that we must come up with an economic framework that is less irrational than the present one and definitely more easily administered, but above all, one that acknowledges the ultimate ethical content of the philosophy of global health promotion.

Wars, health promotion and the debt

As Marc Lalonde (1974) observed, in setting out the conditions which must prevail before health promotion can be effective, it is obvious that a society involved in military conflict cannot practise health promotion! While it would be extremely difficult, if not impossible, to statistically prove that IMF restructuring programmes in the third world in the context of the international debt actually cause wars, a link can certainly be hypothesised.

Large parts of the world have been at war almost without break since the Second World War ended in 1945. Some of these wars have been between nations and of the 'classical' type with identifiable armies, etc., but most have been 'civil' wars and less 'formal'. Almost none of them have been regarded as being newsworthy, but their reality is nonetheless reflected in epidemiological data from the third world,

Table 3.4: Rank of countries sending immigrants to the US as at 1998: range of number sent 1983–1988 ('000s, rounded)

	1998	*Range 1983–1988*
(Total Caribbean)	112	73–112
1 Mexico	95	57–95
2 Philippines	51	41–52
3 Haiti	35	8–35
4 Korea	35	33–35
5 China	29	23–29
6 Dominican Republic	27	22–27
7 India	26	22–28
8 Vietnam*	26	24–38
9 Jamaica	21	19–23
10 Cuba	18	9–33
11 Iran	15	11–16
12 United Kingdom	13	13–15
13 El Salvador	12	9–12
14 Canada	12	11–12
15 Laos**	11	7–24
16 Colombia	10	10–12
17 Taiwan	10	10–17

*85 500 Vietnamese were admitted in 1978; 72 500 in 1982.
**90 000 Laotians were admitted 1980–1983; a considerable drain on a country of only 4 million people.
Source: US Immigration and Naturalization Service, 1990

for it is in the third world that most of these conflicts are taking place. There have been some newsworthy wars – Korea, Vietnam, the Gulf War, the Israeli–Arab wars, Iraq, etc. – but the under-reported ones have been no less destructive for all that. One has only to consider the conflict between the Iraqis and the Kurds, or the Tutsis and the Hutus, to gain some idea of the magnitude of the problem.

It would be oversimplifying things outrageously to claim a simple set of reasons for these conflicts. For instance, conflict over resources is neither the only nor the most important factor of many of these conflicts. But economic problems which induced mass migrations, starvation and wide-scale environmental damage will certainly exacerbate any other causes promoting conflict. It is instructive to look at a list of the two dozen most highly indebted third world nations and to note which ones were involved during 1990–1991 in warfare (*see* Table 3.5). The table also lists

Table 3.5: Debtors at war

Ranking of third world states by gross debt	(US$bn)	War 1990–1991	Ranking of third world states by Debt Service Ratio	%	War 1990–1991
1 Brazil	(113)	–	1 Nicaragua	96	YES
2 Mexico	(113)	–	2 Somalia	81	YES
3 Argentina	(65)	–	3 Mozambique	72	YES
4 India	(61)	YES	4 Madagascar	64	–
5 Egypt	(54)	YES	5 Guatemala	63	YES
6 Indonesia	(54)	YES	6 Algeria	62	–
7 China	(45)	YES	7 Côte d'Ivoire	61	–
8 South Korea	(44)	–	8 Ghana	59	–
9 Turkey	(37)	YES	9 Uganda	53	YES
10 Nigeria	(32)	–	10 Mexico	53	–
11 Venezuela	(30)	–	11 Myanmar	52	YES
12 Philippines	(28)	YES	12 Niger	51	–
13 Algeria	(28)	–	13 Bolivia	46	YES
14 Thailand	(25)	–	14 Congo	46	–
15 Israel	(24)	YES	15 Brazil	44	–
16 Chile	(22)	–	16 Honduras	42	–
17 Peru	(21)	YES	17 Jamaica	42	–
18 Morocco	(21)	YES	18 Colombia	41	YES
19 Malaysia	(20)	–	19 Uruguay	41	–
20 Pakistan	(18)	YES	20 Argentina	40	–
21 Colombia	(17)	YES	21 Indonesia	39	YES
22 Iraq	(15)	YES	22 Kenya	37	–
23 Côte d'Ivoire	(15)	–	23 Venezuela	37	–
24 Ecuador	(13)	–	24 Ethiopia	36	YES
25 Vietnam	(12)	–	25 Philippines	35	YES
26 Turkey	(35)	YES	26 Nigeria	35	–

Sources: OECD, 1990; World Bank, 1989

countries according to the 'Debt Service Ratio' (DSR) on the same basis. The 'Debt Service Ratio' is calculated by working out the percentage of repayments/export earnings. The DSR gives a very clear idea of the disruption caused to the community life and values in a given country by the debt. The debt rankings are from 1988 data (George, 1992).

While structural readjustments generally serve to draw money away from health initiatives and thus prevent their development, it is also plain that by far the most expensive items on which borrowed capital is spent are armaments. This, accordingly, serves to keep the public sector (principally health and education) starved of funds. We therefore have a situation in which some consequences of debt repayments (e.g. environmental destruction, loss of domestic produce, emigration) exacerbate social tensions and thus create an 'enemy within' for the government of the debtor nation. But the debt is incurred (at least partly) in order to try to repress military insurgency. It is very much a chicken-and-egg scenario.

Furthermore, as long as the third world nation is faced with the problem of having to produce for exports in exchange for dollars, the arms trade will prove an irresistible attraction if the country concerned can produce the goods. In fact, it is almost as lucrative as the drugs trade and yet strictly legal! It is beyond the remit of our concern in this book to speculate how third world nations gain the stock of arms to sell, but a passing comment on it will serve to show how destructive it is of attempts to establish global peace – a precondition for equity in health. Some third world nations accumulate huge arms supplies from wars fought in their territory. For years after the rout in Vietnam, Vietnamese arms dealers profited handsomely by selling discarded – but perfectly usable – war material to other third world countries for dollars.

When third world countries import arms they do not always buy from first world countries, but they always pay in dollars. In terms of profits made by the first world banks, therefore, this makes little difference. For instance, in 1990, India was the fourth most indebted nation in the world and yet it was then a leading (in terms of US dollars) arms importer (Wulf and Wulf, 1990). Of course, it has now gone one step better and has produced its own nuclear weapon – as has Pakistan. No doubt such developments have immensely enhanced healthcare among its own people and the prospect of health equity throughout the region!

Of course, we have not yet even considered the possibility that the debt itself may cause a cash-strapped third world country to go to war. An apposite example of this is the first Gulf War. To support the war against Iran, Iraq borrowed extensively from other Arab states, including Kuwait. When that conflict had subsided, Kuwait tried to claim back its loan, to the tune of about US$12 billion. Now Saddam Hussein had long wanted to annex Kuwait and – as was said at the time – if Kuwait had been noted as a producer of carrots rather than of oil, no doubt the first world would not have felt the 'moral' need to defend Kuwait when Iraq struck. Obviously the debt was not Saddam's only motivation for going to war, but it was certainly a major factor.

Even if the reader considers the Vietnam War a bit outdated, let us look at the more recent wars between third world countries, but set in motion and/or exacerbated by their unequal financial involvement with the first world. I refer to such wars as are still running in the Democratic Republic of the Congo, Côte d'Ivoire, Sierra Leone and the Solomon Islands – to say nothing of Iraq and of the Israeli–Palestine conflict. The Solomon Island conflict has been well described in economic terms by the World Bank, which reported on it in a rather upbeat manner in 2003. The reader is left to judge for her/himself. The report is exactly as it appeared in the cited source:

> *The Solomon Islands have struggled with inter-ethnic tension since independence in 1978, although violent conflict only broke out in late 1998. About 20 000 people were forced to abandon their homes. In June 2000 there was a coup, and violence continued particularly in remote rural areas.*
>
> *The effects on the economy and the well-being of the people have been marked. Modest growth in national income has turned into severe decline. Net inflows of foreign direct investment declined from US$33.8 million in 1997 to US$1.4 million in 2000. By 2001, there was a net outflow of US$5.1 million. Debt grew by almost 50% between 2000 and 2001. While aid is about 23% of gross national income, the debt burden is about 58%. See Figure 3.1.*

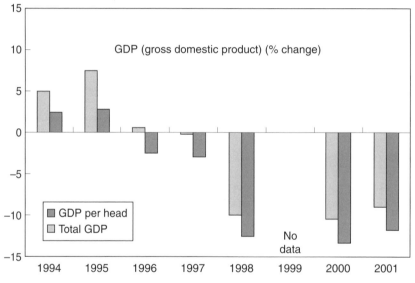

Source: Asian Development Bank, Asian Development Outlook

Figure 3.1: The declining economy of the Solomon Islands at war.

> *The Solomons are far behind on the Millennium Development Goals. Particularly in remote areas, declining funding of essential social services has adversely affected health and education indicators, now the lowest in the region. Maternal mortality rates are particularly high. New vulnerable groups are emerging such as those displaced by the conflict, the unemployed, especially women, and youth.*
>
> *More than two years later, Australia and a few other Pacific neighbours offered to send in a small peacekeeping force. The Solomon Islands parliament approved the force on 17 July 2003. By the end of 2003, a measure of stability had been restored. This may be the chance to prevent conflict as a driver from becoming conflict as a maintainer of chronic poverty.*

Sources: ADB, 2003; BBC, 2003; World Bank, 2003

References

Auden W (1939) In: Oscar Williams (ed.) *A Little Treasury of Modern Poetry*. Routledge, Kegan Paul, London, p.197.

Bunyard P (1985) World climate and tropical forest destruction. *The Ecologist*. **15(3)**: 37–42.

Castro F (1982) *La Deuda Internacional es una Deuda Impagable* [*The International Debt is an Unpayable Debt*]. Government Publications, Havana.

Charveriat C (2001) *Bitter Coffee: How the poor are paying for the slump in coffee prices*. Oxfam, Oxford, pp 7–10.

Christian Aid (1998) *The Jubilee 2000 Petition*. Christian Aid, London.

Du Toit A (2003) *Hunger in the Valley of Fruitfulness: globalisation, poverty dynamics and social exclusion in the Ceres, South Africa*. Conference, Poverty and Development Policy. Manchester, 7–9 April.

FAO/GIEWS (2003) www.ifpri.org/divs/dsgd/dp/papers/dsgdp09.pdf

George S (1992) *The Debt Boomerang*. Pluto Press, London, p.96.

George S and Sabelli F (1994) *Faith and Credit: The World Bank's Secular Empire*. Penguin, London.

Hartwig G and Patterson K (eds) (1998) *Disease in African History: survey and case studies*. Duke University Press, Durham, NC, pp 31–46.

Hillier S (1991) *The Health and Health Care of Ethnic Migrant Groups*. Baillière Tindall, London.

Holmes D (2000) As quoted in *Chronic Poverty Report (2004–05)*. Chronic Poverty Research Centre, Manchester University, Manchester.

Lalonde M (1974) *A Perspective on the Health of all Canadians*. Government Publications, Ottawa.

Leggett J (ed.) (1990) *Global Warming: The Greenpeace Report*. Oxford University Press, Oxford, pp 436–500.

Lines T and Tickell S (2003) *Walk the Talk: a call to action to restore coffee farmers' livelihoods*. Oxfam Briefing Paper 44, Oxford.

Moises N (1993) *The World Bank: its role, governance and organisational culture* (Proceedings of the 1993 Bretton Woods Institutions). Columbia University Press, New York.

Myers N (1989) *Deforestation Rates in Tropical Forests and their Climate Implications*. Friends of the Earth, London, pp 395–6.

New York Times (1991) When south moves north – California reclaimed. 15 January, p.28.

New York Times (2004) Drug trade supports terrorism. 24 May, p.18.

Nissan B (1974) Building the World Bank. In: S Weissman (ed.) *The Trojan Horse*. Ramparts Press, San Francisco.

Organisation for Economic Co-operation and Development (OECD) (1990) *Financing and External Debt of Developing Countries: 1989 Survey*. OECD, Paris.

Organisation for Economic Co-operation and Development (OECD) (2000) Financing the external debt of developing countries. *Technical Notes*. **11**: 75–88.

Potter A (1999) Dealing with two Africas. *British Medical Journal*. **303**: 1558.

Rachman J and Bloch E (eds) (1974) *Multinational Corporations*. Trade And The Dollar Publishers, Chicago, pp 43–57.

Reader's Digest (1998) Stopping the narcotics traders on the high seas. Lafolley, J, pp 74–86.

Reagan R (1981) Inaugural address.

Shoup L and Minter W (1977) Shaping a new world order. Ch. 4 in: *Imperial Brains Trust*. Monthly Review Press, New York, p.117.

Stein B (1986) *The Experience of Being a Refugee*. New Hemisphere, New York.

Time Magazine (1998) Europe's Bad Debt Overseas. 2 August, p.16.

UNICEF (1992) *Children for Health: Children as communicators of facts for life*. UNICEF, Geneva.

UNICEF (1998) *Communities for Development: Human change for survival*. IB Taurus Press, New York.

US Immigration and Naturalization Service (1990) Sources and immigration to the United States 1960–1998. US Immigration and Naturalization Service, publications division, Washington DC.

World Bank (1989) *World Debt Tables 1989–90*. World Bank, Washington, DC.

World Bank (2003) Solomon Islands data profile. In: *Chronic Poverty 2004–2005*, p.45. World Bank, Washington DC.

World Health Organization (WHO) (1973) *Organisational Study on Methods of Promoting the Development of Basic Health Services*. Annex II, Official WHO Records, No. 26. WHO, Geneva.

Wulf A and Wulf H (1990) The trade in major conventional weapons. In: *World Armaments and Disarmament* (SIPRI Yearbook). Oxford University Press, Oxford, pp 211–59.

Zwi A and Ugalde A (1991) Political violence in the Third World – a public health issue. *Health Policy and Planning*. **6(3)**: 203–317.

Chapter 4

The conflict between global health and global finance: a case study approach

Addressing health inequalities

Christian Aid, a group drawn from all of the leading Protestant denominations, perhaps deserves the most credit for drawing the international debt to the attention of lay people in recent years. Their promotion of the Jubilee 2000 Project, which calls for the unilateral lifting of debt from the poorest nations, has attracted considerable media attention. This was reflected in the large street demonstrations which took place in 1998 in Birmingham at the meeting of the G7 nations (plus Russia) and it was widely thought that the most powerful first world nations really would address the debt question in some dramatic way at that gathering. The fact that they didn't served to educate large numbers of 'ordinary people' as to the response of the powerful to issues of social justice.

But, long before Christian Aid made the problem common knowledge, serious attempts had been made, at international level, to address the issue. In 1979 the 32nd World Health Assembly launched the Global Strategy for Health for All by the Year 2000. This strategy gave public expression to a commitment from the governments of the world to enable people to increase control over and to improve their health. The dawn of the new millennium provided a useful milestone against which to evaluate whether progress had been made in implementing such a global strategy for Health for All by the Year 2000. The most recent evaluation report of the implementation of the global strategy (1979–1996) indicates that there have undoubtedly been tremendous global improvements in life expectancy and child mortality and remarkable progress in various disease elimination/eradication efforts (WHO, 1998). However, despite such progress, the report also acknowledges that during this period 'for some health status issues, inequities widened and greater inequities are foreseen' (WHO, 1998, p.1).

Even a cursory glance at the available data reveals the extent of health inequalities between developed and developing countries. Communicable, perinatal and nutritional conditions, for example, accounted for 42% of deaths in developing countries in the 1990s compared to only 6% of deaths in developed countries (WHO, 1998). Life expectancy figures range from 37.5 years in Sierra Leone to 80 years in Japan (WHO, 1998). Infant mortality figures vary from 62% in third world countries to 6.3% in developed market economies. Indeed, 99% of the half a million maternal deaths that occur annually in the world occur in developing countries.

However, we know that health is so much more than merely the absence of disease. Health promotion involves a 'movement towards a positive state of health and well-being' (MacDonald, 1998, p.27). Poverty, other forms of social inequality, and human impact on the environment are increasingly recognised as important, perhaps fundamental, health determinants. An evaluation of Health for All, therefore, cannot ignore the fact that one fifth of the population of developing countries (800 million people) still do not have access to enough food to meet their basic needs (WHO, 1998). These individuals are trapped in 'the grimmest poverty ... Where the burdens of ill health, disease and inequality are heaviest, the outlook is bleakest and life is shortest' (Dr Nakajima, Director General of WHO, press release of the World Health Report, 1998).

No one seriously questions the fact that the health experience of the two thirds of the world's population who belong to the third world is markedly inferior to that of first world countries. In attempting to address this problem, we must first ascertain the factors that condition and constrain health determinants. Is the hope of health for all of the world's population a utopian dream that could never be fulfilled? Is there a lack of political will to translate rhetoric into practice and, if so, why? This chapter aims to contextualise the processes that are acting to reinforce existing global health inequalities. It will also seek to illustrate, through a number of case studies, how programmes implemented in the name of development have often turned out to actually exacerbate health inequalities. In drawing the argument to a close, steps are considered that might be taken to keep the basic tenets of health promotion at the forefront internationally in the drive to provide efficiently for basic human needs.

Reinforcing global inequalities

Although a general overview has already been given as to how the international debt has arisen, it is worth reviewing some of these processes in the context of global health as such.

Debt

When members of the Organization of Petroleum Exporting Countries (OPEC) simultaneously raised the price of oil in 1973, they also – as we have seen – acquired huge reserves of US dollars from their sales of oil, much of which was invested in banks outside of the United States. One of the outlets that the international banks found to soak up the surplus money was developing countries, some of whose dictatorships were eager to take advantage of the loans to bail them out or to squander on grandiose projects (Ransom, 1999). The combination of dictatorship, foreign loans and the transfer of private liabilities onto the backs of the public pervades much of Latin America, Africa and Asia, and between 1970 and 1980 third world debt rose from less than $100 billion to $600 billion (Ransom, 1999). A combination of factors contributed to governments running into financial trouble: prices of raw materials such as coffee, tea and cocoa fell by 30% so that third world income nosedived, and at the same time interest rates soared and oil prices quadrupled. Suddenly the poorest countries in the world were earning less from exports, having to pay more on their loans and on what they needed to import – the result being that many found themselves in a position where they were unable to pay off their debts. In 1982 Mexico defaulted on its interest payments and was soon followed by Brazil, Argentina and others (Thrift, 1989). The international debt crisis had begun. By 1997 the foreign debts of developing countries were more than two trillion US dollars and still growing (World Bank, 2000). For every man, woman and child in the developing world this amounted to a debt of $400, even though the average income is less than a dollar a day (World Bank, 1999).

Clearly a serious implication for health is that debt repayments siphon money away from the health sector. In Ethiopia 100 000 children die annually from preventable diseases, while debt repayments are four times greater than public spending on healthcare (Ransom, 1999). In Tanzania, where 40% of people die before the age of 35, debt repayments are six times greater than spending on healthcare. From the whole of Africa, where four in every 10 children of primary school age are not in school, governments transfer four times more to northern creditors in debt repayments than they spend on the health and education for their citizens (Ransom, 1999). In Nicaragua external debt repayment amounted to $341 million in 1997 – roughly half of all export earnings – and while the total health budget for 1998 stood at $88 million, more than four times this amount was spent on debt servicing (Gaynor, 1999).

Privatisation – destruction of the social fabric

Early in 1999, Brazil teetered on the edge of financial collapse. Such a major event would have had an immense negative impact on global finance. But earlier on, in the mid-1980s, it looked as though the debt crisis might bring the entire world's financial system tumbling down. This did not happen simply because the world financial system changed to meet the threat. In Chapter 1, a brief account of how the debt crisis arose was given. Let us now look at this in more detail.

The end of the 'Cold War' marked the emergence of a single dominant political philosophy, particularly in the powerful donor nations and the organisations linked to them (WHO, 1998). Labonte (1998) labels this philosophy as 'the dominance of a neoliberal economic orthodoxy': one that promotes individualism as preferable to collectivist behaviour and favours market forces to state direction in economic and social management. This philosophy views 'the rational pursuit of self-interest, [as being] ultimately utilitarian creating the greatest good for the greatest number' (Labonte, 1998, p.246).

So much for the theory, but the translation of this philosophy into policy has impacted upon health in a number of ways, in particular as a consequence of what Bennett et al. (1997) termed the 'realignment of the state'. Whereas the Alma Ata declaration viewed governments as the main vehicles for improvement in people's health status (WHO, 1978), since the mid-1980s there has been pressure for governments to take on a smaller role in healthcare. This was articulated by a document produced by the World Bank, 'Financing Healthcare: An Agenda for Reform'. Strenuous attempts were made to interfere directly in the domestic economies of the most affected nations. International finance institutions and bilateral donors gave clear messages to decrease the level of government involvement in healthcare and to promote the private sector. The clear impact of this was that it resulted in aid to developing countries being conditional upon certain economic and political specifications, or 'structural adjustment policies' (SAPs). In simple terms, SAPs are intended to enable the countries to repay their debts by making them export more and spend less. That is, the primary concern is for the welfare of the lender! However, this has led inexorably to the neglect of domestic needs, and means that the IMF intervenes in the management of the economies, undermining the sovereignty of indebted states. In many countries, 20–50% of recurrent health budgets is provided by international aid (World Bank, 1993, in Okuonzi and Macrae, 1995). Two case studies will serve to illustrate how Western political philosophy has infiltrated the health policy and practice of developing countries.

Case study 1: Uganda

Uganda, at the time of its first independence from Britain, was held up as a model of responsible management. Now Uganda is still a very poor country, but in 1993 was ranked by UNICEF as the nineteenth least developed country in the world (Okuonzi and Macrae, 1995). The GDP (gross domestic product) was only US$212 per capita, 90% of which was skewed to 10% of the population. These figures, however, must be viewed in the context of impressive economic growth, which took place during the seven years that the National Resistance Movement (NRM) came into power. Since 1986, for example, the NRM accomplished major rehabilitation of infrastructure and reversed economic decline so that by June 1993 economic growth was at 7.5% per annum and inflation had fallen to an unprecedented negative 3%. Despite this economic progress the debt burden is enormous, accounting for 39% of the GDP. Seventy-seven per cent of all export earnings are used to service debt and interest repayments. Economic growth, therefore, has had only a minimal effect on the quality of life for the majority of the country's population. Balance of repayment and budget deficit problems have continued to force the government to rely heavily on external aid. The situation is particularly severe with respect to education and health. For instance, in the health sector, aid dependence is prodigiously high – 66% of primary healthcare expenditures are supported by international donors. With much hope and fanfare, the government introduced a structural adjustment programme in 1987 under the auspices of the IMF and the World Bank. This led to an increased involvement of international advisers in the process of health policy development and the use of conditionalities on health assistance. A three-year health plan was published in 1992, although it was largely developed by expatriate advisers. A salient feature of it was the proposal that an element of the health plan should be the promotion of user fees. This was strongly contested by the government and, indeed, had its first reading thrown out by the NRM. However, despite this formal rejection, the World Bank negotiated a new loan on condition that the government adopted a national policy promoting user fees.

Such, it would appear, is one easy path to debt-slavery and it illustrates the way in which countries in the stranglehold of debt are often pressurised into adopting interventions which largely reflect the 'values, ideologies, objectives and priorities expressed by organisations in New York, Washington and London, and not those of any national political system' (Okuonzi and Macrae, 1995, p.130).

A clear implication, then, is that any rational debate about healthcare policy can quickly become coloured by vested political and commercial interests. Compromises are often made to prevent the withdrawal of major donor financing.

Case study 2: privatising pharmaceutical provision in India

As we know, SAPs invariably favour private trade as opposed to public initiatives. But, even though the World Bank and other international organisations have placed such a high priority on increasing the role of private providers in social sectors of third world countries for over a decade, there has been little examination of the consequences. Finally, however, concerns have been raised about the application of neoclassical economic theory to developing-country contexts (Bennett *et al.*, 1997). Most basically, there has been a questioning as to the degree to which competitive or contestable markets really exist. In many rural areas the dearth of providers in developing countries and poor accessibility, for example, limit competition or choice between such providers. Additionally, there is some concern that the growth related to private markets may not be equally distributed. Ugalade and Jackson (in Bennett *et al.*, 1997) argue that privatisation disadvantages the poor, making access to crucial, life-enhancing services dependent upon the ability and willingness to pay. Of course, there are those who argue the reverse. For instance, Stren (cited in Labonte, 1998), in a discussion of urban services in Africa, suggests that the growth of private markets has improved the welfare of the poor by providing them with access to services not available to them. In bringing this argument to bear on the healthcare sector, the World Bank has suggested that the private sector can bring in new resources, thus allowing governments to focus upon the poor and on essential services, even expanding services to those who previously did not receive them. However, this oft-cited 'trickle down' claim of neoliberal economics is not supported historically (Hettne, 1995 and Amin, 1997, cited in Labonte, 1998). Indeed, the past two decades of economic and social policies based on privatisation of public services, declining government regulation, and increased free trade and investment, have seen global wealth inequalities more than double (*New Internationalist*, January 1997). Another worry is that the developing country government may be in no position to regulate or manage relationships with the private sector and with the form of competition which arises. We are not, after all, discussing nations with a long tradition of democratic government and entrepreneurial capitalism as their normal modus vivendi.

These concerns are exemplified by Vinay Kamat and Mark Nichter (1997) in their analysis of competition between different pharmaceutical companies in Bombay and in particular the role of the medical representatives ('medreps') in promoting sales. They carried out an ethnographic study which illustrated how medical care in India has acquiesced to strategies employed by the pharmaceutical industries in influencing prescription habits of doctors. It is evident that the medical needs of the patient and the extent to which a doctor makes a rational decision in the interest of the patient both appear to be compromised by the GP's reliance on commercial sources of prescribing information. Large pharmaceutical companies – for example, one the size of Abbott Pharmaceutical – may invest $180–200 in marketing costs per month per doctor visited by its medreps (Kamat and Nichter, 1997). Whatever pharmaceutical company is concerned can then rank-order the GPs on the basis of the number of prescriptions they write for company products during a given period. 'Class A' doctors are those who are high-volume prescribers of expensive medicines. To quote a medrep working for Win-Medicare: 'the truth is, very often, when doctors write a product on the prescription, they are not doing it for the patient, but for the medrep!' (Kamat and Nichter, 1997, p.128).

A standard procedure is for pharmaceutical companies to offer incentives to doctors for prescribing their products. Such promotional strategies include free samples of medicines and gifts, including generous offers of hospitality, and even families of GPs may be targeted as the recipients of attractive gifts. A senior medrep working for Hoechst outlined his '3Cs' sales strategy: 'Convince' the doctor to support the product; 'Confuse' the doctor with the necessary technical details; then 'Corrupt' him with generous gifts and invitations to cocktail parties! In situations involving GPs with fewer resources, as is likely to be the case in developing countries, it is unlikely they will forgo promotional gifts. Another promotional approach widely used by medreps involves creating the impression of a demand for new products among local pharmacy owners. Naturally, pharmacists are often unwilling to stock new products until prescriptions are presented, but medreps persuade the GPs that there are adequate stocks of new products as a means of encouraging them to start prescribing these products. The result is that once a patient receives a prescription for a new product, they frequently have to go from pharmacy to pharmacy before succeeding in getting the prescription filled, creating an impression among the pharmacists that there is great demand for the new product. It is also not unknown for medreps to help pharmacists liquidate slow-moving stock by persuading doctors to generate prescriptions for such products. A common marketing strategy employed by pharmaceutical companies is to identify by market research those sets of symptoms and health issues that most concern the local population. Using these insights, company advertisements and medreps then work to reinforce 'existing' patterns of pharmaceutical behaviour and to influence doctors to meet these perceived health needs and expectations. The effect of all this, of course, is that medicines are being prescribed, not on the basis of appropriate care or medicinal needs, but rather on the basis of the patient's assumptions and expectations.

From this case study, it is easy enough to appreciate the importance of context when considering the impact of the privatisation of unfettered markets in health-care provision. For instance, it has shown how the primary role of medreps is to push their products while at the same time playing down product risks and negative attributes. It has demonstrated, too, the contingencies with which doctors contend in their daily practice.

Overarching these considerations, it renders obvious the way in which the marketing strategies of large pharmaceutical companies prevail. Basically, they can employ their resources in such a way as to dictate the needs of the local consumer. To quote the response of a medrep noted by Kamat and Nichter (1997) in their study: 'This is not a business for those overly concerned with morality.' In this particular instance, in order to gain a sense of moral identity, the medrep cited his participation in medical camps for the poor and noted that participation in such service organisations was particularly popular in medicinal circles (Kamat and Nichter, 1997).

Privatisation, trade and the global market

As a result of increased speed and facility of transport and communication, the market forces model now dominates the world and the world economy has become more integrated than ever before. This increasing economic and social interdependence has been termed 'globalisation'. Although not a new phenomenon, the momentum with which change is taking effect far outstrips that ever experienced before (Labonte, 1998). Nigel Thrift (1989) describes it as 'a world-economic order which is addicted to the knife-edge – a world economic order hooked on speed'. Not unreasonably, this has brought about vast changes to the nature of international trade. Capital has become more footloose (Thrift, 1989) with exchange rates changing every few hours and interest rates changing more frequently. The borders of capitalist industrial production have moved further out from the core industrialised economies. Indeed, financial speculation carried out by one wealthy individual using email can easily outmanoeuvre a single nation's carefully elaborated fiscal plan.

Whereas in the past, transnational companies produced goods entirely within one country or plant and then marketed them abroad, today many large firms have taken advantage of improved transportation and communications technology to shift production and marketing beyond national boundaries. They organise their world network of subsidies to turn the best possible profit by dividing different stages of commodity production. This allows them to promote global brand names and to organise production to take advantage of, for example, design or technical knowledge in one country (usually a first world country) and low labour costs in another country (usually a third world country). As a result, the markets internal to these corporations have dramatically enlarged. According to the UN Conference on Trade and Development, some 40 000 transnational corporations (TNCs) and their foreign affiliates control two-thirds of global trade in goods and services (Leaver and Cavanagh, 1996). For example, General Motors' sales in 1995 were greater than the GNP of 169 countries, including Saudi Arabia, South Africa, Malaysia and Norway (Leaver and Cavanagh, 1996). These changes have led some commentators to conclude that the world has become 'a capitalist stage' and that this is having crucial reverberations – economic, social and cultural – on many countries (Thrift, 1989). It is to these reverberations that we now turn our attention.

The impact of global finance on global health

Although the Ottawa Charter clearly identifies equity and social justice as vital prerequisites for health (Potter, 1997), these values also serve as a counterpoint to the competitive pressures of globalisation. There is no doubt that the easy flow of capital across national borders can and does weaken the influence on an individual government mediating its own national development. If the government wishes to attract capital through TNC investment, it is almost ineluctably forced into softening its regulatory enforcements. At this point, the ruthless canons of competition make themselves felt. Small, poorly endowed nations in competition with one another to raise dollars by selling raw materials to the first world effectively decrease the market value of the commodities they sell. This renders it easy for the TNCs to maximise profits globally by pitting workers' rights, wages and environmental protection in one country against those in other countries. Obviously, this has devastating social consequences for the local population, eroding their rights and standards and resulting in poor pay, cramped and dangerous working conditions, and environmental depression. In Southern California, for example, furniture companies have fled the state's environmental regulations in favour of the lax enforcement climate in Mexico (Leaver and Cavanagh, 1996).

Some large TNCs have greater annual turnovers than many third world nations. Such corporations can avail themselves of tax credits and subsidised insurance on overseas investments as well as export financing. The old regime of tariffs on imported goods, which allowed national states to protect their domestic industries, has been dismantled under pressure from corporations. While in 1947 the average tariff on manufactured imports was 47%, under international free trade agreements it is set to fall to just 3% (Labonte, 1998). Foreign policies such as these have resulted in unequal trading relations between third world and first world. Between 1980 and 1990, for example, the world's share of trade in manufactured goods for the 'Triad' (North America, Europe, Japan/upper-income Asia) rose from 63% to 72% (exports) and 68% to 72% (imports), while for the poorest 102 countries it fell from 8% to 1% (exports) and 9% to 5% (imports) (Labonte, 1998). VSO (Voluntary Service Overseas, 1996) project that the long-term winners and losers from liberalised trade agreements 'place the Triad strongly "in the black" and Africa, lower income Asia and the Mediterranean countries "in the red"'. The *New Internationalist* (1997) argues that 'by the year 2000 sub-Saharan Africa is expected to lose $1200 million annually from its current level of trade'.

The World Trade Organization, established in 1995, monitors and enforces international trade agreements. It is a multilateral body governed by a biennial Ministerial Conference composed of representatives of about 130 nations. Rulings are made by an international tribunal whose decisions are binding and not open to public scrutiny. The overriding intent of the agreements is to remove trade tariffs or other broader restrictions on the import and export of goods and services. Proponents argue that the global free movement of goods and services should benefit poorer countries, with their comparative advantage of cheap labour costs. However, in reality there are factors working against this. Oxfam (1996) argue that reductions in global income inequalities may be achieved by ensuring freer markets for the textiles industries of poorer countries which are large-scale employers. However, revealingly, textiles are one of the goods still excluded from free trade agreement, allowing wealthier countries to impose stiff tariffs to protect their indigenous textile industries. In addition there is evidence that global competitiveness is undermining national policies to protect the environment. In 1991, for example, a GATT (General Agreement on Tariffs and Trade) panel ruled as 'protectionist' an appeal from the United States to ban imports of tuna from Mexico on the basis that Mexican drift net practices violated US environmental regulations and endangered dolphins. Similarly the US were told that they could not ban gasoline imports from Brazil or Venezuela because they failed US clean air legislation (Labonte, 1998).

Investment agreements known as 'Multilateral Agreement on Investments' (MAI) are being negotiated on a more global scale to create a single regulatory framework for investments. These arguments dictate to governments how and when they set investment policy. If governments treat foreign investment in the same way as domestic investments, this must restrict them from directing foreign investment to particular sectors of the economy based, say, on social or environmental objectives. It also prevents them from according preferential treatment to local initiatives. Such provisions make it impossible for local businesses to compete with multinationals and tend to undermine national public health interest. For example, under GATT, the United States forced Thailand to repeal its public health law banning all tobacco imports. These rulings by GATT and the WTO give weight to the suggestion that public health has become a subsidiary goal to economic expediency.

Possible solutions

Earlier in this chapter, we considered the fundamental goal enunciated by the World Health Assembly in 1979: to achieve Health for All by the Year 2000. But we have shown how, in the 20 years since the Alma Ata Declaration, third world debt, structural adjustment policies, the promotion of individualism and the increasing integration of the global economy have acted in such a way as to create an unequal relationship between 'first' and 'third' world countries. The outcome of such processes has been to deprive the citizens of many third world countries of the resources and services required to meet their basic needs. If the World Health Organization is to learn from the past 20 years and to reset its targets so as to achieve Health for All, it might well be better served by focusing on some of the tactical challenges.

Cancellation of world debt

Cancellation of world debt is, of course, the principal objective of Jubilee 2000. This, by itself, is perfectly consistent with one of the basic tenets of health promotion, namely social equity. This chapter suggests, however, that third world debt is enriching the powerful at the expense of the world's majority. Debt has become a modern form of slavery for the poorest of society. There can be little hope of 'health for all' while the chains of debt remain fastened. The Jubilee 2000 campaign calls for the cancellation of the third world debt on the basis of biblical strictures that proclaim:

> *You shall have the trumpet sounded loud.*
> *You shall hallow the fiftieth year.*
> *You shall proclaim liberty throughout the land.*
> *It shall be a Jubilee for you. (Leviticus 25: 9–10)*

This law calls for slaves to be set free, debts to be forgiven, wealth to be restored to the poor and for animals and the land to be given a period of rest. John Mihevc (1999) argues that inherent in the Jubilee concept is a recognition that 'no social, political or economic system can guarantee the well-being of everyone ... The Jubilee vision challenges the triumphant claims of global capitalism – that it is the best and only system for organising society'.

The Alma Ata Declaration needs to detail the mechanisms by which its principles are to be upheld. The cancellation of third world debt is one mechanism by which social equity might be upheld. The Jubilee 2000 campaign is a good example of practical and effective health promotion: it has combined lobbying for policy change and taking the message onto the streets, empowering groups at the local level to understand economic policy-making and to speak out. Of course, one cannot expect complex fiscal problems to be solved that easily, but the idea creates one framework among several that are addressed more fully in the final chapter of this book.

Accountability and sovereignty

In addition to cancellation of actual debt, there is a need to address the flawed process of international lending. Anne Pettifor (1999) argues that structural adjustment policies mean that 'creditors play the role of plaintiff, judge and jury in the court of international debt [using] loans to promote their own interests and negotiations as a way of exercising leverage over sovereign economies'.

While the IMF currently acts as the agent for creditors, Pettifor argues that we could establish an independent Debt Review Body, which could have as its mandate the need to defend both the sovereignty of the debtor nation and to strengthen democracy and accountability, while also being fair to creditors.

Okuonzi and Macrae (1995) also argue for mechanisms of accountability from international donors: 'as the donor community demands stronger mechanisms of accountability in public life in developing countries, it might be argued that similar systems are required to monitor the impact of international actions' (p.30).

There is certainly a need for policy partnerships between international and national actors, rather than the politics of domination which currently predominate.

Collective vs individual

The basis for health promotion is empowerment through neighbourhood advocacy. For instance, the Ottawa Charter for Health Promotion, drawn up in 1986, provided a framework for the process by which Health for All might be achieved. Its significance lay in the fact that it heralded a move away from a focus on the individual as the key agent responsible for his or her health and instead recognising the influence of the collective arena in determining the health experience of individuals. However, as this chapter has shown, the degree to which the concept of individualism permeates the fabric of Western political and fiscal ideologies is paramount. It is intimately woven into the idea of structural adjustment policies and trade agreements with the third world. Indeed, MacDonald (1998) argues that the concept of individual autonomy has permeated the culture of industrialised 'European' nations since ancient Greek times and that 'is a phenomenon which does not apply with the same force in non-European cultures'.

Therefore, in order for health inequalities in third world countries to be addressed in a sustainable way, it is vital to respect the significance of the 'collective'. A corollary of this is that it cannot be assumed that Eurocentric protocols, adopted to promote the health of individuals, can be readily translated to non-European cultures. MacDonald (1998) questions, for example, whether concepts such as 'empowerment' and 'autonomy' – understood to be the basic tenets of 'Western' health promotion – have parallels in the social psychology of cultures in which individualism is not regarded as the primary virtue. Yet the evidence points to the fact that as far as health policy (and other policies) is concerned, a Western cultural perspective has been imposed on developing cultures.

Airhihenbuwa (cited in MacDonald, 1998) argues that Western health promotion models trivialise the effect of cultural diversity within many African societies by placing emphasis on Western models of learning and discourse based on the written word. Health promotion and health service development in third world countries have a better chance of being sustainable if they are built upon indigenous values and systems. MacLachlan (1993) applied the 'bottom up' economic argument to the development of the sustainability of health services in the third world. He argues that, instead of ambitious large-scale health projects with their accompanying costs of drugs, medical equipment, fuel and health personnel, what is needed is something altogether more modest. He states that there were reported to be more than 5000 traditional healers, representing a ratio of 1:120 of the population, and where over 85% of the population had attended a traditional healer at some point. MacLachlan argues for closer collaboration between traditional and modern health sectors, recognising that traditional healers already have authority and credibility among the local populations.

Enforceable social charters and lobbying for change

All that has been discussed heretofore in this book suggests that present global economic markets and investment systems pose a threat to the environment markets, and investment systems pose a threat to the environment and human health. Most public health policy work is directed locally – efforts which, if continued in the absence of global cooperation, are unlikely to be effective. Hart (cited in Labonte, 1998) argues that 'Globalisation is pointing to the need for global governance ... a realignment in the authority exercised by or through extra-national rules and institutions' (p.251).

Labonte (1998) argues that since capital is now global, health-promoting welfare state policies must also be global, or at least supranational. He suggests imposing enforceable reciprocating social and environmental responsibilities into business agreements, thus 'reuniting the false schism (which currently exists) between economic development, social development and environmental protection' (Labonte, 1998, p.251).

In addition to this, there is a need to disburse global trade benefits more equitably and to stem the flow of capital from poor to rich nations. Boyer and Drache (cited in Labonte, 1998) argue for multilateral agreements on taxation and trade and investment profits that could create a pool of capital available to poorer nations for endogenous economic and social welfare development.

As the Jubilee 2000 campaign has demonstrated, national and international citizens' movements might yet play a fundamental role in influencing international economic policy. There are many examples of positive change being effected as a result of the community lobbying for change. For example, the Coalition for Justice in Maquiladoras (CJM) formulated a code of conduct to promote social responsibility in assembly plants on the US/Mexico border. By generating publicity about inadequate working conditions, utilising shareholder pressure, and organising visitor exchanges, CJM prods Maquiladoras to adopt socially responsible business practices (Leaver and Cavanagh, 1996). Boycott, publicity and labelling campaigns are other forms of actions that can effectively challenge corporate power outside of institutional channels. Another strategy is to support alternative production and marketing networks that operate more responsible practices, such as fair trade.

Free trade vs fair trade and the WTO

As we have seen already, many international structures and organisations exist that have the effect of undermining the economic development (and hence health) of various third world countries. The World Trade Organization (WTO) is quickly becoming perceived as one of these. As I write this (August 2004), their meeting at Geneva has already passed its time limit without resolution of the obstacles. Their meeting at Cancun, Mexico (2003), also failed. At Doha (2001), great intentions to improve the situation for the poorer nations were promulgated. But what has happened since? Both the European Union and the US have refined and extended their home-country subsidy programmes. The first world has become even richer and the third world even poorer.

Legislation, such as the Common Agricultural Policy and the subsidising of farmers in the EU, the US and other first world nations, allows those nations to export commodities that are pivotal to third world economies (e.g. sugar, coffee, cotton, rubber, etc.) at far less cost. Even in the 1960s, when this author was in Ghana, locally produced maize could not undercut the price of better quality maize produced (under subsidy) in the US.

The WTO was set up on 1 January 1995, with 104 countries as its founding members. It was a successor to the 1947 General Agreement on Tariffs and Trade (GATT) and it currently includes 147 countries. The WTO is charged with policing member countries' adherence to all prior GATT agreements, including those of the last major GATT trade conference, the Uruguay Round (1986–1994), at whose conclusion GATT had formally gone out of existence. The WTO is also responsible for negotiating and implementing new trade agreements. The WTO is governed by: a Ministerial Conference, which meets every two years; a General Council, which implements the conference's policy decisions and is responsible for day-to-day administration; and a Director General, who is appointed by the Ministerial Conference. The WTO's headquarters is in Geneva, Switzerland.

Patricia Hewitt, UK Secretary of State for Trade, said in a radio broadcast (BBC Radio 4, *Today* programme, 30 July 2004) 'new rules on free trade are needed because the existing ones mostly help rich manufacturing countries and ignore the poor farming countries'. In theory, the members of the WTO meet on an equal footing. In what form in the world can a poor nation, such as Burkina Faso, and the US meet where the former has the power to veto a treaty?

It sounds good, but doesn't work because the first world players have a monopoly of the money, time, lawyers and influence in high places. What it all comes down to is that the first world nations can pay much more in the way of subsidies to their farmers than third world nations can pay theirs. US and EU farmers can actually live quite comfortably on such subsidies while their produce can be sold at a much lower cost to the farmer than his/her third world counterparts have to pay to export in the open market.

Coming back to cotton, Burkina Faso can produce top class cotton in abundance. It is one of its only potential levers on the international market. Free trade, as advocated by the WTO, renders it unable to compete with subsidy-supported cotton from the US. Fair trade, by contrast, would help to balance things out. Benin and Chad are similarly poverty-stricken quality cotton producers. For one thing, first world nations could agree to subsidise crops for domestic use only and not for export. As Patricia Hewitt went on to say in her broadcast cited above:

> *What we have to do is to reform the world trade system so that it's not just free but we get fair trade as well which is what the developing countries need. And for us in Europe that means pulling down our appalling agricultural subsidies that distort trade in the rest of the world and make it impossible for farmers in many developing countries to earn a decent living. We would support the ending of all the export subsidies and all the trade distorting subsidies. There is an important distinction to be made here between subsidies that really damage farmers in developing countries and subsidies that are simply designed to protect our own countryside and our own rural communities. Support for hedgerows and environmental management for instance which we are wholly in favour of, which don't do any damage to the developing world and which do ensure that our own rural communities continue to be properly lived in and properly cared for (Hewitt, 2004).*

Merely as an example of how ludicrous and distorted trade can become under normal WTO rules, consider sugar. We in Europe have never produced cane sugar so easily nor in such magnificent profusion as do many poorer tropical nations. In fact, such heavy production of cane sugar actually became accentuated in many of these poorer nations to generate enough US dollars to meet IMF loan repayments. A good bit of such a country's other resources – forests, fisheries, pastureland and arable acreage – may have been already mortgaged to create an infrastructure to exploit sugar production. If the sugar market should suddenly collapse globally due to first world subsidies to its own farmers, what befalls the hapless third world nations absolutely dependent on it?

There is nothing academic about this discussion. Can the reader really imagine seriously producing commercial quantities of sugar (cane or beet) in the EU? We can do it but at about three times the cost of Jamaica, Cuba, Malawi or Zambia. We do exactly that and then, through agricultural subsidies, reduce the production costs to less than any of those third world countries can do. If we are looking to the WTO for equitable solutions, simply consider other non-third world concerns that can affect its decisions.

In Geneva at this moment (31 July 2004), the WTO believes that progress in its talks is absolutely vital – not just because third world producers are facing ruin, but in order to prevent the coming US presidential elections three months hence from stalling the talks for another one or two years. The imminent changeover in the European Commission is providing the same impetus for speed in bringing the Geneva talks to some sort of 'positive' conclusion. On Sunday 1 August 2004 it was announced that the 147 WTO member states meeting in Geneva had finally reached an agreement on the crucial issue of agricultural subsidies in the first world supporting export of foodstuffs to the third world. Of course, the reader must appreciate that the Geneva 2004 meeting was only intended to develop an agreed 'framework' for change, not to actually legislate one. But even at that modest intention, it looked as though Geneva 2004 would end up like Cancun 2002. The Cancun meeting collapsed altogether when many of the third world delegates simply walked out.

The actual implementation details will be discussed over the next two years (how many will die unnecessarily in that time?) to see if the WTO meeting in 2006 can agree on a plan.

Obviously reform to the WTO will not instantly overcome all of Africa's problems, but it would certainly provide an impetus for continued progress in the right direction. But what could possibly make any of the first world nations out of all 147 nations represented in Geneva agree to severely curtail the interest of its own people? This author sees absolutely no solution except the existence of a transnational body to which all nations belong and to which all are answerable.

Conclusion

Although we are comfortably insulated from its reality, we in the West are part of the global system that maintains third world poverty. The challenge remains to better understand the linkages, to lobby for better terms for third world trade, for the cancellation of third world debt (or some rational modification of its severity), and for more sustainable and appropriate programmes of aid and development. Above all, though, perhaps, we must question our values and the influence we have outside of our immediate environment. In the words of the Honduran Archbishop Oscar Andres Rodrigues: 'we must put aside purely economic criteria and look for human solutions. We cannot have a world run solely by the logic of profit.'

References

Bennett S, McPake B and Mills A (1997) *Private Health Providers in Developing Countries – serving the public interest?* Zed Books, London and New Jersey.

Gaynor T (1999) Under the volcano. *New Internationalist.* May, pp 33–7.

Hewitt P (2004) UK Secretary of State for Trade, speaking on BBC Radio 4 *Today* programme. 30 July.

Kamat VR and Nichter M (1997) Monitoring product movement: an ethnographic study of pharmaceutical sales representatives in Bombay, India. In: S Bennett *et al.* (eds) *Private Health Providers in Developing Countries – serving the public interest?* Zed Books, London and New Jersey.

Labonte R (1998) Healthy public policy and the World Trade Organization: a proposal for an international presence in future world trade/investment talks. *Health Promotion International.* **12(3)**: 7–16.

Leaver E and Cavanagh J (1996) In focus: controlling transnational corporations. *Foreign Policy in Focus.* **1(6)**. http://www.fpif.org

MacDonald TH (1998) *Rethinking Health Promotion: a global approach.* Routledge, London and New York.

MacLachlan M (1993) Sustaining health service developments in the 'Third World'. *Journal of the Royal Society of Health.* **June. 113(3)**: 12–15.

Mihevc J (1999) Starting from scratch. *New Internationalist.* May, p.10.

New Internationalist (1997) January and November. Editorial, p.2.

Okuonzi SA and Macrae J (1995) Whose policy is it anyway? International and national influences on health policy development in Uganda. *Health Policy and Planning.* **10(2)**: 122–32.

Oxfam, World Trade Organisation (1996) *Oxfam Policy Briefing for the WTO Ministerial Conference.* Globalisation, international health and a new international. In: R Petrella *Trade and Health.* World Trade Organisation, Washington DC.

Pettifor A (1999) Break the chains. *New Internationalist.* May, pp 41–2.

Potter I (1997) Looking Back, Looking Ahead: Health promotion, a global challenge. *Health Promotion International*. **12**: 4.

Ransom D (1999) The Dictatorship of Debt. *New Internationalist*. **May**, p.6.

Thrift N (1989) The geography of international economic disorder. In: R Johnston and P Taylor (eds) *A World in Crisis? Geographical Perspectives*. Basil Blackwell, Oxford.

Voluntary Service Overseas (1996) Marafiki Newsletter. VSO, Canada.

WHO (1978) Primary Healthcare: Report of the International Conference on Primary Healthcare at Alma-atay, USSR. 6–12 September.

WHO (1998) *Life in the 21st Century: A vision for all*. World Health Report. World Health Organization, Geneva.

World Bank (2000) World Development Report 2000–1 *Attacking Poverty*. Oxford University Press, New York. www.worldbank.org

World Bank (2003) World Development Report 2002/3: *Sustainable Development in a Dynamic World: transforming institutions, financing healthcare, an agenda for reform*. Oxford University Press, New York.

Chapter 5

The third world helping itself – community health programmes

Forms of financing healthcare

Obviously the way in which any nation finances its healthcare is bound to impact directly on the degree to which the poor can access it. In this regard, the nation itself will usually have what can best be called a 'National Health Policy'. This – ideally – identifies a policy of ensuring access to essential health services on the basis of need, irrespective of ability to pay. But in most third world countries this goal can rarely be realised under present conditions.

Looking at the matter in purely monetary terms, health financing can be addressed in the following three ways:

1 Funding – raising the revenue from direct taxation, indirect taxation, some kind of social insurance or by demanding fees from individual patients.
2 Resource allocation – deciding how much to spend and where to place – hospitals, polyclinics, doctors' surgeries, community nurses, etc.
3 Payment for the providers – securing sufficient finance to pay for personnel involved in health delivery, maintenance and cleaning of the facilities, etc.

The IMF, for instance, since the 1970s has been a strong advocate of some kind of user fee – especially in the context of one of its main structural adjustment policies: to move away from public funding to private provision.

In this regard, the author would draw the reader's attention to an attempt to provide an analytical basis for such decisions in Niger – a large African country which became independent of French colonial control in 1960. It is, in fact, the largest country in West Africa, but is completely landlocked. As reported by Boekel *et al.* (2002), the following assessment was carried out.

During a severe economic crisis in the 1980s, the Ministry of Health in Niger debated different cost-recovery policies for publicly supported health services. To better inform the debate, the Ministry decided to pilot test different financing mechanisms for district-level health services: a fee-for-service model in the Say district and a risk-sharing strategy involving a combination annual district tax and small fee-for-service ('tax-small fee') model in the Boboye district. In these districts, the new fees were accompanied by quality improvements, including greater availability of drugs. The study included the district of Illéla for comparison purposes, and no quality or administrative improvement was instituted there.

The tax-small fee intervention in Boboye resulted in significant improvements in the use of publicly supported health services by women, children and the poor. The rate of use doubled among the poorest quarter of the population. By contrast, the use of services remains low among the poor in the Say district, and use among the poor declined in Illéla.

Notably, the vast majority of people in Boboye and Say districts preferred the tax-small fee model over the pure fee-for-service approach, including more than 80% of the poorest people in both districts. Most said that the main problem with the pure fee-for-service approach was finding the resources to pay for each episode of illness. The study authors noted that the tax-small fee method also seemed to have other positive side-effects. The use of prenatal care services increased significantly in Boboye even though no fees were charged for these services either before or during the intervention. Increase in the use of curative services may have stimulated greater use of preventive services.

In considering the work of the International Planned Parenthood Federation (IPPF) in detail, let us begin by looking at Nepal – a small and very poor nation. In this I have been greatly assisted by two prominent Nepalese health workers: Govinda Prakesh Dahal and Dr Padam Prasad Sinkhada. The former is now completing his doctorate in Britain but is still very much involved with population study in Nepal and with the Family Planning Association of Nepal (FPAN), while the latter was in charge of community health programmes in Nepal until 1997, when he also came to Britain. I last visited Nepal in 1997 to collect epidemiological data.

Involving the community

In Nepal, especially in the rural regions, the infant mortality rate is very high. This is only partly because there are few facilities for safe delivery – e.g. uncertain water and electricity supplies – and because transport is both expensive and scarce. Funded by the Japanese government, the FPAN opened a Family Health Centre (FHC) in the remote township of Itahari, in the eastern plains. This centre distinguished itself – and very much enhanced its impact – by closely involving the local community.

Half a kilometre from the highway running through Itahari, the FHC provides safe obstetric and delivery services to people from 25 village development committees (VDCs). The closest proper health centres for the rural community are at least 20 kilometres away. The FHC at Itahari thus could serve about 2.5 million people, but not everyone could afford these services.

As Dahal and Rana (2002) report, a local benefactor, Ram Chandra Adhikari, donated a US$32 000 block of land to build the Itahari FHC. Through the good offices of the Japanese Embassy in Nepal, the Japanese government donated US$48 700 for the building costs.

Now the community has safe delivery services and access to mother and child healthcare facilities, but they are worried about its sustainable operation.

Says Adhikari, the land donor, 'How long can we lean on a donor's crutch? They have helped us kick-start the project. Now it falls on our shoulders to carry it forward successfully.' Adhikari is willing to contribute anything at his disposal to make the FHC run and serve his fellow community people.

To manage and ensure the smooth running of the FHC, a committee of local people is set up. It is they who set the cost of services provided in the centre. The community is determined to keep the FHC going. They pay for every service – transportation by ambulance, delivery charge, admission fee, bed and medicines – because they know that it is up to them to keep the wheels turning. The ambulance runs on their money.

Rukum Thapa, 24, from Itahari municipality itself, delivered her first child stillborn. Her second delivery, attended by a traditional birth attendant, was botched. The third child was delivered at the FHC. She says, 'The FHC is cheaper, affordable by rural standards and within easy reach. We understand that we have to pay if we receive services or else how will they run it?'

Rukum thinks that the community will make every effort possible to keep the FHC running. They know its importance. She says, 'I learnt it the hard way. I lost my first child. The second, too, lives with a congenital deformity. And the third one is healthy and sound. For me, it is the FHC that helped me bear a healthy child.'

Uma Neupane from Khanar, a village five kilometres away, who had her second child at the FHC, says, 'It's been a great job to open a health centre providing safe delivery and maternal as well as child health services to the rural community.' She, too, is worried about its sustainable operation. Says she, 'Our women are poor. But that doesn't mean they can't pay for services. No poor women can risk life for a fistful of money.'

The women receiving services at the FHC are found to have been powerful advocates of the centre's services. Amrita Choudhary, 23, went through a harrowing experience when delivering a child at home. Her second child was delivered at the FHC. She says, 'Not only did I feel much more comfortable at the FHC, but the presence of the sisters and the surroundings kept my spirits high.' Choudhary now recommends every woman in her community to seek services there.

While the community benefiting from the FHC helps it in several ways such as generating awareness, paying for services, and disseminating information about the centre, Ram Chandra Adhikari, the land donor, has put himself to the task of exploring every possible way to successfully run it. Affiliated to several other social organisations, this respected member of the community said, 'I've been discussing with the district development committee, the municipality and other donors how best to keep it going.'

As in any poor community, the major problem is often gaining access to the services, however good they are. The 24-hour ambulance service offered by the FHC has been a godsend for many since its inception in January 2001. At first, demand for FHC services was very low, but it has been increasing steadily since. The local organisers of the FHC claim that charging fees for use has not prevented this increase, even when the fees had to rise. But what anyone who has worked in the third world knows, if there is any charge at all, not all who need the care will be dealt with.

What is evident, though, is the positive impact that the necessary requirement for volunteers at different levels brings about. It is not only energising in and of itself, but it has already provided opportunities for local people to learn about various health services while on the job and to thus become qualified. In Chapter 6, we shall consider the problem of health finance more deeply.

What about the poorest of the poor in Nepal?

As the author has already pointed out, while some progress can be claimed because the proportion of the world's population living on less than US$1.00 a day has dropped, there has been an increase in the proportion living on less than US$2.00 a day. That is, improvement is being brought about – at least partly – by shifting money from the poor to the very poor, instead of solving the problem completely by shifting money from the first world to both the poor and the very poor.

In Nepal, as in many other poor nations, the rural poor are generally much worse off than the urban poor. In Chitwan, like Itahari, the FPAN branch serves 170 000 people – 38% of the district's population. Thus it has a clinic in Chitwan itself, but also runs local community-based services and 16 outreach clinics. One of the thriving clinics is the Mangalpur outreach clinic, which serves some of the very poorest of the poor. Gillam (2002) reported as follows about it.

A huge banyan tree casts its shadow wide, acting as the clinic's waiting room. Hemlal Ghimere, 54, emerges from the shade to greet us. He's one of the clinic's founder members and is proud that he helped launch the service 13 years ago.

He shows us inside the small wooden building where a clinic is in session. 'A lot of people are benefiting from this outpost – we get at least 50 clients per month,' he says. 'The people in this district are very poor – they cannot afford private clinics.'

Hemlal is now on a working group helping to run the outreach clinic and offers what he calls his social work, encouraging people to use contraceptive devices. He used to be a farmer but doesn't have any land any more after selling it to educate two of his children.

The outreach service in Mangalpur offers counselling in family planning and sexually transmitted infections as well as services and referrals. Mother and child health education and general health services are offered too. It also provides syndromic treatment for sexually transmitted infections and makes referrals.

Attending one session, Sharada Pandey, 32, says she has three children and doesn't want any more. Her husband, however, disagrees so she's decided to opt for injectable contraception instead of sterilisation, as a compromise. She still hopes to persuade him, though.

'My eldest daughter went to school until she was 12. She had to leave then because we couldn't afford it. So now only two of our children are being educated.'

Sharada says the family has no land and she sometimes finds it difficult to manage on the income her husband earns from his bicycle repairs. She comes to Mangalpur outreach clinic because it's close by and the service is free. She says if the clinic closes she would have to go to the city and couldn't afford the fees for private contraceptive service.

Another client, Aita Maya Sunr, is 33 and married with four children. She had her first baby at 19 and started using contraception after having her last child – a much-wanted boy. All her children are at school.

Her husband earns 70 US cents a day making doors and window frames, but when business is slow they have little income at all. For two months in the rainy season Aita Maya helps plant rice and earns about 50 cents per day. The family has a house on a small piece of land, growing rice and maize as well as vegetables for themselves. But sometimes the whole family has to survive on a diet of grains alone.

Eighty per cent of the 18 000 population in and around the area are jobless and there's little opportunity to work except for two months a year during planting season. Most men make less than US$1.00 a day doing this and the women will be paid less.

Hemlal Ghimere believes the clinic is popular because it provides a service that the people want. They trust FPAN. 'It's been in the field a long time – it's very experienced and it provides quality services. When we first opened we started with a community development programme so people got to know what it had to offer.'

He says FPAN provides 75% of the family planning service in this area while the government caters for the rest. The effect of a loss in funding will hit these people hard.

Trafficking for prostitution in Nepal

Dr Padam Simkhada, research fellow at the University of Aberdeen's public health department, visited six NGO-run rehabilitation centres in Nepal and interviewed 42 girls who had returned or been rescued from Indian brothels. His findings formed the basis of a presentation to the Faculty of Public Health's annual scientific meeting, on the topic 'Sexual health knowledge and health-seeking behaviour among trafficked girls in Nepal: implications for public health services'.

Dr Simkhada found sexually transmitted diseases among returned sex workers were common, as were misconceptions as to their causes and treatment. He also discovered that the girls' exploitation sadly continued on their return, as the minority who sought medical help were likely to be conned by quacks with no proper training.

Nepal, a traditionally patriarchal society, has one of the lowest human development indicators in the world. Life expectancy is 59 years and infant and maternal mortality are among the highest globally. A large proportion of the population live below the poverty line, with 38% surviving on less than US$1 per day.

Ninety per cent of the population rely on subsistence agriculture, but this economy is no longer viable, leading in turn to escalating labour migration – particularly among those of prime productive ages. Children are increasingly sent to urban areas to supplement family incomes. Girls may be sent to work in urban carpet factories or the homes and fields of creditors.

Dr Simkhada said:

> Both trafficking and migration operate predominantly through social networks or brokers who may or may not be strangers. Women and girls may be attracted by reports of high incomes and the glamour of urban life, and may be easily deceived by mediators. It is not uncommon for trafficking to take part in stages, with women and girls first trafficked for labour exploitation then later sex trafficked.
>
> Women who become victims of sex trafficking are at high risk of morbidity from reproductive and sexual health problems. Sexually transmitted infections, such as HIV/AIDS, gonorrhoea, syphilis and genital ulcers, are viewed as 'occupational hazards'. They are usually referred to as 'line disease' and are seen as being caused primarily by lack of hygiene or by rough or violent intercourse.

Similar community-based health programmes elsewhere

Legion are the number and variety of such programmes worldwide. The author's purpose here is to briefly touch on only a few to illustrate the point that the third world is far from supine in the face of global financial inequity and to indicate the variety of programmes they can develop. The example of Cuba is often cited. It has managed, through communism, to do remarkable things in health and education for its own people and to produce such a surplus of medical workers and teachers that it is able to lend sustained practical assistance in these areas to other nations – not all of them of the third world.

However, the fact that it has achieved all of theses things through social policies antagonistic to the first world agencies controlling global finance renders its role-model status much more fraught with difficulty than for many other third world nations. Therefore, Cuba will be dealt with in a separate chapter (*see* Chapter 13). In the long term, it may exemplify the best way forward. Meanwhile many of the rest of the third world nations – while gratefully accepting Cuban aid in health – are trying to use their own resources as best they can without antagonising such agencies as the IMF or even some of the larger NGOs.

At this point the reader would find the afore-cited *Real Lives* (issue 8) of 2002 a valuable source of insight into this question generally. It was produced by the International Planned Parenthood Federation (IPPF) of Regent's College in London. As permitted under its remit, I have drawn on it freely in this chapter.

India

The present author first visited South India in 1954. I was in Gujarat State, but India's smallest state, Kerala, was at the time dominating the news. Kerala is a tiny strip of land along the Malabar coast. It can – very roughly – be described as a ribbon of land approximately 600 kilometres by approximately 83 kilometres. It is, however, the most densely populated space in India as well as one of the most beautiful. The Keralans are such a mix of ethnic groupings and religions that life there has rarely been dull. But in 1957 they democratically elected a communist state government.

The impact on all public services was marked, but was most evident in health and education. Rather like Cuba a couple of years later, their public health and literacy statistics rapidly overtook national averages. Their iconic state government soon found itself at odds with the federal government under Nehru and the Congress Party. Part of this was due to the fact that the Indian Communist Party used Kerala's social success as a lever to try to gain a greater say in the national government. Ultimately Kerala's communist government was subsumed and the rebellious state brought more firmly under federal control.

Its achievements in health declined somewhat but its impetus in education has, in many respects, been sustained. But before considering Kerala in detail, let us look at more representative areas in that great country.

The whole of India has made considerable improvements in health and social policy since 1960. The rights of Dalits (Untouchables) – which improved immediately in Kerala in 1957 – are increasingly being taken seriously today in the rest of the country. The former conservative attitudes towards women have changed enormously and their role in politics and health has become indispensable to continued social progress. At the time of my work in Mysore, it was not unknown for newborn baby girls to be buried with the afterbirth – and Gujarat was not unique in that respect. Any idea that contraception might be either a woman's right or – even less – a man's responsibility was barely heard of. Now vasectomy clinics are commonplace. Whereas, before these changes in social attitudes, India's census figures reflected a lower figure for adult females than for adult males, that has now reversed. Consider the situation in Rajasthan – a western desert state in India.

Rajasthan has always been conservative in its attitudes towards women, reports Meenakshi Shedde in *Real Lives* (2000, p.18). In such a backward state, the idea of granting women the right to reproductive health and related choices seemed ludicrous. Yet the Family Planning Association of India (FPAI) has done exemplary work. Before the establishment of FPAI things were very different.

Rajasthan is still a largely feudal state that poses truly challenging social indices. Apart from child marriages, dowry (an expensive groom price), female foeticide and infanticide are common. So is nata prata (traditional relationships) in which married women are bought (if not kidnapped) by prospective husbands, after paying the current husband jhagda (fight money). Moreover, the National Crime Record Bureau estimates that there are 2600 'kidnappings' of girls or women in Rajasthan state in a year, among the highest in India. These 'kidnappings' usually reflect runaway brides – women who were married as children, eloping with men of their choice on reaching maturity.

In such formidable circumstances, the progress achieved by the efforts of the FPAI in the Tonk district of Rajasthan is all the more remarkable. What is more, it continues to make significant progress, despite the fact that its funds have largely dried up. Its four-year Women's Empowerment and Reproductive Health Initiatives Project, started in 1998, received about Rs 30 million (US$600 000) from the UK Community Fund (formerly the National Lottery Charities Board) through the IPPF. Aimed at providing youth with meaningful options beyond early marriage and parenting, it covered a population of over 700 000 in 760 villages, towns and cities.

Men having the snip

In such a socially backward state as said before, the prospect of giving women the right to reproductive health choices seemed preposterous. FPAI Tonk has nevertheless done exemplary work in popularising contraception, and actually has a record of more vasectomies than tubectomies, quite rare in male chauvinist India. The child sex ratio (up to six years), especially relevant in an area of high female infanticide, is 922 girls for every thousand boys in Tonk, while the national average is merely 908. Moreover, where sterilisation occurs in India it is usually female sterilisation. But at FPAI Tonk they actually performed more vasectomies – 356 over the last three years, as opposed to 264 tubectomies. Vasectomies, of course, are much easier and less invasive to carry out, and don't require as much time away from work.

As comments Dr Talek Idreeds of the Tonk branch of FPAI:

> *Non-scalpel vasectomy requires no stitches, it's a five-minute operation. For a tubectomy, you have to open the abdomen. Yet women offer the strongest opposition to their husbands' vasectomy, fearing that their sexual desire will plummet or that they will become weak, thus putting the family's sole breadwinner at risk. In fact, they prefer to take Depo-Provera contraceptive injections, so the husband doesn't find out, even if it has side-effects.*

Over and above women's health, women's education is the other big challenge. It is now being aggressively promoted by women's clubs, locally referred to as 'mahila mandals'. Khareda village, near the town of Toda Rai Singh, has a particularly

effective mahila mandal. Each month its members set aside their individual contributions, so that the monthly total for each 10 people comes to about US$100.
They use this to issue loans to buy such economic necessities as, say, a sewing
machine or direct medical expenses. In this way, they become instrumental in
setting up small businesses for generating further cash.

It is interesting to observe that such money-raising and health-promoting ventures are run by women with neither the permission or (often) the knowledge of
the men.

This underlies an observation made by the author in 1973, while working with
UNESCO in the British Solomon Islands, that, if there has to be a choice, it is about
four times more economically efficient to teach a girl to read than a boy. It is she
who will grow up to run a house, purchase necessities and look after the family's
sexual health and general hygiene. As a childbearer, her education will have much
more impact on the next generation of women and men than will that of a man.

Kerala – a sustained success story

Although Kerala is not the wealthiest state in India, it is one of the country's top-
performing states in health. Its infant mortality rate – 16 deaths per 1000 live births
– is among the lowest in the country, far less than India's overall rate of 68 (IIPS,
2001). In fact, its infant mortality rate is about half that of Brazil and on par with
rates found in higher-income countries such as Argentina and Uruguay. With a life
expectancy of over 70 years, Keralites live almost as long as do Europeans.

The use of health services is high in Kerala, with more than 90% of births
delivered in health facilities and 80% of children fully vaccinated. Moveover, the
government distributes its public health spending almost uniformly across income
groups (World Bank, 2003).

What accounts for this success? Analysts offer many different explanations but
agree that Kerala's unique political and social environment is key. Kerala is distinguished by a highly educated, organised and activist populace that makes strong
demands on the government. Women enjoy a high degree of autonomy and have a
literacy rate of nearly 90% (Heller, 1997).

Keralites place a high value on health and education. Among the poor, health
services have long been considered a right. In the 1950s and 1960s, the poor became
increasingly politicised regarding health. One researcher reported, 'In Kerala, if
a PHC (primary health centre) were unmanned for a few days, there would be a
massive demonstration at the nearest collectorate (the government's administrative centre in a district) led by local leftists, who would demand to be given what
they knew they were entitled to' (Mencher, 1996). In some cases, community
members inflicted physical harm on service providers considered derelict in
performing their duties.

Pakistan

For many years, the Family Planning Association of Pakistan (FPAP) has been
helping women in the highly conservative North West Frontier Province in a
variety of ways, such as holding classes in traditional embroidery techniques,

running youth groups and organising health education camps. It is through tapping the resources of women's education – virtually neglected in some areas until the 1990s – that has produced a groundswell, among both men and women, of concern for health issues generally.

The Kato centres were among the first of these enterprises to get off the ground. We are talking about the North West of Pakistan where women, until recently, have tackled the horrors of life with tenacity and courage in this area where poverty, early marriage, repeated childbearing and high illiteracy and inequality severely limit the lives of women and girls. The FPAP is helping them out in their fight, by opening the Kato Women's Development Centre that has saved them from losing their identity in more ways than one.

The shop Saima runs is one of the 12 that make up the Kato market, the first rural market in Pakistan operated by women. She deals in stitched and unstitched embroidered cloths. And now Shabana is one of the girls who takes orders for embroidery from her.

Safia and Shamim live in Garh, a village nestled in the hills of Haripur. They wade across a stream every day before taking a van to the Kato Centre that also prides itself on preserving the traditional stitchcraft, Phulkari, from dying out. Phulkari means 'flowing' in the local dialect and it does exactly that: it creates a flowery surface with the simplest of tools, a needle and a silken thread – and a high degree of skill. It describes the extraordinary embroidery rural women do on hand-spun, coarsely woven cotton (khaddar) to embellish shawls and bed coverings.

The Japanese government provided a grant under the Grassroots Assistance Scheme which enabled the FPAP to build and equip the Kato Women's Development Centre. The centre is named after Senator Shidzue Kato, a beacon of light for women in Japan and around the world, who died aged 104 in 2001. The Canadian International Development Agency helped the FPAP operate the centre and introduce community mobilisation.

It is here that Safia and Shamim now train girls in Phulkari. 'We are imparting skills to hundreds of women and adolescent girls and helping them to earn money,' says Safia. 'Patience is the most important skill a Phulkari embroiderer could possess,' says Shamim.

Their lessons helped girls understand how Phulkari had been created with the blessings of love, laughter, tradition and memories in every stitch. The girls also learn other skills like making marmalade, pickles and detergent powder.

No longer a girl, Bilquis, aged 65, is also one of the beneficiaries. 'Because of the training I got from the Kato Centre, I am selling detergent powder and making a profit of about Rs 2000 (US$35) a month.'

Now sitting on the charpoys (jute string beds) pulled into the protective shade of a tree, or ensconced against a wall, girls and women in villages and small towns all over Haripur are often busy, happily creating spectacular 'gardens of flowers' for sale in the Kato market. Imtiaz Bibi of Basti Sher Khan has bought a cow calf with the money she got as wages. 'It will soon serve my household needs as a young cow,' says Bibi.

Phulkaris were not originally designed or created with commercialisation and marketing in mind. They were made as special, prized offerings for auspicious occasions such as weddings and other festive times. But now they need to be marketed well to empower their makers economically.

Says Fauzia Naureen who works at her home in Garh village: 'We are on our way. See a cushion takes about a month to be made in the time left after daily chores, but only better marketing can ensure us better wages.'

Youth resource centres

These are another outstanding success of the FPAP. Zakeesh Khan (2002), a youth volunteer with the group, reported as follows after visiting some of its centres around Lahore. Her use of religious metaphors reflects the extent to which religious institutions can be of immense help in mediating community health education.

> *God made us social animals. He didn't create us as isolated individuals, self-sufficient in our needs, born to fend for ourselves and live on our own. We are born to two parents. The three of us, if not more, then make a family. This is the ideal situation. God made it so, we all aspire to it. Even where some of us are unable to make this a reality, we find our own support systems, our own anchors, our own example of how we as human beings lean on each other, seek support, live and work in togetherness ... because this is how God wished it to be and showed us in the most elementary example of them all ... a family unit.*

She went on to explain that a family is just one piece of the bigger picture. Each of us thereon builds his own network of relationships that are based on human social needs. This is the formula to success. It doesn't need to be inculcated; it's inborn. It is even more true for the young people, who are still in the process of discovering themselves. They draw their strength and confidence from each other.

> *As I visited a few youth resource centres (YRCs) in and around the city of Lahore, I tried to identify the originator of this brainchild. I soon realised it was not any single individual. The idea was a built-in social phenomenon; what is needed was some direction, some ready minds and – there you have it.*

The youth resource centre health camps

An interesting point to note is that while these YRCs are a part of the FPAP support programme, they have been providing immense assistance to the FPAP core programme too, organising health camps, mobilising the community to participate and disseminating health-related information. In many cases their members are now being trained as peer educators, health practitioners, community leaders, etc. There are now 28 youth resource centres throughout Pakistan. Many of these have stemmed from the male youth programme running in the country.

While it is encouraging to see YRCs doing so well with young people in so many ill-resourced areas, a lot still needs to be done to make it a more common phenomenon for other communities like Minhaala and Green Town. Women also need to be encouraged to start similar groups, especially since their support systems are much weaker than that of boys.

Networking among these groups would be an added plus, giving more confidence to young people to establish their own YRCs, cover broader areas of activities and yield a wider acceptance of this as an essential human need for a healthier, more progressive society. It will also give a sense of identity to young people and prevent their energies being dissipated in wasteful or dangerous pastimes. The YRCs are a successful model of how youthful inspiration and energy can be the biggest resources to start something small that then achieves something immense.

Pakistan and the refugees from Afghanistan

Refugees from Afghanistan first came to Pakistan in really large numbers during the Soviet presence in the former country in the 1980s. It can obviously be argued that much of this refugee crisis was not necessary and was whipped up by the religious right in both countries, and with considerable funding and military support from the anti-Soviet first world nations. But at the ground level, the matter had to be addressed as a local humanitarian and health issue. As usual, the immense suffering and destruction entailed was of no worry or concern to the revanchist agencies benefiting from it.

Some of these refugees went to Yaka Ghund in the tribal area of Mohmand Agency, 45 km from the border between Pakistan and Afghanistan. Malik Shah, the camp elders' chief, was quoted as saying:

> We were not treated as humans. We would only receive food rations, no medicine, and no education. If somebody got seriously ill, they had to travel on a circuitous route to a bus stop five kilometres away and then to Peshawar, 50 kilometres from here (Mustafa, 2002).

Pakistan, a cash-strapped nation that has already borne the cost of hosting some three million refugees since the start of the Afghan conflict in 1978, has received about 200 000 more refugees since the US-led air strikes in Afghanistan in 2001/2.

Yaka Ghund, with a population of 10 500 refugees, is one of the 100 camps set up in the North West Frontier Province and Baluchistan by the government of Pakistan. Today, with camps filled to capacity, many Afghan newcomers are blending in with local populations in Pakistan, often relying on their families for support. While this takes some of the burden off relief agencies and the Pakistan government, officials here say such self-help may be a transitory solution, because more established refugees often have limited resources.

Funded by IPPF/Business Management Zones (BMZ), the David and Lucile Packard Foundation and the Embassy of Japan, the FPAP is arranging increased access to safe motherhood, family life education and family planning, reproductive health information and services, safe drinking water and non-formal education in 43 camps and subcamps, with the expected beneficiaries being 500 000 Afghan refugees.

Security conditions at or near refugee camps have not only been fragile but posed a serious obstacle to humanitarian effort in the region. 'Work in prospective refugee camps in Quetta and Peshawar was on hold. Aid workers could not move safely or freely, because kidnap for ransom was quite rampant in these tribal areas. We had to convince tribal elders about our project before starting it here,' says Noor-ul-Basar, the coordinator for education.

The author will end this chapter of case study examples with a brief glimpse at Sri Lanka and the efforts of the Family Planning Association of Sri Lanka (FPASL) to promote the use of condoms. It continues to be an uphill task and yet one on which community health desperately depends.

Sri Lanka and the condom

Considerable progress has been reported in the last year in the area of reproductive health in Sri Lanka, but in some parts resistance to the distribution and use of condoms still prevails. The matter is well dealt with in the book *Real Lives*, as previously recommended (IPPF, 2002). Andre Boekel, Public Relations Officer with the FPASL, is the source of this account.

She describes how the first task was to create a climate in which the humble condom was divested of the satanic images imputed to it by both conservative Hindu and Tamil religious leaders and institutions.

Throughout the month of December 2001, along with all the festive banners that were strung across the capital city of Colombo, a striking black one dominated the scenery. The banner depicted a stylised condom, friendly and smiling. This was part of the condom social marketing programme launched by the FPASL. The programme runs to June 2002. Funded by the National STI (sexually transmitted infection)/AIDS Control Programme of the country's Ministry of Health it aims to project the condom – the simplest of protective devices against sexually transmitted infections – in a user-friendly manner.

The campaign aims to overcome the inhibitions and barriers which still exist to the purchase and use of condoms. During this campaign, one of the primary focuses is to project the condom as the best protection against the serious problem of HIV/AIDS. The campaign takes a multipronged approach and has been designed in two stages. During the first phase, a generic campaign on condoms is initiated, stressing the fact that the condom is the best protection against contracting AIDS and other sexually transmitted infections. Despite condoms being easily available, public attitudes indicate that there are still some reservations about them. The campaign serves to 'demystify' the condom, and make it part of every sexually active adult's life: in effect, to change social attitudes and behaviour towards the condom.

There are many social stigmas attached to condom usage – for example, women are hesitant to go to a shop to purchase a condom, and the discussion of its use, even between two sexually active people, is not easily initiated. There are also many unfounded myths surrounding condoms.

One of the prime thrusts of the campaign is to popularise the condom among groups whose behaviour is considered to put them at high risk of acquiring a sexually transmitted infection. These are commercial sex workers, beach boys, officers of the armed forces, homosexual and migrant workers. For these promotions, the print and electronic media are being mobilised aggressively.

The FPA has retained the services of a mobile publicity services company to carry out 105 events in 105 towns, covering 19 districts throughout the country. There will be 35 night shows and 70 day events held as part of this campaign. Banners will be displayed in prominent places in the towns where the events will be held. Some of the activities will be the holding of interactive games and night film shows. There will also be a concerted effort to distribute educational materials as well as gifts and souvenirs.

One more society vulnerable to HIV/AIDS

There are many vulnerable sections of society which could reduce their risk of contracting a serious disease if they relaxed their own restrictions surrounding condom usage. It is important for the public to be comfortable with the concept and the word 'condom'. A popular misconception exists that it is only homosexuals and commercial sex workers who need to use condoms on a regular basis, but there are sections of society such as the clients of commercial sex workers who are also at high risk. There are also people who may be infected with HIV but have not yet developed AIDS.

The help of some 30 community-based organisations in rural areas is being enlisted. These organisations will be provided with financial assistance to produce locally based events, such as drama competitions, street skits, poster competitions, marches and parades. This will eventually result in 300 such events which will no doubt play a big role in helping to popularise the condom with the general public.

Presently, the incidence of HIV/AIDS in Sri Lanka is relatively low, compared with other South Asian countries. This could be attributed to the positive attitude shown by the community towards mass educational campaigns. It is envisaged that such campaigns would stem the spread of HIV/AIDS, which would endorse the campaign's success.

An independent body – Market Behaviour Lanka Ltd – will conduct two studies to assess the success of the campaign. One will be to verify the perception of the community as regarding condoms and the other to monitor the attitudes of the retailers of the condoms.

The whole issue of HIV/AIDS and its threat to both individual health and the global economy overwhelmingly transcends the borders of any individual nation, as Kofi Annan so well pointed out at the 2004 HIV/AIDS conference in Bangkok. He emphasised the degree to which the increasing economic growth of the Asian countries could suddenly be brought to a halt by HIV/AIDS. But this author would go much further and point to HIV/AIDS as another major global cataclysm, along with the ecological ones that lie in store for us, unless we take international action very quickly. We now live in a very small village indeed, and health (and education) planning has to be global to be effective.

The HIV/AIDS issue is so crucial in this regard that the whole of Chapter 11 will be devoted to it.

References

Boekel A, Diop F and Shanti P (2002) Bringing more than bliss to the community. In: *Real Lives*. International Planned Parenthood Federation, London.

Dahal P and Rana P (2002) Where the community turns the wheels. *Real Lives*. **8**: 33–5. International Planned Parenthood Federation.

Gillam S (2002) Reading out to the rural poor. *Real Lives*. **8**: 36. International Planned Parenthood Federation.

Heller P (1997) Social capital as a product of class mobilisation in Kerala. In: P Evans (ed.) *State, Society, Synergy*. University of California, Berkeley.

International Institute for Population Sciences (IIPS) (2001) *National Family Health Survey*. Mumbai, India, p.114.

International Planned Parenthood Federation (IPPF) (2002) *Real Lives*. **8**.

Khan Z (2002) *Real Lives*. **8**. International Planned Parenthood Federation, London, p.16.

Mencher J (1996) Lessons and non-lessons of Kerala: agricultural labourers and poverty. In: Routes to Low Mortality in Poor Countries. *Population and Development Review*. **12(2)**: 198.

Mustafa W (2002) *Real Lives*. **8**. International Planned Parenthood Federation, London, pp 37–40.

World Bank (2003) *India, Raising the Sights: Better Health Systems for India's Poor*. World Bank, Washington, DC.

Chapter 6

Poverty, health and finance

Measuring poverty

Those of us consumed with increasing global health equity have, for about 40 years, now come up with various categorical definitions in the hope of facilitating objective analysis. This has narrowed our focus down to three approaches (Gwatkin, 2000):

1 improving the health of the poor by focusing on their needs
2 reducing poor–rich inequalities – say, by government 'levelling' initiatives
3 redressing health inequalities independently of poverty level.

The first of these argued according to a 'trickle up' theory that, by empowering the very poor, their health and wealth will improve and thus impact on the higher socioeconomic levels. This countered the dominant neoliberal/conservative view that the less that the upper social classes are restricted in their wealth-creation schemes, the greater will be a 'trickle-down' effect. This required a closer analysis of levels of poverty and led to the following two crucial distinctions:

- Absolute poverty – is the lowest amount of money required to purchase the amount of food necessary for a minimally adequate diet with just enough over to purchase other absolutely vital goods and services. This amount is usually referred to as the poverty line. The current international poverty line is US$1.00 per person per day at 1985 exchange rates – as adjusted for transnational purchasing power. The World Bank is the most prominent advocate of this measurement.

  As Gwatkin (2000) pointed out, that figure represented about 25% of the world's population (about 1.3 billion people) and most of them live in South Asia, sub-Saharan Africa and China. The Organisation for Economic Co-operation and Development (OECD) stated that their aim is to reduce this figure by half by 2015.
- Relative poverty – attempts to define the poverty line in terms of a given society, rather than internationally. It is usually done in one of two ways:
  - Through ascertaining how much income one needs to live decently according to local standards. Such 'poverty lines' are often used in first world nations as well. In the US, for example, the Census Bureau stated that in 1999 for a family of four, the figure was US$16 000 a year (Uchitelle, 1999). Currently about 14% of US citizens fall below this level.
  - Define the national poverty line as a proportion – no internationally agreed definition – of a society's per capita income or expenditure. This one definitely lacks credibility for precise comparative analysis. In the UK, the current definition is living on less than one half of the whole nation's average per capita income. It places about 25% of the British population below it (*The Economist*, 1999).

The reader will notice that neither the definition for absolute nor relative poverty considers 'health status' as a factor.

Such approaches to the issue have been changing since 2000. For instance, Amartya Sen (1999a/1999b) was prominent in advocating an approach to defining poverty in terms of a 'human health index', which includes both health and education with income.

Amartya Sen has, indeed, been joined in shifting poverty definitions in this direction by a number of UN agencies. Even the World Bank (2001/2002) reflected such leeway in its World Development Report for that year.

What about measures of health inequality?

There are still a number of influential researchers and institutions who want to focus on a general narrowing of the inequity gap, globally, rather than concentrating only on its lower component. The emergence and development of the study of 'health promotion' takes this line (MacDonald, 1998).

The concern with global inequities in health has gradually moved to centre stage and, along with a similar refocusing on health inequalities within nations, in initiatives such as the Politics of Health Group (POHG) in the UK.

The POHG had its early origins between 1977 and 1985 under the broad umbrella of the British Society for Responsibility of Science, and in turn developed under the aegis of the Joseph Rowntree Foundation. But the POGH under that incarnation gradually faded away. It was revived through the work of a group of whom Marian Duggan and Alex Scott-Samuel (2000) were prominent, at a workshop of the Eighth Annual Forum of the UK Public Health Alliance.

Another grass-roots initiative which, while global in its influence, had a particularly strong input from the UK is the idea of Health Impact Assessment (HIA) and, in this too, Scott-Samuel played an important part. The actual origins of HIA are rather obscure, but their original remit appeared to be environmental. During many of the enormous structural changes being made by man on the environment in the 1970s and 1980s – such as the building of dams, power stations and the like, as well as more modest construction projects – it was recognised that impacts on health were likely to be substantial. In that regard it became increasingly obvious that Health Impact Assessments (and predictions) should be drawn up.

HIAs first took on statutory significance under the socialist Canadian Commonwealth Federation (CCF) party, at that time in power in Canada's province of British Columbia. It became law in 1993 under that administration that an HIA be included for every proposed building project before it could be considered for government approval. HIAs are now having a major impact on third world health and are playing an increasingly pivotal role in the poverty–health debate. In a number of southern third world nations, HIAs began to play a role in decision-making about internationally funded projects.

In 1993, the proposal for a second runway for Manchester airport evoked a demand from a number of socialist health interest groups for an HIA. Scott-Samuel was instrumental in advocating the execution of such an HIA on it (Scott-Samuel, 1996; O'Keefe et al., 2002). Steve Gwatkin, cited previously, was also a major activist in it. The real and potential role of HIAs in the struggle for global equity in health is also discussed in Chapter 14.

Establishing an agenda for global equity in health

The 1984 targets of the WHO Regional Office for Europe (EURO) were all expressed in terms of reducing poor–rich disparities. Much of this came under the familiar remit of Health for All by 2000 (HFA 2000). Whitehead (1990) stated: 'Equity requires reducing unfair disparities ... and ... pursuing equity in health and health care development means trying to reduce unfair and unnecessary social gaps in health and health care.'

The Maximin principle

Equity is a concept that stands apart from 'poverty' and 'inequality' in that so much of health planning, and thought about it, accepts the latter two as empirically measurable, whereas 'equity' is a philosophical – often ideological – desideratum. At the subjective level, we find it wrong for poverty to prevail in contexts that could alleviate it with a change in policy. Consider the Maximin idea of distributive justice recently put forward by John Rawls (1971).

The Maximin principle proposes that resources 'ought to be' distributed more evenly – in such a way that those presently in the minimum position secure the maximum amount of gain. Irrelevant to the 'values' reflected in such a policy is the issue of how this affects the better off, because in the long term, a more socially harmonious society is thereby produced. If we apply this to health, we would agree that preventing the worst off from suffering unnecessary ill health creates gains for the better off. This was recognised even by Edwin Chadwick (1800–1890) in his advocacy of better health facilities for Manchester's 'undeserving poor' in Manchester slums! Indeed, Marchand *et al.* (1998) rather argue from that principle in their approach to equity.

This sort of 'middle ground' of political thought on health equity often brings together the moderates with those who advocate simply shooting the rich or, even more effective, taxing them heavily while not allowing them to leave the country! The more that moderation is achieved between these views and attempts are made to actually implement equity in health, the more bland the discourse tends to become so that it starts to look surprisingly like confusing inequity with inequality.

In the global context it is very difficult to see how these issues can be usefully mediated by such supranational entities as the UN or its agencies (e.g. WHO) without a worldwide system for equity of input and discussion. No existing national government can do that. A good example is provided by the horrifying health conditions being currently imposed by the government of Sudan on the people of Darfur. As I write these words, the government contends that there is enough food in the region to keep the displaced people healthy for 10 months, so that the monsoon rains – which began 18 July 2004 – will not impose starvation. But several independent agencies trying to send aid argue that there is only enough food to last for six to eight weeks, by the end of which time the food stocks in the camps will have run out and the monsoon will be at its height (mid-September), thus guaranteeing a massive spread of infections among an already undernourished population.

Kofi Annan can plead and motions can be passed at the UN headquarters in New York, but there is no mechanism by which first world reserves of wealth can be directly expropriated by the UN. Many in the first world will be content to let the horror unfold. The UN cannot order the Sudan government to allow UN field workers in to organise programmes to reverse the inequities. This author argues that, until we can treat the planet and its people holistically, as far as fundamental human rights are concerned, discussion about global inequity in health will remain just that.

Analysis of health financing strategies

In Chapter 5 we considered an attempt to empirically test three different approaches to health funding in one area of the country. Let us now consider the matter more systematically and with broader application. The WHO World Health Report 2000 enumerates a number of strategies that have the potential of being mediated locally, rather than relying directly on huge fund transfers from the first to the third worlds. This author would regard such strategies as possibly being helpful in the short term only. As for long-term value, many of the ideas put forward, however, represent little more than discussing the positioning of deck chairs on the Titanic!

The actual parameters by which locally supported health financing can be categorised and analysed are laid out most usefully by Sara Bennett and Lucy Gilson (2001) in a publication by the Department for International Development (DFID), to which the reader is recommended to refer for more detail.

Clearly, reforms in health financing can be the only basis for even beginning to act on the question of health equity globally. Eventually, this author argues, these must involve global redistribution of funds. But in this chapter let us concentrate on the DFID analysis. They argue that the current international concern must move away from massive movements of money from the first to the third world in direct aid. They even state that 'equity is largely a secondary issue'.

The various strategies adopted for local funding will diverge widely over different third world nations. *See* Table 6.1, from Bennett and Gilson (2001).

Making locally financed policies 'pro-poor'

What does it mean for a health financing system to be pro-poor? The most important dimensions are that the system should:

- ensure that contributions to the costs of healthcare are in proportion to different households' *ability to pay*
- protect the poor (and the nearly poor) from the *financial shocks* associated with severe illness
- enhance the *accessibility* of services to the poor (particularly with respect to perceived quality and geographic access).

Therefore, how funds for healthcare are raised is pivotal. Furthermore, ensuring adequate pro-poor financing does not, in itself, ensure that appropriate services are delivered. Good financing policies must be supplemented by good policies on organisation and delivery of healthcare. This raises problems of internationally equitable policing of local initiatives (*see* Chapter 14).

Table 6.1:   Major trends in healthcare financing

Trend	Objective	Countries reforming in this way
Introduce or increase use fees in tax-based systems	• Raise more revenues • Encourage more efficient use of resources • Create greater accountability to the consumer	Many countries in sub-Saharan Africa
Introduce community-based health insurance in systems currently based on user fees and tax revenues	• Reduce financial barriers created by use fees • Encourage more efficient use of resources • Raise more revenues	Large-scale initiatives in Thailand and Indonesia; numerous small-scale efforts in many other countries, e.g. Zambia, Tanzania, Uganda, India
Shift from tax-based to social health insurance type systems	• Create independent, sustainable source of health finance • Raise more revenues	Thailand, many countries in the former Soviet Union and Eastern Europe; proposed but not implemented elsewhere, e.g. Nigeria, Zimbabwe, Ghana
Consolidate multiple state insurance funds	• Increase equity and prevent tiering and fragmentation • Increase administrative efficiency	Mexico, Colombia and other countries in Latin America

Financing and provision of healthcare are best if closely linked. Although there are no user fees in a wholly tax-funded system to create barriers to accessing care, there are frequently other barriers to accessibility, for example:

- If the perceived quality of care is very low, even the poor may prefer to pay more to use higher quality private sector services.
- There may be significant time and transport costs associated with accessing care, particularly for the poor.
- Even in a system in which there are no formal charges, informal charges for care may be widely prevalent.

Tackling these problems is important to ensure that the mix of financing mechanisms in any country promotes redistribution between the rich and the poor, a central element of pro-poor financing policies. As the reader will appreciate, this moves us into the realm of taking from the poor to help the very poor.

But who are the poor? In many low-income countries, the majority of the population is formally classified as poor. It is important to distinguish between the majority poor and the minority very poor in developing pro-poor policies in countries where this is the case. For example, a user fee system which succeeds in improving quality of care may benefit the majority poor who can afford to pay the newly introduced fees. But for the minority very poor, fees will create yet another barrier to access to health.

For both the poor and the very poor, the most important cost burden that results from illness comes from the loss of labour associated with severe illnesses and injuries. Although some financing mechanisms may mitigate the costs of care associated with such health problems, they do not address the consequences of ill health, whether through loss of income or loss of services provided by unpaid family members. Pro-poor healthcare financing mechanisms can only play a limited role in tackling the resource constraints that fundamentally shape the health-seeking behaviour of poorer households and thus their ability to capture the benefits of healthcare. This is a very prominent feature with respect to the growing impact of HIV/AIDS in the third world (*see* Chapter 11).

Box 6.1 lists the principal financing mechanisms for healthcare services.

Box 6.1   Principal financing mechanisms

Tax-based financing: health services are paid for out of general government revenue such as income tax, corporate tax, value added tax, import duties, etc. There may be special earmarked taxes (e.g. cigarette taxes) for healthcare.

Social insurance funding: health services are paid for through contributions to a health fund. The most common basis for contributions is the payroll, with both employer and employee commonly paying a percentage of salary. The health fund is usually independent of government but works within a tight framework of regulations. Premiums are linked to the average cost of treatment for the group as a whole, not to the expected cost of care for the individual. Hence, there are explicit cross-subsidies from the healthy to the less healthy. In general, membership of social health insurance schemes is mandatory, although for certain groups (such as the self-employed) it might be voluntary.

Private insurance: people pay premiums related to the expected cost of providing services to them. Thus people who are in high health-risk groups pay more, and those at low risk pay less. Cross-subsidy between people with different risks of ill health is limited. Membership of a private insurance scheme is usually voluntary. The insurance fund is held by a private (frequently for-profit) company.

User fees: patients pay directly, according to a set tariff, for the healthcare services they use. There is no insurance element or mutual support. This is the most common way of paying for privately provided services in developing countries, and is also used as a component of financing for public sector services.

Community-based health insurance: as for social health insurance, premiums are commonly set according to the risk faced by the average member of the community, i.e. there is no distinction in premiums between high- and low-risk groups. However, unlike social health insurance schemes enrolment is generally voluntary and not linked to employment status. Funds are held by a private non-profit entity.

Tax-based financing

This is the most widely used form of healthcare financing in most of sub-Saharan Africa and in South Asia. It also used to be used in the USSR and its European satellites. It is argued that this mechanism is pro-poor because:

- well-run tax-based health funding is generally 'progressive' – the more you earn, the more you pay
- the poor are most easily ruined by unexpected large healthcare costs
- there need be no user charge at the point of user need.

But counter-arguments are not hard to field, for example:

- There is an automatic bias against the rural poor as opposed to the urban poor. The latter are likely to have much easier access to the full range of healthcare facilities.
- Although the general income tax might be progressive, much of the funding tends to come from 'indirect' taxation. These taxes are usually raised in the purchase of goods most used by the less poor – petrol, luxury items, etc. This renders horizontal (countrywide) healthcare provision a less likely option than the vertical planning favoured by many IMF structural adjustment policies.
- Since we are discussing this in the context of third world societies, a tax raised on personal income is not likely to be enough to fund adequate healthcare.

Studies based upon household data suggest that inequitable access to publicly financed healthcare is indeed a substantial problem. Because public primary care services are generally perceived to be of poor quality and the private costs (transport and time costs) of accessing public hospitals are high for the poor (*see* Box 6.2) (Russell, 2000), the poor often prefer to use the services of private doctors. Yet the rich continue to use public hospital care, especially where there are few alternatives. The result is that the poor may use publicly funded services (particularly hospital services) less than the rich.

Box 6.2   Barriers to accessing publicly financed healthcare services in Sri Lanka

---

'If we go to the general hospital we would go in the morning and expect to come back in the afternoon. I would not be able to work and get my Rs 200. So after work I go to the private doctor or only the pharmacy – this is easy and costs about Rs 100.'

'It is often easier to go to a private place close by than to the Kalubovila (government) hospital ... when you consider the time, what you have to spend for the bus. If we feel thirsty, we need to drink something. And if someone is going to Kalubovila two people have to go – while the patient goes to see the doctor another person has to get a place in the medicine queue, so you have to spend for two people.'

Recent work by Wagstaff suggests that, in general, tax revenue financing of healthcare in developing countries is at least mildly progressive, and financing from direct taxes (such as income taxes) is more progressive than other financing mechanisms (Wagstaff, 2000). This suggests that higher-income people pay a higher percentage of their income in supporting tax-funded healthcare systems. But the evidence on tax incidence is not entirely clear, as the calculation of tax burden and incidence is very complex. The incidence of a tax measures the final tax burden on people of different income levels taking into account both the indirect effects of the tax (such as how income tax affects wage levels) and the direct effects.

Social insurance funding

This concept is predicated on the principle that if a desperately poor person is suddenly faced with a need for medical care, this can be paid for out of a medical insurance contributed to by the relatively rich in the community. This takes the element of risk out of the issue, so that the poor are not at a psychological disadvantage in that respect compared with the rich.

As the reader is doubtless aware, many of the first world nations – such as the Netherlands, France, Spain, etc. – provide health cover through a combination of social insurance funding and income tax. But when it comes to third world nations, the amount that the relatively rich can pay for social insurance can only finance a meagre healthcare package for each citizen. In many third world countries, for example, only those in regular employment can draw on the fund. That is, the relatively rich are actually further enriched by the poor in the following ways:

- The government may subsidise the social health insurance fund in order to make the new system more palatable to employers and employees. This can be done directly through government contributions or indirectly through the subsidised treatment of members in public facilities. If government resources are limited, this may involve withdrawal of some financial support for the basic services provided to the poor.
- The development of a social health insurance fund establishes a significant new purchasing power. If the inputs necessary to provide healthcare (such as doctors and nurses) are limited, this may attract inputs away from providing services to the poor.

Ideally this system should go far to eradicate within-country inequities with respect to healthcare access. However, this presupposes that coverage is universal and in many third world nations (and even in the US!) this simply is not so. Consider the case of Korea. The government there successfully expanded its system of social health insurance to the entire population and there was a concurrent expansion in healthcare facilities and health staff to meet the increased demand. Nonetheless, the poor, the elderly and those who live in rural areas still have lower access to healthcare, due to the maldistribution of both health staff and facilities, which tend to locate in urban centres where there is greater demand and ability to pay.

When only part of the population has coverage, social health insurance is likely to increase the disparities in access between the poor and the rich. The nature of the benefit package to be paid for through the insurance mechanism may introduce differentials in the range of services and quality of care offered to the insured and the uninsured. Most schemes (or proposals for schemes) in low and lower middle income countries depend significantly upon government contributions, and government staff represent a large proportion of beneficiaries. In times of economic expansion (as in Thailand during the early 1990s), it may be possible to launch a social health insurance scheme with government financial support, without adversely affecting services for the poor, but when the economy is stagnant this is unlikely to be feasible. Government resources may be redirected away from the healthcare provided to the poor, and health professionals are likely to be attracted towards a better-funded service.

Private health insurance cover

There is no need to explain in detail how this works. Individuals can take out private cover – of various levels of completeness – but in doing so they have to pay regular premiums. It is routinely used by many people in first world countries, even if a national health service already exists. In the UK, where the NHS is available to all, private health insurance can provide quicker access to hospital care.

However, only the relatively well-off can afford it. In the US, it is estimated that some 30% of the population finds itself entirely unprotected (MacDonald, 2000). They cannot afford private insurance premiums and do not qualify for Medicaid or Medicare.

It is therefore not difficult to appreciate how inadequate such a scheme would be in a third world country. Such insurance would only be available to the well endowed economically and probably educationally as well. However, there are some important and noteworthy exceptions to this. Both South Africa and Zimbabwe have routinely run private health insurance for many years and the well-off of both countries depend on it.

While well-run systems of private insurance in the first world usually limit claims made for basic services, this is not at all common in many third world countries. There, private health insurance is often a mechanism by which demands made by privately insured people impact adversely on the health needs of the very poor. In countries with low GNP, it is impossible to raise more than 10 to 20% of delivery cost through mechanisms such as private insurance.

It can be argued, as pointed out in the DFID publication cited above, that private health cover represents a means by which the wealthier will make less use of state provision, thus freeing more government resources for the poor. However, the strength of this argument depends critically on whether any 'freed' resources are actually used to support healthcare for the poor as well as upon the regulation governing private health insurance and how it interacts with the rest of the healthcare system.

- It is important to consider whether or not those purchasing private health insurance are allowed to 'opt out' of the primary financing mechanism or whether they must continue to contribute to the solidarity fund. Allowing the middle class to opt out of the primary financing mechanism may not only damage the potential of this mechanism to subsidise healthcare for the poor, but may also reduce political pressure to maintain high standards of care under this scheme if they seek it outside the public sector.

- The tax treatment of private insurance premiums (i.e. whether private insurance premiums are taxable or not) is an important factor. Proponents of private insurance sometimes argue that making private insurance premiums tax-exempt will encourage more people to purchase private insurance, thus freeing up more government resources for the poor. However, exempting premiums from taxes will also direct significant subsidies to those already purchasing insurance.

However, private health insurance actually uses significant government subsidies, even if the government does not explicitly subsidise private health insurance. For example, in South Africa, not only has the government given tax-breaks on private health insurance contributions, but the following additional means of capturing government subsidies have been identified.

- Expensive cases are 'dumped' on the public system by insurers once their insurance benefits have been exhausted in private hospitals.
- Insured patients frequently claim to be uninsured and thus escape paying for care in public hospitals.
- Fees charged by public hospitals to private insurers do not recover the full costs of care.
- Poor billing systems often fail to charge and recover fees from insured patients.

In Chile it was also found that higher-income persons, covered by the private insurance entities (ISAPREs), captured a larger than average subsidy from government.

In practice, issues of political economy mean that the regulations governing private insurance cannot ensure that this will be a 'pro-poor' financing mechanism.

User fees

It is probably obvious to the reader that, in the third world context, such a system would automatically exclude the majority of people seeking healthcare. But the DFID does propose that introducing such a system might well be pro-poor because:

- tax-financed systems are skewed towards subsidising urban hospital services at the expense of rural and primary care services; introducing user fees for select (urban and hospital) services could redirect subsidies to the rural poor
- increasing resources available for healthcare would allow governments to expand or upgrade their network of rural, primary care services, hence improving the accessibility of such services for the poor.

Among the many counter-arguments which have emerged are the following:

- Low household income levels mean that the revenue-generating potential of user fees in low-income countries is low, limiting the scope to improve the quality and accessibility of rural primary care services.
- It is often not politically feasible to reallocate government subsidies as desired.
- It is difficult in practice to design price discrimination schemes that protect the poor while charging the more affluent.

It is unquestionable, as Jamaica discovered in 1974, that user fees undermine political support for the goal of universal coverage of basic healthcare services.

Wherever user fees were introduced, there has been a concurrent decrease in service utilisation. The magnitude of this drop in utilisation was frequently larger, and the effect of a longer duration, among the poor part of the population. Although there is little evidence on the additional burden that fees may place on household resource levels, at a minimum they are likely to act as an additional deterrent to accessing care (especially for the very poor) while catastrophic costs would have much greater impact.

While the effects to date of user fees on the poor appear almost universally negative, in virtually all cases this has been partly a result of poor design, planning and implementation. Increases in user fees have rarely been accompanied by improvements in quality, and very little attention has been paid to the design and implementation of effective exemption mechanisms. Neither those responsible for implementation nor the wider community have had much involvement in the design of systems that most immediately affect them.

The DFID maintains that, if properly implemented and appropriately designed initially, user fees can deliver benefits to the poor. They look to some very large schemes indeed, such as that in Kenya, to support their view that user fees should not be regarded as automatically suspect by those whose concerns are social justice and equity.

This author's own experience in a wide range of third world communities has made it quite clear that low income could not raise much of the needed healthcare costs. Either the number of services would have to be drastically reduced, or, and in this alternative would reduce user fee customers, raise each user fee cost. The DFID document estimates that that it is probably impossible to raise more than 10 to 20% of delivery costs by that means. The issue becomes further distorted by the wealthier areas generating more user fees than the poorer by introducing differentials between localities within the country. This in turn might well lead to uneven health provision – clinics, etc., even hospitals – between areas. If health spending is to be efficient, there must be an active policy by which the government does the reverse – i.e. actually moves money from the wealthier to the poorer areas.

Community-based health insurance

In situations in which there is high user finance of healthcare, community-based health insurance can work well. There are many examples of this to back up the argument, but not many in the third world's poorest nations. Where such schemes operate, they effectively meet the needs of that particular community's relatively poor.

But, as the DFID report makes clear, the very poor need an infrastructure (transport, communications, etc.) to allow them to access the benefits. Not many third world governments are able to bear such a burden, especially if their debt repayments actually supersede the amounts that they can devote to health. Likewise, such systems would – even in the fairly short term – create geographical inequalities in the same ways that user fees do.

In China, between 1985 and 1999, community-based health insurance represented the principal source of healthcare financing. The Chinese government quickly found out that this involved them in a quagmire of redistribution programmes. The administration of these was recognised as an unsustainable drain on tight health resources.

Thailand seems to run a much more successful community-based health in-surance scheme, under a strongly centralised system of control. But broadly speaking, even in Thailand, such schemes have often failed to meet their objectives. For one thing, it is too difficult to develop such initiatives with sufficient sensitivity both to the technical and managerial structures required and the needs of local communities.

References

Bennett S and Gilson L (2001) *Health Financing: Designing and Implementing Pro-Poor Policies.* DFID Health Systems Resources Centre, London.

Duggan M and Scott-Samuel A (2000) *Towards a Public Health Group for the 21st Century.* Workshop at the Eighth Annual Forum of the UK Public Health Alliance.

The Economist (1999) Labour's crusade. 25 September–1 October. Editorial p.4.

Gwatkin D (2000) Health inequalities and the health of the poor: what do we know? What can we do? *Bulletin of the World Health Organisation.* **78**: 26–33.

MacDonald T (1998) *Rethinking Health Promotion: A Global Approach.* Routledge, London, pp 10–45.

MacDonald T (2000) *Third World Health Promotion and its Dependence on First World Health.* The Edwin Mellen Press, Lewiston, New York.

Marchand S, Wikler D and Landesman B (1998) Class, health and justice: health and society. *Milbank Memorial Fund Quarterly.* **76**: 449–67.

O'Keefe E and Scott-Samuel A (2002) Human rights and wrongs: could health impact assessment help? *Journal of Law, Medicine and Ethics.* **30**: 734–8.

Rawls J (1971) *A Theory of Justice.* Harvard University Press, Cambridge, MA.

Russell S (2000) *Coping with the Costs of Illness: the affordability of health care services for poor households in Sri Lanka.* PhD thesis, University of London.

Scott-Samuel A (1996) Health impact assessment: an idea whose time has come. Editorial. *British Medical Journal.* **313**: 183–4.

Sen A (1999a) Health in development. *Bulletin of the World Health Organization.* **77**: 619–23.

Sen A (1999b) *Development as Freedom: human capability and global need.* Knopf, New York.

Uchitelle L (1999) More cash in hand but poorer. *International Herald Tribune.* 19 October.

Wagstaff A (2000) *Poverty and Health Sector Inequalities.* Bulletin of World Health Organization 80 No. 2, pp 40–65.

WHO (2000) *World Health Report 2000. Health Systems – Improving Performance.* Copenhagen.

Whitehead A (1990) *The Concepts and Principles of Equity in Health.* WHO Regional Office for Europe, Copenhagen, p.414.

World Bank (2001/2002) *World in Global Finance,* pp 491–527.

Chapter 7

Popular opposition to the inequities

Scepticism about the G7/G8

Countries roughly representative of the first world held their first meeting at Rambouillet, France, in 1975. At that time, they called themselves the 'Group of Six' (G6) – France, the US, Britain, Germany, Japan and Italy.

The idea was for the six leaders to discuss current world issues in a constructive and informal manner in a private setting. At that time, the representatives were not accompanied by the army of bureaucrats, advisers, security personnel, etc., as they are now. The idea was not to attract media interest, but to try to solve real problems at ground level. The 1975 discussions were dominated by the oil crisis, already discussed previously in connection with the IMF.

Since then the G6 became the G7 in 1977, when Canada was invited to join, and G8 in 1991 when the USSR joined. Box 7.1 lists all of these summit meetings up through 1994.

Box 7.1   The 'G' summit meetings

Rambouillet, France	15–17 November 1975
San Juan, Puerto Rico, USA	27–28 June 1976
London, UK ('London I')	7–8 May 1977
Bonn, West Germany ('Bonn I')	16–17 July 1978
Tokyo, Japan ('Tokyo I')	28–29 June 1979
Venice, Italy ('Venice I')	22–23 June 1980
Ottawa, Canada (Montebello)	20–21 July 1981
Versailles, France	4–6 June 1982
Williamsburg, Virginia, USA	28–30 May 1983
London, UK ('London II')	7–9 June 1984
Bonn, West Germany ('Bonn II')	2–4 May 1985
Tokyo, Japan ('Tokyo II')	4–6 May 1986
Venice, Italy ('Venice II')	8–10 June 1987
Toronto, Canada	19–21 June 1988
Paris, France ('Summit of the Arch')	14–16 July 1989
Houston, Texas, USA	9–11 July 1990
London, UK ('London III')	15–17 July 1991
Munich, Germany	6–8 July 1992
Tokyo, Japan ('Tokyo III')	7–9 July 1993
Naples, Italy	8–10 July 1994
Halifax, Canada	15–17 June 1995

continued

Nuclear Safety and Security Summit, Moscow, Russia (G7 with Russia)	19–20 April 1996
Lyon, France	27–29 June 1996
Denver Summit of the Eight, USA	20–22 June 1997 (*see also* USIA site)
Birmingham G8 Summit, UK	15–17 May 1998
Cologne, Germany	18–20 June 1999
Okinawa, Japan	21–23 July 2000
Genoa, Italy	20–22 July 2001
Kananaskis, Alberta, Canada	26–27 June 2002
Evian-les-Bains, France	1–3 June 2003
Sea Island, Georgia, USA	8–10 June 2004

It was at the 1996 summit at Lyon that the inequities between the first and third world were first addressed prominently. At Lyon, for instance, the Highly Indebted Poor Countries (HIPC) initiative was launched. At every G8 meeting since, expectations were that the financial/trade/health inequities addressed in this book would result in really practical action by the first world. This expectation has been fuelled as the summing-up statement of each meeting since 1996 has promised to deal with the issue at the next meeting. This attracted great optimism at first, but as the promise has had to be deferred by other 'more urgent current issues' – to quote a Canadian spokesman after the Quebec summit – this surge of optimism has gradually been replaced by increasing anger and frustration.

Of course, there have been some nods in the right direction. For instance, the Cologne Summit (1999) agreed on the Enhanced HIPC Initiative, which promised over US$37 billion of debt relief to some of the world's most needy. In 2000, at Okinawa, the G8 agreed to provide further funding to fight infectious diseases. At the Genoa Summit (2001) emerged the creation of a 'Global Fund' (actual amount not agreed on!) to fight AIDS, tuberculosis (TB) and malaria. This summit really appeared to be getting somewhere as the G8 leaders were joined by the leaders of some of the most important African nations to launch a 'New Africa Initiative' called New Partnerships for Africa's Development (NEPAD). It was promised that, if Africa's leaders each appointed a Personal Representative for Africa, then these leaders could contribute to a G8 Action Plan for the 2002 summit at Kananaskis in the foothills of the Canadian Rockies.

But the Kananaskis Summit was very much dominated by discussions about terrorism. All that was agreed on the global inequity issue was a 'solid commitment' from each G8 member to Africa and agreed priorities for assistance. Much talk, but much less actual movement of funds from G8 countries to the third world, has generally been the result. Even the specific funding 'agreed' in 1999 has not yet been honoured.

The last summit of the G8, in the state of Georgia, USA, in 2004, was even attended by a huge delegation from African nations, so confident were they that their plight – especially with the catastrophic spread of HIV/AIDS – would be properly addressed. Discussions about the Iraq conflict virtually pushed Africa off the agenda.

More promises and gestures in the face of a growing public awareness of the realities – an appreciation much engendered by popular concerns about global warming and green issues – has meant a huge upsurge of protest at G8 meetings. The G8 response to this – especially after such huge protests as those in Seattle, London and Genoa – has been to surround its meetings with elaborate and well-armed 'security'. 'Scepticism' has increasingly been replaced by 'confrontation'.

I would argue that – unpleasant and inconvenient for the smooth administration of life in the first world as this is – it reflects a basic reality. Injustice on a global scale – very much as on a community level – cannot be sustained. Moral issues cannot be consigned to 'theory' but must find expression in reality. That is why, despite the catastrophes we face, I remain basically optimistic. Numerous action groups among ordinary people in the first world have sprung up in the last five years, and they are increasing. Websites at which these can be accessed are provided in the following account of the public protests at the G8 Summit in Genoa, 2001. The account is from the Wikipedia free encyclopedia.

Genoa G8 Summit protest

One of the bloodiest protests in Western Europe's recent history, resulting in at least three demonstrator deaths and several hundred demonstrators hospitalised after police attacks and torture in custody, was the Genoa Group of Eight Summit protest, from 18 to 22 July 2001.

The response from protestors to such police tactics has included accusing them of brutality in interrupting their right to non-violently protest. They claim that the Group of Eight Summit is, in any case, a non-legitimate attempt by eight of the world's most powerful governments to set the rules for the world at large. However, police and many politicians argue attempting to blockade a meeting is in itself a violent event and an attempt to impede the processes of democratically elected governments. They also argue that police use the minimum force necessary to achieve their goals, and that protestors' claims are exaggerated.

All in all, there were several hundred demonstrators injured and several hundred arrests during the days surrounding the G8 meeting; most of those arrested have been charged with some form of 'criminal association' under Italy's anti-mafia and anti-terrorist laws. As part of the continuing investigations, police raids of social centres, media centres, union buildings and law offices have continued across Italy since the G8 Summit in Genoa. Many police officers or responsible authorities present in Genoa during the G8 Summit are currently under investigation by the Italian judges, and some of them have resigned.

Some have since admitted to planting Molotov cocktails in order to justify the Diaz School raids, as well as faking the stabbing of a police officer to frame activists [*see*: fair.org: http://www.fair.org/activism/genoa-update.html].

In Genoa, where over 300 000 demonstrators gathered to protest the G8 Summit from 18 to 22 July 2001, the police conducted night-time raids upon convergence centres and campsites. Around midnight on 21 July, the police conducted a raid upon the two schools known as Diaz-Pascoli and Diaz-Pertini, in which activists had been sleeping and doing media, medical and legal support work. The Diaz School raids resulted in 93 arrests, at least 61 activists severely injured, and a parliamentary inquiry [*see*: http://www.guardian.co.uk/international/story/0,3604,526484.html].

Police baton attacks during this raid left several activists, including journalist Mark Covell, in comas, at least one with brain damage, and another with both jaws and 14 teeth broken. In May 2003, Judge Anna Ivaldi concluded that the activists arrested during the Diaz School raid had put up no resistance whatsoever to the police.

In an unrelated incident, one of the protestors, Carlo Giuliani of Genoa, was killed by a Carabiniere while holding a fire extinguisher and engaged in a conflict between Carabinieri in a jeep and a group of protesters. Property within the city of Genoa was severely damaged by these events, and there were over 400 demonstrators severely injured. For the first time in its republican history, Italy temporarily suspended the constitutional freedom of movement on the national territory.

Since the G8 Summit was held inside a 'Red Zone' in the centre of town that had been evacuated of inhabitants and surrounded by a temporary wall, there was no chance for protesters to communicate with the participants. Only one activist, Valerie Vie, secretary of a French branch of the Association for the Taxation of Financial Transaction for the aid of Citizens (ATTAC), managed to publicly breach the Red Zone. There were several border riots leading up to the summit as well, as police attempted to prevent suspected activists from entering Italy.

An activist who had been heading to Genoa, Susanne Bendotti, was hit by a vehicle and killed on 21 July at the French–Italian border in Ventimiglia; another Genoa activist, Maria Jose Olivastri was found naked and strangled in a ditch in Padua, two weeks after the summit.

Genoa demonstrator Eduardo Parodi, a close friend of Carlo Giuliani, died shortly after Genoa after experiencing severe health problems that may have been related to the use of CS gas. Rumours of further deaths and of Genoa demonstrators who remained missing after the summit continue to circulate. *See* photos from Genoa on: http://www.nadir.org/nadir/initiativ/agp/free/genova/pics1.htm.

Globalisation perceived as inimical to equity

In Chapter 14 the author addresses the issue of possible solutions to the growing inequity between the first and third worlds. He argues that any viable solutions must be global. Just as mismanaged global finance can worsen health inequities, it will be argued that global finance, ethically managed, can be a principal solution. It is therefore somewhat of a paradox that groups formed to oppose inequity and injustice in health should often categorise themselves as 'anti-globalisation'.

The 'anti-globalisation' movement has become very widespread largely due to emotional calls to combat the inroads of multinational corporations – and of first world (especially US) capitalism in particular – into efforts on the part of third world nations to run their own affairs.

This widespread opposition remains largely a grass-roots effort. It deserves close scrutiny on the part of all of us who are concerned to remedy the problems. We can learn lessons from it – both methodological and cautionary. The prefix 'anti' has always struck me as being a poor way to describe a movement whose aims are so positive. Therefore, in this context I will simply refer to it as the 'movement' throughout this chapter.

Some factions of the movement reject globalisation as such, but the overwhelming majority of its participants are aligned with movements of indigenous people, human rights, NGOs, anarchism, green movements and, to a minor extent, communism. Some activists in the movement have objected, not to capitalism or international markets as such, but rather to what they claim are the non-transparent and undemocratic mechanisms; and the negative consequences of unregulated globalisation. They are especially opposed to 'globalisation abuse' being misrepresented as neoliberalism, and international institutions that are perceived to promote neoliberalism without regard to ethical standards, such as the World Bank (WB), International Monetary Fund (IMF), and the Organisation for Economic Co-Operation and Development (OECD) and the World Trade Organization (WTO) and 'free trade' treaties like the North American Free Trade Agreement (NAFTA), Free Trade Area of the Americas (FTAA), the Multilateral Agreement on Investments (MAI) and the General Agreement on Trade in Services (GATS).

Activists often also oppose business alliances like the World Economic Forum (WEF), the Trans Atlantic Business Dialogue (TABD) and the Asia-Pacific Economic Forum (APEC), as well as the governments which promote such agreements or institutions. Others argue that, if borders are opened to capital, borders should be similarly opened to allow free and legal circulation and choice of residence for migrants and refugees. These activists tend to target organisations such as the International Organisation for Migration and the Schengen Information System.

It is also worth noting that many nationalist movements, such as the UK Independence Party (UKIP) and the French National Front, are also against globalisation. They are usually not considered part of the 'mainstream' anti-globalisation movement, which tends to adopt left-wing approaches.

Diversity within the movement

There are many different causes championed by movement members, including labour rights, environmentalism, feminism, freedom of migration, preservation of the cultures of indigenous peoples, biodiversity, cultural diversity, food safety, organic farming, opposition to the green revolution and genetic engineering, and ending or reforming capitalism. Many of the protesters are veterans of single-issue campaigns, including forest/anti-logging activism, living wage, labour union organising, anti-sweatshop campaigns, homeless solidarity campouts, urban squatting, urban autonomy, and political secession. Some protesters identify themselves as revolutionary anarchists, socialists, Gaians, or communists; others agree ideologically but don't immediately identify themselves as such and still others want to reform capitalism, e.g. democratic Greens, some pagans, etc.

Although movement members see most or all of these goals as complementary to one another, the number of different, and sometimes contradictory, issues has been a point of annoyance for the people they are protesting against. Critics claim many views are inconsistent and unrealistic. Many of these concerns can be said to represent specific issues about which the protestors fear a loss of self-determination, because they believe that the global financial institutions and agreements undermine local decision-making methods. Local or national sovereignty is seen as key to protecting cultures, and ecologies.

As such, one common thread among the disparate causes is that the World Bank and IMF are perceived as undermining local decision-making methods. Local or national sovereignty is seen as key to protecting cultures and ecologies. Governments and free-trade institutions, on the other hand, are seen as acting for the good of transnational (or multinational) corporations (e.g. Microsoft, Monsanto, etc.). These corporations are regarded as having abilities that human persons do not have: moving freely across borders, extracting desired natural resources, utilising a diversity of human resources. They are perceived to be able to move on after damage to natural capital and biodiversity in a manner impossible for a nation's citizens. Activists also claim corporations impose a kind of 'global monoculture'. Some of the movements' common goals are, therefore, an end to the legal status of corporate personhood and the dissolution, or dramatic reform, of the World Bank, IMF and WTO.

Some aspects of the movement's agenda are shared by major (pro-capitalist) economic theorists who argue for much less centralised systems of money supply, debt control and trade law. These include George Soros, Joseph E Stiglitz (formerly of the World Bank) and David Korten. These three in particular have made strong arguments for drastically improving transparency, for debt relief, land reform and restructuring corporate accountability systems. Korten and Stiglitz's contribution to the movement includes involvement in direct actions and street protest. As many supporters of the movement do not share basic assumptions about capitalism and economics itself, their particular agenda may not dominate the movement or its perceptions. But it potentially provides greater credibility.

Organisation within the movement

Although over the past years more emphasis has been given to the construction of grass-roots alternatives to (capitalist) globalisation, the movement's largest and most visible mode of organising remains mass decentralised campaigns of direct action and civil disobedience. This mode of organising, sometimes under the banner of the People's Global Action network, tried to tie the many disparate causes together into one global struggle. Exposure to the other causes helps create a sense of solidarity and may lay the groundwork for a consensus process and basis of unity for the movement overall, which could eventually include any, all or none of the doctrines listed above.

In many ways the process of organising matters overall can be more important to activists than the avowed goals or achievements of any component of the movement.

As Ralph Nader (2002) has put it: 'You may support some of the goals. You may even like some of the decisions. But you can't reasonably support the way these decisions are being made.'

The movement's organisational model is notable. Despite (or perhaps because of) the lack of formal coordinating bodies, the movement manages to successfully organise large protests on a global basis, using information technology to spread information and organise. Protesters organise themselves into 'affinity groups', typically a non-hierarchical group of people who live close together and share a common goal or political message. Affinity groups will then send representatives to planning meetings. However, because these groups are easily and frequently penetrated by law enforcement intelligence, important plans of the protests are often not made until the last minute. One common tactic of the protests is to split up, based on willingness to break the law. This is designed, with varying success, to protect the risk-averse from the physical and legal dangers posed by confrontations with law enforcement. For example, in Prague, the protest split into three distinct groups, approaching the conference centre from three directions: one engaging in various forms of civil disobedience (the Yellow march), one (the Pink/Silver march) advancing through 'tactical frivolity' (costume, dance, theatre, music and artwork), and one (the Blue march) engaging in violent conflicts with the baton-armed police, the protesters throwing cobblestones lifted from the street [*The Guardian* report: http://www.guardian.co.uk/imf/story/0,7369,373703,00.html].

These demonstrations come to resemble small societies in themselves. Many protesters take training in first aid and act as medics to other injured protesters. Some organisations, like the National Lawyers Guild and, to a lesser extent, the American Civil Liberties Union (ACLU), provide legal witnesses in case of law enforcement confrontation. Protesters often claim that major media outlets do not properly report on them. In response, some of them created the Independent Media Centre, a collective of protesters reporting on the actions as they happen.

Influences on the movement

Several influential critical works have inspired the anti-globalisation movement. They are worth reading.

- Naomi Klein's book *No Logo* (2003), which criticised the production practices of multinational corporations and the omnipresence of brand-driven marketing in popular culture.
- Vandana Shiva's book *Biopiracy* (1998), which documented the way that the natural capital of indigenous peoples and eco-regions is converted to forms of intellectual capital recognised as commercial property, without sharing the private utility thus derived.
- Amartya Sen's *Development as Freedom* (winner of The Bank of Sweden Prize in Economic Sciences in Memory of Alfred Nobel 1999), arguing strongly against traditional macroeconomics, and for a system of money supply where currency would be based on free time.

Perhaps more influential than any printed book is the vast array of material on spiritual movements, anarchism, libertarian socialism and the Green movement that is now available on the Internet. The previously obscure works of Arundhati Roy (1998), Starhawk (1999) and John Zerzan (2002) in particular inspired a critique favouring feminism, consensus process and political secession, opposing a 'tyranny of number', by which the critics seem to mean any global measurements of people or profit at all. Perhaps the only axiom shared widely by such critics is, in line with this critique, that biodiversity is good, extinction bad. Arguably, most advocates of globalisation would agree with this too, so it may be a straw man.

Other than this vague 'biodiversity good, extinction bad, numbers harmful' summary, which would no doubt enrage many followers of specific ideologies, there seems to be no leader who is universally accepted by 'the movement'. In this respect it resembles the peace movement, environmental movement, ecology movement, Green movement, and various forms of anarchism and fundamentalism, all of which generally abhor usurpation of power by 'leaders', while paradoxically elevating previously obscure figures or doctrines. Some call this an anti-monoculture movement, and make strong links between ecological, social and ideological diversity doctrines.

Other direct confrontations

We have already discussed the upheavals at the Genoa Summit, but there have been others. The first major mobilisation of the movement happened on 18 June 1999. Anti-globalisation protests were organised in dozens of cities around the world, especially London, UK, and Eugene, Oregon. The protest in Eugene, Oregon, turned into a mini-riot where local anarchists drove the police out of a small park. One anarchist, Robert Thaxton, was arrested and convicted of throwing a rock at a police officer. As of 2004, he is still in prison.

The second major mobilisation of the movement, known as N30, occurred on 30 November 1999, when protesters blocked delegates' entrance to the WTO meetings in Seattle, USA. The protests forced the cancellation of the opening ceremonies and lasted the length of the meeting until 3 December. There was a large, permitted march by members of the American Federation of Labor – Congress of Industrial Organizations (AFL-CIO), and another large, unpermitted march by assorted affinity groups. The Seattle riot police, in conjunction with the National Guard, assaulted protesters with truncheons, pepper spray, tear gas and rubber bullets. Over 600 protesters were arrested and dozens were injured. One demonstrator miscarried her baby after being exposed to CS and OC gas. Three policemen were injured by friendly fire, and one by a thrown rock. Some protesters destroyed the windows of storefronts of businesses owned or franchised by targeted corporations such as a large Nike shop and many Starbucks windows. The mayor put the city under the municipal equivalent of martial law and declared a curfew. As of 2002, the city of Seattle had paid over $200 000 in settlements of lawsuits filed against the Seattle Police Department for assault and wrongful arrest, with a class action lawsuit still pending.

Law enforcement reaction

The role of state-sanctioned 'law enforcement' actions at Genoa has already been cited above.

Although local police were surprised by the size of N30, law enforcement agencies have since reacted worldwide to prevent the disruption of future events by a variety of tactics, including sheer weight of numbers, infiltrating the groups to determine their plans, and preparations for the use of force to remove protesters. At the 2000 protest of the Republican National Convention in Philadelphia, John Sellers, a key organiser of the Ruckus Society, one of the groups organising the protests, was arrested on charges of jaywalking and held in jail on $1 000 000 bail for sufficient time to impede the organisation of the protest. Many protesters have been prevented from crossing borders for the purpose of joining a protest, either because their names matched a list of known protesters or because of their appearance. In the UK, a coach heading to a rally was turned back and escorted back to London – a police operation later found to be illegal by the courts.

At the site of some of the protests, police have used tear gas and pepper spray, concussion grenades, rubber and wooden bullets, truncheons, water cannons, dogs, horses, and occasionally live ammunition to repel the protesters. In Quebec City, municipal officials built a ten-foot-high wall around the portion of the city where the Summit of the Americas was being held, which only residents, delegates to the summit, and certain accredited journalists were allowed inside. Although police claimed that violent elements in the protesters required a firm response, they allegedly fired tear gas and rubber bullets indiscriminately, dispersing peaceful assemblies and even teams of medics assisting the wounded. It is claimed they also gassed areas not involved in the protests, firing off the mountaintop where the confrontations were taking place into the city below. The medical centre and independent media centre were evacuated by police at gunpoint.

Influence on the developing world

Some people claim that the major mobilisations have taken place mainly in the developed world, where there are strong traditions of free speech, police restraint, civil rights and the rule of law. In these countries, one of the objectives is to demonstrate that the protesters self-govern better than they could ever be controlled by violent force. On 15 March 2002 in Barcelona, 250 000 people 'rioted' for days with apparently no serious injury to individuals on either side – far fewer casualties than would be expected in a typical European soccer riot. There was, however, much damage to private and public property – which is, arguably, unnecessary in public protest.

In Argentina during the winter 2002 economic crisis, millions of ordinary citizens took to the streets for days, with similar results to the Barcelona 'protests', forcing several changes in the federal government. On 19 and 20 December 2001, demonstrations (called 'cacerolazos') in Buenos Aires forced the resignation of then-president De La Rua, though over 32 demonstrators were killed. Since then, Argentine citizens have continued to try and develop 'alternative' neighbourhood-based economic systems, social structures and local systems of autonomous self-government. A popular slogan within the uprising was: 'Que se vayan todos! Que no se quede ninguno solo!' This means, 'Everybody out [of the government]! Nobody stays!', indicating protesters' frustration, not only with corruption in government, but with the entire governmental structure. Whether these protests are beneficial to the functioning of fledgling democracies is debatable, given the ability of the voters to change their representatives periodically anyway.

In India, the views of Vandana Shiva, Amartya Sen and Arundhati Roy are very popular. Effectively they enjoy full celebrity status. The acceptance and interest in their ideas and in the methods of Mohandas Gandhi are forming a major and specific challenge to both Hindu and Muslim fundamentalism. The three have also had a substantial impact on views within the anti-globalisation movement.

Criticism

The anti-globalisation movement has been heavily criticised on many fronts by politicians, members of right-wing think tanks, mainstream economists and other supporters of free trade policies. Participants in the movement dismiss these criticisms as carping from a tiny minority who can express their opinions via what they call the corporate media. They claim that the criticisms themselves are self-serving and unrepresentative of informed popular opinion.

One of the most fundamental criticisms of the movement is simply that it lacks coherent goals, and that the views of different protesters are fundamentally contradictory. A survey that was made recently during such a protest has shown that at least 40% of the people protesting could not define the meaning of the word globalisation nor list actual reasons against what they are protesting.

For instance, it is argued (especially by *The Economist*) that one of the major causes of poverty among third world farmers are the trade barriers put up by rich nations. The WTO is an organisation set up to work towards removing those trade barriers. Therefore, it is argued, people really concerned about the plight of the third world should actually be encouraging free trade, rather than attempting to fight it. Further in this vein, it is argued that the protesters' opposition to free trade is sometimes aimed at protecting the interests of Western labour (whose wages and conditions are protected by trade barriers) rather than the interests of the developing world. This contrasts with the 'goals' of those in the movement, in favour of improving the conditions of ordinary farmers and workers *everywhere*.

Anti-globalisation activists counter that free trade policies create an environment for workers similar to the prisoner's dilemma, in which workers in different countries are tempted to 'defect' by undercutting standards on wages and work conditions, and reject this argument in favour of a strategy of cooperation for mutual benefit.

Another criticism is that, although the movement protests about things that are widely recognised as serious problems, such as human rights violations, genocide and global warming, it rarely proposes detailed solutions. Those solutions that *are* advocated are often what some people regard as failed variants of socialism – e.g. *see* the debate between Michael Albert, Marvin Mandell and Barry Finger [http:// www.zmag.org/socdebate.htm]. Proponents of the movement point to the existence of web resources like the Philadelphia IMC alternatives site [http://www. phillyimc.org/alternatives] and the annual World Social Fora where numerous solutions are proposed and debated and empirical data on social experiments are exchanged. However, even some supporters of the movement, such as George Monbiot, believe this is a serious problem in the movement. In a forum discussing 'life after capitalism' he states he was 'as unconvinced by my own answers as I was by everyone's else's' [http://www.monbiot.com/archives/2004/06/01/the-age-of-consent].

Some have criticised its claim to be non-violent. Aside from the indisputably violent tactics by a minority of protesters (possibly aggravated by the police), some see an enforced blockade of events and public throughways as a violent action, in and of itself. Many protesters counter that blockades are a time-honoured technique of civil disobedience.

Finally, the motivations of the organisers of the protests are often questioned. Some believe that the key organisers are really Trotskyites, who are simply using whatever grievances they can find to enlarge their protests, with the aim of provoking violent revolution. The counter-argument to this is that the movement has a very horizontal power structure, so that the powers of any key organisers are limited, and that the communications structures in rich countries make it totally unrealistic for violent revolution to occur there, since the vast majority of ordinary people reject violence once they have sufficient evidence of it. As such, a revolution is so improbable, activists believe organisers cannot be so mistaken as to advocate it.

The Iraq War and its impact on the movement

In 2003, the movement showed wide and deep global opposition to the war in Iraq. Following the most spectacular show of numbers on the weekend of 15 February 2003, when about 10 million or more anti-globalisation protesters participated in global protests against war on Iraq (pre-war), the *New York Times* (17 Februrary 2003) dubbed the movement as the 'world's second superpower'.

Although the global protest did not stop the invasion itself, supporters believe it demonstrated to the world the seeming inconsistency between the claim that the invasion defended and promoted democracy, and the fact that the leaders of many formally democratic countries (Spain, Italy, Poland) were acting against the wishes of the majority of their populations in supporting the war. Noam Chomsky claimed these leaders showed their contempt for democracy (*New York Times*, 2003) Critics of this type of argument have tended to point out that this is just a standard criticism of representative democracy – a democratically elected government will not always act in the direction of greatest current public support – and that, therefore, there is no inconsistency in the leader's positions given these countries are parliamentary democracies. The author's views on the role of war in advancing health among the dispossessed (*see* Chapter 1) have already been discussed. But certain life-saving medical procedures and products were hastened onto the scene by war, e.g. penicillin, DDT, etc.

Useful websites

All of the following websites provide ongoing details about the issues crucial to this book.

- International Forum on Globalisation (http://ifg.org)
- Focus on the Global South (http://www.focusweb.org)
- Global Exchange (http://globalexchange.org)
- World Social Forum 2004 (http://www.wsfindia.org)
- Mumbai Resistance 2004 (http://www.mumbairesistance.org)
- International Monetary Fund (http://www.imf.org)
- World Trade Organization (http://www.wto.org)
- World Economic Forum (http://www.weforum.org)
- People's Global Action (http://www.agp.org)
- World Bank Group (http://www.worldbank.org)
- The Free Trade Area of the Americas (http://www.ftaa-alca.org)
- Stop the FTAA (http://www.stopftaa.org)
- FTAA Resistance (http://ftaaresistance.org)
- Independent Media Center (http://www.indymedia.org)
- United for Peace and Justice (http://unitedforpeace.org)
- Landless Workers' Movement (http://www.mstbrazil.org)
- Our World Is Not For Sale (http://www.ourworldisnotforsale.org)

- ZNet global economics site – are the alternatives practical and ethical? (http://www.zmag.org/CrisesCurEvts/Globalism/GlobaEcon.htm)
- Anti-Capitalist Convergence – DC (http://www.abolishthebank.org)
- Mobilization for Global Justice (http://www.globalizethis.org)
- Infoshop.org (http://www.infoshop.org) – archive of the anti-globalisation movement.

References

Klein N (2003) *No Logo*. Flamingo Books, London.
Nader R (2002) *Crashing the Party: taking on the corporate government in an age of surrender*. St Martin's Press, New York.
New York Times (2003) The world's second superpower. 17 February, p.12.
Roy A (1998) *The God of Small Things*. Oxford University Press, Oxford.
Sen A (1999) *Development as Freedom*. Oxford University Press, Oxford.
Shiva V (1998) *Biopiracy: the plunder of nature and knowledge*. Green Books – Gaia, London.
Starhawk (1999) *The Spirit Dance: A rebirth of the ancient religion of the Great Goddess*. Harper, San Francisco.
Wikipedia: www.wikipedia.
Zerzan J (2002) *Running on Emptiness*. Feral House Publishers, Oregon.

Chapter 8

Milk and imperialism

Links between global health and Western wealth

In this chapter the author will consider one particularly well-known example of how first world financial interests impact adversely on third world health. This is the issue of creating a market for bottle-feed baby-milk formula in third world nations and the ethical issues it raises. A brief introduction to the subject is followed by a detailed analysis of its implications for the health and economy of the third world.

While working in Accra for UNESCO in 1962, the author was impressed one April day by the sudden appearance of large, well-produced hoardings advertising a well-known milk powder for the bottle-feeding of babies. The advertisements featured pictures of two mothers – on the left, a Ghanaian mother holding her baby to her breast, and on the right, another Ghanaian mother holding her baby in one arm while she bottle-fed it. The mother on the left was poorly dressed, had huge pendulous breasts and was decidedly down-at-heel and haggard. The one on the right had small, tight breasts under a suit of clean and fashionable clothing and appeared young, fit and very much 'with it'. Along the bottom of the hoarding was a strip reading: 'Which mother do YOU want to be?' The message, of course, was clear. What perhaps was not so easy to appreciate is that similar campaigns had run in the first world nations during the 1940s and 1950s, but they had been rendered largely ineffective by several factors. Among these were: increasing access to education for Western women, a more discerning purchasing power among mothers; and 'breast is best' campaigns. NGOs proliferated in countries such as the United States and Britain to provide tips to new mothers who had decided to breastfeed, and – above all – certain manufacturers of 'baby-milk formula' were being slated for trying to profit from people's ignorance. Life was becoming tougher for milk manufacturers in the first world. They responded in two ways: by diversifying into production of commodities such as breakfast cereals; and by shifting the milk powder business into the third world, where access to basic education for women was less available, and where nervous, recently formed indigenous governments were less likely to interfere.

Support for third world services

Ghana was not the only (nor the first) third world country to undergo this experience. Ministers of health and individual hospital directors in such countries found themselves being offered funding to establish maternity care units and even money to staff them, provided that the emphasis was to be on encouraging new mothers to bottle-feed. The whole package was made even more attractive with a programme under which mothers were given three weeks' free supply of formula when they left the hospital. Such an offer would be extraordinarily difficult for a cash-strapped third world government to resist.

When the mothers returned home with their babies, however, certain problems arose. Many mothers, unable to afford further supplies of powder, would try to make the free supply last as long as possible. Generally this was done in one or both of two ways: they would make the formula for each feed more dilute than specified in the directions on the packet; or they would add other powders – such as corn meal or maize – to the commercial powder.

This author often witnessed these practices and had a difficult time persuading some mothers that colour and texture of a powder were not sufficiently precise criteria by which to decide whether or not it could be used as a 'stretcher'. But yet more problems quickly made themselves felt at the village level.

Market forces, SAPs and private enterprise

While in the maternity unit, the young mother would have usually been able to rely on the water supply she was using in mixing the baby-milk formula. But in the village a reliable source of clean water was much more problematic. Routinely, young babies died of enteric infections and diarrhoeas caused by use of polluted water. This risk greatly increased once mothers either added inappropriate stretchers to the formula or diluted it beyond the specified levels.

Moreover, as part of the IMF/World Bank structural adjustment policies, third world client governments were encouraged to cut back on public sector spending and to push money into support for private initiatives. The cutbacks on public sector spending certainly knocked large-scale rural water reticulation and purification plans on the head. This is something which the author frequently witnessed first-hand throughout the 1980s, in a range of third world countries.

But the return to the village of mothers who now needed a dependable supply of commercial milk formula opened up new opportunities for rural private enterprise initiatives – something which IMF/World Bank loans were dedicated to encouraging. In Ghana, Kenya and Papua New Guinea – widely separated cultures with widely divergent ethnologies – this author was amazed at the similarity of private sector intervention in this context! After she has been back from maternity care for, say, five or six weeks, the new mother is likely to be running out of her free supply of formula. Of course, she cannot replenish her supply locally and this must rely on a 'trader'. The 'trader' is a man (usually) who owns a pick-up truck, often kept in precarious running order by a combination of ingenuity, hay-binding wire and faith! Every fortnight or so, he will drive to the capital (or some other larger town) to purchase commodities ordered by people from the village and not available locally.

In short, he is an entrepreneur. His charges for each item so purchased must be enough to cover expenses – of which petrol is an obvious one – but exceed that level by an amount dictated by 'market forces'. These are largely determined by how great the customers' need for the product in question is. In the case of young mothers, when their supplies of formula milk have dried up, their need is quite clearly a life or death one, as far as the baby is concerned. This author witnessed a mother being told that a package of Lactogen, costing one shilling and six pence in town, 30 miles away, would have involved her paying the trader four shillings! The negotiations were fearful to behold. He even offered her five shillings for the baby, confident that he could sell it at a profit in town. The author intervened, handed over what currency he had – enough for 11 packages of Lactogen at the going rate – and then had to leave. He often wonders what happened when that supply of Lactogen ran out. Maybe the baby died in the meantime and its mum set herself up in business selling Lactogen locally!

Let us now consider the matter in more analytic terms.

Status of breastfeeding in the third world

Obviously the desire to lead a healthy life is a worldwide phenomenon, along with the wish to raise well-nourished children and provide them with opportunities for the future. Most governments regard it as a priority to invest in public health measures and programmes to improve health. However, resources are usually scarce while so many other demands are made upon them.

It is a truism that breastfeeding is a natural resource that can have a major impact upon health and family planning goals. If more women were to breastfeed their infants for longer periods of time, fewer infants would die, women and children would be healthier, and public health and family planning programmes would save money (Labbock and Nazro, 1995).

Generally speaking, there has been an increase in many countries of women opting for the breastfeeding route. This has come about largely because national policy-makers, health professionals, support groups and families have begun to recognise the many benefits of breastfeeding and have strengthened their support for it. Over and above those global trends, though, a north–south divide is evident. There are far more industrialised countries in which breastfeeding rates are low but rising, and third world ones in which breastfeeding rates are high but falling. If considered globally, the figures reflect a decline in rates of breastfeeding.

We now address the benefits of breastfeeding and outline the main causes of the decline in global breastfeeding rates, identifying specific actions that health pro-moters and policy-makers can take in order to promote and preserve this natural resource. The constant aim of this chapter is to stress the evidence of copious research, which demonstrates that:

- breastfeeding saves infant lives
- breastfeeding promotes the child's growth and development
- breastfeeding improves women's health and welfare
- breastfeeding complements family planning
- breastfeeding saves money (Labbock and Nazro, 1995).

Breastfeeding as part of the health promotion agenda

It has been stated (Jones, 1997) that breastfeeding is one of the purest forms of health promotion and is of vital importance to infants and their mothers for nutritional, immunological, and psychological reasons (Cunningham, 1987). Breast milk is unique in its composition, varying its contents during and from one feed to another according to an individual baby's needs. These compositional changes are set in motion by the mother's hormonal response to her own infant's needs and also to the climate of the country, altering the proportion of fluid in relation to the local temperature and humidity. In situations in which an infant feeds directly from the mother's breast, the milk cannot be contaminated whatever the quality or quantity of a local water supply. It is also true that breast-fed babies are protected against diabetes, pneumonia, ear infection, polio and many other conditions.

From the mother's own point of view, the message is also supportive, for the practice has an immediate positive effect on maternal health, reducing post-partum haemorrhage. In addition, it is generally believed to reduce the risk of pre-menopausal breast cancer (Newcombe *et al.*, 1994), osteoporosis (Cumming *et al.*, 1985), and some forms of ovarian cancer (Schneider, 1987).

Additionally, we know that exclusive breastfeeding during the first six months usually results in hormonal suppressions of ovulation, and this prevents pregnancy before the mother's menstrual cycle resumes. With longer intervals between births, mothers and babies are healthier, producing lower maternal and infant mortality and lower fertility rates. This confers greater maternal control in spacing births, giving mothers more time to regain their strength and health status. It also allows them to give appropriate time and energy to older children while sustaining breastfeeding for the youngest one. A frequently quoted statistic is that infants born less than two years after their next sibling are twice as likely to die as infants born after this gap. A three-year gap increases this protection (Rustein, 1984).

Third world economics and breastfeeding

From the purely management perspective, there are important economic advantages in breastfeeding to families, health providers, family planning programmes, and national budgets. Consider also the cost of substitutes: where one-half to one-third of the population live in poverty in large urban areas, the cost of manufactured breast-milk replacements to provide adequate nutrition, plus the necessary feeding equipment, constitutes a significant portion of a family's income. Other members of the family may be inadequately fed as a consequence of buying infant formula or, conversely, the infant formula may be watered down to make it go further, with obvious malnourishment consequences. The death rate is higher, malnutrition starts earlier, and the morbidity incidence is greater in formula-fed babies (Labbock and Nazro, 1995).

UNICEF (1997) states that if the 51% of Indian mothers who exclusively breastfeed were to stop, replacing all the breast milk with infant formula, it would cost $23 million. In Indonesia, a study in the 1980s calculated that the mothers produced over one billion litres of breast milk annually; equivalent supplies of commercial milk would cost $400 million. Savings in health costs and reduced fertility rate related to breastfeeding were estimated to be another $120 million. In Haiti, where just 3% of infants are breast-fed, infant formula costs $10 per week per child – more than twice a typical income.

A UNICEF study has been carried out which shows cost comparisons in improving the maternal diet by an additional 500 calories per day above the mother's normal diet so that she can breastfeed properly, versus the equivalent cost of formula for the baby. They found in India that five days' worth of extra food cost less than 15 rupees (45 cents) whereas the comparative cost of infant formula over the five days cost 130 rupees ($3.70). In the Philippines, the Jose Fabello Hospital saved

8% of its annual budget ($100 000) within one year of taking steps to promote and support exclusive breastfeeding.

It has been stated by the Director of the World Health Organization that the lives of 1.5 million infants could be saved every year if, for the first six months of life, infants were breast-fed exclusively and given no solids or other liquids, not even water.

To ensure continuance of health development and survival after six months of age, it is preferable that breastfeeding continue, supplemented by nutritious food.

Addressing the global decline in breastfeeding rates

In some ways a 'Dr Spock' of his day (the eighteenth century), William Cadogan was an influential doctor, called the father of paediatrics, whose writings were translated and reprinted throughout Europe. He is quoted as saying:

> It is with great pleasure I see at last the preservation of children become the care of men of sense. In my opinion, this business has been too long fatally left to the management of women, who cannot be supposed to have a proper knowledge to fit them for the ask, not withstanding they look upon it to be their own province (Cadogan, 1740).

We know now that, in the past, uneducated women often knew more about baby care than many highly educated men. However, despite the fact that such women carried a vast amount of practical undocumented knowledge relating to infant feeding and child rearing, they often lacked the confidence to admit it. The minimal formal education of most mothers ensured that male medical doctors became increasingly influential in the area of infant feeding (Palmer and Kemp, 1996).

But Cadogan set the cat among the pigeons when he observed that the breast-fed infants of English working-class women thrived, while the babies of the rich – who received pre-lacteal feeds of butter, honey, sugared wine and water (Filder, 1986) and were either sent to a wet nurse or fed artificially – often died. Once Cadogan had educated the rich about the importance of exclusive breastfeeding and the exclusion of pre-lacteal feeds, infant and maternal mortality rates fell. One important reason for this drop in mortality rates could be that effective expulsion of the placenta led to a reduction in post-partum bleeding. Along with this, there was less engorgement and mastitis, all of which can lead to a lower incidence of septicaemia and a fall in death rates. But becoming regarded as a guru of the nursery obscured the fact that Cadogan made a number of errors. For instance, he sought to limit the number of feeds to only four in 24 hours with night feeds being forbidden, as he thought infant diarrhoea was caused by overfeeding. It is probably unnecessary to remind the reader that this was before the emergence of the Germ Theory.

Even today, Cadogan's influence is still so strong in certain quarters that his restrictive regime of feeding (though thankfully not a restriction on feeding times) is often still attempted wherever Western medical influence has superseded local cultural norms. Because of restricted feeding episodes, many babies were underfed and mothers' lactation diminished, necessitating supplements of cow's milk. Mothers found that they became dependent upon doctors to advise them about hazards connected to artificial feeding. However, the poor could rarely afford this advice, nor did they have the conditions for preparing artificial feeds, and so their babies died in greater numbers. Thus, despite the improvement in economic growth, and increases in food, fuel and medical knowledge, infant mortality rates in Europe and North America went up in the nineteenth century (Palmer, 1993).

During the 1920s the relationship between milk manufacturers and health professionals grew, with the baby-food companies providing sponsorship and funding. Such practices rendered it difficult for the health professionals to feel confident enough to speak out against baby-milk manufacturers who used unethical practices. All of this seriously affected infant-feeding policies throughout the world (Jelliffe and Jelliffe, 1978).

Professional opposition to breastfeeding

Increasingly health professionals militantly opposed breastfeeding, justifying their stand with new medical rules. As a result, many women tended to lose their confidence and skills in breastfeeding. The wealthy led the way by bottle-feeding, and breastfeeding became seen as 'peasant-like' and second-best. As fewer mothers have breast-fed and public pressure has resulted in loss of visible breastfeeding (even in households) so the skills and knowledge, acquired automatically from observation of friends and family, have been lost. It can be said that 'the "civilised world" has taken us backwards when it comes to ability and inclination to breastfeed' (Tootill, 1995).

Alongside these developments, the proportion of home births declined. In this way as hospital childbirth increased, strict institutional regimes, nurseries and artificial feeding further militated against successful breastfeeding. It is shameful to admit that nurses and even midwives continued to spread the edicts of the (largely male) doctors with due reverence!

The Health Visitors' Association (HVA) was established in 1896 to educate ignorant mothers. However, promoting the medicalised approach soon caused lactation to decline, and breastfeeding also decreased. Mothers were disempowered, being made to feel that they could not rear their children without the guidance of health professionals.

Impact on the third world

Trade and exploration, of course, generated the spread of European values, including incorrect health education messages. By the end of the Victorian era, this had become almost worldwide. Jones (1997) states that in Malaysia in 1926, British nurses reported that 'some mothers had not even seen a clock and those who had could not understand what it had to with the feeding of an infant'. Needless to say, the cost of infant formulas has national financial implications as well as for families. Expenses devoted by developing countries to the import of infant formula often use up scarce foreign exchange needed for other essential priorities. Furthermore, it costs the country more in the use of scarce healthcare funds treating illnesses relating directly to the decline in breastfeeding.

Current statistics suggest that approximately 44% of infants in the developing world (fewer in industrial countries) are exclusively breast-fed. Among the factors responsible for the decrease in breastfeeding rates worldwide, surely the relentless promotion of breast-milk substitutes by 32 multinational infant-feeding companies – such as Nestlé, Abbott-Ross, Mead Johnson, Nutricia and Wyeth – must be the greatest. We know that in a few developing countries, in which breastfeeding rates remain high, such as Rwanda (90%) and Burundi (89%), there is little marketing of powdered milk (*see* Table 8.1).

Table 8.1: Breastfeeding rates in developing countries

10% and under		*50% and over*	
Developing countries with exclusive breastfeeding rates of 10% or less	*%*	*Developing countries with exclusive breastfeeding rates of 50% or more*	*%*
Niger	1	Rwanda	90
Nigeria	2	Burundi	89
Angola	3	Ethiopia	74
Ivory Coast	3	Tanzania	73
Haiti	3	Uganda	70
Central African Republic	4	Egypt	68
Thailand	4	Eritrea	65
Cameroon	7	China	64
Paraguay	7	Mauritania	60
Maldives	8	Bangladesh	54
Senegal	9	Turkmenistan	54
Dominican Republic	10	Bolivia	53
Togo	10	Iran	53
Trinidad/Tobago	10	India	51
		Guatemala	50

Data refer to infants under four months of age
Sources: DHS, MCIS and other nationwide surveys, 1987–1996 (UNICEF, 1997)

It was not until the 1970s that the negative effects of infant formulas on infant health and survival rates first became apparent. Along with this came the identification of the fact that advertising had a role in the promotion and use of infant formula, especially in the developing countries. In 1977, frustration in response to the aggressive global marketing led to a consumer boycott specifically against Nestlé, and this spread from the United States to 10 other countries including the United Kingdom. Eventually this led to a reduction of inappropriate advertising and promotion of baby-milk substitutes. These developments have been central in the fight to protect and promote breastfeeding.

The World Health Organization's response

The World Health Organization approved the International Code of Marketing of Breast-Milk Substitutes in 1981. The document had been drafted by WHO, together with the United Nations International Children's Educational Fund (UNICEF). Non-governmental organisations and representatives of the infant food manufacturers had contributed as well. In theory, the Code established minimum standards to regulate marketing standards by setting out the responsibility of companies, health workers, governments and others. It also provided standards for the labelling of breast-milk substitutes. The most salient provisions of the Code were:

- no advertising of breast-milk substitutes
- no free supplies of samples
- no promotion of products through healthcare facilities
- no contact between company marketing personnel and mothers
- no gifts or personal samples to health workers
- no words or pictures idealising artificial feeding, including pictures of infants on labels of the products
- information to health workers should be scientific and factual only
- all information on artificial feeding, including labels, should explain the benefits of breastfeeding and the cost and hazards of artificial feeding
- unsuitable products should not be promoted for babies.

New mothers are particularly vulnerable to psychological and commercial activities, such as providing free or subsidised supplies of infant formula; bottles and teats on maternity wards must have eroded the confidence and good intentions of many mothers to breastfeed. Clearly, for the minority of children who cannot be breast-fed, infant formula is an important product. However, sales and promotional activities relating to infant formulas have sometimes been based on false claims as to its value in comparison to that of breast milk. It is of no small interest that included in the provisions of the Code is the statement that health facilities must never be involved in the promotion of breast-milk substitutes and that free samples should never be given to pregnant women or new mothers!

A long-term aim was that the Code would gradually be enshrined in legislation. But its progress in being translated from minimum voluntary provisions into national law has been desperately slow. In September 1997 only 17 countries globally had approved laws that put them into full compliance with the Code (*see* Appendices C and D). In 1997 came a report entitled 'Cracking the Code', and published by the Interagency Group on Breastfeeding Monitoring (IGBM). It highlights the violations of the Code and work still to be done. IGBM is made up of 27 organisations, including churches, health experts, academic institutions, agencies such as UNICEF UK, Save the Children Fund, Voluntary Service Overseas (VSO) and others. 'Cracking the Code' is the first major community-based study undertaken of the prevalence of the Code violations and of the urgent need for enforcement. Serious violations of the Code by multinational infant food manufacturers in four countries – Bangladesh, Poland, South Africa and Thailand – are thoroughly documented. By implication, this publication also highlighted the negative impact of IMF/World Bank promotion of structural adjustment policies.

Breastfeeding vs market forces

Featured in the IGBM study was a statistical analysis of interviews with 800 pregnant women and new mothers and also with 120 health workers in 40 facilities in each country. Many violations of the Code emerge in their accounts. For instance, infant formula companies had been distributing marketing literature promoting formula over breast milk and giving free formula to maternity hospitals and mothers at ratios of one in 12 mothers in Poland and one in four mothers in Thailand. Giving free samples of milk substitutes to new mothers represents a particularly insidious way of promoting formula, because even a few days of infant formula using a teat and bottle makes a baby fussy about taking the breast. The mother's lactation will naturally have become reduced through lack of stimulation and may not be capable of increasing again. In this way the mother is then forced to feed and buy formula when the free supplies cease, at great cost to the baby, its family, and the state in both health and economic terms.

The whole sordid process is facilitated if the free samples are actually given to the mother by paramedical staff at a clinic or hospital. Obviously health workers, such as doctors and nurses, are seen as giving the product the health professionals' stamp of approval by handing out these 'gifts' but in doing so they are acting unethically by condoning the violation of the Code. Unsurprisingly, the International Association of Infant Food Manufacturers (IFM) soon complained that the IGBM study was biased and unscientific. The reader can easily ascertain, however, that the experimental design and the random sampling framework used to investigate the violations were standard epidemiologically sound techniques of the kind used by governments, research organisations, WHO, UNICEF and others for assessing prevalence of health conditions internationally.

Reacting to modern research showing falling breastfeeding rates, the global strategy of UNICEF's Baby Friendly Hospital Initiative (BFHI) was launched with *The Ten Steps to Successful Breastfeeding* (Gockay *et al.*, 1997). Established in response to the resistance to change, implementation has nevertheless been slow, especially in industrialised countries. Getting health professionals to change their ways can be far more difficult than getting mothers to acknowledge the benefits of breastfeeding! However, it has been unambiguously established that infant formula manufacturers have used their marketing practices to exploit medical mistakes, such as the unnecessary administration of dextrose or formula.

Implementation of the BFHI in Chile has raised breastfeeding rates of 4% in 1985 to 25% one year after the launch in 1991. A national survey in 1996 suggested exclusive breastfeeding rates of 40% for the first six months after birth. Training of health workers became a crucial part of the equation, as was strong support from the Ministry of Health and sustained advocacy from UNICEF, and the introduction of the BFHI is gradually spreading globally with the developing countries showing the way forward.

We are now in a stronger position to consider the cost in both health and economic terms, and to make an analysis of some of the insidious reasons for the decline in breastfeeding. It is interesting to see that the decline in breastfeeding began in the 'civilised world' and has gradually spread to the developing countries, but only after having been promoted as the best start for babies because of the extent that mothers from wealthier countries were represented as rearing their babies on instant formula! Unquestionably, the Code has had the effect of making health professionals aware of insidious promotion of baby milks. Seductive presents of pens, calendars, obstetric calculators and posters, all bearing the name of infant formula companies, will have appeared to many mothers to be an endorsement by health professionals of the wisdom of using formulas.

It has been in third world countries that the awareness of the major damage caused by the drop in breastfeeding rates was first seen. Likewise, it is in third world nations, in which the state of health and economy are more fragile, that the remedies are now commencing. The response to the Baby Friendly Initiative and the legislation relating to the Code of Marketing have been implemented far more effectively in those countries than in their industrialised counterparts.

The breastfeeding issue worldwide

Mothers, as a group, have been disempowered over the centuries, and as advocacy needs to start 'from the bottom up', help with the practicalities of teaching breastfeeding is vital to facilitate a restoration of this empowerment. One approach would be the promotion of a more holistic approach to childbirth and infant feeding, with the latter being seen as a natural process requiring only minimal interference. Of course, such matters need to be approached sensitively, and in full awareness of cultural and other contextual factors.

Research has shown that few reasons why women do not breastfeed are nominated, and they fall mostly into three categories:

- women who cannot do it because of a medical reason, e.g. breast cancer, AIDS (those not HIV-positive and fit)
- women who resolve not to breastfeed because of personal or socially induced resistance
- women who cannot survive the initial difficulties which sometimes arise in the early days, despite wishing to breastfeed.

No one doubts that there will always be some role for the use of infant formulas, but there is considerable divergence in the views of health professionals about the amount of information given, regarding formulas and the sterilisation of feeding equipment, antenatally. For instance the *Code of Conduct – Guidelines for Professional Practice* published in 1996 by the United Kingdom Central Council of Nursing, Midwives and Health Visitors (UKCC) states: 'the registered practitioner must not practise in a way which assumes that only they know what is best for the patient, as this can only create dependence and interfere with an individual's right to choose'. In other words, a politically correct awareness of the autonomy of patients compels nurses to respect whatever choices the patients make. Gough (1996) claims that overemphasis on an individual basis to promote breastfeeding could be seen as victim blaming, if not unethical, of a nurse. Susan Bates (1996) of the Health Visitors' Association stated:

> *Patients are entitled to choose how to feed their infants and as much information as possible should be provided to help parents make informed choices. Having made their choice, mothers should be given as much help as possible to establish infant feeding with minimum difficulty – it must not become a witch-hunt.*

Undoubtedly, the huge multinational infant formula companies have a major influence on feeding practices worldwide and also have the vast resources to promote them. On the other hand, the financial resources for promoting breastfeeding tend to be minimal and mostly generated by voluntary bodies, such as the International Baby Food Action Network (IBFAN). Possibly legislation is the key, and if the codes of practice for manufacturers can be monitored more closely and more countries bring in enabling legislation, matters will improve more quickly. Money hitherto spent on counteracting multinational advertising can be utilised in more appropriate ways. One obvious such initiative could be providing the kind of practical support to initiate breastfeeding from which new mothers now benefit in first world nations.

With no obvious legal restraints preventing it, the instant formula manufacturers' lobby continues wilfully to misinterpret the Code. Despite the word 'International' in its title, the manufacturers' body insists that the Code applies only to third world countries. These companies still continue to promote breast-milk substitutes unethically and to flout the International Code of Marketing of Breast-Milk Substitutes (ICMBSI). While this continues, concerned parties are likely to maintain pressure, perhaps by maintaining the boycott of Nestlé, who produce 40% of the world's baby milks.

This author suggests that the two-pronged attack needs to continue, both 'bottom up' and 'top down'. The 'bottom up' approach involves local communities, empowering women to make informed choices about infant feeding and also to give them back the skills that were once second nature with the aid of practical tuition and support. The 'top down' strategy is the global action of organisations and pressure groups continuing to monitor and publicise violations by the baby milk manufacturers to continue boycotts of the same.

Now third world countries are actually taking the lead over industrialised countries in implementing changes which will raise breastfeeding rates. All things considered, this should not be so surprising, as the effects of the possible damage caused by infant formula feeding are more catastrophic in these countries.

It might be appropriate to finish with a comment from The Right Reverend Simon Barrington-Ward, until recently chair of the International and Development Affairs Committee of the Church of England's General Synod:

> *For babies everywhere, the benefits of breastfeeding are undisputed. But for babies in developing nations breastfeeding is imperative: their very survival depends on the immune boosting properties of mother's milk. For them, infant formula is not just inferior; it can cause disease or even death. Poor families often over-dilute costly formula with unclean water and mix it in unclean bottles, adding to the risk. Yet despite international pleas and a marketing code agreed in 1981, manufacturers still market infant formula with other substitutes unethically around the world. It is time for them to stop.*

There has been no really sustained improvement and the rest of this chapter deals with one of the worst offenders, Nestlé. There are others, but Nestlé controls 40% (as of 2004) of the market globally.

Nestlé and its impact on the third world

As we have seen, breastfeeding has everything to recommend it. It is cheap, involves no transport costs and is the least polluted feed available. Breast milk also carries protection against many infections to which the baby would otherwise be prone. Because it provides optimal nutrition, it can reduce the entire family's poverty – which is a major cause of malnutrition. It has been shown to reduce the risk of breast cancer (*The Lancet*, 2002). In fact, UNICEF and WHO estimate (2004) that 1.5 million lives can be saved annually through increased breastfeeding (IBFAN, 2004a).

But breast milk has to compete in a rapidly growing market for breast-milk substitutes, now worth $10.9 billion (*Euromonitor*, 2001). The International Code of Marketing of Breast-Milk Substitutes and its Resolutions, and other policies which attempt to protect breastfeeding and ensure responsible marketing of breast-milk substitutes, challenge such growth and are opposed by companies. Nestlé controls approximately 40% of the baby food market, and as the world's largest food company (with over 11 000 brands of processed foods), it is able to exert a powerful influence on government policies and market trends. For over two decades Nestlé has been dogged by criticism of its baby-food marketing and is the target of an international boycott campaign. Because of this Nestlé has curbed some of its more blatant malpractices, removing pictures of babies on infant formula tins and stopping some media advertising. It has also spent millions of dollars on public relations strategies which include sponsorship, glossy brochures and attempts to link its name with and to influence the UN system. Nestlé's Sustainability Review, its Infant Feeding in the Developing World, and its Infant Feeding Policy are all examples which present Nestlé as a responsible company, even a leader in sustainable development and environmental protection – a company that is eager to listen to criticism and to act on it. But all these documents fail to stand up to scrutiny. In reality there has been no real change of policy nor any commitment to a marketing strategy that will match the public relations promises.

Worldwide independent monitoring consistently shows that Nestlé, more than any other company, systematically violates the International Code and its Resolutions, promoting its products in many ways which damage infant health. The few limited changes Nestlé has made do not counterbalance the harm caused by its marketing and its persistent undermining of legislation and trading standards which seek to protect infant health.

The author is grateful to IBFAN for permission to use the following material, which they published in 2004 (IBFAN, 2004b).

Despite Nestlé's persistent reference to its compliance with the International Code, the company's policy and instructions, against which all staff behaviour are measured, are substantially weaker than the International Code and the subsequent relevant World Health Assembly Resolutions. During a public hearing at the European Parliament in November 2000, UNICEF's Legal Officer stressed how much more stringent the International Code is in approach, coverage and scope than Nestlé's policy and instructions. Nestlé boycotted the hearing. The following 10 points show the questionable intentions of Nestlé's whole approach.

1 The International Code applies to all nations, not just developing countries. Nestlé's policy and instructions apply only to what it calls 'developing countries'

and so do not cover countries such as Poland, Hungary, Korea or Taiwan. For the smallest, most defenceless of consumers, such double standards make no sense at all.

2 The International Code covers all breast-milk substitutes, including any products marketed in ways which undermine exclusive and sustained breastfeeding. Nestlé's policy and instructions apply only to 'infant formula'.

3 Nestlé's policy and instructions fail to include the 10 Resolutions which have been passed at the World Health Assembly since 1981 and have the same status as the International Code itself. They are important because they clarify, update and strengthen the International Code's provisions in the light of research and current marketing practices. WHO has confirmed that the International Code and the Resolutions enjoy equal status and should be read together as one and the same document.

4 Nestlé ignores the fact that the International Code was adopted as a minimum requirement to be implemented in its entirety. Where countries have laws stronger than the International Code, companies must abide by those stronger laws. However, where countries have weaker measures Article 11.3 of the International Code requires companies to ensure that their conduct at every level conforms to it, and to do so independently of any measures taken by governments.

5 Hundreds of violations of the International Code from 14 countries were published in IBFAN's report, *Breaking the Rules 2001* (IBFAN, 2004a) and were brought to Nestlé CEO Peter Brabeck's personal attention in 2001. He has dismissed the vast majority as invalid and, so far, done very little to end the practices which endanger infant health.

6 Nestlé claims to be the first company to implement the Code. However, it is the responsibility of governments to implement it and then the companies must comply with it. Nestlé, more than any other company, undermines government efforts to implement the Code and Resolutions. In India, for example, it not only lobbied against the law for many years, but when facing criminal charges over the language and text of its labelling, it issued a Writ Petition against the Indian government, attempting to have key sections of the law struck down, including some articles directly implementing the Code. The Writ Petition still stands and some see it as an attempt to delay the legal action taken against Nestlé which could see its Managing Director imprisoned. In Zimbabwe, before the government brought in its strong law in 1998, Nestlé threatened to pull out all investment, arguing that 'it would not be economically viable for the company to continue operating under such regulations'.

7 Nestlé's policy and instructions refer only to direct consumer advertising of infant formula. The International Code calls for a ban of all promotion of all breast-milk substitutes – either direct to mothers, to health workers or to the public. The aim is to protect health and ensure that parents receive independent, objective information about infant feeding. Under the International Code, health workers are responsible for advising parents on infant feeding.

8 The International Code calls for all information about and on products to be restricted to scientific and factual matters with no idealising pictures or text, such as 'maternalised' or 'humanised'. One advertisement for Nativa infant formula, intended for health workers in Côte d'Ivoire, claimed that Nativa is even better than breast milk: 'Nestlé: Meeting the need for certain micro-nutrients which the human organism cannot produce, but which are needed

to orchestrate a gamut of physiological functions essential for optimal development.' Mr Brabeck dismissed the violation.

9 Nestlé's Sustainability Review states: 'Free infant formula donated over the past 12 months was only for social welfare cases.' (BFAG, 1998). As long ago as 1994, World Health Assembly (WHA) Resolution 47.5 stated that there should be 'no donations of free or subsidised supplies of breast milk substitutes ... in any part of the health care system'. *Breaking the Rules 2001* found free or low-cost supplies of infant formula in 10 of the 14 countries studied. On 1 May 2002 UNICEF staff found boxes and boxes of donated Nestlé's Bear Brand Prebio 2 follow-on formula in a Bangkok hospital. None of the staff seemed to be sure why the samples were donated, but the excuse was given that they might be for mothers infected with HIV. Less than 3% of mothers are known to be infected with HIV in Thailand. The mothers who are infected are provided with free formula which is purchased through the Ministry of Public Health in a bidding process and made available to all hospitals. There is therefore no need for hospitals to accept free supplies from companies.

10 All over the world baby-food companies aggressively promote expensive, packaged 'complementary foods' resulting in mothers using them as breast-milk substitutes, often feeding them through a bottle. In 1994 WHA (World Health Assembly) Resolution 47.5 stated that complementary feeding should be fostered from six months of age, and in 2001 WHA Resolution 54.2 emphasised the importance of exclusive breastfeeding for six months and the use of indigenous nutrient-rich foodstuffs. At its AGM in April 2001, Nestlé promised to encourage exclusive breastfeeding for six months, but has since stepped up its promotion of Cerelac complementary food from four months in many countries. Full colour glossy advertisements, with idealising pictures and text and offers of free samples, appear regularly in Indian newspapers with blatant health claims about micronutrients. In 2001 and 2002 the Codex Alimentarius draft guidelines (Codex sets global food standards) proposed that health claims should not be used on labels of foods for infants and young children. The 2002 WHA Resolution (55.25) specified that the marketing of micronutrients should not undermine breastfeeding or optimal complementary feeding.

Nestlé's use of the HIV/AIDS pandemic

Some businesses will exploit absolutely calamitous situations to their own advantage and – except for the fact that Nestlé controls such a huge percentage of the market – it is probably no worse than many other firms in its cynical use of the desperation and fear caused by HIV/AIDS in some of the poorest countries.

Nestlé has been using the HIV/AIDS pandemic to push the use of its infant formula, *Pelargon*, in Africa. It launched a Nutrition Institute in August 2001 and has been visiting policy-makers in southern Africa, making unsubstantiated claims that *Pelargon*'s high acidity will kill germs and that this makes it safe to use with infected water. Nestlé has done much to distort mothers', health workers' and policy-makers' perceptions, playing up the risk of HIV infection from breastfeeding and playing down the risks of artificial feeding. IBFAN believes that, when partnerships are formed between NGOs and companies such as Nestlé, which have a vested interest in mothers choosing artificial feeding in the context of HIV, women's rights to truly independent and objective information on this subject are undermined. The WHA Resolution passed in May 2001 (WHA 54.2) reaffirmed this right, stressing the need for independent research into HIV and stating that mothers should be protected from commercial influences.

Other questionable practices revealed by IBFAN

We have already considered the problems that an unreliable and impure supply of accessible water poses for third world mothers using powdered milk. This author has often, in his third world country work, run across the situation that only people who can pay for individual lots of bottled water have access to reasonably reliable water. But what happens when firms like Nestlé also corner this market?

Nestlé is the world's largest manufacturer of bottled water, with over 50 brands and 16% of a fast-growing $33.7 billion market. Nestlé faces criticism about its damage to the environment and local ecosystems in many countries.

The promotion of bottled water can undermine commitment to the provision of affordable piped water. Irresponsible promotion and labelling and brand names such as 'Pure Life' can falsely imply sterility, undermining breastfeeding and safety messages about boiling water for babies. Bottled water is not sterile and must be boiled before use. Mineral water is unprocessed and may have unsuitable levels of salts for use in infant feeding.

At its AGM in March 2002, Nestlé faced criticism from shareholders about the impact of its water business on the environment and concerns from Perrier workers about the use of plastic bottles (supplied by Coca-Cola). Nestlé responded with promises to sell 3.5 million bottles of Perrier in China!

In Brazil Nestlé has been accused of 'pillaging' the 'circuito das Aguas' (a Brazilian geological marvel) and 'destroying an ecosystem which took nature thousands of years to create' (IBFAN, 2004b). Naturally, Nestlé is ever anxious to counter such negative commentary by claiming that it is developing internal safety watchdogs.

According to the Nestlé Sustainability Review, Nestlé is instituting an ombudsman system. This could be a sign that it is recognising that it has a problem. However, this will mean nothing unless the terms of reference are clear. An internal ombudsman – paid by the company – is totally different from an independent ombudsman paid by a government or other party. The allegations of malpractice reaching up to senior management provided by former Nestlé Pakistan employee Syed Aamir Raza remain unanswered. Mr Raza claims he was threatened by Nestlé in 1997 when he challenged the company to stop its malpractice. He resigned soon after witnessing the death of an infant as a result of unsafe bottle-feeding. Unless the ombudsman system is accompanied by a complete change of policy on Nestlé's part, employees will continue to be placed under intense pressure to maximise sales, as Mr Raza was. To protect someone like Mr Raza an ombudsman would need to have greater power than the CEO Mr Brabeck, who is now the driving force behind the company. Mr Brabeck continues to make unsubstantiated attacks on Mr Raza's character.

Nestlé has refused to provide information about audits it refers to in the Sustainability Review and readers must accept on trust that only four problems were uncovered. EME, the auditors called in to investigate in Pakistan in 2000, were specifically instructed not to look at the evidence of Syed Aamir Raza and were limited to interviewing doctors from a list provided by Nestlé. Baby Milk Action's offer to provide documentary evidence of malpractice, including the bribing of doctors, was not passed on to the auditors by Nestlé.

In IBFAN (2004a), the following comment appears:

> In July 2001 Nestlé and all the baby food companies cited as violating the International Code in IBFAN's report, *Breaking the Rules 2001*, were excluded from the FTSE4 Good Index for socially responsible investment.

All of these matters are more fully dealt with – and embrace companies other than Nestlé – in IBFAN's publication 'Breaking the rules – stretching the rules' (2004a). It presents evidence of violations of the International Code of Marketing of Breast-Milk Substitutes (ICMBSI).

In closing this chapter, though, the author presents IBFAN's summary (2004a) of the State of the Code by Country (*see* Appendix G). The nine categories it specifies are as follows, where Code shall refer to the International Code.

1 Law: These countries have either:
   a) enacted legislation encompassing all, or nearly all, provisions of the Code along with the clarifications and additions from subsequent World Health Association Resolutions, or
   b) introduced early measures to control the marketing of breast-milk substitutes, bottles and teats, prior to the Code or shortly after 1981 (27 countries in total in 2004).
2 Many provisions law: These countries have either:
   a) enacted legislation encompassing some, but not all, provisions of the Code, or
   b) introduced early measures which partly control such marketing prior to the Code or immediately after it was adopted (33 countries as of 2004).
3 Policy or voluntary measures: In these countries, the government has adopted a voluntary code or health policy encompassing nearly all the provision of the Code. However, there are no enforcement mechanisms (18 countries as of 2004).
4 Few provisions law: In these countries the government has adopted only a few provisions of the Code. For the purposes of Appendix G, the general food labelling laws are not considered part of the Code (22 countries as of 2004).
5 Some voluntary provisions or guidelines applicable to the health sector: In these countries, the government has:
   a) adopted some, but not all, of the Code as a voluntary measure to which the industry has agreed to comply, or
   b) issued guidelines for health authorities to complement all of the Code and of subsequent WHA resolutions (18 countries as of 2004).
6 Measure drafted, awaiting final approval as of 2004 (33 countries as of 2004).
7 Being studied: A government committee in these countries is still studying how best to implement the Code (24 countries as of 2004).
8 No action: These countries have taken no steps to implement the Code (10 countries as of 2004).
9 No information available (seven countries as of 2004).

Appendix G shows the status of the Code in 192 countries. The nine categories (*see* above) indicate each country's current position.

- 27 countries in Category 1 have implemented most of the Code and subsequent WHA resolutions by means of a comprehensive law, decree or other legally enforceable measure. Yemen, Cape Verde and Argentina are new entrants to this category. A few countries in Category 1 have strengthened their existing laws, namely Brazil, India and Sri Lanka.
- 33 countries shown in Category 2 have implemented many but not all provisions of the Code as law. Pakistan joined after a nine-year struggle, during which industry ensured it can influence implementation of the law. Azerbaijan, on the other hand, made a quantum leap from draft to law.
- 22 countries in Category 4 have taken measures to legislate on only some aspects of the Code. This form of Code implementation falls short of the minimum envisaged by the World Health Assembly when the Code was adopted.
- 18 countries in Category 3 have implemented the entire Code as a voluntary measure or as a national health policy. Although such measures are not legally enforceable, they can be effective if properly monitored. Thailand has been removed from this category since the old voluntary agreement expired. An additional five countries listed in Category 3 have drafts based on the Code and subsequent WHA Resolutions and are therefore highlighted under Category 6. Some countries appear under more than one category. The most significant one is highlighted in green and is the one which counts for the IBFAN Scale.
- 33 countries in Category 6 have draft laws. Botswana, Malawi, South Africa and Zambia are countries to watch in the coming years, due to a hive of activities concerning the Code and infant feeding, not least their responses to the HIV pandemic. Two notable inclusions in Category 6 are Afghanistan and the newly independent Timor-Leste. Gabon's draft has become law as this chart goes to print. It remains in this category until International Code Documentation Centre (ICDC) has received the text for full analysis. Due to lack of political will or resistance from industry, many other countries in Category 6 have lost momentum in implementing the Code.
- In summary, 65% of the 192 countries have taken some measures to implement the Code. There are still countries, including the United States, that have done nothing. There is no information available for a handful of countries.

The data in Appendix G was published by, and used with the permission, of:
IBFAN, PO Box 19, 10700 Penang, Malaysia
Printed by Jutaprint, Penang
Production by Adrian Cheah and Raja Abdul Razak
ISBN 0128.9209

Note

1 In the UK, the Breastfeeding Help Line – Tel: 01624 670 383 – gives direct practical assistance to parents having problems with breastfeeding.

References

Baby Food Action Network (1998) *Engineering Consent*. Cornerhouse, London.

Bates S (1996) Culture change. *Nursing Standard*. **10(45)**: 17.

Cadogan W (1740) *An Essay Upon Nursing and the Management of Children, From Their Birth to Three Years of Age*. John Knapton, London.

Cumming SR, Kelsey JL and Nevitt MC (1985) Epidemiology of osteoporosis and osteoporotic fractures. *Epidemiology Review*. 7: 178–208.

Cunningham A (1987) Breastfeeding and health. *Journal of Paediatrics*. 110: 658.

Euromonitor (2001) *Baby Food in South Africa – a market report*. Euromonitor International, London.

Filder V (1986) *Breasts, Bottles and Babies*. Edinburgh University Press, Edinburgh.

Gockay G, Uzel N, Kayatark F and Neyzi O (1997) Ten steps for successful breastfeeding. Assessment of hospital performance, its determinants and planning for improvement. *Child: Care, Health and Development*. **23(2)**: 187–200.

Gough P (1996) Heavy handed. *Nursing Standard*. **10(43)**: 17.

IBFAN (International Baby Food Action Network) (2004a) Breaking the rules: stretching the rules. In: *Evidence of Violations of the International Code of Marketing Breast Food Substitutes*. IBFAN, Penang, Malaysia.

IBFAN (International Baby Food Action Network) (2004b) *Nice Design – Shame About the Text: Nestlé's Infant Feeding Policy and Sustainability Review – Another PR Cover-up*. IBFAN, Penang, Malaysia.

Jelliffe E and Jelliffee P (1978) Don't let baby hit the bottle too soon. *Nursing Times*. 74: 15–16.

Jones E (1997) Cracking the Code – monitoring the International Code of Marketing of Breast-Milk Substitutes. *Modern Midwife*. **7(2)**: 27–9.

Labbock M and Nazro J (1995) *Breastfeeding: protecting a natural resource*. Georgetown University, Institute for Reproductive Studies, Washington, DC.

The Lancet (2002) Breast cancer and breastfeeding: collaboration reanalysis of individual data. *The Lancet*. **July.** 360(9328): 187–95.

Newcombe I, Allen G and Pearson L (1994) Lactation and a reduced risk of premenopausal cancer. *New England Journal of Medicine*. 330: 81–7.

Nursing and Midwifery Council of UK (1996) *Code of Conduct: Guidelines for Professional Practice*. Nursing and Midwifery Council of UK, London.

Palmer G (1993) *The Politics of Breastfeeding*. Pandora, London.

Palmer G and Kemp S (1996) Breastfeeding promotion and the role of the professional midwife. In: SF Murray (ed.) *Baby Friendly – Mother Friendly*. Mosby, London, pp 1–23.

Rustein S (1984) Infant and child mortality: level, trends and demographic differentials. *WFS Comparative Studies*. 43(rev. edn): 212–6.

Schneider AP (1987) Risk factors for ovarian cancer. *New England Journal of Medicine*. 317: 558–9.

Tootill B (1995) Infant feeding in a refugee camp. *Professional Care of Mother and Child*. 108: 150–1.

UNICEF (United Nations Children's Fund) (1997) *Progress of Nations 1997*: www.unicef.org/pon97.

Chapter 9

The impact of first world wealth on third world health: British American Tobacco in China

Smoking – a third world problem?

In the previous chapter, we considered the impact of the multinational powdered milk industry on third world health. In this chapter, we consider a similar problem, but with respect to tobacco products rather than milk. The present author spent some time in North Vietnam during the war years and just after, and was constantly dismayed at the extent to which even young children had developed a firmly based cigarette dependency. The situation apparently (and unsurprisingly) was even worse in the South. The liberation of Vietnam from foreign military control, and its unification, had the potential suddenly to erase this kind of addiction. But postwar Vietnam's need to reach a modus vivendi with the powerful first world nations, and allow the incursion of multinationals, has only exacerbated the problem.

The primary focus of this chapter, however, is China. Countries like Vietnam are certainly valued by the big tobacco firms based in the first world, and are exploited accordingly. But the real prize is China, embracing as it does about 25% of the world's total population.

But before going further, allow the author to make a caveat. Although the chapter title refers to one tobacco multinational – namely, British American Tobacco (BAT) – and one third world country, China, this does not imply that BAT tobacco products have a worse unit-impact on health than do others, or that China is unique (per head of population) in its uptake of BAT products. Indeed, WHO and other agencies have available similar statistics on a whole range of tobacco manufacturers and their third world targets. For the author to draw meaningfully on all of them would produce a book exclusively about that topic. In the eyes of all types of multinationals, China represents the single largest potential market and BAT has a long – if interrupted – history of engagement with it. The following is a brief resume for the moment, but it will be developed in detail in Chapter 10.

When the communists assumed control in China, the company found itself seriously at odds with the political context and BAT left the country in 1952. However, they returned in the 1980s and have been a dominant and growing presence to the present day. BAT was not the first tobacco product corporation from the first world to start up business in China after the downfall of Mao Tse Tung. Both Imperial Tobacco and Gallaher came first and both have since developed licensing agreements with state-owned tobacco firms.

But BAT is now involved in a joint venture factory that will doubtless soon make BAT the biggest international brand in China with its State Express 555 and Kent brands. This will be the first time that a first world company will be allowed to own a factory in China. Moreover, it will have the authority to promote and sell its products throughout China, rather than being confined to a few provinces. As McGregor and Urquart go on to explain in their *Money and Times* article (McGregor and Urquart, 1994) – commissioned by the London-based Action on Smoking and Health (ASH) – the proposed scale of production (up to 100 billion cigarettes a year) will eclipse all other such deals put together.

Gallaher, which has a reciprocal deal with Shanghai Tobacco to make its Memphis brand, in return for making and distributing the Golden Deer brand in Russia, is only making 100 million cigarettes.

Imperial Tobacco's 10-year reciprocal agreement with Yuxi Hongta to produce and distribute Imperial's West brand of cigarettes in two southern Chinese cities is thought to be for 500 million cigarettes. Japan Tobacco and Philip Morris, aside from importing their brands, have yet to announce any such deals.

It was unsurprising, therefore, that Paul Adams, BAT's chief executive, also agreed that the factory could be one of the company's most significant deals (Wilmore, 2004, p.14):

> It will be up there with RJR, but this is a different character of deal, this is all about our ability to grow. There are 300 million existing smokers in China and, unlike some, we are not creating a new market, we are supplying an existing market. The 555 brand is known in China and there is consumer demand for the product.

BAT is believed to have used its historic connections with China to facilitate the deal and is thought to have been working with Chinese tobacco groups for over 10 years – initially supplying marketing and technical expertise to oil the wheels of the deal.

Some analysts predicted that the move would enable BAT to challenge Altria's Philip Morris for the number one position in the global tobacco sector.

Martin Steinik, of JP Morgan, said: 'I see this as the most important deal at BAT for some time. China has been the Holy Grail of tobacco and this deal could make BAT the world's biggest group.'

JP Morgan is estimating that the new factory, which will be the largest in the group, could add 3% to BAT's overall earnings growth within five years. But there were concerns that the deal, although possibly the most lucrative of all the current tie-ups, was potentially the most risky.

One analyst questioned how effective BAT's joint partner, China Eastern Investment Corporation, would be, especially against the entrenched regional tobacco companies, whose quasi-monopolies make the movement of different cigarette brands between provinces difficult. Risks aside, the deal marks the first significant move by the Chinese government to open up its previously highly protected market.

China's reluctance to open its market is unsurprising given that the industry paid the equivalent of 10% of the national tax revenue of China last year, a figure that is expected to rise by another two to three percentage points this year.

Previously, the reliance of the central and provincial governments on revenues from local tobacco monopolies prompted Beijing to ban foreign joint ventures in 1995, on the grounds that the market was 'saturated'.

However, the government now wants to streamline the industry and improve efficiency, a programme that would result in the closure of nearly half of the country's 150-odd cigarette factories. China's 300 cigarette brands are also expected to be slimmed down to 100 to encourage better brand leverage by the survivors. Currently, the two leading brands, Hongmei and Hong Ta Shan, have less than 6% of the total market. The reform also envisaged the gradual opening of the market to foreign brands, which now have less than 10%, and allowing limited production joint ventures. External pressure has also been brought to bear. Under the terms of its accession to the World Trade Organization, China is also reducing tariffs on imported cigarettes, which were as high as 70%. Mr Steinik said some of the softening has come as China has struggled to catch up with the world's leading tobacco companies in terms of tobacco grades, brands and structure – making a joint venture a necessity to sharpen competitiveness.

In *The Guardian* (Saturday 17 July 2004), as the author was writing this chapter, an article appeared, confirming that the deal has now been consummated. Jonathan Watts reports from Beijing that clearance has been given for BAT to build an £800 million factory, putting the firm in the world's largest tobacco market.

Why BAT needs the third world

We in the first world have many social mechanisms at our disposal through which advocacy about health concerns can be mounted. Many authors/agencies, such as Doll and Crofton (1996), Callum (1998) and ASH (2004), have campaigned, published and researched the adverse effects that cigarette smoking has on the health of men, women, children and babies. Our elected governments cannot completely ignore the increase in research and evidence to support the fact that smoking kills. As a result smoking rates among men aged 16 and above in the United Kingdom had fallen from 50% in 1976 to 27% in 1996. In the same way smoking rates among women living in the United Kingdom aged 16 and above had fallen from 40% in 1976 to 20% in 1996 (Office for National Statistics, 1996). Since then rates of smoking among young women have been rising. High-profile emphasis on evidence-based research and campaigns has contributed to the implementation of legislation in the form of a Tobacco White Paper, *Smoking Kills* (DoH, 1998). In publishing this White Paper the UK government has pledged to invest £60 million over the next three years to enable smokers who want to give up to do so. Moreover, the proposals to limit the extent that the tobacco industry uses the media to encourage young people, women and other social groups to start smoking have also been outlined within the White Paper and EU-wide bans on cigarette advertisements are to be implemented by the year 2005.

Generally, therefore, the first world has become a fairly hostile market environment for the tobacco pushers. This had led to multinationals looking further afield, to countries in the developing world which are not as advanced in their fight against this legal and addictive habit (Foulds, in Doll and Crofton, 1996). Evidence abounds to show that multinational companies, such as BAT, are not overwhelmingly concerned if the market for their product in the developing world shrinks. Big bucks are elsewhere and, as far as BAT are concerned, the biggest prize is that of getting their product onto the Chinese market (BAT, 1990; Hu, 1997).

The continual search for cheaper labour by multinational companies promotes widening income differentials, and in their search for new markets companies sell damaging products to developing countries (Unwin et al., p.1401).

On 16 July 2004, BAT reported from its London office that the deal had been finalised, effectively allowing BAT to merge with China Eastern Investment to build the factory. No details about exactly where the plant will be located have yet been released, but it is anticipated that it will take at least two years to establish it.

Once it is running at full capacity, it will exceed production in all of the rest of BAT's factories worldwide. It is anticipated that its companies – Dunhill, Lucky Strike, Kent and State Express 555 – will then corner 5% of China's tobacco sales. In *The Guardian* article (2004), BAT's chief executive, Paul Adams, was quoted as saying: 'For us it represents a major growth opportunity while contributing to the Chinese government's excellent efforts to continue developing the performance of the country's tobacco industry.'

China, of course, like most other third world countries, has far lower health and safety standards in its plants than would have to be complied with in the first world. Likewise the local customers are given much less statutory health protection and there are far fewer restrictions on advertising. The health warnings on the actual cigarette packets are ambiguous and in small print. They do not appear on the front of the packet, but on the sides. There is no national law in most third world nations, including China, on smoking by minors.

WHO has warned that one-third of all Chinese men alive in 2004 will perish from lung cancer and other tobacco-related illnesses. Indeed, consideration of international respectability pressured the Chinese government to sign the UN Framework Convention on Tobacco Control. This requires it to tighten restrictions on cigarette sales and consumption.

On the other hand, according to *The Guardian* article (2004): 'The government is addicted to tobacco income, which accounts for ten percent of its tax revenues.'

Over and above the pliability of a third world government desperate to attract US dollars, psychosocial changes among the Chinese people render them more susceptible to consumerist values. There are great increases noted in the proportion of Chinese women taking up smoking. On a visit there in 1976, the author was struck by the resistance of Chinese women to the practice. It was regarded as demeaning. The change has bought another 3 million customers at least into the market.

At present throughout the world, about 4 million people die each year from tobacco-related deaths. It is anticipated that this will rise to 10 million by 2025, and out of these 7 million will occur in developing countries (Peto *et al.*, 1994). Expectations are that 2 million of these deaths will occur in China alone (Peto *et al.*, 1994). In that nation 4% of women are smokers compared with 63% of men (Zolty, 1999). Also, annual tobacco use has increased fastest in this region, i.e. from 1100 cigarettes per adult in 1971 to 2010 per adult in 1991 – an 83% increase, compared to a 0.0% increase in Europe (McGinn, 1997). In 1992 the National Household Expenditure Survey showed that the amount of money spent on cigarettes by individuals in China was $9.05 per annum (Hu, 1997, p.136), whereas money spent on healthcare was $6.92 per head of population (State Statistics Bureau, 1993, 1998).

Related negative impacts on health

The impacts of global financing of first world corporate power should not be regarded by the reader as being confined to directly measurable and attributable factors. Even using data provided by the World Bank, it is estimated that premature deaths caused by tobacco-related illnesses will further exacerbate deaths caused by AIDS and TB. Even complications in childbirth will see an increase. Money spent on tobacco products will be withdrawn from essential food purchases and access to clean water by the poor in those societies.

Consider the impact of these related factors on China's healthcare system, as one out of every two smokers worldwide is Chinese (Peto *et al.*, 1998a, 1998b). Figures for 1996 show that tobacco sales in China generated $10 billion in tax revenue on profits (Hui, 1997). Min (1996) argues that the amount of money that the tobacco industry turns over to the treasury is overshadowed by the economic loss that is caused by people smoking.

> *We should not be depressed simply because the total world market appears to be declining. Within the total market, there are areas of strong growth ... new markets are opening up for our exports, such as Indo-China and the Comecon countries: and there are great opportunities to increase our market ... This industry is consistently profitable. And there are opportunities to increase their profitability still further (BAT, 1990).*

A closer look at how BAT benefits in China

To gain some insight into why China is such a good market for BAT, one needs to look at the geographical structure of the country. Its population size at 1.519 billion is the largest in the world (UN, 1998) and about 350 000 000 of China's inhabitants are tobacco smokers (*Tobacco International*, 1993).

Urbanisation levels in China have increased dramatically over the last 20 years, rising from 17.9% in 1978 to 32% in 1996. Worldwide, there are 32 big cities with populations of more than 1 000 000 people. Beijing is one of China's 'five mega cities' where the population is in excess of 11 000 000 (Lai-guian, 1996). Major demographic changes like this, especially those involving growths in population, are viewed by the multinationals as situations worth exploiting. New city inhabitants are more likely to be influenced by the flashy advertising campaigns that multinationals such as BAT can afford to launch (Amos, in Doll and Crofton, 1996).

Again, China's shift to a market forces economy provides another reason as to why it is attractive to multinationals such as BAT. Changes made to China's market economy in 1979 meant that, although China was under communist rule, a market economy was encouraged. The consequent opening up to trade had immediate fiscal effects. China's gross domestic product (GDP) rose from $43.6 billion in 1979 to $904 billion in 1997 (Yao and Liu, 1998). Likewise, China's export market has also increased by 52% annually. Much of this increase is due to multinationals such as BAT, who have invested more than $220 billion into this developing country. Consequently, 'China has become trapped between a flashy corporate culture of fast cars and sharp suits, and a moribund political system that still demands obeisance to Marxist ideals' (Tomlinson, 1999, p.158). Such a wide-scale shift from a state-controlled to a market economy has resulted in major changes being made to state and private organisations. Gone are many of the former political constraints and both public and private organisations are now free to do business with foreign investors. Profit has become the benchmark and unprofitable businesses have been eradicated. All commercial organisations must now sell their products in a competitive market (Mackerras *et al.*, 1998). Other changes brought about by the economic reforms include the end of life-long employment and even of fixed salaries. Workers employed in the public and in the joint public/private sector organisations now have fewer rights and can more easily be sacked, disciplined and fired at the whim of employers. Legislation governing labour market contracts introduced in 1983 has given employers the right to treat their new employees differently to the old ones and pay increases are modelled on the capitalist notion of performance, rather than those of seniority that prevailed in communist China (Zhang *et al.*, 1998, p.180).

So much for the 'why' of BAT's interest in China. Let us now consider the 'how'. To understand the way in which BAT has infiltrated the Chinese tobacco industry and exploited the health and wealth of the Chinese people, one needs to analyse the development of BAT itself. British American Tobacco was formed in 1902 to take over the overseas businesses of American Tobacco and Imperial Tobacco. BAT became a public company in 1912 and its international brands of cigarettes include Benson and Hedges, Lucky Strike, Kent 555 and Kool. BAT produces 900 billion cigarettes annually. At present, the company controls 16% of the world tobacco market and has market leadership in 55 countries (Darby, 1999). Of course, they manufacture other products, such as the Lucky Strikes Original mail order catalogue in the UK, Holland and Spain. As well as that, they own a Benson and Hedges coffee bar in Malaysia, and a travel agency in Asia. It now has emerged that BAT has plans to produce beer and bourbon under the Lucky Strike name. BAT's main strategy is to earn extra money and to avoid the increasing restrictions that have been placed on tobacco advertising in the developed world markets. Accordingly, over the next five years BAT have allocated £250 million to the development of the Formula One Team, who are responsible for marketing BAT's products in the developing world (Pandya, 1999, p.37).

As far back as 1999, BAT reported that it had earned £738 million; this was after £613 million had been deducted to pay off the tobacco settlement (Jackson, 1999). On the stock market BAT shares were sold for 553 pence/stock in 1999, and their stock market value was £8.79 million. Recently BAT and Rothmans International merged. Therefore, BAT now own Rothmans, Peter Stuyvesant, Dunhill and Du Maurier tobacco brands. It was a major merger, costing £13 million, thus giving the strength to compete with the largest tobacco group in the developed world – Philip Morris, the US tobacco company that owns Marlboro (Pandya, 1999). It has been suggested by Jackson (1999) that this merger is another of those defensive alliances in which actors in a disappearing world all pull together for security.

Despite the fact that BAT is in the unscrupulous business of selling a product that eventually kills its users, they do operate a comprehensive equal opportunities policy. According to their own literature, the reason for this is that BAT wants its workers to be as ethnically and culturally diverse as the customers in the developing world who it wants to attract.

If people choose to invest in tobacco companies, or to work for them, that is their own responsibility. However they forget that profiting from tobacco specialisation and sales to developed countries is unethical (Financial Times, 1999, p.23).

Financial analysis of BAT's past connections with China makes evident the fact that, up until 1949, China was BAT's most profitable market. As early as 1911, BAT posters advertising tobacco were on display in China (Cochran, 1980) and BAT sponsored events such as theatre performances (Ting Wen-chiang, 1960). During the revolution, BAT's 12 factories were confiscated, although expropriation was paid. Should BAT re-establish itself in the Chinese market, it will merely be recovering the factories that it lost (*Financial Times*, 1999, p.23), but at considerable financial gain.

First world finance bodies in the Chinese tobacco trade

A number of global factors facilitated BAT's infiltration of the Chinese tobacco market. China does not yet export cigarettes to the developed world, but it does face the pressure of having to adhere to the unilateral trade sanctions that are related to tobacco production (*Tobacco Control*, 1997). For example, under section 301 of the US Trade Agreement Act (1974), and following threats from the US of the implementation of tariffs on US$3.9 billion worth of Chinese exports:

> *China signed a Memorandum of Understanding with the US in October 1992. This agreement stated that China had to drop all their statutory licence requirements for cigarettes, cigars, smoking tobacco, and cigarette filters being imported into China by the end of 1994: and to lift all scientifically unjustifiable phytosanitary restrictions on tobacco. 'Phytosanitary' means related to health, but is a curious term of uncertain intent (Tobacco Control, 1997, p.77).*

Much more to the point is China's debt predicament, for it is the particular debt that China has with the World Bank that has facilitated BAT's infiltration into China and thus contributed to the high level of tobacco-related ill health that is experienced by Chinese people. There can be no doubt that China is the World Bank's largest customer and that country received $14 billion in loans in 1996 (*The Economist*, 1996, p.32). In addition, it was given a 'soft loan' of $8.8 billion following this. A limit exists beyond which a country cannot borrow from the World Bank: no country can owe more than a tenth of the bank's total lending capacity. China has almost reached this level. China has large budget deficits and no surplus money with which it can pay off this debt. The World Bank has stated that China can only have additional funds if it is prepared to accept new performance guarantees. But China dislikes performance guarantees, as they regard it as insulting to be held to ransom by foreigners (*The Economist*, 1996, p.32). As a group, G7 oppose China being given additional loans by the World Bank, and the US government supported this in 1996 (*The Economist*, 1996), as they believe that China is too poor to qualify.

Due to these restraints on its financial manoeuvrability, China is reliant on foreign investment to raise revenues to finance healthcare, while at the same time smoking-related ill health among its population has increased as a result of BAT. Financial losses occasioned by the care of individuals who develop smoking-related ill health or diseases are enormous. The annual healthcare costs and indirect productivity losses, for example, were $11.3 billion in 1995 (Walker, 1996). It is no wonder that the Chinese health service continues to experience problems in paying for healthcare. However, the irony is a tobacco tax is viewed as an effective way of financing healthcare and health promotion activities as well as paying for the treatment and prevention of smoking-related diseases (Hu, 1997, p.136). The healthcare system has encountered problems in fitting in with the changes brought about by the economic reforms and in some urban areas the healthcare system has collapsed (Zhang *et al.*, 1998, p.179). In recent years increasing pressure has been brought to bear on the Chinese government to finance healthcare by means of private health insurance. The World Bank, the World Health Organization and UNICEF are helping China to pilot systems among urban and rural populations, so that a suitable healthcare system can be established (Zhang *et al.*, 1998). Naturally, in terms of helping the Chinese government to reduce healthcare costs, the World Bank could, if they wanted to, simply apply sanctions that reduce the part that the tobacco industry plays in China. Doubtless such actions would help to reduce the incidence of smoking-related diseases and thus diminish healthcare costs, but is it reasonable to expect a bank to assume a social service role?

The Asian Monetary Fund

Can we assume that a more 'regionally loyal' facility would fare better? In an attempt to solve this problem Japan has proposed an Asian Monetary Fund 1996 (*The Economist*, 1998, p.19). The Japanese government believes that the economic problems that affect the Western Pacific region can be solved by way of setting up an Asian Monetary Fund. Even though there have been increasing calls from the United States, Canada, France and Germany 'for an expanded IMF, a financial supervisory organisation parallel to the IMF, or even a second Bretton Woods conference to rethink the world's financial architecture from scratch', first world nations have generally objected to this. The very vehemence of objections leaves one with the distinct impression that G7 members do not want China to be self-sufficient. Their lack of support *ipso facto* condones the exploitative pressures that tobacco multinationals such as BAT have placed upon China.

We can say with confidence that the IMF has also contributed to the increase in tobacco-related ill health that Chinese people have been exposed to over the last 20 years. It is of no small interest that the IMF has not acknowledged the adverse way in which interest rates within the Chinese economy have increased as a result of the increased rates of 'private indebtedness and low inflationary expectations' (*The Economist*, 1998, p.19). Clearly, in this author's view, this is the reason why the IMF's strategy for Asia has been unsuccessful. It has resulted in recession and increased rates of unemployment and social and economic unrest that gave rise to a decrease in the value of the yen on the stock market. One effect of this is that governments in Asia Pacific countries seem to have slight faith in the IMF's strategies (*The Economist*, 1998).

The Chinese National Tobacco Corporation (CNTC) and Western multinationals

If we are to effectively assess the manner in which multinational tobacco companies have exploited China, we need to examine the way in which they are taking advantage of their merger with the Chinese National Tobacco Corporation (CNTC). CNTC is the largest cigarette manufacturer in the world, and in 1992, CNTC produced 32.85 million cases of cigarettes (Hu, 1997, p.136). The Corporation has eight factories, 150 drying plants, 30 research institutes and employs 520 000 workers who produce 500 brands of cigarettes (*Washington Post*, 1996). Consequent upon pressure from the US, Beijing has agreed to allow multinational tobacco imports to compete with CNTC. Altogether CNTC has 30% of the world tobacco market. However, its principal market is domestic, and it is not accustomed to competitive sales. Rather it is used to allocation and distribution. Thus, if CNTC is to survive, it will have to become as ruthless as Western companies (Pollock, in Doll and Crofton, 1996). Mackay (in Hu, 1997) conjectures that CNTC will go the same way as all the Eastern European and South American monopolies that have been taken over by the multinational cigarette companies.

> *As recession grows the world economy is overshadowed by powerful ... global monopolies. These powerful industrial ... interests are in conflict with those of civil society. While the spirit of Anglo-Saxon liberalism is committed for 'fostering competition', G7 macroeconomic policy (through tight fiscal and monetary controls) has in practice supported a wave of corporate mergers and acquisitions as well as the planned bankruptcy of small and medium-size enterprises (Chossudovsky, 1998, p.18).*

These, and similar, economic reforms have resulted in multinationals such as Philip Morris, BAT and Japan Tobacco Company (JTC) forming joint projects with CNTC. For instance, BAT is now working with the Hangzhou cigarette factory. Similar projects with Rothmans in Jinan have also been established. To some extent this mutes competition, for the joint working agreement means that there is cooperation, and sharing of resources such as technology, workers and tobacco blending techniques (*Tobacco Control*, 1997).

> *In turn, large multinational companies (particularly in the US and Canada) have taken control of local level markets ... through the system of corporate franchising. Small franchises are either eradicated or impounded as 'franchisees' into the net of the global distributor. This process enables large corporate capital ('the franchise') to gain control over human capital and entrepreneurship. A large share of earnings of small firms and/or retailers is thereby appropriated while the bulk of investment is assumed by the independent producer (Chossudovsky, 1998, p.19).*

Targeting Chinese health with Western advertising

No one seriously questions the view that first world multinationals have taken advantage of their position in China, and have used their wealth to launch high-profile media campaigns that thrust strong persuasive Western images of smoking as fashionable and desirable behaviour. It is also obvious that it has been successful and that as a result large numbers of Chinese youth and young women have been encouraged to take up smoking (Peto *et al.*, 1998). When confronted with this (self-evident) claim, the tobacco industry asserts that its advertising is only intended to influence brand choice and not to encourage people to smoke! However, research has shown that children mostly smoke heavily advertised brands (Currie *et al.*, 1994; Difranza *et al.*, 1991; Ernster, 1985; Hastings *et al.*, 1994; USDHHS, 1994). If one has any doubt about the truth of the matter, consider findings of a survey carried out among elementary schoolchildren aged between 10 and 12 in Beijing, which revealed that 28% of boys and 3% of girls had smoked a cigarette in the last month. Fifty per cent of them reported that they had smoked a cigarette at between five and nine years of age, and most significantly the majority smoked the most heavily advertised cigarettes (Bao-Ping Zhu and Ling-Chiu Sum, 1996). Multi-national cigarette companies have been flouting advertising restrictions by pub-lishing tobacco advertisements that do indeed advertise their products, but which omit the word 'cigarette'. As an example of this, large billboards can be seen in Chinese cities with the slogan 'Marlboro World' or simply '555' (Hui, 1997). In addition, there has been a dramatic growth in cigarette advertising in Western Pacific countries that targets groups such as women. Western promotion tech-niques work and high-profile Western media performers such as Madonna and Paula Abdul have taken part in concerts and events that have been financed by tobacco companies such as BAT (Amos, in Doll and Crofton, 1996).

Naturally enough, BAT wants cigarette smoking to be viewed as glamorous, sophisticated, sexy, healthy, sporty, liberated, rebellious and slimming. Values such as these are having a detrimental effect on the health of Chinese people, and CNTC have started to copy their Western-style marketing strategies. For example, 'Chahua' and 'Yuren' are low-tar cigarettes marketed by CNTC for women. 'Yuren' cigarettes are long and thin with a white filter and a mild taste and the name means 'pretty woman' (ASH, 1998). It is now appreciated that the increased amount of advertising by multinationals in China has also contributed to the increase in the number of the Western cigarettes that are smuggled into China. The financial incentive for this is that Western brands cost a lot more than do the cigarettes manufactured by CNTC. But smuggling is also of benefit to multinationals such as BAT, for it allows easy access to the product and ignores any restrictions on imports. It goes without saying that the main casualties of smuggling are the Chinese people, whose health suffers (Pollock, in Doll and Crofton, 1996).

BAT's denial of the health risks vs the statistical evidence

Consistently BAT has denied the health risks that are associated with smoking, thus contributing to the increase in smoking-related ill health in China. Patrick Sheehy, BAT's chairman (1990), declared at a company AGM that 'cigarette smoking has not been proven to cause disease'. BAT has also claimed that passive smoking does not affect health and that nicotine is not addictive! (Wilmore, 2004, p.15) The contrary view is said to be a 'scientific mistake', as research scientists have not taken into account other contributory factors. Not only that, BAT claim that their advertising and marketing activities are not aimed at young people, and they continue to use the old argument that their advertising campaigns only target adults, and that the sole purpose of this is to encourage adults to change brands

(BAT, 1990, p.278). Hastings (1999) argues that these claims are extremely weak, as the overall aim of marketing is to appeal to specific groups, and that this is done by tailoring the price, availability and image of a product through packaging, advertising and promotion.

Chinese analysis of mortality patterns in their own country during the 1960s reveals that the main causes of death were infectious diseases, respiratory illnesses and accidents. However, since the 1970s, cancer, strokes and heart disease have become the main causes of death in rural and urban areas and around Shanghai. Again, after 1989 coronary heart disease and strokes became the main causes of death in China (McGinn, 1997). Data published in 1997 showed that cigarette smoking caused 750 000 deaths per year in China. Moreover, this is predicted to rise to 3 million by the time young smokers of today reach middle age. Naturally the risk of death is the same for Chinese as for Western smokers, but the actual course that smoking-related diseases take in China is much different to that in the developed world. For example, in China, tobacco causes more deaths from chronic lung disease than from vascular disease, and it causes as many deaths from tuberculosis as from coronary heart disease. Interestingly, there are cultural differences which mean that the risk of developing lung cancer as a result of smoking is different in China from that among people living in the developing world. Worldwide, by the end of this century, cigarette smoking will be causing 4 million deaths per year. Should smoking rates stay the same, by the year 2030 the number of deaths will increase by 10 million annually of which 70% will occur in the developing world (Peto and Wolansky, 1998).

It has been convincingly argued by Amos (in Doll and Crofton, 1996) and by Peto *et al.* (1994) that variations in rates of smoking are not random but mirror the different evolutionary stages of the smoking epidemic in each country. China is at stage two, as explained in Chapter 10, and as a result smoking rates among men will increase from 60% to 80% with few stopping smoking. Gender differences also apply, with rates among women being one to two decades behind those of their male counterparts. However, these rates are predicted to increase (Amos, in Doll and Crofton, 1996). Likewise, the rate at which people are taking up smoking in China is much greater than when it occurred in developing countries 75 years ago (McGinn, 1997).

It has been predicted that in the future smoking prevalence among the young, those living in towns, the better educated and the affluent will increase (Weng, 1987). Because of the intensive marketing of tobacco and a reduction in the social taboo for women to smoke, an increase in smoking rates among women will also occur. The rural and uneducated are particularly vulnerable and ignorance of the health risks that are associated with it contribute to an increase in smoking rates (Weng *et al.*, 1987). Again lack of funding for control measures and the difficulty in implementing these, especially in rural areas, will add to the number of people who smoke (Mackay and Crofton, in Doll and Crofton 1996).

China's attempts to sustain health policies

China's government does officially recognise its obligation to protect its citizens and Article 21 of the Chinese Constitution explicitly states that the state is responsible for promoting the public's health. Nevertheless, the Chinese government's dilemma is similar to that of the governments of developed countries, whereby the revenue that tobacco tax brings is relied on to fund healthcare (*Tobacco Control*, 1997). China desperately needs money to finance a health promotion campaign that comprises an anti-smoking media campaign and/or school health education programmes. It is entirely fatuous to assert that a proportion of cigarette tax revenues should be used to fund these activities (Hu, 1997, p.136).

Although progress has been made in banning cigarette advertising, increasing import duties on cigarettes, and banning cigarette smoking in some public places, the health of the Chinese people continues to be affected by smoking (Hu, 1997, p.136). Countrywide implementation of legislation is difficult, especially in rural areas, as multinational companies are establishing stronger bonds with CNTC (Frankel, 1986). A consequence of this is a growing resentment towards tobacco legislation, and sophisticated cigarette marketing and promotion; and, as discussed above, foreign cigarettes are becoming more fashionable among the young. In addition, the smuggling of tobacco-related products is also predicted to increase (*Tobacco Control*, 1997).

It is certainly encouraging to note that there are some health promotion initiatives that have gained momentum in China. As an example of this, in March 1996 Xian City government designated one of the city's main pedestrian thoroughfares a smoke-free zone; 340 no-smoking signs were put up and tobacco advertisements were banned. Statistical evaluation of the project after only six months showed that the number of people smoking on the street had declined from 3.5% to 0.6%. In addition, the number of smoke-free shops increased from four to 198. Fires caused by smoking in premises on this street fell from two to nil, and deaths fell from seven to nil, while tobacco sales in this area decreased from $15 000 to $10 000, and smoking prevalence among men working in shops on this street fell to 2.5%. Even the television tower that advertised Kent cigarettes lost $75 000 a year (Mackay, 1997, p.9).

Increasing concern regarding the adverse effects of smoking on the health of the Chinese people, and of its correlation with the increase in multinational tobacco companies in the country, has led the international/regional non-governmental organisations (NGOs), like the International Union Against Cancer (UICC) and Consumers International (CI), to encourage their member organisations to take a public and political stand on the tobacco epidemic, and to fund the projects, research, meetings and the visits of experts. A good instance of this is the Ninth World Conference on Tobacco or Health in 1994 (hosted in China), where representatives from the world's six different developing regions met to discuss regional development and plan future strategies (Mackay and Crofton, in Doll and Crofton, 1996). It was agreed that this conference had quite a positive impact in China as visiting foreign consultants, oncologists, cardiologists and respiratory physicians were invited to share their expertise, and to highlight the importance of smoking by creating a local medical climate which is influencing policy-makers in China to address this extensive problem (Mackay and Crofton, in Doll and Crofton, 1996).

Health organisations need to develop transnational strategies that counteract those that the tobacco industry has developed. Regional organisations, such as the Asia Pacific Association for the Control of Tobacco, are organising regional annual meetings at which delegates suggest moves to restrict the power of multinational tobacco companies in China (Mackay and Crofton, in Doll and Crofton, 1996).

Evidence is growing that the Chinese anti-smoking lobby is becoming stronger. For example, the Ministry for Public Health announced its plans to ban tobacco advertising in China. In Beijing, cigarette advertising in all forms has been banned, including advertising in newspapers and magazines, on billboards and on electronic notice boards (Hui, 1997). Neighbourhood advocacy was not far behind, with the establishment of a tobacco campaign group, the Chinese Association on Smoking and Health (CASH). CASH's campaign for legislation is to be implemented to help smokers to quit; they also coordinate control initiatives, and member associations have been set up in a large number of Chinese provinces. CASH is a proactive body, and has hosted yearly international seminars on tobacco control policy, smoking cessation and the effects of passive smoking. They have involved the media, health personnel and young people in their campaigns. In addition, they have been successful in campaigning for preventing the sale of cigarettes in China on World No Tobacco Day. They were successful, too, in their campaign for tobacco smoking to be banned in public places (from 1997) such as on railway carriages, in taxis, buses and subways, at airports and train stations, and on all the flights of China's airlines. Tobacco control is not a priority area in all the Chinese provinces, but lack of resources to launch it has caused delays in many (Mackay, in Doll and Crofton, 1996).

The role of schools in getting the 'no tobacco' message across has been recognised in developed countries, in which school health education programmes have been effective in increasing young people's knowledge of the health risks of smoking, broadening their awareness of influences such as advertising and social pressure, and developing their confidence, self-esteem and social skills to help them to ignore powerful media messages that encourage them to smoke (Currie *et al.*, 1994; Ernster, 1985; USDHHS, 1994). But in developing countries, poor knowledge levels among young people about smoking and its adverse effect on health is consequent upon a lack of health education programmes. Also, structural barriers such as widespread rural problems and high levels of illiteracy exacerbate the situation. School programmes are desperately needed to counteract the increasing promotion/sponsorship activities of tobacco countries (Currie *et al.*, 1994; Ernster, 1985; USDHHS, 1994). Of course, one of the reasons why the governments of some developing countries have not devised and implemented national tobacco legislation is that they are inexperienced and, accordingly, ill equipped to draw up policies that will combat the new epidemic or counter the persuasive sophistication of the transnational companies (Mackay and Crofton, in Doll and Crofton, 1996).

Conclusion and recommendations

Statistics verify that the Chinese population is now smoking ever-larger numbers of cigarettes, which in turn is having an increasingly adverse impact on the morbidity and mortality rates in China. We also know that foreign investors and tobacco multinationals have used unethical strategies to encourage developing countries such as China to expand the market for tobacco products. The Chinese government has only recently begun to appreciate the cost to themselves of this. In every respect, tobacco use is a threat to sustainable development (Bellagio, 1995; McGinn, 1997).

On the other hand, the World Bank and the IMF need to support China and other developing countries by addressing their criteria for extending loans. Indeed, it can be easily argued that lack of financial support and increased pressure on countries such as China to pay money back has contributed to the increase in smoking-related diseases. Foreign investment has not enabled China to provide a comprehensive healthcare system for its people, as the foreign investment from multinational tobacco companies is slowly killing the people of China, and escalating healthcare costs, while decreasing productivity.

Health promotion proponents in developed countries have a responsibility to people who live in developing countries such as China. However, to do this effectively, individuals need to think of themselves as being members of a global community. Inadequate domestic legislation has allowed the development of the tobacco business in China, with its vigorous unethical marketing, sponsorship and advertising campaigns. These in turn have led to adverse smoking-related health problems, causing approximately 750 000 deaths per year. It has been said that this number will increase to 3 million per year by the year 2025. Unless effective tobacco control programmes are implemented, additional ethical dilemmas will arise, such as that of employment versus nutrition, in which employment within the tobacco industry finds itself weighted against malnutrition, brought about by large percentages of household finances being used to purchase tobacco; and the depletion of fertile forests, as trees are used to manufacture cigarette papers. Some advances in tobacco control have recently been made in China, and in this there is a potential for further development (Richmond, 1997). Bans tend to have only partial effects, and are frequently undermined by indirect advertising/sponsorship/brand-stretching (Chapman, 1985; Charlton, 1986). As in the West, these include strategic sponsorship of sport, cultural events, television and radio programmes, medical organisations and pop concerts. Strategies to address this issue must be implemented, otherwise the apocalyptic tobacco death toll predicted for China in 2025 will become a reality (Mackay and Crofton, in Doll and Crofton, 1996).

References

Action on Smoking and Health (ASH) (2004) *Big Tobacco and Women. What the Industry's Confidential Documents Reveal*. 22 November. Website: http://www.ash.org.uk/smoking

Bellagio V (1985) Statement on tobacco and sustainable development. *Journal of Canadian Medical Association*. 15 October 1998, p.12.

Bao-Ping Zhu and Ling-Chiu Sum (1996) Cigarette smoking and its risk factors among elementary school students in Beijing. *American Journal of Public Health*. March. pp 104–8.

British American Tobacco (BAT) (1990) Talk given to trainee managers at the Chalwood College of Management by BAT on the competition represented by RJ Reynolds Company, 6 August.

Callum C (1998) *The UK Smoking Epidemic*. Health Education Authority, London.

Chapman S and Leng W (1985) *Tobacco Control in the Third World: A Resource Atlas*. International Organisation of Consumers Unions.

Charlton A (1986) Children's advertisement awareness related to their views on smoking. *Health Education Journal*. **45**: 75–80.

Chossudovsky M (1998) *Globalisation of Poverty: impacts of IMF and World Bank reforms*. Zed Books, London and New York.

Cochran S (1980) *Big Business in China: Sino-Foreign Rivalry in the Cigarette Industry, 1890–1930*. Harvard University Press, Cambridge, MA and London.

Currie C, Todd J and Thomson C (1994) *Health Behaviour of Scottish School Children. Report 4. The Cross-national Perspective: Scotland Compared to Other European Countries and Canada*. Health Education Board for Scotland, Edinburgh.

Darby I (1999) BAT-Rothmans faces Marlboro in global struggle. *Marketing*. **21 January**: 13(1).

Department of Health (1998) *Smoking Kills*. Tobacco White Paper. Department of Health, London.

Difranza JR, Richards JW, Paulman PM and Wilkinson F (1991) RJR Nabisco's cartoon camel promotes Camel cigarettes to children. *Journal of the American Medical Association*. **266**: 3149–53.

Doll R and Crofton J (1996) *Tobacco and Health*. The Royal Society for Medicine Press, London.

The Economist (1996) A problem with the Bank: China. 13 July, p.32.

The Economist (1998) The case for an Asian Monetary Fund. 7 November, p.19.

Ernster VL (1985) Mixed messages for women: a social history of cigarette smoking and advertising. *New York State Journal of Medicine*. **316**: 725–32.

Financial Times, leader: 'Smoke signals', 13 January 1999, p.23.

Frankel G (1986) US Aided Cigarette Firms Conquest Across Asia. *Washington Post*. 17 November. p.A01.

The Guardian (2004) BAT breaks China barrier. Main section, 17 July, p.25.

Hastings G (1999) Young People and Smoking Seminar: Marketing Presentation at the HEA. April.

Hastings GB, Ryan H, Teer P and Mackintosh AM (1994) Cigarette advertising and children's smoking: why Reg was withdrawn. *British Medical Journal*. **309**: 933–6.

Hu T (1997) Cigarette taxation in China: lessons from international experiences. *Tobacco Control*. **6**: 136–40.

Hui L (1997) *Tobacco Smoking in China Set to Decrease. Tobacco Control*. **6**: 136–40.

Jackson T (1999) Squaring up to the Marlboro man: BAT's deal with Rothmans makes it the only serious rival to Philip Morris. *Financial Times*. 12 January, p.12.

Lai-guian AA (1996) Viewpoint – China and Vietnam: urban strategies in societies in transition. *Journal of International Affairs* (George Washington University). **Summer**: 20–34.

Mackay J (1997) Battling upstream against the tobacco epidemic in China. *Tobacco Control*. **6**: 9–13.

Mackerras C, Taneja P and Young G (1998) *China Since 1978* (2e). Longman, London.

McGinn AP (1997) *Preventing Chronic Disease in Developing Countries: State of the World 1997*. Earthscan Publications, London, ch. 4, pp 60–77.

McGregor R and Urquart L (1994) BAT goes in search of the Chinese Holy Grail. *Money and Times*. 17 July, p.4.

Min C (1996) Smoking and drinking: smoking and health. *International Medical Journal*. December. **3(4)**: 305–6.

Office for National Statistics (1996) *General Household Survey Data*. General Household Survey, Stationery Office, London.

Pandya N (1999) Company vitae: British American Tobacco. Jobs and Money section. *The Guardian*, 13 March, p.37.

Peto R, Lopez A and Boreham J (1994) *Mortality from Smoking in Developed Countries*. Oxford University Press, Oxford.

Peto R, Alberton F and Roberts H (1998a) Emerging Tobacco Hazards in China: 2 Early mortality studies from a prospective study. *British Medical Journal*. **317**: 1423–4.

Peto R and Wolansky V (1998b) *The Growing Epidemic: proceedings of the 10th World Conference on Tobacco and Health* (Beijing, China, 24–28 August 1997). East-West, for World Health Organization, Singapore.

Richmond R (1997) Ethical dilemmas in providing tobacco to developing countries: the case of China. *Addiction*. September. **92(9)**: 1137–41.

State Statistics Bureau (1993) *Attempts to Decrease Smoking-Related Disease*. Statistical Year Book. Available in English from Embassy of Peoples' Republic of China, Cultural Section, London. p.1022.

State Statistics Bureau (1998) Report of the Chinese Association on Smoking and Health. Statistical Year Book. Available in English from Embassy of Peoples' Republic of China, Cultural Section, London. pp 897–8.

Ting Wen-chiang (1960) Free enterprise in China: the case of a cigarette concern, 1905–1953. *Pacific Historical Review*. **29(4)**: 389n.18.

Tobacco Control (1997) Smoking in China: 'the limits of space'. Editorial. *Tobacco Control*. **6**: 77–9.

Tobacco International (1993) Chinese smokers pass the 300 million mark. Editorial. *Tobacco International*. **7**: 3–5.

Tomlinson R (1999) China's reform: now comes the hard part: over the past 20 years, China has transformed itself from an economic nonentity into a force to be reckoned with. *Fortune*. March. **139(41)**: 158–9.

United Nations (UN) (1998) *World Population Nearing 6 Billion: Projected.* UN Population Division, Department of Economic and Social Affairs.

United States Department of Health and Health Services (USDHHS) (1994) *Preventing Tobacco Use Among Young People: a report of the Surgeon General.* USDHHS, Atlanta, GA.

Unwin N, Alberti G, Aspray T and Mbanya R (1998) Economic globalisation and its effect on health. *British Medical Journal*. **316**: 1401–2.

Walker T (1996) Chinese smoking curbs fail to break the habit. *Financial Times*. 15 May, p.6.

Washington Post (1996) China's Growing Tobacco Trade. 20 November, p.11.

Weng J (1987) Smoking prevalence in Chinese aged 15 and above. Report of 1984 First National Prevalence Study. *Chinese Medical Journal*. **100(11)**: 886–92.

Wilmore I (2004) BAT, Big Wheeze: the alternative British American Tobacco Social and Environmental Report. Action on Smoking and Health, London.

Yao S and Liu J (1998) Economic reforms and regional segmentation in rural China. *Regional Studies*. **32(18)**: 735.

Zhang T, Yang S and Tanihara H (1998) Health and environment: from China to Japan: How long shall we go – from the viewpoint of Yanagawa health insurance system. *International Medical Journal*. September. **5(3)**: 179–87.

Zolty B (1999) Gender issues: smoking men are still the main victims. *World Health*, 51st Year, No. 5, September–October. World Health Organization, Geneva, pp 36–40.

Chapter 10

The tobacco impact worldwide

Beyond China

Chapter 9 concentrated on China because it constitutes roughly a quarter of the world's population. The impact of first world involvement in its economy – and hence on the health of its people – is expanding enormously. China desperately needs US dollars because of its own perceived need to industrialise fast – or face total exploitation at the hands of first world multinational corporations and banks.

To balance this equation, it has had to open its markets to such concerns as BAT – and many others. Paradoxically, it needs to mortgage the health and lifespan of many of its own people to sustain much-needed public services of the country as a whole.

In this chapter, the author will be drawing on a number of other sources to illustrate how the first world tobacco product manufacturers, through aggressive (and often illegal) promotional strategies, effectively undermine the painstaking efforts of people all over the globe to enjoy health. The present situation indicates clearly that tobacco products, and the agencies promoting them, represent obstacles that must be overcome if we are seriously to address the issue of global inequities in health. As the last chapter argues, this cannot be accomplished under the present system of national autonomies in trade.

Much of the material for this chapter is informed by the publications and press releases of the American and British Cancer Societies (ACS and BCS), the World Health Organization (WHO) and the International Union Against Cancer (IUAC). The latter three have now, jointly, produced two Tobacco Control Country Profiles. Material in this chapter is drawn principally from the most recent of these (ACS, IUAC and WHO, 2003).

This second edition gives current data on the production, consumption, trade and morbidity/mortality of tobacco-related disease for 196 countries (Costa e Silva and Thun, 2003). As they point out, tobacco use worldwide represents a global pandemic.

The tobacco pandemic

About 1.3 billion people – using 2003 figures – now smoke cigarettes and other tobacco products. That breaks down to approximately one billion males and 250 million females. We cannot really say 'men' and 'women' – as the reports usually do – because, in some of the Asian countries in particular, one often sees children under 10 years of age smoking and/or begging for cigarettes.

As mentioned before, there has – over the past 30 years – been a steady decline in smoking in the first world. Even in this context, more school-age girls are taking up smoking than are boys. This can be traced rather convincingly to clever changes in tobacco advertising (MacDonald, 1989), when many of the major producers started to address the 'problem' posed by young girls not taking up smoking to the same extent that boys did. By 1991, the total trend started falling, while that among girls continued to rise.

By 2003, it was noted that the smoking levels had been relatively static since 1999, except for China where it was still rising by leaps and bounds. Basically as tobacco use declined in most industrialised countries, the geography of smoking changed – and continues to do so – from the first to the third world. By 1995, more smokers lived in the third (about 933 million people) than in the first (about 209 million) (Oluwafemi, 2000). Further, about 35% of males in the first world smoke, while nearly 50% of males in the third world do. Close to 66% of Chinese men smoke.

These trends inevitably reflect themselves in mortality rates, with a delay of about 30 to 60 years. It is estimated that about 4.9 million premature smoking-related deaths occurred in 2003. These figures were relatively evenly divided between the first and the third world (WHO, 2000). In excess of 6000 of these deaths occurred in China alone. Bearing in mind that Asia accounts for about one-third of the world's population, deaths from smoking (assuming current trends persist) will reach about 8.4 million by 2020 yearly (Lopez, 2001).

A conceptual framework for tobacco use

The World Health Organization has produced a conceptual framework that identifies four stages of the evolving tobacco epidemic (*see* Figure 10.1).

Their idea is that these four stages must not be seen as discrete, but as linked into a continuum. This model was due, initially, to the work of Lopez *et al.* (1994). Let us

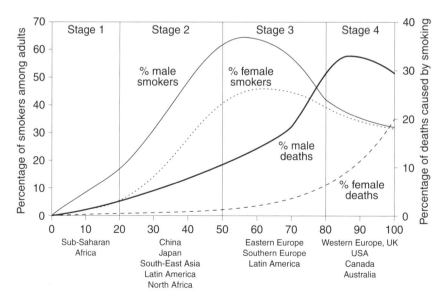

Source: Lopez *et al.*, 1994. Reproduced by permission of BMJ Publishing Group.

Figure 10.1:   Four stages of the tobacco epidemic.

examine it in more detail to appreciate the global scale, and relative geographical intensities of this threat to health.

- Stage 1:
  A low prevalence of cigarette smoking, mainly engaged in by males. It involves less than 20% of the cohort, and is not associated with an increase in incidence of cancer of other smoking-related diseases. This stage includes a number of sub-Saharan countries in Africa that have not been penetrated by tobacco corporations of the first world. Such countries are obviously frightfully vulnerable to strategic subtleties of the very well-financed transnational tobacco product manufacturers. Unless preventive measures are taken at the international level, this author predicts that it is only a matter of time before they fall into the same trap.
- Stage 2:
  Countries at Stage 2 live with smoking rates in excess of 50% in males. As well, increases in rates of smoking among females are a prominent phenomenon, and there is a marked shift towards smoking being taken up at an earlier and earlier age. Among the males there is a pronounced increase in cancer and other smoking-related diseases. Into this category are now included numerous Asian, North African and Latin American countries. It is customary in these countries for legislation on tobacco control to be laxly enforced, or commonly not enforced at all. Social, educational and certainly political support for such controls are neither widely understood nor promoted.
- Stage 3:
  By this stage the epidemic reflects itself in a noticeable decrease in prevalence of tobacco use among males. There is also a less conspicuous decline in smoking among females. In fact, gender-based prevalence rates are drawing closer together. Despite this, the incidence of smoking-related illnesses is still on the increase, with such illness accounting for 10% to 30% of total mortality. About 75% of these deaths are of males. In both Eastern Europe (countries of the former USSR) and Southern Europe, many countries are now at this stage. Among the more educated of these populations the non-smoking message seems to be making headway.
- Stage 4:
  In this stage, the downturn in smoking rates among both females and males has been quite steep. Mortality due to smoking-related diseases peaks at 30% to 35% of all male deaths. Forty to 50% of such deaths occur in middle-aged men (35 to 60 years) and then it drops. The data for female smoking-related diseases accounts for 20% to 25% of all deaths. Presently included in Stage 4 are the first world nations and several areas of the Western Pacific.

It goes without saying that this WHO model is not likely to be universally applicable, due to variations in cultural and social values across and between ethnic groups. For instance, despite China's huge (and growing) appetite for tobacco products, Chinese women are again becoming less involved. Somewhat below 5% of them indulge (WHO, 2003), and this is no doubt because for centuries Chinese culture has regarded smoking among women as demeaning – tantamount to socially disgraceful.

It is salutary (both literally and figuratively) to look at Thailand. In that country, cigarette-smoking rates dropped by more than 30% in only four years, from 1996 to

2000. The reason? From 1995 the Thai government banned cigarette sales and advertising.

But, despite such exceptions, the WHO paradigm is widely useful in planning any global campaign against this sinister epidemic.

Are we winning?

Despite such negative statistics as provided by the still developing situation in China, a number of recent surveys have suggested that international tobacco control is improving. Of course, there are strict time limits as to how long this improvement can continue. While the author was working at Duke University at Raleigh-Durham in the American state of North Carolina, he was struck by the fact that much of the good life there was financed by the huge acreage of tobacco fields in the state. Those fields were in the 1960s associated with Winston Salem Tobacco. But there are plenty of other tobacco areas in the US whose economic well-being depends heavily on tobacco.

A much less wealthy third world country, dependent on trading relations with the first, cannot launch a secure tobacco control mechanism in the face of first world financed pressure. For one thing, the World Trade Organization (WTO) has immense legal clout which it routinely wields on behalf of US business interests.

It is also worth reminding the reader that large-scale production of tobacco, and the need to find markets for it as a pivotal part of the country's economic welfare, is not only confined to the first world. Many third world nations are heavily depend-ent on exporting tobacco. One of these large-scale producers is none other than Cuba. It finds itself in the paradoxical position of providing enormous numbers of doctors and other health workers without charge to numerous third world countries as a reflection of its internationalist and socialist policies. By marketing tobacco in such quantities (and of such quality, I am told!), Cuba is effectively undermining equity and health in some of the countries it is aiding!

For the short-to-intermediate term, though, we can rejoice in any improvement in tobacco control. Cigarette consumption, per capita, is continuing to decrease in the first world (those at Stage 3 or 4). *See* Figure 10.2. Average per capita consump-tion (APCC) is estimated with the formula:

$$\text{APCC} = \frac{(\text{Production} + \text{imports} - \text{exports})}{(\text{Population aged 15+ years})}$$

The APCC in the pan-American region – which also includes a number of third world countries – had halved between 1975 and 2000. Obviously, most of this decline occurred in the US and Canada because of strong support for such health issues as: laws protecting clean indoor air in working environments, increases in taxes on cigarettes, legislation requiring health warnings on tobacco products, etc.

Countries in the Western Pacific, such as Australia and New Zealand, have had strong and (especially in Australia's case) flamboyantly high-profile anti-smoking campaigns since 1965. The result has been a gradual decline in the use of tobacco products since 1987. That 'latency period' – between organised and sustained anti-smoking campaigns and their effects – seems to be about average whenever it has

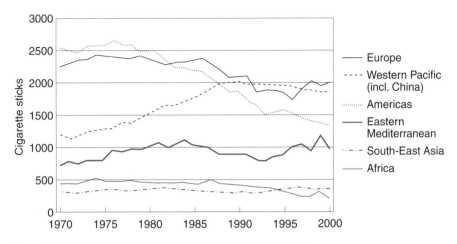

Source: United Nations Statistics Division (2003). Commodity Trade Statistics Database.

Figure 10.2: Average per capita cigarette consumption in persons aged >14 years by WHO region.

occurred. During the latency period, the anti-smoking movement has to achieve a number of grades.

1 It has to gain respect in civil society as being responsible and with an important message.
2 It has to attract media interest of sufficient intensity that most people recognise the acronym of its title, e.g. virtually everybody in Australia knows of the anti-tobacco group BUGA UP – Billboard Users Graffiti Against Unhealthy Promotions. BUGA UP is discussed in more detail in the next few pages.
3 There has to be sufficient pressure to gradually bring about changes in legislation in such a way as to enhance tobacco controls. This is an absolutely crucial element and the great variety of ways of bringing it about naturally reflects the temper and culture of the country concerned.
4 Legislation thus passed has to be actively pursued by such authorities as the police, educational personnel, etc. Much to the surprise of many people, the passage of such legislation, rather than creating initial antagonism, has widespread support. One has seen this in such heavy-smoking countries as Spain and France.

A brief account of BUGA UP

The Australian campaign has been spectacularly successful and is therefore worth some comment. The name of their group was almost certainly built around an appealing acronym rather than the other way round. The campaign was begun by a group of medical doctors in Sydney, under the leadership of one Dr John Chesterfield-Evans, who is reputed to have stated: 'I consider four hours a week spent "refacing" hoardings promoting tobacco as better spent than sitting in my surgery telling people that they have cancer.'

The story may be apocryphal but is very much in character because the group became most evident to the public by 'buggering up' the huge hoardings promoting tobacco products. Legally, this activity is called 'defacing' and in the many court cases following, it was routinely prosecuted as 'malicious injury'. But note that the BUGA UP people always called it 'refacing' because they actually – and most cleverly – changed the advertising message by removing some letters from the advertisers' blurb and replacing them with others that changed the message to one of opposite meaning. For example: a voluptuous young woman is offered a cigarette by a bronzed and handsome yacht owner. She looks into his manly and amorous eyes and coos: 'What a STIRLING idea!' Stirling, of course, is a brand of cigarette. Once BUGA UP had 'refaced' the poster, the woman was screeching: 'What a STINKING idea!'

The present author was a member of the group in the early 1980s and was once prosecuted for 'malicious injury' for altering posters. As did numbers of others accused in such actions, I objected to the phrase 'defacing' the adverts and claimed that someone had merely 'refaced' them so that they told the truth!

Even the originators of BUGA UP surely would not have predicted either the speed or impact with which their activities would affect legislation. Their antics attracted immense press coverage – especially as so many of the activists were 'respectable' community figures. Most of Australia's newspapers relied heavily on tobacco advertising, hence often their coverage was hostile, some of it luridly false. But most of the court cases, including mine, ended in failure for the prosecutors. This later led to radio and TV programmes in which some of us were invited to explain our actions more fully. By and large, members of parliament became sympathetic. Australia was one of the first countries to widely legislate against tobacco interests, further bolstering its image as a clean and healthy nation. Its moves in this direction unquestionably had an international impact.

It appears, from the 2003 data, that a decline may even be gathering modest pace in China, although much more data over time is required to sustain such a hope.

As the above-cited *Tobacco Control Country Profiles* (second edition) points out (ACS, IUAC and WHO, 2003), it is most useful to repeatedly conduct such surveys across whole clusters of countries as a major component of Health Impact Assessment. Such surveys grant us a much better historical perspective than do prevalence surveys from individual countries. *See* Figure 10.2 for the data on the WHO regions we have been discussing, namely: Europe, the Western Pacific, the Americas, the Eastern Mediterranean, South-East Asia and Africa.

Statistically speaking, and in terms of on-the-ground health legislation and health promotion, there are certain limitations to the sales-weighted estimates of tobacco consumption that have been reported thus far. They give no indication as to who is doing the smoking. National peculiarities in legislation sometimes render this difficult to measure. For instance, in the US it is illegal to *sell* tobacco products to minors, but it is not illegal for people to *give* them cigarettes to smoke. So the actual sales figures for cigarettes in this country give us little indication of use among children. Also, overall estimates of consumption in this and many other countries are rendered difficult because of the increasing engagement in smuggling (Shafey *et al.*, 2002).

They cite the interesting example that countries such as Bosnia and Herzegovina, Brunei, Croatia, Cyprus, the Republic of Korea and the United Arab Emirates report cigarette imports that are far in excess of known exports plus any kind of realistic estimate of what the level of domestic use is. What happens to all of these 'extra' cigarettes? They get smuggled to large first world countries which have punitive taxation on tobacco as part of their health strategy. One plausible assumption is that the people in such places as listed above are provided with money from the tobacco manufacturers themselves to import their cigarettes in the first place. It would seem likely that they might well be involved in mediating the actual smuggling. We are here discussing financial profits that far exceed the entire national budgets of many third world countries.

Trying to measure smoking initiation among minors

Drawing directly from the second edition of *Tobacco Control Country Profiles* (ACS, IUAC and WHO, 2003), the following information addresses the issue well. We know that in most countries under scrutiny, people are usually initiated into smoking when still minors.

The prevalence of smoking and other forms of tobacco use among adolescents provides a sensitive measure of the initiation of tobacco dependence, provided that the survey methods are standardised to allow valid comparisons over time. A major initiative by the Global Youth Tobacco Survey (GYTS) Collaborative Group is administering confidential, self-administered school-based questionnaires to monitor tobacco use by adolescents aged 13 to 15 years in approximately 150 countries. More than 1 million students have already completed GYTS surveys, which provide the data on tobacco use among adolescents for 51 countries in this monograph. Surveillance using GYTS promises to be a relatively inexpensive and effective approach for measuring youth tobacco exposure.

Currently, longitudinal data on tobacco use among adolescents are available for only a few economically developed countries. An encouraging decrease in cigarette smoking among adolescents occurred in the United States between 1997 and 2001 (*see* Figure 10.3), based on nationally representative surveys of high-school students participating in the Youth Risk Behavioural Surveillance System (YRBSS) (Centre for Disease Surveillance and Prevention, 2002). The prevalence of smoking during the preceding 30 days decreased between 1997 and 2001 among males and females in each of the three largest racial and ethnic subgroups. This decrease occurred despite major increases in expenditures on tobacco promotion by the tobacco industry. This encouraging trend indicates that it is possible to reduce smoking initiation by adolescents if tobacco control measures that are known to be effective are actually implemented.

In contrast, Figure 10.4 illustrates that lifetime smoking prevalence among 15- to 16-year olds increased significantly from 1995 to 1999 in 10 of the 23 countries that participated in the European School Survey Project on Alcohol and Other Drugs (ESPAD) (Swedish Council, 2000) in both years. Lifetime prevalence was defined as reporting the use of cigarettes at least 40 times. Tobacco use among adolescents is believed to be increasing in many other countries. Over the next five years, countries that periodically measure various forms of tobacco use among adolescents through GYTS will be able to evaluate longitudinal trends. *See* Figure 10.3.

Figure 10.4 reflects even more interesting data over a wider range of countries.

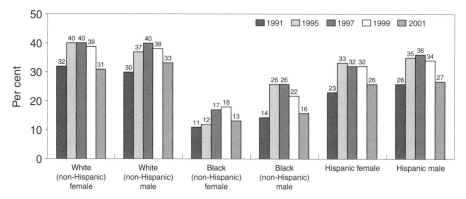

Source: Youth Risk Behavior Surveillance System, 1991, 1995, 1997, 1999, 2001, National Center for Chronic Disease Prevention and Health Promotion, Centers for Disease Control and Prevention.
Reprinted from Cancer Prevention and Early Detection Facts and Figures, 2003, American Cancer Society.

Figure 10.3: Prevalence of cigarette smoking in the last 30 days among high-school students in the US, 1991–2001.

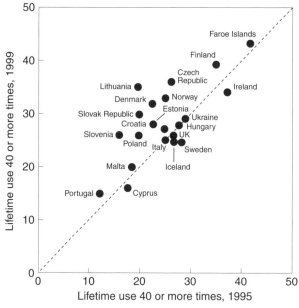

Source: European School Survey Project on Alcohol and other drugs.
http://www.ipdt/investigacao/espad99/indice.htm

Figure 10.4: Comparison of cigarette smoking among students aged 15–16 years in 1995 and 1999 in selected countries. Countries above the dotted line experienced increases in smoking prevalence.

Profiles of female tobacco use

At one time, wherever tobacco was used, smoking was very much a male-dominated activity. But, as indicated previously in this chapter, that situation has been changing rapidly over the last decade or so. Figures for 2003 now show that, globally, tobacco use is still higher for males (47%) than for females (12%) (Gajalakshmi *et al.*, 2000).

However, as shown by MacDonald (1989), even two decades ago the tobacco manufacturers had started to target the potential female market. Many firms now have, it is said, a professionally qualified psychologist on their staff whose role is to advise on advertising strategies that would exploit the psychological and cognitive vulnerabilities of young girls. If absolutely proven, of course, this would constitute selling tobacco to minors, which is a criminal offence. But it is rather difficult to prove.

The themes of tobacco marketing to women typically associate smoking with feminism, sophistication, weight control and Western-style independence (Samuel and Yoon, 2001). The rapid increase in smoking prevalence that occurred among women in Spain, Italy and Greece since the 1970s (South East Asia Tobacco Control Alliance, 2002), decades after the increase in female smoking in other Western countries, demonstrates that cultural prohibitions against tobacco use by women can be eclipsed by social change and aggressive tobacco marketing aimed at women. Recent increases in female smoking prevalence have been reported from Cambodia and Malaysia and Bangladesh. Adult smoking prevalence is actually higher in women than men in five countries: the Cook Islands, Nauru, Norway, Papua New Guinea and Sweden. In the 1999 ESPAD survey of 15- to 16-year-old school-children, girls were more likely than boys to report having smoked at least 40 times in their lifetime in eight countries (Bulgaria, Denmark, Ireland, Italy, Malta, Norway, Slovenia and the United Kingdom) (Swedish Council, 2000). A more typical pattern among adults has been the convergence of male and female smoking prevalence occurring in many countries in Europe and North America (WHO South East Asia Regional Office, 2003).

The WHO Framework Convention on Tobacco Use, Article 20, specifies that: Parties are obligated to establish, as appropriate, programmes for national, regional and global surveillance of the magnitude, patterns, determinants and consequences of tobacco consumption and exposure to tobacco smoke. This involves the development of effective national and regional systems for the epidemiological surveillance of tobacco. It also involves the integration of such programmes into global efforts to facilitate the exchange of information, and to analyse and disseminate surveillance data regarding tobacco.

Substantial efforts are underway to strengthen the infrastructure of global tobacco surveillance through the regional WHO offices. Local tobacco control advocates at the grass-roots level provide the underlying momentum for this work. Training programmes led by the Centers for Disease Control (CDC) and WHO have greatly improved the quality, standardisation and potential availability of data on tobacco use by adolescents. The expertise developed to collect, analyse and report data on youth tobacco use will facilitate the collection and analysis of other kinds of surveillance data. The development of strong and effective partnerships within countries will strengthen the local capacity for tobacco control. Passage of the draft WHO Framework Convention on Tobacco Control will provide continuing opportunities for grass-roots involvement in monitoring overt and covert violations of the convention regarding tobacco marketing.

Other indicators used in tobacco surveillance

Obviously teenagers and women do not exhaust the types of cohorts that could usefully be investigated in tobacco surveillance. Health workers, pregnant mothers and their partners, teachers, etc. – the field is wide open and the need for information critical, especially in the third world, where so many other factors are potential underminers of health.

It used to be a truism in the 1960s (after Richard Doll's work had become widely known) that hospital doctors gave up smoking in significant numbers before nurses reflected the same trend. But doctors in practices outside of the hospitals gave up more slowly than their hospital-based colleagues. Looking at it now, with the benefit of more accurate data, we can say that doctors seem quick to start up smoking in Stages 1 and 2 of the epidemic. They then often become strong anti-smoking advocates, promoting dissemination of information about how to quit and in making people more fully aware of just how dangerous the habit is.

By the good offices of such bodies as the Tobacco Free Initiative, the Centers for Disease Control, etc., WHO has been intimately and supportively involved. For instance, they have worked together with the World Medical Association and the International Council of Nurses to develop standardised approaches to data collection. To this end they have developed a standardised instrument to measure the prevalence of tobacco use and also of the knowledge, attitudes and behaviours towards smoking of all health professionals. General practitioners are important in this request because the 'family doctor' was – until very recently – a major role model.

The survey is intended to guide the development of appropriate control strategies for both care-givers and their patients. Initial data collection has been completed in Bahrain, Iran, Kuwait, Oman and the Republic of Korea. In three countries, Kuwait, the Republic of Korea and Bahrain, analyses have been completed and the reports are being disseminated and publicised through mass media.

Another indicator that reflects strategic initiatives by the transnational tobacco companies, in conjunction with national and local governments, involves trends in tobacco cultivation, processing and/or manufacture. Table 10.1 lists countries in which the acreage devoted to tobacco cultivation increased by more than 20% between 1970 and 2000. Although investments in tobacco production may be seen by local political leaders as providing a short-term economic benefit, such investments ultimately displace other, less destructive economic activities and strengthen and entrench the political base for a tobacco economy.

Land use for growing tobacco is but another reflection of the distortions caused by the control over third world health exercised by first world wealth. In Chapter 3, this issue was considered with respect to the income which can be generated by growing maize for local use compared with that which can be generated by coffee crops – or even cocaine, for that matter.

Table 10.1: Countries in which the number of hectares devoted to tobacco cultivation increased by more than 20% from 1970 to 2000

	1970	*2000*
Africa		
Zimbabwe	43 668	90 769
Malawi	41 354	118 752
Tanzania	17 500	44 000
Ghana	1630	4500
Rwanda	1100	2800
Niger	720	6200
Kenya	500	14 160
Mali	87	372
Chad	12	145
America Region		
Brazil	245 207	309 989
Honduras	4493	11 214
Guatemala	4150	8374
Panama	730	1100
Uruguay	481	830
Haiti	150	400
Other		
China	394 053	1 441 537
Malaysia	3237	9129
Syrian Arab Republic	10 212	16 726

References

ACS (American Cancer Society), IUAC (International Union Against Cancer) and WHO (World Health Organization) (2003) *Tobacco Control Country Profile*.

Centre for Disease Surveillance and Prevention (2002) www.wrongdiagnosis.com/s/smoking/basics.htm

Costa e Silva V and Thum M (2003) Introduction and review of global tobacco surveillance. In: *Tobacco Control Country Profile* (2e). ACS, IUAC and WHO, Atlanta, GA, pp 7–12.

Gajalakshmi C *et al.* (2000) Global patterns of smoking and smoking-attributable mortality. In: F Chaloupka (ed.) *Tobacco Control in Developing Countries*. Oxford University Press, Oxford.

European School Survey Project on Alcohol and Other Drugs (ESPAD) (2000) Swedish Council Report. Swedish Council, Stockholm, p.47.

Lopez A, Collishaw N and Pika T (1994) A descriptive model of the cigarette epidemic in developed countries. *Tobacco Control.* 3: 242–7.

Lopez P (2001) Future worldwide health effects of current smoking patterns. In: C Koop and M Schwartz (eds) *Critical Issue in Global Health*. Jossey-Bass, San Francisco, CA.

MacDonald T (1989) *Legal Drug Pushers Need New Clients – Are Your Kids Hooked Yet?* BUGA UP, University of Sydney.

Oluwafemi A (2000) *Regional Summary, Tobacco Control Country Profile*. The 11th World Conference on Tobacco OR Health, Kenya, pp 131–2.

Samuel J and Yoon S (2001) *Women and the Tobacco Epidemic*. WHO, Geneva.

Shafey O, Cokkinides V, Cavalcante T, Teixeira M, Vianna C and Thun M (2002) Case studies in international tobacco surveillance – cigarette smuggling in Brazil. *Tobacco Control.* 11: 215–19.

South East Asia Tobacco Control Alliance (2002) *Women and Tobacco.* Tobacco Free Asia. Penang, Malaysia.

Swedish Council for Information on Alcohol and Other Drugs (2000) *The 1999 ESPAD Report.* Vol. 2003. Department of Epidemiology and Public Health, Karolinska Institute, Stockholm, Sweden.

WHO (World Health Organization) (2000) Smoking and health among adolescents – a world perspective. In: C Currie *et al.* (eds) *Health and Health Behaviour Among Young People.* WHO Regional Office for Europe, Copenhagen.

WHO (World Health Organization) South East Asia Regional Office (2003) *Women's Health in South East Asia – Tobacco Use.* WHO, Singapore.

Chapter 11

The third world and HIV/AIDS

The changing HIV/AIDS pandemic in the third world

In a book the author wrote a few years ago (MacDonald, 2000), he devoted his attention to the situation in Africa. At that time and till now the cataclysm of HIV/AIDS (Human Immunodeficiency Virus/Acquired Immune Deficiency Syndrome) was racing through many communities, preventing the education of children, undermining rational economic planning and tearing communities apart. It illustrated most graphically the main theses of this book – namely, that the poverty and degradation of the third world is, in large measure, the result of first world financial control through global capitalism.

Only four years later AIDS has changed some of its focus. Through immense effort on the part of its own people and government, the situation in Uganda has been turned around and Uganda is rapidly becoming a model of what can be done to put health at the top of its political and social agenda and how to do it. One way, of course, is to extricate the country from its dependence on multinational pharmaceutical companies, which had been making an enormous profit in marketing antiretroviral drugs in such countries.

The trouble with that, of course, was not only that once again the first world was becoming wealthier through the third world becoming even more deprived, but that obviously only a small proportion of Uganda's population could afford the drugs. Attempts to engage in local manufacture of the necessary antiretrovirals were blocked by ruthless imposition of TRIPS regulations (*see* Chapter 1).

The US delegate to the WTO fought for eight months to stall negotiations designed to assess the safety and efficacy of much cheaper generic copies of the first world's antiretrovirals. As Fiona Flick (September 2003) reported:

> *A long awaited trade deal to give poor nations access to cheap lifesaving drugs for diseases such as AIDS, malaria and tuberculosis was agreed on August 30th 2003, after eight months of stalling mainly due to US objections.*

At that meeting of the WTO (*see* Chapter 4) there were only 146 nations represented and they all hailed it as a 'major breakthrough'. But some aid organisations were less enthralled. For instance, Médecins Sans Frontières argued that 'it threw up new legal, economic and political obstacles' to poor countries wishing to import (from other larger third world countries such as Brazil or India) cheap generic copies of patented drugs. In that respect, of course, it may still have been good news to US and other first world pharmaceutical companies. Until now, under the WTO 'compulsory' licence, patents for lifesaving drugs could not be waived for countries that could produce their own generic copies. It was illegal to import or export them.

The agreement came about in the face of a joint statement from African nations, which pointed out that 2.2 million Africans had already died from AIDS between the Doha meeting where the matter was first raised in 2001 and 2003.

Just before considering the situation in Africa up to 2000, though, let us look at the sinister progress of AIDS through the third world countries.

Consider the following statement from the Chronic Poverty Report (2004–2005) (*see* Box 11.1).

Box 11.1   Are rich countries and their citizens really committed to reducing poverty? Targeting MDG 8

The bold Millennium Declaration from 189 countries that 'We are committed to making the Right to Development a reality for everyone and to freeing the entire human race from want' is not yet matched by bold actions on the part of the developed world.

Goal 8 of the Millennium Development Goals declares the establishment of a global partnership for development. It promises the Least Developed Countries (where the greatest concentrations of chronically poor people live) tariff and quota-free access for their exports; an enhanced programme of debt relief for HIPC and cancellation of official bilateral debt; and more aid for countries committed to poverty reduction.

What has followed this declaration? Trade talks at Cancun have failed as OECD countries refused to open up their highly protected agricultural markets; debt reduction has proceeded at a snail's pace; and rich countries have made promises of more Overseas Development Assistance (ODA) at Monterrey but have not committed anything like the necessary resources.

MDG Goals 1–7 – all of which are the primary responsibility of developing countries – have agreed targets that are regularly monitored. There is less emphasis on quantifiable targets, however, for MDG Goal 8, which is about what rich countries do.

The *Morning Star* (12 July 2004) published the following account by a social work student in Mumbai. The account is entirely factual except that Sonali is not the protagonist's real name. It had to be changed in this account for family reasons (Somandahan, 2004).

> *On seeing Sonali's frozen body, I was overwhelmed. Less than three months ago, this child played hopscotch with me. It was painful to see her still, in a morgue in Mumbai, India's economic capital.*
>
> *I was angry with her parents, who had infected her with HIV and died, leaving her to the care of a support home. And I dared not think about the fate of the 55 other children like Sonali with whom I worked.*
>
> *The first time I saw her, she was playing with her friends, a very jovial and friendly child. She loved to laugh and dance to the tune of the latest Hindi film songs.*
>
> *A good student, she loved the school.*
>
> *Nearly a month later, I came to know that she had fallen ill.*
>
> *Tuberculosis. Her immune system was weak.*
>
> *On hearing that she was in the local municipal hospital, I visited her.*
>
> *It took me some time to find her because she was given the last bed in the children's ward, facing a corner.*

It was an act of discretion on the part of the nurses, who otherwise treated her with indifference.

A few weeks later, her tuberculosis worsened and affected her brain. When I visited her again at her corner bed, she was in pain. A nurse was massaging her head. She was nearly comatose and was not responding to any of her visitors.

The doctor on rounds told us that several tests needed to be done.

But Sonali's care home could not afford these expensive tests. With drastic cuts in public health funds, the hospital could no longer conduct free tests.

After some convincing, the doctor agreed to give a concession. But she was dismayed that she could not give specific drugs that could prolong the child's life.

Less than a mile away, there is a well-equipped hospital, a 'five-star hospital', as the local people say, which could have given Sonali the best of care.

But it was far beyond her reach. Medical costs and drugs are expensive and access to medical care is a block that defines life and death. Sonali is not a case in isolation.

The child felt a little better and was brought back to the support home.

She started smiling again, and her friends were happy.

But, soon enough, her condition deteriorated. Severe headaches. Her little friends would stay up until early morning, massaging her head, chatting to her.

Sonali was again sent back to her corner bed in the municipal hospital, where her condition deteriorated further. She stopped eating and now her food and medicine had to be administered intravenously.

Last time that I saw her alive, she could not recognise me. And she did not answer when I called. In a more caring world, maybe, just maybe, she would have lived longer in less pain (Somanadahan, 2004, p.7).

Let us look briefly at India and China. From 2000 until 2004, the AIDS pandemic has gained rapidly. The same thing is already happening in the Russian Federation. The latter has suffered a disastrous increase in poverty and an almost total withdrawal of their once excellent state-run health service since the collapse of the Soviet Union barely 15 years ago. This almost certainly is responsible for the rapidity of advance of AIDS in that country.

Altogether in India, China and the Russian Federation (RFA), AIDS rates are now increasing rapidly. Indeed, this is now impacting severely on the not-at-risk group. Because of its uneven prevalence over all, infection is often easier than not. The Chronic Poverty Report (2004–2005) asserts that low overall prevalence rates serve to mask huge local differences. It is to be hoped that the Asian states (as well as the first world) learn from Africa's successes and failures. Yet again, this is an opportunity for the first world to make a more concerted, and less profit-driven, effort to ameliorate the situation. It is a global problem. We cannot stand aside from it. The United Nations programme for HIV/AIDS (UNAIDS) has stated that:

China presently has about one million people with HIV/AIDS. UNAIDS expect the incidence of HIV to soar in the context of ever-widening socio-economic disparities and massive amounts of migration. These prevalence rates are estimated to rise tenfold by the end of the decade. In 2001, China launched a five-year AIDS action plan, signalling a growing recognition of the huge task at hand (UNAIDS, 2002).

After South Africa, India has the most people living with HIV/AIDS of any country, an estimated 3.97 million as of the end of 2001, and rising. If HIV/AIDS is not brought under control, it is likely to undermine progress made in reducing poverty, particularly in the southern states. In July 2003, a National Parliamentary Convention on HIV/AIDS was convened, in which over 1000 political leaders from mayors to ministers took part. The Executive Director of UNAIDS described the event as 'historic':

> *Never before, in any nation of the world, has there been such a large and committed gathering of the leaders from every level of decision-making, dedicated to the common cause of fighting AIDS (UNAIDS, 2002).*

Third world women and AIDS

The recent International HIV/AIDS Conference in Bangkok is coming to an end as these words are being written and are expected to reveal a deeply worsening situation worldwide, while acknowledging great progress in certain areas. In the third world, women are particularly vulnerable because in so many cases they are in no position to assume their human rights. They often acquire AIDS through having the attention of HIV-positive and promiscuous males forced upon them. When the author was in India in 1981, it was not uncommon for very young girls to be raped, and thus become infected with sexually transmitted diseases (STDs).

Many third world cultures do not acknowledge women's rights over a range of issues involving access to information, property and inheritance, etc.

Human Rights Watch (2003) points out that both in law and in practice, women are disadvantaged especially in sub-Saharan Africa, South Asia and the Middle East. An unequal or absent means of inheriting, managing and trading property, especially land, is a major maintainer of poverty among women and their dependants. The effect of this discrimination is multiplied when it emerges suddenly and brutally after a husband's death, by which time many households are already reduced to extreme poverty. Throughout southern and eastern Africa, a high proportion of widows and their children are left destitute when their dead husband's relatives snatch their property – theft in the guise of tradition, fostered by unequal and unenforced laws.

Nepal also is well known to the author. Govinda Prasad Dahal has been of particular value in this regard (Dahal, 2004). In his research into the sexual behaviour of young men in Nepal, he found that one in 12 single men were sexually active but of these, 20% engaged in 'risky sex'. This he defines as: 'Persons with multiple partners in the last 12 months, plus persons with one non-regular partner where a condom was not used.' The vulnerability of women in such a context is not difficult to imagine.

In fact, at the International AIDS Conference in Bangkok, Dr Peter Piot, Executive Director of UNAIDS, has referred to this whole problem as 'the feminisation of the epidemic'. Dr Andrew Farber, reporting from the conference as a member of NHS Health and Development Networks, has said that: 'Women are physically more susceptible to HIV infection. Male to female transmission during sex is twice as likely to occur than female to male and women now make up nearly 60% of all those infected with HIV in sub-Saharan Africa.'

Campaigns of public sexual health education in the third world are gradually increasing. The strategy goes under the acronym of ABC (Abstinence, Be faithful, Condoms). But despite this, marriage and long-term monogamous relationships do not protect women from HIV. In Cambodia, recent studies indicate that 13% of urban and 10% of rural men reported having sex with both a sex worker and their wife or steady girlfriend. In Thailand, a 1999 study found that 75% of HIV-infected women were likely to have been infected by their husbands. In parts of Africa, it appears that marriage actually increases women's HIV risk. In some African countries, married 15- to 19-year-old women have higher HIV infection levels than unmarried sexually active females of the same age.

In the light of these facts, there was considerable criticism in Bangkok of reliance on the ABC approach to AIDS prevention being pushed by initiatives such as the US president's emergency plan for AIDS relief. Clearly, ABC will fail to protect married women unable to negotiate condom use with their husbands.

However, as already suggested, social, cultural and psychological factors impinging on many third world women merely accentuate their biological susceptibility. Certain key areas for community action have been identified by the Global Coalition of Women and AIDS. This is an international pressure group and their call for action is enshrined in a UN report, *Woman and HIV/AIDS: Confronting the Crisis*, which was released at the Bangkok conference. However, the International AIDS Conference also made it clear that there would be no quick fixes. In terms of prevention, for example, access to the female condom, itself far from ideal, remains poor. Microbicides, chemicals placed into the vagina to prevent HIV transmission, are still being tested and will not be available within the next five years. Even then they may be less than 50% effective. An HIV vaccine seems as elusive as ever.

But there are some signs of hope. Sonya Gandhi, leader of the ruling Indian Congress Party, spoke at the closing ceremony of the conference of her commitment to controlling HIV in India. For the first time, the Indian government is to put its own resources, in addition to donated funds, into the fight against AIDS. Graca Machel, patron of the leadership programme in the conference and the wife of Nelson Mandela, identified the need to develop female leaders. Kofi Annan talked of the need for societies to recognise that educating girls is not an option, but a necessity. The ability of the international community to turn these statements into practical action will be judged at the next international AIDS conference in Toronto in 2006.

The Guardian (19 July 2004) described the international AIDS conference as 'the most political, most desperately passionate and most exuberant scientific meeting on the planet'. Others have described it as a party. But now the party is over for another two years. Randall Tobias, the US president's global AIDS coordinator, summarised by saying that he hoped that Bangkok would be 'a turning point into an era of compassionate action. All of us share a great responsibility, and time is short'.

Back to Africa

Despite the phenomenal successes of countries such as Uganda over recent years, HIV is spreading exponentially in other areas of that continent. Over large regions, such as Sudan, Dafur and Chad, viciously destructive wars are still being fought. This obviously undermines all of the involved communities, first economically and then, because of that, healthwise. War has never been known as a particularly good context for human rights or gentlemanly behaviour and is an excellent breeding ground for HIV infection. It doesn't always require a war, though. Take Malawi as a case in point. The Chronic Poverty Report (2004–2005) provides the following information on page 43 of its report.

The food crisis in Malawi in early 2002 resulted in several hundred, perhaps several thousand, hunger-related deaths. Starving Malawians resorted to eating unripe and unconventional foods, including flour fortified by maize cobs and sawdust, much of which made them ill. Malnutrition was high, not only among young children, older people and the ill, but also among working adults. An estimated 30% of the population required emergency aid.

The famine can be explained in two ways. The technical view is that an environmental shock (bad weather), limited information, and import bottlenecks resulted in famine. The political view attributes blame to different actors, depending on who one talks to: the IMF for recommending the sale of strategic food stock; Malawian politicians for selling off the entire food reserve, and making money on the side; complacent government and donor officials; and profiteering traders inflating prices. The truth lies somewhere in a combination of the technical and political views.

In addition to these immediate causes of famine, there are a number of underlying vulnerability factors that left poor Malawians unable to cope with a production shock that was actually less severe than the drought of 1991–1992:

- declining soil fertility and neglect of smallholder agriculture, particularly in remote areas
- deepening poverty that decimated asset buffers (foodstocks, savings)
- weakened informal systems of social protection in poor communities
- the demographic and economic consequences of HIV/AIDS.

Better weather in mid-2003 has been followed by a period of low rainfall. Recent reports describe a country struggling through the lean season, on the brink of another food crisis.

The Zimbabwe situation until 2002

The author had access to information about HIV/AIDS in Zimbabwe up until 2002. After that, due to the political situation there, such data and informed comment became less dependable. In many ways Zimbabwe represents an archetype of a third world country in which health programmes have been drastically undermined by totalitarian rule. In Chapter 1 Zimbabwe was used as a good example of a country trying to resist the inroads of first world corporate interests. Its government had stipulated that it would only borrow from the IMF/World Bank up to the extent that repayment on the loans would not exceed 10% of export earnings. We have seen how short-lived this policy was.

As one of many third world nations, and as one among several in Africa itself, Zimbabwe was in no position to dictate to either the IMF or the first world banks behind it. If it needed loans, Zimbabwe would have to agree to structural adjustment policies and everything stemming from them. No doubt, had there existed some huge pan-African bloc negotiating as a whole with the IMF, things might have been different, but that was not the case. Second, Zimbabwe along with South Africa, Zambia and Tanzania have been among the world leaders in levels of HIV/

AIDS prevalence. And finally, this author's continuing access to health institutions and to health personnel in Zimbabwe has allowed him to document, especially on the basis of the HIV/AIDS epidemic, pivotal issues in the matter of global health promotion. This has been especially valuable in illustrating how intrusive non-medical cultural factors are and, at the same time, how entrenched gender in-equalities interfere with health promotion. It is the overriding aim of this chapter to show how IMF funding renders these obstacles to health promotion more, rather than less, problematical.

Health promotion, empowerment and African women

Lalonde (1974) stated that a very important element of health promotion is empowerment, a process whereby individual people are encouraged to assert their own autonomy and their self-esteem sufficiently to be able to identify their own health agendas, rather than being told what to do or what is good for their health. But any initiative aimed at engendering empowerment must have a focus, and the focus of this chapter is on women's empowerment generally in the third world and with special emphasis on promoting safer sex in the face of HIV and AIDS. A number of factors render this concern of pivotal relevance. For instance, the vast majority of the third world's women are poor and lacking in basic education. They can be largely categorised as illiterate women, both married and single, who are perhaps the most disadvantaged of all groups in the world. The author deals here primarily with Zimbabwe, but this is an arbitrary choice, and much the same could be said of Nepal, or many other third world countries in which this author has worked. By definition, empowerment must involve some conflict of social values. This chapter argues that it is possible to empower women, but that prevention programmes have not taken into account the cultural, social and economic constraints and the male gender roles imposed on most African women which obstruct the empowerment process. As will also become evident, the fiscal constraints imposed by structural adjustment policies to meet IMF criteria are rendering the problem even more intractable.

HIV/AIDS in the African context

It is generally agreed that men and women in most sub-Saharan African countries are equally at risk of acquiring HIV. With approximately 80% of the risk attributable to heterosexual transmission, prevention, at least in theory, is within the reach of every adult. HIV's prevalence is currently conservatively estimated at 1 million people with about 25% of the adult, sexually active population infected. In fine, this means that about a quarter of working people in Zimbabwe are HIV-positive (Loewenson and Kerkhoven, 1995). The figures relating to Zimbabwe's HIV/AIDS epidemic can be summarised as follows as of 2000:

- 35% urban HIV prevalence
- 20% rural HIV prevalence
- 1.2 million people HIV-positive

- 200 000 people have developed AIDS
- 90 000 have died of AIDS.

Fiscal considerations, of course, are a major constraint. Because of the continued absence of a preventive vaccine or until therapy recently to cure AIDS, measures for prevention remained the mainstay of Zimbabwean public health promotion strategy. Interventions, such as behavioural change or factors influencing changes in behaviour, such as regular condom use and loyalty to one sexual partner (Mbizvo, 1997), are prominent. Interventions towards HIV prevention are promoted at the clinics, workplaces, in the community, at nightclubs, soccer matches, political rallies, bus stations, within the family, and during lunch-breaks at both government and non-government enterprises.

Among social scientists and health professionals, however, there is widespread concern that many women in the developing countries may not have the power to negotiate change for either themselves or their partners (Worth, 1989). Behavioural change that is driven by crisis is difficult and painful for everyone, but modifying behaviour to prevent HIV transmission poses a special challenge to women (Ulin, 1992). It should come as no surprise that in Zimbabwe the focus of women's health needs has tended to be limited to those that are related to pregnancy, childbirth and child health to the exclusion of women's health in general, particularly sexual health.

Obviously, there are many sources of empowerment, but in this author's opinion, to promote safer sex would certainly empower women. The promotion of safer sex per se, and throughout the country, is what should have priority, but IMF targets only direct money to vertical and regional specific remit programmes. A health promotion-based initiative would have to converge on two themes, according to Webb (1997) – behavioural empowerment and structural empowerment.

> *Behavioural empowerment allows girls and women to have more control over their sexual activity, either through resisting sexual advances or through negotiating safer sex. It is the increase in decision-making ability of the women that renders them less vulnerable to infection as the incidence of unsafe sex is reduced (Webb, 1997).*

Structural empowerment involves nothing less than the reduction of economic dependence on men and the improvement of women's socio-legal status (Webb, 1997).

Why women are especially vulnerable

Any consideration of a society's sexual health will rely heavily on initiatives directed at women. But this is especially so with HIV/AIDS for four reasons.

- Women in Africa are being portrayed as the 'dangerous victim of the AIDS outbreak'. The devastating level of infection documented on prostitutes is gratuitously interpreted to mean that, without them, the epidemic would not be occurring (Bassett and Mhloyi, 1991).
- In comparison with men, women have an increased risk of exposure to HIV infection and increased vulnerability to developing AIDS for reasons related indirectly and directly to their gender.

- Contextual socio-cultural factors, including the following: widowhood; inheritance; polygamy; low power to make decisions in sexual matters; and lack of access of information (De Bruyn, 1992).
- Poor diet, poor hygiene, prostitution, and the necessity for some students and young women to use sex as an economic resource (exploitation by 'sugar daddies') (Schoepf, 1983).

Ethnological considerations would lead us to believe that women have greater vulnerability. All STDs, including AIDS, are transmitted more efficiently from men to women. Research indicates that men appear to pass on HIV more efficiently than women during unprotected vaginal intercourse, making women more likely to be infected by men than for men to be infected by women.

The cultural context in which any health strategy has to operate is crucial. For example, Stein (1990) comments that the success of current HIV prevention strategies among heterosexual couples depends not so much on efficacy as such, as on the strategy's acceptability to the male partner and on the informed cooperation of both partners. The author argues that until women have it within their power to exercise protection independently, the use of condoms as a way of practising safer sex will require women to resort to persuasive or coercive tactics. This alternative may be difficult for many women, especially in the face of economic dependency and societal expectations of a more compliant female role.

Once again, we must turn to anthropology for further contextualising insights. To appreciate the plight of the Zimbabwean women, it is necessary to briefly consider Zimbabwean marital customs. In the societies of Shona and Ndebele, the main purpose of marriage is to produce children for the husband's lineage. In order to secure the right to the children, the husband's family needs to pay a bride price (lobola) and other sums of money to the wife's family. A wife is expected to be obedient to her husband and in-laws, hard working and respectful. However, the most important requirement is that she be able to bear children. In the author's experience, Zimbabwean societies prefer sons to be born, rather than daughters. Sons are preferred as they can carry on their father's lineage, while daughters get married to other men and do not carry on their father's lineage.

Local culture and HIV prevention

As in many other cultures, the death of a woman's husband in Zimbabwe is invested with huge consequences. Chabal *et al.* (1995, cited in Campbell, 1997) report that childlessness is a source of shame and humiliation and is reflected in different funeral rites for childless people. These rites are intended to prevent the deceased from returning as a ghost to wreak havoc because of their anger at not having children. As the woman's husband pays lobola for the right to the couple's children, the position of a married woman is severely threatened if she does not bear children. Often, her in-laws and husband will blame her for the infertility. In the author's experience, although the infertility problem may lie with the husband, that possibility is often ignored and not even acknowledged by men. Biased and ignorant views ensure that the woman is almost always blamed for infertility. The husband's family may even send the wife back to her family and demand a refund of the lobola, or demand a female relative as a second wife to bear children in her stead, thereby effecting polygamy. Both partners may resort to sex with other partners to effect a pregnancy, thereby putting both partners at greater risk from contracting HIV. Thus, marriage affects the family relationships of men and women in different ways. A married man remains part of his family of origin all his life, while a wife leaves her family to become part of another one.

This immediately makes it obvious that no real improvement in the situation can be expected unless a long-term view is adopted, featuring the strengthening and furthering of general basic education. But, between 1989 and 1996, Zimbabwe reduced spending on primary schooling by 48% and on secondary education by 31% in order to meet SAP criteria! In many rural areas this entailed the outright elimination of access to schooling where such had existed before.

This author argues that although the health promotion message is that of empowering women, it is well nigh impossible to begin to attain that goal because of the poverty and gender-related factors that prevail in the everyday life of the women. Moreover, the eradication of those factors requires a political commitment of more use of public funds for education. But HIV prevention strategies can only empower women to a limited extent. Beyond that they will require the cooperation and support of their male counterparts.

Male condoms: culture and consequences

Persuading men to use condoms, especially during recreational sex, has long been reported as difficult in all societies. But some argue that this represents an even greater problem for African men and for a number of cultural reasons. This is especially so if the men are already married. Many studies have pointed out that many people do not enjoy using condoms and prefer to have intercourse without them (Campbell, 1997). Attention has been drawn to the fact that women often have difficulty in negotiating condom use because of the power imbalances between the sexes. The author argues that even when women ask their husbands and partners to use condoms, they often encounter male refusal, are accused of adultery or promiscuity, are suspected of already being infected with HIV or are said to accuse their partners of infidelity (Schoepf, 1983). This view is supported by Wight (1992), who points out that condom use often implies sexual activity outside the primary relationship, or even promiscuity. The limited control that women have in determining their own lives forms part of the social substrate of the current epidemic. The subordination of African women in patrilineal societies places them at a special disadvantage with regard to their ability or willingness to intervene and to reduce their own risk of HIV infection. For many women, faced with divorce or dire poverty on the one hand and the risk of HIV infection on the other, the choice becomes one of social death or biological death (Bassett and Mhloyi, 1991).

Wilson (1990) argues that studies of sub-Saharan Africa suggest that, although there is a high level of knowledge about HIV transmission, this knowledge has not resulted in effective and appropriate sexual risk reduction practices, specifically condom use. Maposhere *et al.* (1995) revealed that only 38% of Harare men reported condom use. Campbell and Kelly (1995) point to beliefs that it is harmful for a man not to be sexually relieved when he feels the urge. Fears that men will go elsewhere to find sexual relief may prompt women to have sex with their partners in an attempt to ensure sexual fidelity. In this way, a woman's own and her children's economic stability is ensured by her sexual compliance, even within a context where sexual activity outside the relationship is common or even expected.

In predominantly agrarian societies, production of offspring is held to be of high importance. Thus, in African societies the greatest deterrent to the use of condoms may be their contraceptive effect. The limited success of family planning programmes in sub-Saharan countries is testimony to the powerful social and cultural constraints on any effort to reduce fertility. Indeed the resistance of African families to contraception has hindered efforts to prevent vertical transmission of HIV (Ulin, 1992).

In addition, stresses within individual families play a major role. For instance, studies from several sub-Saharan African countries document women's fears of family conflict, economic loss and lowered self-esteem if they advocate condom use (Bledsoe, 1989, and Perlez, 1991, cited in Ulin, 1992). Nonetheless, these women are acutely aware of their own risk of acquiring AIDS and the vulnerability of their children if they should become infected. At the centre of this conflict of values is the condom. For many the condom is not a symbol of reproductive health but of the painful process of negotiating behavioural change.

Even in developed nations, some women feel ambivalent about insisting on condom use. African women with whom this author has discussed the matter often say that, if they do carry male condoms, they feel embarrassment about every stage of condom use. They put their reputation at risk, by buying condoms, carrying them and asking for their use. All these aspects are very difficult for them. Having a condom on one's person indicates a lack of sexual innocence, an unfeminine identity and that of a woman actively seeking sex (Lear, 1995). The author, in speaking with numerous Zimbabwean women, agrees with the view that men will assume that such a woman is cheap and easy and most probably a prostitute.

Are female condoms the answer?

One solution may be to promote the use of female condoms. The current introduction of female condoms may empower women (Stein, 1990). Since it is used by the woman rather than the man, it gives women greater control over sexual decision-making. Ironically, while empowering women to some degree, it may free men from taking responsibility for their own health (Richardson, 1990). Thus there is a certain ambivalence among women about the real advantages of the female condom.

Also, the female condom is much more expensive than the male equivalent and few women can afford it. Research carried out by Ray *et al.* (1995) on commercial sex workers and family planning clinics in both urban and rural areas showed all three groups reacting favourably and even preferring them to the traditional male version. Sex workers are particularly insistent that it is important, recognising the advantage of having more power to negotiate the use of condoms simply by virtue of the exchange relationship between buyer and seller. However, to the extent that most women lack a voice in sexual decision-making, AIDS prevention campaigns may be over-optimistic in expecting sudden behaviour change. Winters (1997) reports that the government of Zimbabwe and other donor agencies are helping to empower women by selling the female condoms at subsidised prices for women in the lower socioeconomic groups. Such categorisation in itself raises problems, of course. Although the female condoms are being sold at subsidised prices, they are not systematically or efficiently distributed across the country. The author thinks that the World Health Organization (WHO) and other international bodies must play their part in facilitating availability of female condoms for all women. Surprisingly, it is an enterprise that has not yet attracted a great deal of response from NGO aid groups.

Sexually transmitted diseases as an 'acceptable risk'

Speedy response to STD infection is crucial, and thus an important way of empowering women would be to educate them to seek help in the event of them contracting such an infection. Research indicates that the transmission of HIV is facilitated by genital ulcer disease which causes lesions and disrupts the mucosal barrier, and this in turn facilitates HIV transmission (Subuga *et al.*, 1990, cited in Pitts *et al.*, 1995). Bassett and Mhloyi (1991) suggest that the link between STDs and AIDS is twofold. First the presence of STDs serves as a marker of sexual activity outside the family unit, thus indicating areas where AIDS is likely to spread. Second, in Zimbabwe, nearly half of genital ulcer incidence is due to chancroid infections in men.

Women experience fewer STD symptoms, and even when they do, they tend to avoid STD care because of stigmatism and because they accept discomfort as part of their reproductive lives. Over 80% of women with STDs receive no care, thus increasing HIV vulnerability (Pitts, 1995). The author argues that even if the women go to clinics, the nurses at the clinics often convey a very judgemental attitude to these women because STDs are regarded as a sign of promiscuity on the women's part. There is no privacy, and confidentiality is not assured. This, in turn, makes the vulnerable women avoid the STD treatment which they so need in order to reduce the risk of HIV contraction. Again, this illustrates a real inadequacy in a policy of reducing public spending on general education and directing IMF funding to vertical, interventionist, practices and projects.

In many societies, cultural double standards honour men who have many sexual partners while stigmatising women who have sexual relations outside marriage. Having STDs is almost regarded as a rite of passage into manhood and proof of sexual activity! The author advocates the view that women should be educated about the signs and symptoms of STDs and the importance of seeking early treatment. The author is in agreement that more research is necessary to examine possible intervention strategies which may develop women's power, increase their ability to negotiate sexual matters and persuade men that the use of condoms is not unmanly. Pitts (1995) also argues that the belief that men have rights to multiple sexual partners needs to be challenged, and many health programmes will continue to be only partly effective in changing behaviour until these issues of inequality between the genders are more fully addressed.

Impact of the lack of basic education

This author found (MacDonald, 1998) that about 30% of a sample of 500 London 16–18-year-old girls had seriously incomplete knowledge of the actual basic anatomy underlying their sexual health. It is not surprising that in Zimbabwe studies suggest that most women do not know how their reproductive organs work. There are some cultural beliefs that put women more at risk of HIV infection. For example, there is widely held belief that the vagina should be dry, tight and hot for a man to enjoy sex. The herbal ointments that these women use should be discouraged, as they may damage the vaginal wall and open the way for HIV and other STD transmission (Brown *et al.*, 1993). Such mythology can only gain widespread credence in societies in which schools do not widely, and from an early age, address human sexuality as a routine part of the curriculum. Lack of such education also encourages unquestioning acceptance of male dominance values. For instance, in many of these communities the success of a couple's sex life is measured in terms of the amount of pleasure the man receives and women define their satisfaction by the degree of pleasure they give.

In 1994, Civic and Wilson found that when couples practise dry sex with a condom, there is a very good chance of the condom breaking, thus exposing the couple to a high risk of contracting HIV. Results of the same study suggest that, although individuals may accept handouts of condoms and initiate condom use, they may not use them effectively.

But let us not ignore the existing sources of women's empowerment, for even in male-dominated societies women have a certain degree of autonomy which expresses itself in women's groups. Rural women have always found strength in informal organisations, mobilising themselves around specific needs and activities and using neighbourhood groups and other informal networks to accomplish their aims. To quote March and Taggy (1982):

> *Women's associations promote confidence, organise leadership and resources and thereby create leverage for women, although they may not prevent the overall structural authority of men over women, they do redistribute power and resources in some very important way.*

Thus we see that women who share common experiences, and face common risks, can make a conscious decision to take action with the expectation that the benefits to all will ultimately outweigh the costs. Through informal associations and networking, African women in the general population typically rally behind each other to solve numerous common problems (March and Taggy, 1982). However, Ulin (1992) argues that this source of strength seems not to have been recognised and utilised by the policy-makers who direct AIDS campaigns. Women's collective perception of their ability to act as AIDS prevention agents could be a critical determinant of both female and male behaviour change. But such 'local group autonomy' does not fit in with privately funded SAP initiatives.

Empowering function of local advocacy groups

It goes without saying that empowerment of one segment of a society cannot occur without wider impact. Although these solidarity groups aim to empower women, they too can threaten the man's power and superiority. Many women can go so far, up to a certain extent permitted by their husbands, but no further. Afshar (1998) commented that men do not like to be threatened by women. As a result, because of this fear, they prevent their wives by violence and force from enacting what they have learned from the solidarity group, thus disempowering the woman again. This observation is supported by Webb (1997), who points out that such actions make the implementation of the empowerment process extremely problematic, inhibiting any widespread changes in the position of women in the short term.

These considerations suggest a way forward, for if empowerment to alter risky behaviour lies within the women's solidarity groups, then these informal associations of African women may be a powerful potential vehicle for normative change. Nevertheless, women's empowerment is only half the solution. Men too must acknowledge their joint responsibility and all members of society must be willing to redefine sexual roles in relation to the health of the family and the community. But this can only happen if the local women's solidarity groups are accorded a higher profile in government funding. The perceived respect which such groups are seen to attract would be pivotally effective in discouraging village men from trivialising or opposing them.

Entrenching poverty – an SAP bequest

It has been argued throughout this book that structural adjustment policies often exacerbate, rather than ameliorate, the financing of health initiatives in third world countries. Again, the most important factor governing HIV/AIDS prevention programmes is that of poverty. This poverty affects the women most because of the lack of economic opportunities, and the social inequality of women increases their vulnerability to HIV/AIDS and STDs. During the years 1991 to 1993 the economic security of every citizen in Zimbabwe became increasingly threatened by the introduction of the Economic Structural Adjustment Programme (ESAP). The programme was imposed by the World Bank on Zimbabwe to repay the International Monetary Fund loan. Though this programme aimed to improve living conditions of the population by making the economy more productive and competitive, for the great majority of people of low socioeconomic status its immediate effects were exactly the opposite (Meursing, 1997).

Sexual health has been even further jeopardised in Zimbabwe by economic recession. That, together with ESAP programmes, has aggravated the transmission and undermined the control of HIV infection in Zimbabwe and Africa in two major ways: directly by increasing the population at risk through increased urban migration, the subsequent impoverishment and women's powerlessness, and prostitution; and indirectly through a decrease in healthcare provision (Saunders and Abdulrahman, 1991).

As is often the case, the forces of nature have also not been cooperative. The economic strain caused by ESAP was compounded by the severe drought of 1991 and 1992. George and Sabelli (1994) state that approximately $50 000 is leaving Zimbabwe every hour to pay back the IMF loan. Stoneman (1994, cited in George and Sabelli, 1994) commented that, at the behest of the World Bank, Zimbabwe has also turned one of Africa's best healthcare and educational records into a virtual shambles. As one woman put it: '"Health For All by the year 2000" is not going to be achieved. Instead, because of ESAP, it will be Death For All by the year 2000. The elite will not die but they will be very lonely, there will be no one to live with them.'

Consider just some of the negative impacts so far engendered. Many women can no longer afford hospital births. Children are leaving school early; girls will be the first to be withdrawn from school in order to assist in the home. In Zimbabwe approximately 70% of hospital bed occupancy is HIV-related. The World Bank estimates that the direct hospital cost per Zimbabwean AIDS patient averages US$614. On top of all that, women – once they have become infected – have a shorter survival expectancy than men. There are several reasons. Women have less access to healthcare. Unlike men, they engage in numerous activities which do not stop when they are ill; they are also expected to care for their sick husbands or relatives, regardless of their own health. When women are unwell, fewer household members care for them (Barnet and Blackie, 1992). In interviews of Zimbabwean hospital workers, this author was told that often relatives will encourage a man who appears fit and well to leave his AIDS-stricken wife and find another one, with no understanding that he may pass the infection on to another woman.

Any serious attempt at reversing these negative effects must involve policy changes. Clearly, strategies to address the impact of AIDS on women are most likely to be effective if they approach the problem at different levels, working to reverse women's social, economic and legal disadvantage simultaneously of AIDS on their lives (Danzier, 1994). This is the complete opposite of the sort of IMF-favoured 'vertical planning'. For example, enhancing opportunities for women's economic independence may require legal and economic reform, and changes in social and educational policy, as well as community programmes for social reform. All of these require more government commitment to public policy initiatives, rather than the blind action of market forces. At the same time, efforts need to be made at the community level to change customs and attitudes which perpetuate women's disadvantages. Again, this challenges basic education provision even more than it challenges specific healthcare.

Solutions to the women's health crisis

In conclusion, this author would say that realistic solutions to the real problem of women's health must transcend the purely clinical. To empower women with respect to HIV/AIDS, the epidemic demands renewed focus on poverty reduction and female economic participation. There must be greater focus on proven poverty-reducing approaches, including: land redistribution; abolition of education and health fees; and vocational training to prepare students, including orphans, for self-employment.

Good health promotion practice should focus on advocacy, and progress in addressing the impact of AIDS on women also requires that women be empowered by giving them opportunities and resources for self-help. Barnet and Blackie (1992) found that, in the absence of formal support networks, women developed ad hoc mechanisms for coping with the impact of the epidemic. By meeting at markets, churches, roadsides and in homes, discussing with each other their and other women's concerns, exchanging comic tales about AIDS and condoms, these informal counselling sessions can be a means for women to gain the courage to fight against the injustices of their society.

Most importantly, serious efforts have to be directed at critically analysing social and cultural factors. Society as a whole shares both the burden of AIDS and the responsibility for its prevention. However, our current limited means for preventing HIV infections have put women in the difficult position of having to find ways to control male sexual behaviour. Perhaps the AIDS and gender debate is best defined by Jonathan Mann's (1997) famous statement: 'male dominated societies are the greatest threat to public health in the world today'.

Whatever process is used, this chapter has tried to argue that social scientists working on AIDS prevention strategies have to acknowledge and address the cultural, social, and economic constraints and gender inequality issues that obstruct the empowerment process for women. By addressing these issues, HIV prevention strategies will help empower women, families and communities to mobilise their human resources to promote at each local level the well-being of all their members.

A diluted WHO target on HIV/AIDS

The WHO 56th World Health Assembly in Geneva (19–28 May 2003) passed a resolution on 'Global Health Sector Strategy for HIV/AIDS', backing away from re-endorsing its year 2000 strategy, called the three-by-five target. That referred to the aim of ensuring that 3 million people with AIDS receive antiretroviral treatment by 2005. Instead, they changed the target's language to 'bearing it in mind' – and this was done at the request of some first world countries in the EU. The concern remains that the global fight against HIV/AIDS continues to be grossly under-funded, with the failure to facilitate access to available treatment to the millions dying of the disease in Africa and other developing regions. This represents a denial of the fundamental human right to health. India submitted an amendment to the AIDS resolution, calling on countries to increase expenditures on global AIDS programmes, recalling the commitment by all member countries to the UN at the 2001 UN General Assembly Special Session on HIV/AIDS to give US$7–10 billion per year by 2005, but it was not accepted. NGOs such as Health GAP, Act UP Paris and other Fund-the-Fund allies advocated a dues-based commitment to full funding of the Global Fund to Fight AIDS, tuberculosis and malaria. However, no explicit language to this effect was forthcoming.

Huge obstacles, linked to the financial interests of the first world pharmaceutical companies, still remain, as Owen Dyer reports in the *British Medical Journal* (3 April 2004).

International health charities have accused George Bush's administration of trying to block developing countries' access to cheap AIDS drugs by questioning the quality of 'three in one' generic combination drugs.

At a meeting in August 2004 in Gaborone, Botswana, the US global AIDS coordinator, Randall Tobias, said that the World Health Organization's drug pre-qualification programme is not a sufficiently stringent approval process to ensure consistency and quality of fixed dose combination drugs.

He told delegates from national drug regulatory agencies, the pharmaceutical industry and non-governmental organisations that the United States was unwilling to spend the A38bn ($15 bn; Euro12 bn) promised in the presidential emergency plan for AIDS relief (PEPFAR) on drugs of unknown quality.

Médecins Sans Frontières and other NGOs working with AIDS patients in Africa accused the US government of trying to escape the 2001 Doha agreement on affordable drugs by the side door (*BMJ*, 2001, **323**: 1146). The objections raised by Tobias also threaten implementation of the World Trade Organization's August

2003 agreement that specifies how countries with limited or no capacity to manufacture drugs can gain access to cheaper generic medicines (Fleck, 2003).

Sharonann Lynch, of the charity Health GAP, said the US government is trying to ensure that the money from the US AIDS relief plan goes to brand-name manufacturers. 'These objections make no sense. The generic drugs are bioequivalent compounds, and the WHO pre-qualifications process uses staff from Canadian and European regulatory bodies that the US recognises.'

The cheapest generic combination pills cost about US$125 per person per year under a price agreement negotiated with manufacturers by former US president Bill Clinton. The same combination from brand-name companies costs about US$496 per person per year.

Addressing Congress on 18 March 2004, Mr Tobias, a former chief executive of Eli Lilly, said the US government's objections were motivated by concern for the safety of patients with AIDS. 'We have been reading stories lately about some problems with some drugs around the world, where people with the best of intentions have made acquisitions of drugs that have turned out to not have the consistency, safety, and effectiveness that people had hoped.'

What is to be done?

The HIV/AIDS pandemic, deeply rooted in so many of humanity's economic, social, cultural, biological and religious customs, will be with us for some time. But it is not really deniable that it is exacerbated enormously because of the iniquitous exploitation of the third world by the first. Therefore, we have a number of fronts on which to work, such as the following.

1 Continued medical research on its epidemiology and other purely clinical aspects.
2 Education. Much of the harm done by HIV and other STDs relies on it being immodest to discuss it openly. Children need to know about it and how to avoid it long before puberty. Cautionary advice has a much greater likelihood to be ignored once the hormones get going. Shame and ignorance are the two most logical and effective agents in promoting the suffering, family dislocation, financial ruin, grief and death caused by AIDS.
3 It is obvious that abstention works if it is used but it rarely is, or not for long. Condoms for both males and females are much more reliable, whatever religious orthodoxies might preach.
4 Respect for human rights is the foundation stone of a psychologically healthy society and a biomedically healthy one as well. That is why health promotion, with its emphasis on empowerment, is so crucial in combating such scourges as AIDS and STDs generally. We have to learn to respect ourselves for only then can we respect one another.
5 Internationalism – a situation in which we regard our common global citizenship as of paramount importance – is basic to all of the rest. Such a goal would require a large degree of voluntary investment in some kind of transnational governance, and it will require great imagination, compassion and determination to bring it about. These issues are given some airing in the final chapter of this book.
6 The principles of health promotion need to be applied with the same degree of foresight and community involvement in the third world as they are in many

first world nations. I have already referred to the work of Dr Padan Simkhada (*see* Chapter 5) in Nepal. He recently was a delegate to the Bangkok International HIV/AIDS conference. He makes this point well in the following comment, made in an email to the author on 6 August 2004.

> *Focusing on prevention of HIV and on expanding access to antiretroviral treatment for people living with AIDS is critically important to the fight against HIV/AIDS, but alone this strategy is not enough to tackle the problem.*
>
> *Sustainable and more appropriate prevention and treatment of HIV/AIDS requires empowering people to act and bring about change in their own terms. Combating HIV/AIDS in developing countries requires more than disease specific biomedical interventions. It must be linked to broader development strategies. It requires improving the conditions under which people are free to choose safer life strategies and conditions for themselves. For example, at the individual level, better education or better employment makes individuals more likely to protect themselves from contracting HIV. At the same time, improved economic, cultural, political, human rights and social conditions for disempowered or marginalised groups such as migrant workers improve the effectiveness of HIV/AIDS prevention and treatment programmes (Padam Simkhada, Research Fellow, Medical School, University of Aberdeen).*

Such levels of empowerment must rely heavily on the support of the wealthier nations in a globalised system of international trade and aid regulations.

References

Afshar H (1998) *Women and Empowerment – Illustrations from the Third World*. Macmillan Press, London.

Barnet T and Blackie P (1992) *AIDS in Africa: its present and future impact*. Belhaven Press, London.

Bassett MT and Mhloyi E (1991) Women and AIDS in Zimbabwe: the making of an epidemic. *International Journal of Health Services*. **21**: 143.

Bledsoe C (1989) *The Cultural Meaning of AIDS and Condoms for Stable, Heterosexual Relations in Africa; recent evidence from the local print*. Media paper presented at the IUSSP Seminar on Population Policy in sub-Saharan Africa, Drawing on International Experience, Kinshasa.

Brown JE, Ayowa OB and Brown RC (1993) Dry and tight sexual practices and potential AIDS risk in Zaire. *Social Science and Medicine*. **37**: 989.

Campbell T (1997) How can psychological theory help to promote condom use in sub-Saharan African developing countries. *Journal of Royal Society of Health*. **117(3)**: 186–91.

Campbell T and Kelly J (1995) How can psychology theory help promote condom use in sub-saharan African developing countries. *Journal of Royal Society of Health*. **117(3)**: 211–14.

Chabal T, Campbell T and Sheth S (1995) Issues raised in a counselling support group for HIV positive people in Zambia. *Journal of the British Association of Counselling*. **6(3)**: 211–14.

Chronic Poverty Report (2004–2005) *What Should Be Done About Chronic Poverty?* Chapter 5. The Chronic Poverty Research Centre, Manchester University, Manchester, pp 50–62.

Civic D and Wilson D (1994) Dry sex in Zimbabwe and implications of condom use. *Social Science and Medicine*. **42**: 91–8.

Dahal G (2004) *Quantifying Population Health: emerging issues and prospects*. Paper presented at University of St Andrews, 6 February.

Danzier R (1994) The social impact of HIV/AIDS in developing countries. *Social Science and Medicine*. **39(7)**: 905–9.

De Bruyn M (1992) Women and AIDS in developing countries. *Social Science and Medicine.* **34(3)**: 249–62.

Dyer O (2004) Bush accused of blocking access to cheap AIDs drugs. *British Medical Journal.* **328**: 738.

Fleck F (2003) WTO finally agrees cheap drugs deal. *British Medical Journal.* **327**: 517.

The Guardian (2004) Blair's Plan to Help AID Victims. 19 July, p.5.

George S and Sabelli F (1994) *Faith and Credit: The World Bank's secular empire.* Penguin, London.

Human Rights Watch (2003) Double Standards: women's property violations in Kenya. *Kenya.* **15(5)**: 25–8.

Lalonde M (1974) *A New Perspective on the Health of Canadians.* Information Canada, Ottawa.

Lear D (1995) Sexual communication in the age of AIDS: the construction of risk and trust among young adults. *Social Science and Medicine.* **41(9)**: 1311–23.

Loewenson R and Kerkhoven A (1995) *Socio-Economic Impact of AIDS Issues and Options.* Study prepared for Sida Sweden Executive Summary. Department of Epidemiology and Public Health, Karolkinsa Institute, Sweden.

MacDonald T (1998) *Rethinking Health Promotion: a global approach.* Routledge, London.

MacDonald T (2000) *Third World Health Promotion and its Dependence on First World Health.* The Edwin Mellen Press, Lewiston, NY, pp 155–75.

Mann J (1997) *Center for Disease Control: HIV/AIDS in the world.* Report based on a workshop: HIV/AIDS in the World. Centers for Disease Control, Atlanta, Georgia.

Maposhere C, Manyeya S and Zhuwau T (1995) *Male Condom Accessibility and Availability within Health Centers in Zimbabwe.* Study prepared for the National Aids Coordination Programme, Department of Health, Harare, Zimbabwe.

March KS and Taggy R (1982) *Women's Informal Associations and the Organisational Capacity for Development.* Monograph Series No. 5. Rural Development Committee, Centre for International Studies, Cornel University, Ithaca, NY.

Mbizvo M (1997) *Towards a Strategy for HIV prevention in Zimbabwe: what interventions work?* Symposium report. University of Zimbabwe. University Dissertations and Thesis Stacks, Harare, Zimbabwe.

Meursing K (1997) *A World of Silence: living with HIV in Matebeleland, Zimbabwe.* KIT Publications, Amsterdam.

Perlez J (1991) AIDS outweighed by the desire to have a child. *New York Times.* 26 April.

Pitts M, Bowman M and McMaster H (1995) Reactions to repeated STD infections: psychological aspect and gender issues in Zimbabwe. *Social Science and Medicine.* **40(9)**: 1299–304.

Ray S, Bassett M, Maphoshere C, Manangasira P, Nicolette JD, Macheleano R and Moyo J (1995) Acceptability of the female condom in Zimbabwe: positive but male-centred responses. *Journal of Reproductive Health Matters.* **5** (May): 68–79.

Richardson D (1990) AIDS education and women: sexual and reproductive issues. In: P Aggleton, P Davies and G Hart (eds) *AIDS: individual, cultural and policy dimensions.* Flamer Press, London, pp 157–65.

Saunders D and Abdulrahman S (1991) AIDS in Africa: the implications of economic recession and structural adjustment. *Health Policy and Planning.* **6(2)**: 157–65.

Schoepf BG (1983) Women, AIDS and economic crisis in Central Africa. *Central Journal of African Studies.* **3**: 662–5.

Somandahan S (2004) Sonali's story. *Morning Star.* London, 12 July, p.7.

Stein B (1990) Woman and contraception in developing societies. In: P Aggleton, P Davies and G Hart (eds) *AIDS: Individual, Cultural and Policy Dimensions.* Flamer Press, London. pp 98–107.

Ulin P (1992) African women and AIDS: negotiating behavioural change. *Social Science and Medicine.* **34**: 63–73.

UNAIDS (2002) Joint UNAIDS /Parliamentary forum on AIDS 2003. *Chronic Poverty Report* (2004–05), p.43.

Webb D (1997) *HIV and AIDS in Africa.* Pluto Press, London.

Wight D (1992) Impediments to safer heterosexual sex: a review of research with young people. *AIDS Care.* **4**: 11–21.

Wilson L (1990) When health education is not enough. *Journal of the Canadian Students Association for Overseas Aid.*

Winters J (1997) Social marketing of condoms (female too) gets going (again). *AIDS Analysis Africa.* **7(2)**: 6.

Worth D (1989) Sexual decision making and AIDS: why condom promotion among vulnerable women is likely to fail. *Studies in Family Planning.* **20**: 297.

Chapter 12

Peru – a detailed case study of one third world country until 2000

About Peru

The third largest country in South America, Peru embraces an area of 1 285 216 square kilometres. It is thus equivalent to approximately the size of France, Spain and the United Kingdom combined. Just 'three percent of the country is cultivated as 53 percent is covered in tropical rainforest harbouring a wealth of plants, animals and natural resources' (CIDA, 1996). It has three distinct geographical zones. The Costa, or coast, is a narrow strip sandwiched between the Pacific Ocean and the Andes Mountains stretching from north to south for over 2200 km with a largely urban population. It is the most productive area of the country (most of the crops for export are found here) and has traditionally been the dominant economic region. In contrast the Sierra is dominated by the Andes, making it difficult for human habitation, which is also true of the Selva, or jungle, which covers a large proportion of the country and is the beginning of the great Amazon basin. The climate varies from tropical in the east to dry desert in the west. Peru was the centre of the great Inca Empire, which was conquered by the Spanish in the sixteenth century, and remained under Spanish rule for 300 years before winning independence in 1821.

In sociological turns, Peruvian society is a melting pot of native Andeans, Afro-Peruvians, Spanish, immigrant Chinese, Japanese, Italians and Germans and, to a lesser extent, indigenous Amazon tribes, who have lived together for so long that many Peruvians can claim to have a mixed blood. The total population is just over 26 million and is, according to UNICEF (1998), increasing at the rate of 1.97% per annum with the result that the population is predominantly young, with 0–14 years: 35%; 15–64 years: 60%; and over 65: 5%. Life expectancy at birth for the total population is 69.97 (male: 67.78 years; female: 72.25). The official languages are Spanish (spoken by approximately 70%) and the Native American Quenchua language.

Movement into debt

Like many Latin American countries, Peru has seen generations of autocracy and decades of fierce military rule and, also like the rest of Latin America, is still coming to terms with constitutional democracy. Political instability has meant that the economy has shifted confusingly from feast to famine over recent decades and the population has suffered as a result of it. One consequence of this is that Peru has had to borrow large amounts of money from International Financial Institutions (IFIs) and this has resulted in the country acquiring enormous debt with accompanying interest. Even the latter has become unpayable as these debts have grown. Finally, in order to repay the external debts, Peru was persuaded by the International Monetary Fund and the World Bank in 1974 to shift towards a more market-oriented economic system in a bid to increase economic efficiency by a process of structural adjustment. Quickly this resulted in a range of economic policies – including budgetary austerity, devaluation of the local currency, trade liberalisation, commercial agricultural production, and privatisation of public sector industries – being implemented in the country. Paramount in these economies, cuts in health, education and social services, and food subsidies are examples of the adoption of and implementation of the structural adjustment policies which are having a devastating effect on the health of the Peruvian people.

But structural adjustment policies have only deepened the existing deprivation in the country by undermining opportunities for investment and economic growth, together with employment. Rather than improving people's lives, resources that are desperately needed for investment in the people are diverted instead to creditors. It has been stated by the International Red Cross that currently over 60% of the population is living in poverty, with 22.5% in extreme poverty. Peru also has one of the worst nutrition levels in the world, as stated by Oxfam (1998), with 11% of children under five years of age being severely underweight. It has been estimated that chronic malnutrition of children in rural areas is approximately 40%, while the diets of the Amazon tribes are 50% below acceptable levels. It goes without saying, of course, that the infant mortality rate is also high at 52% per 1000, according to UNICEF.

Through structural adjustment policies, not only has the health status of the population deteriorated, but it has further indebted the country to the international financial community. This has made it still more dependent economically on the West, with access to equitable healthcare being a long way off in the future. Analysis, apparently, has not been lacking. The World Bank commissioned a study in 1989 on the effects of structural adjustment on the Peruvians (Glewwe, 1989), which indicated that increasing prices of public services, such as education and healthcare, would further decrease health status of the poor households and also affect non-poor households. However, these warnings have not deterred the World Bank and the IMF from still persisting in following their economic goals.

The economic and political context

In 1975 Peru took its first steps toward structural adjustment after the *coup d'état* directed against the populist military government of General Velasco Alvarado. Before this, and throughout the 1960s, Peru's current account deficits and external borrowing to finance them were kept at safely low fractions of GDP. Indeed, for both 1971 and 1972, the deficits were barely 1% of GDP. From then on the nation's balance of payments became an almost constant problem. Because the military government had borrowed so much for their own uses, tempted by the plentiful supply of foreign exchange, it reduced the pressure for them to take corrective action. It is averred by George (1989) that by 1975 this had resulted in a deficit of $1.5 billion (10% of GDP). As a consequence, foreign creditors started to withdraw backing as the debt repayments began to accrue along with the interest. This, in turn, forced the government to take action to meet debt repayments.

Economically reforms in the mid-1970s had been carried out under a military junta led by General Morales Bermudez. These were directly negotiated with the creditor banks and without the involvement of the IMF at this stage. Nevertheless, despite the reforms, very little progress had been made and Peru was still unable to meet its debt repayments. Finally, in 1978 a second economic package was put in place, directed under a formal agreement with the IMF. Ineluctably, this resulted in price increases and provoked the first general strike the country had known since 1919. Inflation ate up savings and purchasing power dropped drastically. Despite the IMF quote with which this chapter concludes, the IMF prescribed a further one third cut in the government's budget. This entailed a sharp chronic under-employment which already affected half the population. Among other adverse effects, prices of fuel, public transport and basic foodstuffs doubled as all government subsidies were outlawed. As riots broke out, Peru was placed under martial law and a so-called 'democratic' government was elected in 1980 under President Belaunde Terry.

The new president was ardent in his commitment to privatisation policies. IMF reforms continued to become more cohesive under Belaunde Terry but unfortu-nately the economy continued to decline and debt continued to escalate. There was also further weakening of state enterprises established under the previous govern-ment. With inflation at 100% and political violence breaking out between anti-government and pro-government forces, the government was eventually rejected and was replaced by the quasi-socialist Alan Garcia of the Alianza Popular Revolu-cionaria Americana party (APRA) in 1985.

President Garcia had committed himself during the election campaign to paying higher prices to farmers with a view to reactivating food production and bringing about a redistribution of income in favour of the rural areas. His alternative economic package started with a sharp challenge to the IMF and external creditors that Peru would immediately limit its debt repayment to only 10% (World Bank, 1989, p.10) of its export revenues to improve the country and decrease poverty. Because of this, Peru was immediately blacklisted by the IMF for further financial assistance.

Devoting less to debt repayments caused the country's reserves to increase, and this extra money was put into health and education and self-help projects. The implementation of price freezes reduced inflation and the levels of consumption accordingly increased. In the cities, wages increased and direct investment in the production of food by the Andean Indian populations was implemented for the first time in 400 years. Throughout the first 18 months of the APRA government, GDP increased significantly, inflation was beginning to be controlled effectively, and consumption had increased markedly.

Unfortunately, persistent balance-of-payments problems – another aspect of the first world wealth impacting on third world health – had brought a measure of economic recovery to Peru which could not be sustained in the long term. For instance, the programme allowed for significant tax incentives to large corporations and a consequent expansion of the money supply. Thus, in the longer term, tax incentives and commercial subsidies accumulated to cause the appropriation of a large proportion of Peru's foreign exchange earnings. Within a decade the country's foreign reserves were substantially depleted and inflation started creeping up again. Disastrously, between December 1997 and October 1998, real earnings decreased by 50 to 60%. Health and education felt the impact first as public services started closing down and there was a further decline in the health status of the population. Not unnaturally associated with this was a rise in insurgent and criminal violence.

As the APRA government approached collapse, shortages of the most basic goods, such as water and electricity, were the norm. Visiting Lima in 1990, economist Jeffrey D Sachs described the country as 'slipping away from the rest of the world' (*The Economist*, 1996, p.21). These events ushered in a new pro-IMF government in 1990, which emphatically rejected Garcia's position and requested renewed negotiations with external creditors as 'its external debt in 1991 had gone up to $14 billion' (Oxfam, 1997, p.6).

Peru under Fujimori (1990–2000)

Alberto Fujimori's party, Cambio 90/Nueva Mayoria, won a landslide victory in 1990's election and held power for five years. He was then re-elected for a second term in 1995. A stalwart advocate of market forces, the economic shock package adopted by Fujimori in August 1990 (known as 'Fujishock') was intended to crush hyper-inflation, which was still out of control. Naturally he felt firmly committed to the IMF package and perceived it as necessary to make further 'adjustment' measures such as to increase prices of food and public services (which were already inaccessible to most, along with healthcare and education, for which user fees had previously been introduced). *See* Table 12.1.

Table 12.1: The impact of the August 1990 shock treatment on consumer prices

Lima Metropolitan Area, August 1990 (Intis)			
Commodity	*Before 3 August 1990*	*After 9 August 1990*	*Percentage increase*
Kerosene (gals)	19	608	3100
Gasoline (84-oct. gals)	22	675	2968
Propane gas (924 lb)	41	1120	2632
Bread (36 g/unit)	2	25	1150
Beans (kg)	240	2800	1067
White Potatoes (kg)	40	300	650
Flour (kg)	220	1500	531
Milk (litre)	60	290	383
Spaghetti (kg)	180	775	331
Vegetable oil (litre)	220	850	236
Rice (grade-A kg)	94	310	230
Powdered milk (410 g)	100	330	230
Eggs (kg)	170	540	218
Chicken (kg)	213	600	182

Source: *Cuanto* (1990)

Additionally, Fujimori raised the price of gasoline, together with imposing substantial cuts in real earnings to alleviate inflationary pressures. These measures resulted in a 60% decrease in real earnings (*see* Table 12.3). From one day to the next the price of fuel increased – by 446% in a single month – and, even worse, the IMF supported the package. Moreover, there were no promises and no loans attached to it, as Fujimori had hoped. *See* Table 12.2.

Table 12.2: Estimates of percentage increases of Lima consumer prices (by Peru National Statistics Institute and Tomas Cuanto) during 1990

Percentage increase	*INEI*	*Cuanto*
Food and beverages	446.2	288.2
Transport and communications	571.4	1428.0
Health and medical services	702.7	648.3
Rent, fuel and electricity	421.8	1035.0
Consumer Price Index	397.0	411.9

Source: Instituto Navoual de Estadistica (INEI), Anuario estadistico, 1991, Cuanto (1990), Peru en Numeros, ch. 21 (Lima, 1991)

As might have been expected, though, Fujimori's willingness to negotiate, together with his acquiescence in the accompanying programmes of economic reform, led the IFIs to resume discussions, and the IMF decided in September 1991 to lend Peru the money to clear its arrears. The main condition was that it continue with the adjustment process already underway, despite the fact that poverty was increasing in the country.

In April 1992, Fujimori – under increasing pressure from an unstable economy and an escalation in violence by the Shining Path (Sendero Luminoso), a leftist guerrilla group – suspended democracy in Peru and arrested many of its key leaders. Rumours of corruption in the government were widespread, and plans were also implemented to crush critics of his administration, such as trade unions, peasant leaders and student leaders. Amnesty International reported that this was accompanied by a wave of human rights violations by the security forces. Almost immediately, the IFIs responded by suspending negotiations on external credit.

Despite all this, negotiations with creditors, the IMF and the World Bank were reinstated, and arrears to the IMF and the World Bank were repaid in 1993. Further privatisations were implemented with the introduction of private pensions and the continuation of a plan to privatise all state-owned companies by the end of the decade. Altogether nearly $6 billion worth of state-owned enterprises have been privatised since 1990. The impact on the rural economy was swift; there was a major contraction in agricultural production, with the exception of the illegal coca cultivation. Wide-scale land privatisation and huge increases in the price of fuel and transportation contributed to alienating the peasant communities from the market economy and subsequently invoked a return to subsistence agriculture. The upshot has been that the peasant communities became reserves of labour for commercial agriculture, which rapidly assumed precedence.

Life for the urban population did not go unaffected and with a 30-fold increase in the price of cooking oil, many people in Lima, including some in the middle classes,

Table 12.3: Index of real wages (1974–1991)

(1974 = 100)*			
Year	Minimum Legal Income	White-collar private sector	Blue-collar private sector	Wages in govt sector
1974	100.0	100.0	100.0	
1975	93.1	100.6	88.3	
1976	85.6	83.3	95.1	
1977	75.3	72.4	79.2	
1978	58.4	62.2	71.3	
1979	63.6	56.9	70.9	
1980	79.9	61.1	75.0	
1981	67.9	62.1	73.5	100.0
1982	62.2	67.0	74.4	91.7
1983	64.6	57.4	61.6	66.3
1984	49.7	59.6	52.5	58.2
1985	43.5	48.8	45.5	46.4
1986	45.1	61.0	60.8	48.4
1987	49.0	63.9	65.6	59.2
1988	41.5	44.2	41.3	53.5
1989	25.1	36.3	37.6	35.3
1990	21.4	18.7	20.1	18.8
July	20.9	13.8	16.2	21.1
August		7.5	8.3	8.9
September ^	19.4	11.1	12.9	8.6
December	13.8	14.6	16.3	6.1
1991				
April	15.3	15.7	19.4	8.6
May	14.1			7.8

* The base year of the index for government-sector wages is 1981. ^ Includes *gratificacion*.
The private sector categories include white-collar and blue-collar earnings in private sector employment in the Lima Metropolitan Area.
Since 1963, the Minimum Legal Income was equal to the reference unit (*unidad de referencia*). From June 1984 to August 1990 it was equivalent to the reference unit plus additional bonus payments. From August 1990, the government abolished the Minimum Legal Income (*Ingreso Minimo Legal*) and replaced it with the so-called *Remuneracion Minima Vital*.
(The category General Government includes earnings in the central and regional governments and decentralised public institutions.)
Source: Estimated from official data of INEI, Anuario estadistico, 1991, Cuanto, Peru en Numeros, 1991, ch. 21 and Cuanto Suplemento, No. 13 (July 1991)

could no longer afford to boil their water or cook their food. 'Public schools, universities and hospitals had been closed down as a result of an indefinite strike by teachers and health workers (their wages were on average SU$45.70 a month [in July 1991], 40 times lower than in the US)' (Chossudovsky, 1998, p.201). Due to high unemployment and migration as a coping strategy to economic change, according to Oxfam (1998a, p.7) 'as much as 50 percent of the economically active population (which is only 20 percent of the total population) now work in the informal sector, with many working at below what the government considers a subsistence wage'. In a further lurch to the right, the government moved even further to free the labour market in 1995 by eliminating rules protecting workers from dismissal. Obviously, this renders them much more vulnerable to exploitation.

Though Peru's economy is still growing, its essential fragility is evident. Recent growth rates have been 12% in 1994, 4% in 1995 and 6% in 1996 (*The Economist*, 1995, p.21) but this has been at the price of its people's health and welfare. It is to be noted that GNP per capita has barely reached the 1965 level.

Fujimori's conservatism

Up to the time of his flight to Japan, the IMF and the World Bank still dominated in their negotiations with Fujimori. And he really seemed determined to set up a market economy in Peru despite it being detrimental to his own people. In what proved to be his final year in office, he again criticised those who had demanded sudden changes, and he went on record as stating that 'progress will take time' (Gestion, 1999). He was then still waiting for the loan package promised by the IMF and the World Bank. Up until the time of his departure, the IMF still only provided policy guidelines and technical advice without formal loan support. To qualify as eligible for loans, the government had to provide evidence to the IMF that it was seriously committed to economic reform. Such a process involved a test of credentials, often taking the form of a so-called 'Letter of Intent' submitted to the IMF identifying a government's major orientations in macroeconomic policy and debt management (*see* Appendix E for Peru's Letter of Intent of 1998). The figures stated on page 4 of that letter, reporting reductions in extreme poverty, are somewhat lower when compared to other reputable sources!

Needless to say, Fujimori's popularity thereafter rapidly dwindled and many Peruvians believed in his last months that the army held all the power. In 1998 a major polling firm asked thousands of voters, in what is called a 'highly reliable' national sample, their opinion of the president. Only 31% said they approved, against 61% disapproving (*The Economist*, 1998, p.38). Despite his unpopularity, Fujimori was still campaigning for a third term in 2000, even though it was against the country's constitution. In the end, amid accusations of corruption, his nerve evidently broke and he sought asylum in Japan, a country that has no extradition treaty with Peru. Still under question is the role of the military, the human rights record, and queries about the independence of the judiciary. These are all subjects generating significant public debate and a degree of political uncertainty.

As can be imagined, for the average Peruvian these years of economic problems have had a serious effect on their health. The financial difficulties have led to a tremendous deterioration in nutritional intake. Many families have been split up as the main breadwinner has had to leave home to seek work elsewhere. Despite education being supposedly free and compulsory between 6 and 14, poor parents both in rural and urban areas do not have the money to buy pencils, notebooks and textbooks in state schools. Furthermore, many children have to work instead of attending school to contribute income to their families. Other children have even been abandoned as their parents just cannot afford to keep feeding them. Yet Fujimori was, to the end of his days in power, commended by the international financial community for his successful national economic policies.

Health in Peru under adjustment

It has been claimed throughout this book that economic reform through structural adjustment policies undoubtedly affects the population's health status, especially the poor, who have been most hard hit. For example, price inflation and the removal of food subsidies means that consumers cannot afford to buy even the most basic commodities. In turn, this has resulted in a decline in the population's nutritional status. More than 83% of Peru's population (UNICEF's mid-1991 estimate), including the middle class, do not meet the minimum calorie and protein requirements, and child malnutrition is the second highest in Latin America.

Pressure to generate extra income to spend on essentials, such as food and healthcare, has limited the population's ability to undertake such health-related activities as feeding and caring for children properly, and it militates against the feasibility of sending children to school. Decreases in the need for unskilled agricultural labour as a consequence of land reform, and privatisation of agricultural land to commercial enterprises, have resulted in mass migration of rural people to the cities to look for work. The consequent urban overcrowding has substantially increased the risk of airborne infections. It has been pointed out by Wise (1998), for example, that since August 1990 tuberculosis has reached epidemic proportions and its deleterious impact has been heightened by malnutrition.

As we have already observed, healthcare in Peru is provided by both the public sector through hospitals and by centres run by the Ministry of Health (MOH), the Instituto Peruano Seguridad Social (IPSS), the armed forces and by private sectors. But it is the balance between the two that is pivotal. About 75% of the population are reliant on public health services, and the incidence of disease, not surprisingly, reflects any large-scale inequities. As would be expected, most (and the best) of the health facilities were and still are concentrated in metropolitan Lima, followed by the principal coastal cities, and the rest of the country. According to UNICEF (1998, p.10), whereas 'Lima has a doctor for every 400 persons on average and other coastal areas have a ratio of one doctor for every 2000, the highland departments have one doctor for every 12 000 persons'. Similar levels of variation apply with respect to hospital beds, nurses, and other medical specialities.

Decreases in public expenditure have meant the introduction of user fees for healthcare provision, which has heightened the poor health status of the population. Most people cannot afford to pay for healthcare and thus go without it. McPake (1994) provides evidence that supports the claim that user fees result in a decline in the uptake of services, especially among the people who are most socio-economically deprived.

'Increases in maternal mortality and the incidence of communicable diseases, such as diphtheria and tuberculosis, have been attributed to such policies', avers Andrew Creese, a health economist at the World Health Organization (Creese, 1997, p.203). Even for those who can afford to pay, the actual quality of healthcare and of equipment in existing hospitals is poor. According to the US Embassy in Lima, 40% of all equipment in hospitals and centres throughout the country has not been replaced for over two decades, and the resources that are in place are mainly provided by international donors.

Contextual factors are also affected. Because of reduced public expenditure, the water and sanitation infrastructure has become decrepit and unreliable, directly exposing the population to a wide variety of waterborne diseases. In a report produced on Peru by the US embassy in Lima, it was stated that only 67% of the population have access to safe water (urban 84%, rural 33%), with 72% having access to sanitation (urban 89%, rural 37%). Poorly managed sanitation and inadequate water supplies in rural areas, in particular, have contributed directly to contaminated drinking water and food (e.g. fish) and have also discouraged the use of water for health-related purposes (e.g. washing). Certainly this has been associated with outbreaks of cholera (1991 is an example). Likewise, schistoso-miasis, skin and eye infections and guinea worm disease have all risen over recent years, as a direct result of inadequacies in water supply. The government is so concerned with the rise in waterborne diseases that it had pledged to invest $2.5 billion for improving drinking water systems and US$625 million for irrigation systems by the year 2000. These goals have not yet been met as of 2004.

Chossudovsky (1998) has argued that in some areas of Peru there is a total absence of state health provision. For example, in the Selva region, due to lack of healthcare, there is a resurgence of diseases such as malaria and leishmaniasis. Most rural people tend to address their health problems principally by self-medication with herbs and other remedies. Only as a last resort is access to biomedical treatments sought, and only if these are available. Unfortunately this is rarely the case in rural Peru, as Larme (1998) points out.

Other areas with no state healthcare provision are the rainforests of northern Peru. The administrative department of the Amazonas, where over 35 000 Aguaruna and Huambisa Indians live, is another area in which state healthcare is conspicuous by its absence. A subsistence economy prevails there and the life expectancy of its people is just 50 years (Oths, 1998). As would be anticipated, the most common illnesses and causes of death are gastrointestinal and respiratory disorders and measles. Of course, all of these are preventable diseases if there is access to adequate healthcare. In southern Peru the province of Nunuo is an area with high levels of poverty, also lacking in healthcare provision. It was studied over a two-year period in 1993, and was found to have significant variations in diet, nutritional status and growth patterns among the population with '57 percent of the children showing evidence of stunting, or low height for age' (Leatherman, 1993, p.1039).

On top of all this, and almost certainly as a further consequence of reductions in healthcare provision, there has been a breakdown in the government's public health programmes. For example, vaccination programmes have deteriorated dramat-ically (under adjustment) and subsequently immunisation coverage for measles, polio and DTP series (diphtheria/tetanus/pertussis) was just '43 percent for Peru's urban areas and ten percent for rural areas' (Oths, 1998, p.1017).

Despite the fact that Peru is a Roman Catholic country, family planning is permitted and was brought into law in 1985. On the other hand, family planning programmes have also been adversely affected by cuts in public health expenditure. Undoubtedly, in this the government has been very short-sighted as these programmes can have far-reaching effects in improving the health of women. Not only do they enhance reproductive health and lessen the reliance on abortion, but they render it more likely that the children are valued. Abortion remains one of the major causes of maternal mortality, estimated at 265 deaths per 100 000 live births. The Ministry of Health estimated in 1996 reports that maternal mortality in certain rural regions was 700 per 100,000 live births. Here we are discussing a country in which induced abortion is only legal in very restricted cases, but recent estimates put the number at 260 000 per annum (Schnedier, 1998).

A survey conducted by the Peruvian government in 1996 indicated that most women wanted to space or limit births, and that natural family planning methods are the most common practice in Peru. Notwithstanding this, voluntary surgical contraception (such as tubal ligation) was the third most utilised form of contraception in Peru, which is the same for the rest of the world. Mensch *et al.* (1996), using as sample size 7841 women aged 15–49 from different districts in the country, suggested that if the quality in family planning services were improved, contraceptive prevalence would be 16–23% greater.

Government strategy in Peru is to target areas for improvement where contraceptive use is low, and although this is necessary in order to reduce the population rate, there is an in-built problem. All women have to be targeted, especially those in rural areas where there is still a considerable suspicion of birth control. This is especially so among men, among whom there exists a culture which values fertility as a sign of sexual prowess. Campaigns to educate women in controlling their fertility are essential, as supported by various studies. Bansal (1999) also found that women with higher educational attainment are more likely to control their fertility rate than are the less educated. Cutbacks in education budgets are hence likely to adversely affect the provision of appropriate and intelligent sex education in schools and universities.

The increase in prevalence of HIV also may be linked to structural adjustment. The first case of AIDS was diagnosed in 1983. Realising the numbers were rising, health officials in 1986 conducted nationwide testing for HIV-1 infection and confirmed that HIV-1 infection was at epidemic level in Peru, particularly among high-risk groups such as male homosexuals, drug users and unlicensed prostitutes. Of course, there is now also a risk of infection increasing rapidly in these groups. These findings are supported by other studies, e.g. McCarthy *et al.* (1996). Despite the government being aware of the epidemic, another study by Caceres and Rosaco (1997) found that in Lima there was a lack of basic AIDS information and a gross lack of promotion of condoms and safer sex, together with an absence of intervention programmes for homosexually active men. These programmes would undoubtedly cost money, which the government still in 2003 was unable or unwilling to commit.

Not only has there been an actual decline in facilities for state healthcare provision, but the introduction of user fees, to pay for what existing services there are, has meant that it has been left to the people themselves and to non-governmental organisations to fill the huge gaps in care that do exist. Let us now consider these alternative healthcare initiatives.

Circumventing impacts on health of SAPs

An integrated public health policy has now been missing in Peru for three decades. Economic growth has taken priority over issues of equity and poverty reduction. In the long term, health promotion strategies in Peru need to aim towards influencing those who are instrumental in shaping policies in the country. Only at this level can real changes be made to the health status of the population. Most NGOs are trying to incorporate this approach into their activities. Salil Shetty, who runs ActionAid, has recently been quoted as saying that 'Traditionally the role of NGOs was assistance. But now they are asking more questions of government and developing an advocacy role' (Woolf, 1999, p.8).

The larger NGOs, such as Oxfam, assume a broader strategy involving lobbying the IMF and the World Bank to provide debt relief, as it is the debt (and the compound interest) the country is incurring that lies at the root of many of Peru's health problems. In Oxfam's view, debt servicing should be regarded as unsustainable when it absorbs resources needed to meet targets for improving human and social development. The same point was made by the Cuban leader, Fidel Castro, when he defined 'unpayable debts' (1974). The best strategy for Peru, as for any other third world country, is to redirect debt repayments straight into healthcare and poverty reduction. This process could be monitored by international bodies and presumably would ultimately change the health status of the population in the long term.

Many Peruvians, despite their depleted resources, have undertaken innovative and committed efforts to solving the problems they face and have set up and implemented successful strategies around the country. Undoubtedly, these have had positive, if localised, effects. One such strategy, as described by Durning (1989), was accomplished in Lima's El Salvador district. In the face of the extreme poverty of the district's inhabitants and a population that has shot up to 300 000, the initiative has scored impressive successes. The basis of success has been a vast network of women's groups and neighbourhood associations embodying a democratic administrative structure. Together the community has planted half a million trees, built 26 schools, 150 day-care centres and 300 community kitchens, as well as training 100 door-to-door health workers. Such impressive results speak for themselves. Illiteracy has fallen to 3%, one of the lowest rates in Latin America, and infant mortality is 40% below the national average. This is empowerment in action, for the people determined their own destinies, and improved their quality of life, often with powerful opposition from the government. In health promotion terms, it stands as a prime example of a community empowering itself through neighbourhood advocacy and in the face of adversity.

One can cite other examples of people energised to address their health needs. Hewett (1986) cites a community in northern Peru, home to the Aguaruna and Huambisa Indians. Until 1970, at least, healthcare was non-existent and, due to contaminated water and lack of sanitation, the incidence of intestinal parasites was hugely prevalent throughout the entire community. Additionally, infectious diseases – particularly the common cold, whooping cough and measles – caused deadly epidemics. As a result of the deteriorating health status of the community, a Spanish development group moved into the area and pioneered a health promotion programme based around the concept of community health promoters. This aid was mediated in such a way that it was the people themselves who took over the project and who built their own health post from natural materials. They also initiated a communal fund for medicines. Health promoters were elected from their own community and were then trained by the Spanish development group, which within three years could withdraw from the area. Now the population is much healthier and there are almost 100 health promoters in the area organising preventive health programmes, and giving talks on various topics, including hygiene and the transmission of diseases, care of the newborn and nutrition. The community also organises collective work, such as protecting fresh water springs and generally improving community facilities. About 30 women health promoters have been trained to promote health specifically with mothers and children.

Again, one must not neglect to mention the numerous NGO projects around the country. A good example is 'HOPE Around the World', which trains healthcare workers to prevent disease and improve the health of mothers and children in 79 remote jungle communities east of the Andes Mountains. Oxfam also has a presence in Peru supporting urban and rural reconstruction of houses and water supplies, following such disasters such as *El Niño* in 1997 and the earthquake in Nazca in 1996. On account of inadequate water supplies and sanitation in 1998, there was an increase in outbreaks of diarrhoea and dehydration. Naturally this was most evident among infants and young children. Easton (1997), at the Rehydration Unit at the Cayetano Heredia Hospital in Lima, states that it experienced a 35% increase in number of cases of diarrhoea following *El Niño*. Oxfam are also working in coordination with other international agencies to strengthen people's abilities to resist further natural disasters. Examples of other Oxfam projects include encouraging local people to run community services that are missing in their areas, such as street vendors' associations. These projects have already been established in three municipalities of Lima.

Naturally, the International Red Cross (IRC) also operates in Peru and continues to provide emergency assistance. This consists largely of food parcels, blankets, cooking utensils and clothing for civilians affected by the internal conflict, especially in the upper Huallaga valley and the jungle region of Junin Department.

But health promotion is poorly represented as a national policy and government health promotion initiatives are few and far between in Peru. As a result of the deteriorating health of the population, and especially the negative publicity about the worsening health of children in Peru, the government in 1993 did set up a health initiative, the School Breakfast Programme. This was directed at school children in the Peruvian Andes, as discussed by Jacoby (1998). It came into being primarily due to mounting evidence underscoring the importance of nutrition for the learning capacity and academic performance of children. However, this programme differed from previous programmes, which had traditionally been managed by untrained staff and politicians eager for the publicity to be gained from distributing food to the poor. This programme instead involved a multidisciplinary collaboration of experts. They set about providing all the children with breakfast at school for one year and then evaluations were conducted. These reflected a significant decline in the prevalence of anaemia and an improvement in verbal skills, with better levels of school attendance and lower drop-out rates. Results such as these cannot be ignored and have prompted the Peruvian government to continue supporting the programme. They have also agreed to implement similar ones around the country. Certainly this is a step in the right direction, a small but promising start.

Conclusion

It is this author's view that the consequences of structural adjustment policies in Peru have had, and still are having, devastating effects on the health of the population. Average incomes may have shown some increase, but almost half the population is still living below the poverty line. We know that empowerment and neighbour-hood advocacy are basic to health promotion, and yet these can only prevail in the context of 'democratic' government (however broadly that is defined). Can we say that Peru is 'democratically' governed? *The Economist* (1995, p.21) remarked:

> *Fujimori is closely tied to the army with a vastly expanding intelligence service (over 750 members strong) to keep his critics at bay. An opposition press survives as one of the few checks on presidential power. But a phone call from Fujimori is sufficient to have critical television programmes removed from the air.*

In fiscal terms, President Fujimori was committed to the reform programme, as supported by the World Bank and the IMF, and this despite the effect it first predictably and then demonstrably had on his people. It is known that adjustment policies have merely diverted resources away from the domestic economy and the people themselves and the services they require to live a decent life. Peru has also been encouraged by such policies to keep importing large quantities of consumer goods, including food staples, from rich countries, rendering it even more depend-ent on the first world. This process has brought about an enlargement of the balance-of-payments crisis and the growth of the debt burden. Flying in the face of distressing evidence, the World Bank (1993) continued to maintain that adjusting is more beneficial to health and welfare than not adjusting, and that any negative impacts are purely temporary. This claim is contrary to the evidence, not only in Peru, but in many indebted countries in the third world.

Closely similar measures of budgetary reductions are applied in more than 100 indebted countries. Management of fiscal and monetary policy is relinquished to the IMF and, accordingly, state bureaucracies are dismantled and policies scrapped. Many examples prevail of countries which do not comply and are then blacklisted by the IMF. Chossudovsky (1998) argues that this is a new form of economic and political domination – a form of market colonialism. The anomaly here, though, is that if people are already disadvantaged because of limited means, financial and otherwise, market forces are not at all free but are dictatorial in terms of what individuals can or cannot achieve.

The message from a variety of sources, such as non-governmental agencies, independent academics, UNICEF, and even quarters of the World Bank, is abun-dantly clear and suggests that many countries implementing structural adjustment policies have suffered significant welfare reversals over the past decade. In a recent report the World Bank accepts that the state does have a role to play in 'protecting the vulnerable' through social welfare programmes and declares that 'the state is not there merely to deliver economic growth, but that it also has an obligation to ensure that the benefits are shared though investments in basic education and health' (World Bank, 1997, p.4). Such rhetoric aside, though, this has been denied to the people of Peru under the IMF/World Bank's adjustment policies.

UNICEF (1987/88) has published the only empirical study of effects of adjust-ment policies on health (George, 1989). This work is germinal in that it draws attention to the serious health effects of structural adjustment policies. However, it only analyses the earlier phase of adjustment, and therefore focuses primarily on stabilisation rather than on structural adjustment. For a more comprehensive picture to be obtained, research needs to take account, as recommended by Costello *et al.* (1994), of substantial time lags. These may initially be offset by coping strategies and it does take considerable time for health status to deteriorate. This surely suggests that one of the main roles of health promotion in the meantime is to lobby for changes by governments, the World Bank and the IMF. It is this essentially political, social and discursive aspect that tends to be marginalised. Unfortunately, many NGOs adopt as policy the view that they should not engage in such advocatory activity.

In 1978 the Declaration of Alma Ata promoted primary healthcare as the key to achieving an acceptable level of health throughout the world in the foreseeable future. However, it is precisely primary healthcare, as well as any type of adequate state healthcare, that is being denied the people of Peru and unquestionably this is due to the structural adjustment policies imposed on the country by the World Bank and the IMF.

It might be useful to close with an excerpt from the IMF's answer to such criticisms. 'Contrary to widespread perception, the IMF has no effective authority over the domestic economic policies of its members. It is in no position, for example, to force a member to spend more on schools or hospitals' (Driscoll, 1998). Can such a statement be accepted within the context of what we know of structural adjustment?

The author has experienced various difficulties in accessing reliable information about these issues in Peru since 2002. His comments, therefore, are largely only valid up until then.

References

Bansal RK (1999) Elementary education and its impact on health. *British Medical Journal.* **318**: 141.

Caceres CF and Rosasco AM (1997) The correlates of safer behaviour among heterosexually active men in Lima. *AIDS II.* **Suppl.** 1: S53–S59.

Canadian International Development Agency (1996) *Latin American Conspectus.* Ottawa Information, Canada, p.5.

Castro F (1974) *La Deuda Impagable.* Casa de las Americas, Havana, p.11.

Chossudovsky M (1998) *Globalisation of Poverty: impacts of IMF & World Bank reforms.* Zed Books, London.

Costello A, Watson F and Woodward D (1994) *Human Face or Human Façade?* Centre for International Child Health, London.

Creese A (1997) User fees. *British Medical Journal.* **315**: 202–3.

Cuanto T (1990) Basic Information Peru Living Standards Survey. Lima, Peru. www.world bank.org/lsms/country/pe90/docs/pe90.pdf

Driscoll DD (1998) *What is the International Monetary Fund?* IMF, Washington DC.

Durning AB (1989) Grass roots groups are our best hope for global prosperity and ecology. *Unte Reader.* **34**: 40–9.

Easton A (1997) *El Niño* causes diarrhoea outbreaks. *British Medical Journal.* 6 December. **315**: 1485–8.

The Economist (1995) The dark side of the boom. 5 August, p.21.

The Economist (1998) Peru: possible presidents. 17 October, p.38.

The Economist (1996) Peru's balance of payments crisis. 17 December, p.21.

George S (1989) *A Fate Worse than Debt*. Penguin, London.

Gestion A (1999) *Peru and the New Capitalism*. Seminar given at Department of Economic and Social Sciences, University of West Indies, Jamaica (unpublished).

Glewwe P (1989) *The Poor in Latin America during Adjustment: a case study of Peru*. LSMS Working Paper 56. World Bank, Washington.

Hewett NC (1986) A primary health care project in the Amazonian jungle of northern Peru. *British Medical Journal*. 27 September. **293**: 805–7.

Jacoby ER (1998) When science and politics listen to each other: good prospects from a new school breakfast programme in Peru. *American Journal of Clinical Nutrition*. **67 (Suppl. 7)**: 95.

Larme AC (1998) Environment, vulnerability and gender in Andean ethnomedicine. *Social Science and Medicine*. **47(8)**: 1005–15.

Leatherman T (1993) Changing biocultural perspectives on health in the Andes. *Social Science and Medicine*. **47(8)**: 1031–41.

McCarthy MC, Wignall FS, Sanchez J, Gotuzzo E, Alarcon J, Phillips I, Watts DM and Hyams KC (1996) The epidemiology of HIV-1 infection in Peru, 1986–1990. *AIDS*. **10**: 1141–5.

McPake B (1994) User charges for health in developing countries: a review of the economic literature. *Social Science and Medicine*. **39**: 118–20.

Mensch B, Arends-Kuenning M and Jain A (1996) The impact of the quality of family planning services on contraceptive use in Peru. *Studies in Family Planning*. March/April. **27(2)**: 59–75.

Oths KS (1998) Assessing variation in health status in the Andes: a biocultural model. *Social Science and Medicine*. **47(8)**: 1017–30.

Oxfam International (1997) *Poor Country Debt Relief: false dawn or new hope for poverty reduction?* Oxfam.

Oxfam International (1998a) *Marking Debt Relief Work: a test of political will*. Oxfam.

Oxfam International (1998b) *Oxfam at Work in Peru*. Oxfam.

Schnedier M (1998) *Testimony of Assistant Administrator for USAID in Latin America & the Caribbean before the House International Relations Committee on International Operations & Human Rights*. Washington, DC.

Wise J (1998) WHO identifies 16 countries struggling to control tuberculosis. *British Medical Journal*. 28 March. **316**: 955.

Woolf A (1999) Action, not just aid. *The Guardian*. 24 February, pp 8–9.

World Bank (1989) *Peru, Policies to Stop Hyperinflation and Initiate Economic Recovery*. World Bank, Washington, DC.

World Bank (1993) *World Development Report 'Investing in Health'*. World Bank, Washington, DC.

World Bank (1997) *The State in a Changing World*. World Bank, Washington, DC.

Chapter 13

Cuba – model or monster?

Cuba in the news

Before considering why Cuba – a small third world country – should be so well represented in the world's media output, let us consider it along the lines of difference in the first and third world's media. For a good example of the first world's media view of Cuba, look at a recent account by Matthew Campbell (2004) in the *Sunday Times* of 18 July 2004.

His story is dramatically headlined: 'Elderly Cubans left to starve as drought brings cut in rations'.

The report goes on to point out that the drought in Cuba, which has been intense for more than two years in some parts of the country, is proving to be a major economic problem. There have been food shortages and the milk cattle industry and the eastern part of Cuba is seriously imperilled by the lack of water and the drying up of pasturelands. But the line taken in the *Sunday Times* article goes much further. It claims that the impact of the drought is greatly exacerbated by: '... inefficient distribution (of food) ... drought sweep one of the world's last communist strongholds'.

Having worked in Cuba for six years, this author has always been struck by how efficient food distribution has been. Cuba has been 'blockaded' by the US – and now, through US trade legislation, as will be explained later, by many other first world countries. In effect, the UK, the rest of the EU, the US, Russia and various other countries now support the blockade for one simple reason. If any country dares to trade with Cuba, US law prohibits that country from trading with the US. Since the US is by far the world's wealthiest market, not many countries can compete effectively for markets if they do not trade with the US. There have been some courageous exceptions. Canada, for instance, manages a limited trade with Cuba and often turns a blind eye to other non-Canadian countries and agencies doing so under Canadian trade. But this is highly precarious and – unless attitudes alter in the US government – President Bush's current strategies for bringing down the Cuban government will cause yet more grief for Cuba and for democracy generally.

Before dealing directly with the claims made in the *Sunday Times* article – and the reliability of Matthew Campbell's sources – let us consider first what the trade embargo with Cuba is for. We are told that the Cuban government is profiting from stolen goods. Before their revolution in 1959, vast tranches of Cuban industry and commerce were owned by foreign (mainly US) citizens and corporations. A number of wealthy Cuban individuals and concerns were also involved in this. But when the revolution first 'triumphed' (as the Cubans say), the revolutionary government gradually began expropriating this property. Thus, trading with Cuba today renders any country doing so complicit in the original 'crime'!

As well as this, we are told that the Cuban authorities are seriously in breach of human rights and of various UN and other international agreements relating to human rights. The media (in most of the first world) regularly disseminates colourful accounts of victimisation of 'dissident Cubans' and of organisations supporting them.

Both of these 'justifications' seem rather odd, however. In Cuba, both health and education are enhanced and promoted and Cuba has been internationally famous for that since the early 1960s (*see* MacDonald, 2000).

Although some of the school buildings are desperately in need of repair and of a high level of maintenance, the education that goes on in them is one of the best by world standards. This author knows whereof he talks, being intimately familiar with standards in some of Britain's best public schools and of educational standards in several other first world countries – e.g. the US, France, Germany, Spain, Australia, Canada, etc.

Later on this chapter will consider both the academic and the social impact of Cuban schools.

Take the hospitals and other medical facilities. Again, although many of them could do with much more cash for maintenance, the treatment one receives as a patient is first rate. And, like schooling, this is available to every Cuban as required. Their maternity and other community-based services are often better, and more accessible than they are in the NHS. They are far better than in the US, as reflected in UNESCO and WHO figures. This is because the heavy reliance on private medical care there guarantees that the coverage is patchy. Access to services in the US is clearly correlated with wealth (*see* Figure 1.1).

Then, too, what about some of the countries that the US does not blockade or try to undermine, for grand theft or scant regard for human rights? One can think of many in which health and education are not universally available and which have frequently harboured criminals, lived off stolen property and in which human rights is a joke, e.g. Colombia, Argentina, El Salvador, etc. – even Israel. One cannot but wonder at the double standard and to suspect corruption.

From the first days of the new administration in Cuba, exiles (including the former dictator Fulgencio Batista) took sanctuary in Florida. The Florida vote – in US federal elections – is regarded as crucial. It tends to be Republican, and this is very much tolerated by the anti-Castro vote, which has over the years been organised into various pro-Republican groupings. One of the first of these was the Cuban American National Foundation (CANF), but there are many others. They have immense leverage in US politics and regularly spew out 'press releases', etc., exaggerating Cuban domestic crises – or even inventing some – always attributing the problems to communist totalitarianism.

Who are the 'elderly Cubans'?

Matthew Campbell's article in the *Sunday Times* draws rather heavily on such suspect sources. The author is not thus impugning Campbell's integrity, because these sources prominently present themselves as purveyors of impartial information on Cuba. When he was teaching in a Florida college in the 1960s, this author often sought information about Cuba from such sources. They are so prominent that it is difficult for a newcomer even to know of alternative unbiased sources. www.Cubanet.org, for instance, is widely known for its unreliability.

So when we consider those two 'justifications' for the embargo – strongly promoted of course by the CANF and by groups cited in the *Sunday Times* article – they seem rather unbalanced. In Cuba both education and health are famously enhanced and promoted. *See* MacDonald (2000) and numerous other sources.

There have developed in Cuban since 1959 a huge array of grass-roots, community-led initiatives, some of which have become nationally powerful. Some of these will be dealt with in this chapter. Among them, the Third Age Movement has assumed considerable clout.

Cuban pensioners can hardly be compared with, say, UK pensioners. The UK pensioners are – by and large – a fairly moderate and well-behaved group. They are not highly organised as a group, either politically or socially. Part of the reason for this is that there is a huge variation in their personal pension arrangements. Some are enormously wealthy, others barely scraping by. A common attitude here is that their status as pensioners is no one else's business. It is a private matter and not generally a matter for public discussion.

Contrast this with the hell-raisers in the Cuban Third Age Movement! They do work and organise as a group and are well featured in the media. There is no way that they can be quietly set to one side by the government. In the early days, the revolutionary government tried to quietly sideline women and some thought that by promoting the Cuban Women's Federation (FMC), they could put them in a box and keep them from interfering too much. As has been amply demonstrated, this didn't work and their prominence in Cuban affairs is well attested. Macho is no longer as macho in Cuba as it is elsewhere in other nations in the region.

The same phenomenon is evident with the Third Age. And they have a Third Age University (Universidad de la Tercera Edad or UTA). They have a solid representation in various branches of government. They are not renowned for their obsequiousness or decorum! There is no way in the world that they would put up with the treatment described in that *Sunday Times* article. It would immediately be raised in the media and at the highest levels of government. A goodly proportion of the residents in the homes described by Matthew Campbell were activists in the earliest days of the revolution. They know how to organise. The best way to find out about them is to go to Cuba and see.

Robert Quick, deputy director of the National Health Service University (NHSU) for Yorkshire and the Humber, has had intimate and, as well, very recent experience of the 'old people's homes' referred to in the *Sunday Times* article. In March 2004 he led a tour of 20 NHS Chief Executives (who are participating in an NHS leadership programme) to Cuba for a fact-finding tour. Then in June 2004, he took a group of 24 NHSU students. He has had ample experience of Cuba (20 visits in 14 years). Most of those visits have been in connection with Medical Aid programmes or with the organisation of study tours. These visits, and notably the ones in 2004, included Houses of the Third Age (old people's homes in the US and UK). He stated categorically on 9 August 2004, in an email to the author:

> *We visited a House of the Third Age for Women in Havana (10th October Municipality). The facilities were poor, there was no air-conditioning and the building was in need of repair (like most buildings in Havana). We interviewed staff and residents. In fact, two residents were fluent in English and so we did not need an*

interpreter. There seemed to be no concerns about supply of food or drinking water. Staff were well motivated and residents enthusiastic to talk about the support they got. The House of the Third Age has a number of day patients too.

My own experience over visits to similar establishments in Cuba over the past few years is that usually residents and patients in care institutions (hospitals or residential centres) get better nutrition than most because they are seen as a high priority. We and not government officials usually selected the facilities to visit.

As well, there is a real dichotomy between the way in which the media in the US and the UK usually report on Cuba and the way it is often treated by the media elsewhere. Working as a doctor and a teacher in a variety of third world countries – Angola, Mozambique, Ghana, India, Vietnam, Nepal, etc. – I continually hear accounts from people about how Cuban doctors, nurses and teachers contributed their services freely in health and education work. This is all well documented and will be discussed in further detail in subsequent pages. It is an important part of Cuban foreign policy.

One does not have to be either a conspiracy theorist or a hopeless cynic to realise some agenda other than objective judgement is pulling the strings here!

Let us now look at Cuba's revolution and the extent to which its social policies have so dramatically improved health (and education) not only in Cuba but world-wide.

Some background

Since Cuba's levers of power were seized by revolution on 1 January 1959 that tiny island third world country has hardly been out of the news. The column inches of newsprint, the hours of commercial radio and television news-time and the number of books published about Cuba since that date have been totally dispro-portionate to its military or economic clout.

The reasons for this are several, interrelated and complex, but are extremely instructive for people concerned with strategies for global health promotion. Revolutionary Cuba has seemed to specialise in refuting predictions based on 'common sense' and in giving the lie to well-established stereotypes. Consider, for example, the Great Literacy Campaign – 42nd in a list of postwar national literacy campaigns in poor nations, but the only one to succeed. Subsequent ones in other countries have succeeded, largely to the extent that Cuba has shown the world how to go about it. Then there was the matter of health and education.

At the time of the 'triumph of the revolution', Cuba was grotesquely under-equipped and understaffed in both health and schooling sectors. It was estimated, in September 1958 (MacDonald, 1985), that even to provide only primary schooling for all children between the ages of 6 and 11 years, living in towns or cities of population in excess of 1000, would require 9.5 times the number of teachers then available in Cuba. Healthcare was even worse. Rural areas were largely bereft of any provision for healthcare at all. Consistent with this neglect, there was very little electrification outside the urban areas. The peasantry lived in mud huts called bohios, unencumbered by any provision for sanitation.

The infant mortality rate (IMR) in Cuba on the eve of the revolution was 61 per 1000 live births and the average lifespan was 56 years. Not only that, but both of these parameters were characterised by large standard deviations – a common enough feature of third world epidemiological measures – reflecting Cuba's gross social and economic inequities.

Moreover, both educational and health infrastructures deteriorated even further immediately after the revolution. Almost all the teaching staff of Cuba's only medical school, along with 40% of Havana's doctors and 35% of those in Santiago, fled to Miami, along with ousted dictator Batista and his entourage. Not only did Cuba thus lose its skills, but most of its hard currency as well. In particular, Batista was said to have physically removed crate-loads of US currency from the National Bank in Havana.

In sum, 1959 found Cuba a small third world nation with fewer teachers than it had before, almost no way of training doctors, hardly any qualified GPs or dentists and no money – and a leader who urged that illiteracy be eradicated in a year and who proclaimed that two of the revolution's priorities were universal access to schooling up until age 16 and a health service available to all free at point of access! It struck many responsible people in Cuba as rather like the opening scene of a comic opera (MacDonald, 1998).

People-centred government

But the revolution worked. Within five years, Cuba – even to the casual visitor – looked astonishingly different to other Caribbean nations. Hardly any children between the ages of 6 and 16 were to be seen on the streets during school hours; in the evenings adults of all ages were encountered in droves going to evening classes after work. Polyclinics were to be found even in remote rural localities, the IMR had dropped to 12 per 1000 live births and a rise was already measurable in life expectancy. By 1974, there were 16 medical schools and the Cuban doctor–patient ratio was better than that of the US or the UK. The IMR was down to 9.1 per 1000 live births; life expectancy was 73 years for women and 71 for men. Nineteen universities flourished and Cuban literacy levels were put by UNESCO as the world's highest.

Health promotion was being discussed as a philosophical issue in 1975 in Canada, but had not yet been identified as such as a WHO objective. But in Cuba it was happening. Healthcare organised by street committees, and involving almost total grass-roots participation, was seen as much more than intervention in the event of illness but as a socially positive objective. Cuba was experiencing health promotion in all but name. But of even greater import, in third world terms, was the fact that Cuba's ideologically inspired social policy led it to send medical teams to other countries which could not afford their own.

Cuba had become unique in health and educational terms. Although a third world country, its people were dying of first world diseases. The huge death rate of children due to parasitic and enteric diseases, a routine feature of most third world countries, had almost vanished from Cuba. Its social and cultural life flourished, with folkloric theatre groups, a highly innovatory film industry and a massive upsurge in literary output, reflecting a scale of human values and social optimism that had rarely occurred before.

Obviously this brief account does not detail how these astonishing achievements were brought about. It is a complex story, almost unbelievable in some of its details, and has already been carefully detailed in a previous book by this author (MacDonald, 1999). Suffice to say, it beautifully validated many of the claims made for its potential by the first world pioneers of health promotion in the 1970s (Lalonde, 1974; MacDonald, 1998).

Consider the basic theoretical structure of health promotion: personal autonomy and high self-esteem, leading to neighbourhood advocacy, ultimately to inter-sectoral collaboration. In revolutionary Cuba, intersectorality was built into the enterprise from the beginning. This author worked in both the Ministry of Education and in the Ministry of Public Health. Interchanges between the two were accepted as operationally natural. Likewise, social workers, teachers and police worked in tandem through locally organised teams.

Cuba as 'virus'

In so many respects Cuba could be perceived as being a model for global health promotion. It is a small country, limited to some degree in terms of natural resources – it has no oil for instance, and its soil is such that its capacity to pasture milch-cows is severely compromised – and financially strictly in the third world league. Yet it has developed a social policy that has produced a healthcare system and an educational outreach that are the envy of many first world nations. Moreover, it has accomplished these outcomes without becoming caught up in the debt trap and without living beyond its means. Why, then, is the Cuban model not more widely adopted?

The answer lies in that matrix of the fiscal relationship between the first and the third world described in Chapter 1. By achieving its social and political objectives largely outside this framework, and outside its control by first world capitalism, Cuba is correctly perceived as being an enormous menace to the system of first world finance. In fact, President Ronald Reagan actually referred to Cuba in 1983 as a dangerous 'virus' capable of 'infecting' all of the other Central and Latin American countries in their dealings with the United States. Some pro-Cuba lobbyists and the left-wingers in the first world countries took exception to Reagan's remark, but it was astonishingly accurate.

If other Latin American countries were allowed to follow the Cuban example, or even if only Brazil did, the major US banks would be ruined. The interest payments on loans to Brazil alone generate enormous profits for the stockholders of Citicorp Bank in New York. For third world countries in significant numbers to emulate Cuba would spell the collapse of first world banking and hence the downfall of the market system and capitalist financial structures as we now know them. In that context, Cuba is indeed a very dangerous virus. Cuban leaders themselves have implied as much. Consider Che Guevara's now famous 1960 comment: 'Cuba is Chapter One of a twenty-three Chapter book' (*New York Times*, 1960), an obvious reference to the 22 Latin American nations still languishing in the sort of economic dependency on the US from which Cuba had escaped.

Recently oil deposits have been found under the sea floor in Cuba's waters. This may prove to be a threat to the country's welfare. On 10 August 2002, the deposits were classified as 'not of commercial use' but by January 2005 new Cuban and new international analyses have suggested otherwise.

The foregoing provides rationale enough for the United States blockade of Cuba. But it is that blockade which has put Cuba's health programme under the most severe of tests. There are various ways in which it could survive the rigours of that ordeal. For instance, one way would be for other financial crises to undermine first world economic dominance sufficiently for the balance to tip globally in favour of a system like Cuba's. Their idea of a global health strategy based on a linking of 'red' and 'green' social paradigms is discussed in the final chapter of this book.

But before we can consider the possibility of such strategies, it is useful to briefly analyse the impact of the blockade of Cuban public health initiatives.

The long blockade

The United States has interfered with Cuban social and economic life by various 'quarantines', blockades and embargoes since 1960. In fact, the use of the word 'blockade' for what the US is doing to Cuba is almost universal, but it is technically inaccurate. US government commentators refer to it as an 'embargo'. The differences all relate to the purpose of the enterprise, rather than its effect. Under UN law, one country may only blockade another during a time of war. But the US is not at war with Cuba. Therefore, for it to refer to the US blockade as a 'trade embargo' lets it off the hook of being accused of being in breach of UN law. But what is the difference between an 'embargo' and a 'blockade', and how can it be that both are the same as far as Cuba is concerned?

Prior to the revolution, Cuba was almost totally dependent on the United States for virtually all commodities which it could not produce itself. In addition, even its domestic infrastructure was 94% US-owned – including the telephone service, the hospitals, the water supply company, etc. This had been the case since 1898, so obviously if America were to cut its supply of spare parts, etc., Cuba would either have to manufacture them themselves or purchase them abroad. The first option could not be considered, because Cuba's dependence had been sealed by the US simply not building appropriate local factories. The second option was problematical because parts made abroad were aimed at the European market and were made to metric specifications rather than US-Imperial.

In 1960 it therefore seemed a realistic option for the United States to impose a 'trade embargo' on Cuba in the hope of it leading to the collapse of the government. This, at first, did not prevent Cuba from purchasing food products (such as alfalfa for feeding milk cattle), educational materials or pharmaceuticals from the US. But it did prevent Cuba from obtaining oil and oil products, such as petrol. A less stalwart and a less popularly supported regime might well have caved in under that pressure, but the Cubans did not. They did two things which the US found extremely inconvenient: they made treaties of friendship with 'non-aligned' nations (*see* Chapter 1) outside of the Organisation of American States (the OAS) – dominated by US financial interests – and they bought crude oil from the USSR. The USSR (then under Khrushchev) was only too glad to oblige, as it gave them a propaganda foothold in the US sphere of influence, and they shipped their oil to Cuba under an exchange system with Cuban sugar production.

Of course, crude oil is not petrol, so Cuba faced the problem of refining it. It had oil refineries, but these were owned by Standard Oil (Esso, a US firm) and by Shell (a British firm). Both refused to refine Soviet crude oil. The Cuban government therefore moved to expropriate the refineries. To each of the two companies they offered compensation to the value that the companies themselves had declared on their tax returns. Of course, these were very low valuations, but the companies could hardly admit vast tax fraud. Shell agreed, cut their losses and left Cuba. Esso refused. The US government realised that the embargo, although it was causing some hardship in Cuba, was not enough to topple the regime. They then organised an invasion of the island, using the soldiers drawn from the ranks of disaffected Cubans who had fled to Miami and from other Spanish-speaking Central and South American states.

The invasion failed and after a week, Cuban forces had captured 1200 of the force and had repelled the rest. This represented a serious propaganda humiliation to the United States and they looked for other ways to intensify the 'embargo', making it more like a 'blockade'. They did not have to wait long. Khrushchev and Castro worked out a deal in which Cuba would receive favoured trading-status if the USSR could establish long-range missiles on Cuban soil directed at targets in the US. Once the US government realised what was happening, the US President (Kennedy, at the time) and Khrushchev were brought into direct confrontation. The fate of the world literally hung in the balance. After five days of negotiation between the two superpower leaders (Cuba was not consulted, which came as a distinct blow to its national pride!), Khrushchev ordered the removal of the missiles and we all breathed easier again.

This resolution was presented in the US as a victory for Kennedy and in the USSR as a victory for Khrushchev. In fact, it was more of a victory for the third world. In exchange for the Soviet withdrawal of missiles from Cuban soil, the US had to withdraw missiles, directed at Soviet targets, from Turkey. They also had to undertake never again to attempt an invasion of Cuba.

From then until 1992, the US maintained the embargo against trade with Cuba but kept toughening it in the detail, rendering it more and more difficult for Cuba to obtain medical, educational and nutritional items, but in such a way as to stay clear of an actual breach of international law. Cuba responded by becoming extremely versatile in manufacturing pharmaceuticals and even inventing new ones. For a detailed review of this remarkable period in Cuba's history, see this author's 1999 book *Health Care in Cuba.*

During this period from 1962 to 1992, Cuba's healthcare system kept improving and it was sending dozens of medical experts abroad. Cuba's impact on the third world was thus very great indeed and continues to be so. It represents a genuinely viable alternative and for this reason it has become even more imperative to the US government that it be destroyed.

In 1992 the trade embargo was tightened to the extent that any nation that traded with Cuba was disallowed from trading with the US for 180 days thereafter. This represented a serious blow to Cuba's high-tech healthcare system, for it had already lost 60% of its trade due to the 1991 collapse of the Soviet bloc. From then on, successive US governments have kept refining the embargo, increasing its effectiveness against beleaguered Cuba. In 1994 the Helms Burton Act came into play, by which even if a third nation wished to sell food, pharmaceuticals, parts for medical machinery, educational materials, computer software – anything at all – to Cuba, it would have to apply for a US licence to do so or else lose its US markets. By providing licences, the US government can insist that it is not preventing items for health or education from entering Cuba, but the evidence proves otherwise. The 'embargo' really is a 'blockade' now, and this is how.

Each licence application, say for a particular medication or even for textbook supplies, must name a specific potential recipient. In the case of a pharmaceutical, the patient must be named, his/her medical condition detailed, the doctor in charge must be named, as must the health facility. The application form is 38 pages long and, since it has to be completed for each case, any company in Europe or Asia wishing to sell to Cuba has to be willing to complete hundreds of these each year – and can then expect to find obstacles in the way of their US markets. Few businesses can afford to be that ethical in their determination to trade in one small market! Even worse, each licence takes about six months to process so that if a particular child suffering from leukaemia, say, has been named on the licence and he/she has died without treatment while awaiting the outcome, the application is invalid even though the same pharmaceutical may be needed by that time for another patient!

President Bush tightens the noose

In recent months, President George W Bush (2004) has overseen a draconian tightening of the embargo. Cuban émigrés to the US are now severely restricted in the amount of money they can send back to their families. The idea that a third world citizen, on gaining legal entry to a first world country, can send some of his earnings back to his family is an honoured one. But now, for Cubans, it is being curbed. Even more bizarre is the legislation which puts a strict limit on the amount of money émigrés, or even ordinary American citizens, visiting Cuba can spend there. When the legislation first was announced, many people thought it must be a joke. In a 'democracy' can its citizens be so controlled by the state?

The legislation – according to US President Bush – is designed to create such hardship and chaos that the Cuban revolutionary government will collapse. Stephen Gibbs, the BBC's correspondent in Cuba, has reported thus from Cuba, in an article in *The Independent on Sunday* (Gibbs, 2004). The obvious severity of the drought imposes immense strains on the already beleaguered Cuban Government. This would, of course, represent another victory for first world corporate capitalism and have disastrous health impacts in many third world countries whose health and education programmes are sustained by Cuba. But Stephen Gibbs reports that he remains cautiously optimistic.

> But the resilience of the Cuban people in the face of the drought argues against those who suggest that all this hardship might finally push the people to do something to change their leader.
>
> As one young Cuban computer engineer, queuing to collect his rations cheerfully puts it: 'what would Cuba be, without a crisis?' (Gibbs, 2004).

This rather protracted explanation of how the US has been able to thwart health promotion in Cuba is important if we are to gain an insight into the options realistically open to the third world. And despite Cuba's energy and innovatory spirit in trying to maintain its internationally acclaimed healthcare system in the face of the might of the US dollar, the blockade has caused temporary setbacks. Cubans – especially those with young children and old people – are now dying and/ or suffering unnecessarily purely because of the blockade. For instance, by 1994 Cuba's IMR had dropped to 6.2 per 1000 live births – lower than that in the US and about equal with that in such nations as Britain and Germany. By early 1998, it had risen to 7.1 per 1000 live births; this was soon remedied and by July 2002 it had dropped to 6.3 per 1000 live births.

With respect to life expectancy, the figures for 1995–98 were an average of 74.83 years, but this has continued to rise, reaching 76.15 years in 2002 (Perez, 2004).

Can Cuban public health survive the blockade?

Cuba's advances in healthcare and promotion depend very strongly not only primarily on the sorts of pharmacologically and clinically centred interventions considered above, but on a broad social awareness of the link between social factors, lifestyles and health. Here, too, the US blockade is proving seriously obstructive. For instance, Cuba is the only country in the Caribbean, Central or Latin America with a universally guaranteed pure water supply. This is a remarkable achievement. Even in such tourist meccas as the Dominican Republic or Barbados, one is warned not to rely on tap water for drinking. Bottled water has to be purchased. Of course, the local poor cannot afford to do that and thus IMRs are inflated by enteric diseases and deaths by typhoid are not uncommon.

But there is now evidence (since late 1997) that the blockade is rendering it impossible for Cuba to maintain this high standard. The parts they need for pumping apparatus and water purification plants would be most cheaply and easily obtained from US manufacturers. Cuba's entire sewerage and water supply system was US-owned before the revolution and built to US non-metric specifications. Of course, since the revolution it has been massively extended with apparatus consistent with the original. Now, under the Helms Burton Act, any attempt to purchase a vital component is subject to the licensing restrictions discussed above. Again, each piece has to be applied for individually on a separate licence, and US firms are not able to devote the time and paperwork for such a comparatively insignificant market. Additionally, in the case of materials for water or sewerage systems, the Cubans have to specifically prove that the materials are not for any potential military use.

Most of Cuba's original water reticulation system has not been renewed since prior to 1959. It cannot be long before it all needs replacing. Faced with this possibility, Cuba has to consider whether or not to purchase elsewhere. But even then, few suppliers (South Korea is a frequently mentioned possible supplier) would be willing to incur the penalties against trading with US markets should they trade with Cuba. On top of all this, any such solution would involve Cuba having to pay far more per item, plus the cost of its shipment from a much greater distance, as well as having to reconstruct the entire system to render it compatible with the new supplier's codes.

One can think of many other specific, product-related obstacles imposed by the Helms Burton Act, but even more threatening is the impact of the US blockade on the whole ethos underlying Cuban health promotion. To explain that, it is necessary to show precisely how Cuba's political and social policies link, through intersectorality, creating what this author refers to as an 'attitudinal net' as a precondition for health promotion. It is necessary to consider this in some depth because, so far, it is the only viable approach to third world health promotion which has worked in practice. But to do this we must momentarily address a more general health promotion phenomenon.

Health promotion and social attitudes

One distinct way in which health promotion must differ in its implementation in the third world to that in the first relates to the material conditions on which it is to be based. The decade 1975 to 1985 saw the development of health promotion initiatives in most of the first world economies. In many respects it was also an upbeat decade, economically, with much confidence in the 'new face' of conservatism, privatisation, popularisation of stock and share ownership and innovatory approaches to starting small businesses. It was a decade which, in the first world, witnessed a distinct shift of attitudes from deference to one's 'betters' to a more participatory approach. The 'middle classes' seemed to extend in both directions. Access to the media became easier and, especially in Britain, computer and word-processor use by 'ordinary' people increased dramatically. In many ways it represented a social renaissance.

At the community level this created a growth in awareness of one's rights and of empowerment. The 'gospel' of health promotion thus fell on receptive ears, and most first world health promotion initiatives were therefore strongly 'middle class' in their orientation. In other words, they tended to be the sort of idea- and book-oriented initiatives that were appreciated by articulate people who played key roles in their communities.

In a sense, this meant that the health promotion movement in the first world did not have to worry overmuch about establishing its bases. Other social factors had already seen to that and, indeed, some people argued that that was why health promotion arose when it did. Likewise, in the third world, the nature of health promotion must be determined by its social bases and if the social bases are hostile to it, then the social bases have to be changed if health promotion is to become global. The first world models of health promotion reflect certain disadvantages and defects stemming from these considerations. For instance, it is now becoming more obvious that such liberation phenomena as computer access are also socially divisive.

Privatisation has further exacerbated the situation by noticeably broadening the gap between the educational achievements of British children whose parents could afford to send them to private schools and those who had to make do with what the state provided. The UK Educational Research Council analysed the results of Key Stage II tests given to children at age 11, who were completing their primary schooling. They noted that by June 1998, the gap in achievement levels between the two cohorts of schoolchildren was 'about three years' (*Evening Standard*, 1998).

Obviously this was more a reflection of methodologies, facilities, access and opportunities, than of innate ability. What we are tending to see in this, and in all sorts of other ways, is the gradual creation of two-tiered societies in first world nations – with the upper tier being articulate, with good self-esteem and a high level of empowerment, and the lower tier being more fragmented, less able to articulate its social agenda and much more disempowered by such factors as poor housing, less education and higher levels of unemployment – and maybe lack of access to the Internet! If this interpretation is correct, it would suggest that health promotion initiatives in the first world, although up-front and visible, enthusiastically articulated and well represented in terms of legalisation and credibility, may be primarily addressed to the top tier.

In most of the third world, of course, the social divide is much wider between the rich and poor, and a broadly educated 'clerical' and literate middle-class pathway between the two is very much less evident. Such was the situation, for instance, in Chile when Salvador Allende's 'Marxist' Unidad Popular Party found itself elected in 1970. Empowerment of previously marginalised and oppressed groups among the lower classes quickly began. Evening adult literacy classes were packed out and people who had previously assumed that they were of no account plucked up courage and began to find themselves elected by their colleagues to local barrio councils and the like. As we know, it all came to a sticky end. The gap between the two tiers was so great, and middle-class support so ambivalent, that it was easy enough for US-controlled corporations, especially in the copper mining industry, to work through the military to reverse the whole process. But during its brief period of efflorescence, one of the first issues reflecting popular empowerment of the barrio poor in Santiago (and probably elsewhere in Chile) was hygiene and public health. Mothers did not simply come to the newly available family clinics with their young children – they demanded information. Illiterate though many of them were, they were not content simply to receive instruction about medication and baby care – they wanted to know why and how. They were experiencing the sort of empowerment referred to by Wilson (1976).

Differences in the Cuban context

The Cuban experience is now exceedingly instructive in this respect – and its achievement precariously vulnerable over a wide spectrum to non-military and covert sabotage by first world financial interests. For instance, consider some of the differences between the ascension to power of Allende's government in Chile and Castro's in Cuba. Allende won in a conventional multiparty election. The vote for him was almost solid in the wretched slum areas of the main cities because the Unidad Popular was the only party that really addressed any of their concerns. It got in – narrowly – with a shift in middle-class votes. Chile had, in the previous decade and like a number of third world countries, expanded access to education (especially technical and scientific subjects) to meet its trading needs. Many of these young modern thinkers looked for a break with oligarchic traditions and Allende seemed to represent a breath of fresh air. But once Unidad Popular came to power, it had an immense uphill job to do to educate its polling booth supporters as to the implications of what was involved.

Fidel Castro, however, was not elected. He and the political system he headed and represented only came to power after at least six years (more among some of the groups supporting him) of assiduously cultivating grass-roots support among the rural and urban populations. Therefore within days of the revolution's triumph, Committees for the Defence of the Revolution (CDRs) were set up, each representing groups of 100 to 500 local people. Everyone in Cuba belongs to a CDR and these form one of several identifiable bases for neighbourhood advocacy and empowerment. While the popular press in both the United States and Britain widely presented the CDRs as 'neighbourhood spy networks' designed to identify counter-revolutionary plotters and covert CIA agents, that was only a very minor part of their remit. The bulk of their time now, in fact, is spent in cataloguing their neighbourhoods' health and educational needs, prioritising them and elaborating strategies for meeting them.

In other words, health promotion came to Cuba after the bases for neighbourhood advocacy had already been established. Empowerment in Cuba really was a precondition for health promotion, as first world thinkers such as Lalonde (1974), Tannahill (1985), and Ashton and Seymour (1988) – and many others – have always suggested should be the case. Indeed, the formation of CDRs itself quickly gave rise to further grass-roots empowerment organisations, some of them – like the now immensely influential Cuban Federations of Women (FMCs) – at first an acute embarrassment to any factions in the government who may have hoped to 'direct' revolutionary activity from above (MacDonald, 1998).

No other political revolution in history seems to have been quite so successful in encompassing local empowerment and personal autonomy and using them in implementing social policy. For instance, in conversations this author has had with numerous aid workers visiting Cuba from the then communist states of Eastern Europe and from the Soviet Union itself, it became clear that Cuban communism struck them as quite different from the more top-down authoritarian models to which they had been accustomed. When in the Soviet Union in 1981, this author often saw a very colourful and attractive poster on primary classroom walls headed: 'How can I Be a Good Communist?'. The major theme seemed to be obedience: for instance 'Good little Communists value health. They eat what their parents and teachers give them. They don't argue about bedtimes and always follow the rules of their local health council.' This would not have gone down well in Cuba! The nearest thing to it in Cuba was a Young Pioneers' leaflet which the author read in 1984. It stated: 'Your health is important to you and to everyone around you. Do you know how your body works? Find out whatever you can.'

The vulnerability of Cuban health promotion

But, as stated earlier, health promotion in Cuba is not only based on different criteria to that in most other third world countries and to those of the first world, it is also uniquely vulnerable. Neighbourhood empowerment implies an unimpeded access to information, first of all. However, the US blockade, especially as refined under the Helms Burton Act and under President Bush, renders that increasingly difficult. Confidence and community self-esteem rest on human dignity, and yet the blockade has impacted badly on supplies to Cuba of basic food items which it cannot produce, as well as soap, cleaning agents, paints, etc. Schools, the pride and joy of Cuba's revolution, are now looking increasingly shabby, even though 40% of its (much depleted) GNP is devoted to health and education – the highest in the world.

As of 2004, Cuba has not closed down any school or hospital, despite the fact that some of them now would not pass fire safety inspections in a first world country. Much wealthier third world countries under full US support – and, of course, without a blockade – do not have universal access to schooling and even in some urban areas run what schools they do have on a two-shift system (e.g. Jamaica). Cuba takes great pride in the fact that they are not yet in that situation. But for how long can they maintain this unique achievement in the teeth of an increasingly threatening US?

Cuba's grass-roots social organisation flourishes on community involvement at all levels. But even this is increasingly seriously compromised by the blockade. For instance, Cuba's continued progress relies on the faith, commitment and optimism of its young people. Cuban youth have, since the revolution, been very much in public evidence in reflecting the socially positive values of helpfulness and uplifting ideals. But to sustain these, their 'spiritual needs' (the term used by Fidel Castro in a 1997 speech to the Cuban Teachers Union) must be met. What he meant by their 'spiritual needs', we probably would refer to as 'aesthetic needs', for what he was bemoaning was the difficulties Cuba was having providing facilities for discos – such as sound systems, etc. Cuba has had a long tradition of popular music culture (along with most of the other Caribbean and Latin American countries) and it is perfectly reasonable to believe that were this seriously curtailed for long, it would do much to create disaffection in young people.

It may seem extraordinary to think that such an issue has important health promotion implications, but it unquestionably does. In fact it is interesting to note that one of the several Cuba Solidarity Organisations in Britain (the Revolutionary Communist Group) specialises in collecting funds to supply sound systems to the Cuban Communist Youth Council for setting up in local communities. If anyone doubts the importance of this sort of thing, let them ponder the words of Plato who stated (*Dialogues, Book II*) that: 'Music reflects the soul of a people and any government which does not support it cannot sustain the loyalty of the people.'

There are even wider avenues of vulnerability to the maintenance of health promotion in Cuba. The blockade has forced Cuba to compromise seriously with the moral and ethical roots of its social policy. For instance, the need for hard currency – a need which Cuba could easily have met through normal trade without the blockade – has meant that Cuba has had to promote itself as a tourist attraction, but until 1988, its almost puritan ideological values in placing human dignity above money meant that it did not go out of its way to seriously promote tourism. Its trading links with the Soviet Union and its satellites, third world countries and non-US first world countries were sufficient to maintain its sense of dignity and pride.

But the collapse of the Soviet Union, together with progressive US interference with its trading network, quickly reduced its resources. By 1992, Cuba began to look destitute. Shops were empty, rationing had to be intensified, medical equipment could not be obtained and – at the grass-roots level – Cubans found themselves stooping to all sorts of humiliations in order to secure money and commodities. Prostitution, once a vast and thriving industry in pre-revolutionary Cuba, had been eliminated since 1959. However, by 1994 it was creeping back again in and around hotels where foreign visitors stayed. The government found itself compelled to allow people to work for, and trade in, US dollars. It had hitherto resisted this because it was socially divisive and hence caused alienation and represented a barrier to equity. But on this it was forced to retreat as an alternative to sacrificing all of the other social and moral gains of the revolution thus far.

The effect of this was – as the government had always feared – the division of people into a two-tier society: those who could work in a dollar economy and those who were 'relegated' to that of the Cuban peso. Even more detrimental to national pride was the fact that many highly qualified Cuban medical and scientific personnel found it worthwhile to work as lift operators and porters in hotels attracting international clients because their tips (in US currency) exceeded their peso salaries as professionals in the Cuban economy. It really is a moot question as to whether Cuba's social system – so emphatically based on national collective pride and a belief in the dignity of labour – can psychologically survive such derogation. Obviously it is hoped, in first world financial circles, that it cannot. The collapse of the Cuban model would represent a great gain for them!

Dollar-earning Cubans rally to promote health

But let us not be too pessimistic. The revolutionary values of human dignity and social response to one another's needs are now deeply entrenched in the thinking of ordinary Cubans. On 1 July 2004, according to a report on BBC Radio 4, a Cuban trade union leader indicated that tourist industry workers – hugely privileged because they earn US dollars in tips – provided one million dollars (£559 650) to the health service.

It was further reported by Britain's left-wing newspaper, the *Morning Star* (26 July 2004), that – at an event held to recognise their contribution – the Confederation of Cuban Workers (CTC) decorated 32 workers and 27 workplaces for their altruism. Their contribution had gone specifically to 'fighting cancer and promoting mother–child health care'.

The campaign, organised entirely at the grass-roots level, and taking off at different dates in different CDRs, used the slogan 'My contribution to life'. It quickly spread all over Cuba. It is probably difficult for many of us in the first world not only to imagine that kind of spontaneous altruism, but for it to represent a major news item in the media. We do tend to reserve such attention for various pop idols, fashion gurus, enormously wealthy tycoons, etc. – people who make millions – not who give it away for the social good!

The report continues that the enterprise makes possible the purchase of citostatic drugs, special radioactive isotopes for cancer research and treatment, incubators and fans for newborn infants and instruments, along with other medical equipment. These latter are chronically in short supply because of the US embargo and its legislation to reduce hard currency from reaching Cuba.

Starting 11 years ago, in 1993, the programme has apparently been gathering pace ever since. Its protagonists are the sort of people held up to Cuban youth as role models. Its donations to the country's health services, as of 2004, total US$17 million. This author pointed out, in his 1999 book, how the Helms Burton Act was causing high levels of stress among child leukaemia victims in Cuba because of the difficulties put in Cuba's way to secure the appropriate medication. But the programme described above is partly addressing that particular sector.

The National Programme to Fight Cancer in Children was established in 1987. Since 2000, it has been funded by the campaign. Partly as a result, the survival rate of cancer patients is nearly at parity with the UK figures.

When Cuban children start at their first pre-school, one of the opening ceremonies of the day involves them saying, instead of a pledge of allegiance (as US children do), that: 'Seremos como Che. Seremos internacionalistas' (We shall be like Che. We are internationalists). Just as the Pledge of Allegiance in US schools seems to impact on the attitudes of most US adults, the equivalent routine in Cuba really does seem to transcend selfish and acquisitive tendencies.

The workers do not only donate money, but they also contribute in their spare time to medical facility repair and upkeep. They are often seen about on the streets taking patients out for walks, etc.

Potential of the Cuban experience

The dramatic successes in healthcare under the Cuban system mark it as an obvious model for third world development. But, as we have seen, it appears to be so easily isolated and undermined that the question must be raised as to whether it has any long-term validity at all. Financial power in the first world is a fact and cannot be discounted easily. However, the situation is not altogether bleak for the following reasons.

- The Cuban model does work internally and would work even better in a country which has sufficient natural resources, especially oil, to be less dependent on trade for survival. Of course, one of the preconditions for such a set-up would be a social revolution and the preparation of the sort of psychological bases described earlier.
- Even when a third world country is heavily tied into the international trading matrix for its basic needs, it is well positioned to be politically self-sufficient if it has oil! As a WHO consultant, this author has had to spend time in Libya, a country that had been 'trade embargoed' until 1999, although not as severely as has Cuba, since the Lockerbie air disaster in 1988. Yet hard currency is not a problem for them because they are sitting on so much oil which the first world needs. They have therefore been able to mount and sustain a healthcare system to which all of its people have access (Abdulbasset, 1997). Health promotion in Libya poses a different set of psychological problems from those which prevail in Cuba, and tends to be 'administered' from above rather than elaborated at grass-roots level. But that may represent a cultural difference rather than a financial one.
- General instability in market economies within the first world has, since 1997, raised afresh the possibility of a viable critique along Marxist lines of capitalism as a world system. If Cuba can survive another few years of the US blockade, it could well act as a beacon to the social reorganisation of some first world economies.
- The globalisation of financial markets has had many deleterious effects on third world health generally, and hence on prospects for global health promotion. But, especially if that system is forced to give way to more rationally planned and regulated government-controlled economies, globalisation may well remain as a sound basis for organising it. In that case, the globalisation of equity in health might not have to fly in the face of market globalisation, but become part of its very infrastructure.

The fact that the Cuban model is not so ideologically driven that it cannot temporarily adapt to survive in a market-forces matrix might be seen as indicative of its essential resilience. Its psychological basis appears to be much stronger than that which prevailed in the Soviet system or in that of its Eastern European allies. Cuba's highly successful implementation of a national health promotion enterprise has been shown to be, in every sense, a logical expression of its basic social philosophy. Its capacity to adapt to this, and to share it so effectively with other nations and cultures, has already established Cuba as a likely model for other third world countries to follow.

This had great relevance with respect of diseases, either largely indigenous to the third world (malarias, some filterable virus disorders, childhood enteric diseases, etc.) or of diseases which, while of deep concern in the first world, have a different aetiology in the third. The most compelling example of this is HIV/AIDS and its incidence in some African countries.

On 4 August 2004, it was announced that, currently, more than 17 000 Cuban doctors are working in 65 countries. Ten thousand of these are serving in Venezuela. Consult: http://www.vnagency.com.vn

HIV/AIDS in Zimbabwe – Cuba's response

As already discussed in Chapter 11, the situation in Zimbabwe is not atypical of such other African nations as Uganda, Zambia and Tanzania. In 1998 the incidence of HIV/AIDS in Zimbabwe was quoted at 13% by WHO (WHO, 1998). This far exceeded the figure for any first world country and reflected a host of factors, including difficulties in obtaining condoms easily and at no cost, cultural attitudes to manliness, inadequate sexual health education and a high level of heterosexual promiscuity. With respect to the latter, most HIV/AIDS transmission in African countries is heterosexual-based rather than homosexual. Meanwhile there is now competition between various first world pharmaceutical houses in the search for a cure or at least a suppressant that can greatly delay the progress of the condition from HIV to full-blown AIDS.

One treatment in particular involves simultaneous administration of three or more different drugs with a common duo of AZT and Interferon, but this line of treatment had to be field-tested. All such regimes are of enormous cost and, since they are sold privately, only very wealthy first world clients can contemplate using them. To test them, HIV-positive Zimbabweans who were 16–21 years of age were tested on one such 3-in-1 cocktail. The testees were told that the material was being tested and that therefore an improvement could not be guaranteed. However, they were also told that even if it did not work, there were no longer-term harmful side-effects. The testees signed forms asserting that they understood the terms and conditions and that their continued weekly payments involved them agreeing to serve as long as the pharmaceutical company concerned needed to use them.

The treatment turned out to be 84–86% successful in greatly slowing the development of the disease, to the extent that in 17% of the cases, adverse symptoms vanished totally while in the rest they no longer were troubling enough to interfere with the prosecution of ordinary life. However, this was not a cure – only a suppressant – and the patients would have to continue taking the three drugs daily for the rest of their lives. After 18 months of field trials, the validity of the treatment was established to the satisfaction of company officials and the African trials were terminated.

This meant of course, that the testees would have to stop treatment, because it was no longer available free. The company had done nothing unethical in the legal sense, because they had paid each volunteer for each test, but it meant, in fact, that third world victims had been used to test a therapy from which only first world victims could benefit, given the costs involved. It would be extremely difficult to mount a logical argument compelling a private company to provide free treatment for life to selected African victims – namely the original sample – but not to all.

Under global administration, this problem would of course not arise. Profit would not be a factor because the medication would be supplied from the first to the third world as a global cost. Moreover, other third world countries – such as Cuba – which had elaborated a particularly effective and supportive approach to HIV/AIDS in the community, would be free to share its expertise with another third world nation because they would have themselves coped with a similar aetiology for the disease. First world-based AIDS workers would not be able to do that with the same degree of effectiveness. The Cuban approach to HIV/AIDS is entirely innovatory (Waller *et al.*, 1993) and its application – together with the most advanced pharmacology available in the first world – would quickly make a global impact on the incidence of the condition.

Cuba's healthcare relationship with the third world is most unusual. Earlier in this chapter, references were made to the fact that Cuba sends its doctors to other third world countries as a form of 'third world solidarity'. Few countries, even first world nations, could afford to export their doctors in this way, sometimes for two or three years at a time. But Cuba still does so, even under the harsh economic impact of the US blockade. To end this chapter, an account of one such Cuban aid programme to another third world country will be detailed.

Cuban doctors in post-apartheid South Africa

South Africa held its first non-racial elections in 1994, bringing Nelson Mandela and the ANC (African National Congress) to power. At that, there was a mass exodus of many white people – especially of professionally qualified people – from South Africa. Among these were so many doctors that entire areas of rural South Africa were left bereft of medically trained people. In fact, ANC officials calculated that 2000 medical posts had been vacated and, of these, it was estimated that 600 doctors were needed as a matter of absolute urgency. In desperation more than hope, South Africa approached beleaguered Cuba. Cuba's response was to provide the complete slate of 600 doctors.

The following inspiring account of this remarkable enterprise is quoted from a 1998 article by Suzanne Daleyudeni, and which appeared in *Cuba Si*, the official magazine of the Cuba Solidarity Committee.

> *In the two years since he arrived at the tiny hospital here deep in the misty hills of KwaZulu/Natal, Dr Abel Gonzalez Perez has learned the Zulu words and phrases for lie down, relax, breathe deeply and where is the pain?*
>
> *But he has not yet mastered all the phrases he might need. So on a recent morning he resorted to pantomime to communicate to a pregnant young woman awaiting a sonogram that the traditional layers of fabric she wrapped around her hips in an effort to look pleasingly hefty had to be pushed much farther down if he was to do his work.*
>
> *The young woman stared. He tried again, this time pulling at his own clothes. She stared some more. Finally, with a shake of his head and an apologetic smile, he reached around her waist and yanked at her clothes himself. It was about ten minutes later when he leaned around the screen of the ultrasound equipment to announce 'Intombazana!' – 'It's a girl!' – that the woman finally smiled.*
>
> *The people of this desperately poor rural community ravaged by malnutrition and AIDS have been flocking to the hospital here lately in part to see this doctor who has the power to tell the sex of a child before it is born. But partly they come just because there is a doctor here.*

Posts like the one here – hours from the nearest town, at the end of the 25-mile-long dirt road – had little hope of being filled.

Now Gonzalez is one of four Cuban doctors at the hospital here earning, they say, about twice as much as they would earn in their own country and struggling with relative good cheer to understand the sometimes perplexing ways of the local population. In the two years since the first two Cuban doctors arrived, they have reopened the surgery centre, brought in the sonogram equipment, expanded the hospital from 120 to 200 beds and reduced by half the number of babies who die at birth.

South African health officials say they are delighted with the performance of the 359 Cubans who had been deployed since 1996, when the first 60 arrived. Only two had been sent back to Cuba: one did not show up for work; the other, an anaesthetist, left after two operations in which the patients died.

South Africa's governing African National Congress party has long had ties to Cuba, which supported it when it was outlawed. Health officials said they talked to several countries about hiring doctors but that Cuba was the first to respond and, as a country that has long produced an excess of doctors, was able to send the large numbers South Africa needed.

'We did not care too much what the Western thinking was on this issue', said Vincent Hlongwane, a spokesperson for the health ministry. 'There aren't too many countries that can give you 600 doctors without collapsing their services and that's what we wanted.' Hlongwane said that for the most part the Cubans, who are being paid South African wages that range from about $20 000 to $60 000 depending on experience, have been a success.

They sign three-year contracts, which are then renewable each year.

'The feedback we are getting is that we are getting more than we paid for,' Hlongwane said. 'They are a caring lot and they are not materialistic. They are doing more than their contracts ask them to do.'

Cuba currently has doctors working in more than 40 countries. In fact, two of the doctors at Qudeni's Ekombe Hospital have worked elsewhere in Africa before.

But Dr Eduardo Paz Paula and Dr Leocadio Blanco, the first to arrive, were hardly prepared for how far into the back hills they were going. During their two-week orientation, as they toured Durban's top hospitals and were wined and dined by the country's top health officials, they kept asking where Ekombe was. No one knew. When the time came to get into the car, Blanco said, the drive got eerier and eerier as the late afternoon fog set in and the road turned to gravel. 'We kept asking the driver, ''Where are you taking us?'' I kept saying, ''My friend, are you lost?'' But he said ''No.'' When we finally got here, it was a big shock, I tell you.'

By early in the morning, Ekombe's cluster of whitewashed one-storey buildings are crammed with patients. The paediatric ward is full of children suffering from malnutrition – not the skeletons of starvation, but the bloated, expressionless faces and bodies that result from a diet of cornmeal and nothing else. Dr Alfredo Hevia Martin, the fourth Cuban doctor, moves down the line stroking swollen faces and examining patches where skin has sloughed off, another symptom of malnutrition, and deciding whether to administer plasma to boost their systems. Very often, the adults are in good shape and the nursing babies are fine. It is the toddlers and slightly older children who suffer most.

Dr Hevia has begun cataloguing the community, arguing that a true knowledge of how its members live will help establish proper primary care. Travelling in a *four-wheel-drive vehicle with a nurse as an interpreter, he has already visited 60 families, noting that few in the area have an income exceeding $60 a month. They live in tiny round huts with a fire in the middle and poor ventilation, which makes them easy prey to tuberculosis.*

Illiteracy is standard, and the doctors have given up on the fancy anti-AIDS posters that their patients can't read. They carry condoms in their pockets along with a Xeroxed cartoon showing how to use them.

The doctors have also reached out to the local healers, trying in particular to enlist their help against what is widely called here 'the Zulu enema', a homemade remedy for colicky babies that kills one or two infants a week. Originally a herbal mixture, the doctors say, mothers these days use toxic ingredients like shoe polish, liquid soap and even battery acid.

Blaming the problem on advice from 'deadly grannies', Hevia is clearly frustrated. 'There is nothing in the medical books about how to treat a Zulu enema', he said. 'Go look it up. Not a word. We see five or six a week. One or two we cannot save.' (Daleyudeni, 1998)

With experience like this in its repertoire it is difficult to see how Cuba could not play a pivotal role as a worldwide model of how to organise and administer global health promotion.

References

Abdulbasset E (1997) *Health Promotion in Libya.* MSc dissertation, Brunel University, London.

Ashton J and Seymour H (1988) *The New Public Health.* Open University Press, Buckingham, ch. 8.

Campbell M (2004) Elderly Cuban left to starve as drought brings cut in rations. *Sunday Times,* 17 July, main section, p.21.

Daleyudeni S (1998) Cuban doctors are saving lives in rural South Africa. *Cuba Si* – Journal of the Cuba Solidarity Campaign. Spring. **25(4):** 11.

Evening Standard (1998) Standards in state education fall behind private sector. 13 November, p.9.

Gibbs S (2004) Drought brings Cuba to its knees. *The Independent,* 31 July, pp 30–1.

Lalonde M (1974) *Perspectives on Health of All Canadians.* Canadian Government Publications, Ottawa.

MacDonald T (1985) *Making A New People.* New Star Books, Vancouver.

MacDonald T (1998) *Schooling the Revolution.* Praxis Press, London.

MacDonald T (1999) *Health Care in Cuba: An Analysis of Development Since 1959.* Edwin Mellen Press, Lewiston, Lampeter and Queenstown.

MacDonald T (2000) *Third World Health Promotion and its Dependence on First World Health.* Edwin Mellen Press, Lewiston, Lampeter and Queenstown.

Morning Star (2004) Cubans' donations aid health care. The People's Press Printing Society, London, 26 July, p.3.

New York Times (1960) Conversations with Fidel Castro. 2 November, p.3.

Perez A (2004) Speaking at the Cuban Ministry of Public Health, Havana, 26 April.

Tannahill A (1985) What is health promotion? *Health Education Journal.* **44(4):** 167–8.

Waller J, Adams L, Lyms B, Redgrave P and Schatzberger P (1993) *AIDS in Cuba – a portrait of prevention.* Cuba Solidarity Committee, London.

World Health Organization (1998) *World Health.* WHO, Geneva, p.28.

Wilson M (1976) *Health is for People.* Darton, Longman and Todd, London, pp 116–20.

Chapter 14

Possible routes to global health equity

Capitalism and first world consumerism:
the underlying problems

The situation so far described is far too serious to be swept under the carpet by benign generalities. The whole of civilisation is threatened by it, as is possibly the continued existence of life on the planet. But we must not panic or run wildly after 'heroic' solutions or excesses based on narrow ideology. Such can worsen the situation. Instead, let us try to take the problem apart and consider it dispassionately.

If we do so, it is not an exaggeration to say that – as things stand now and for some time to come – there is only one superpower and that is the US. It is to them we must look for significant headway in resolving the difficulties. Because they control such a huge proportion of the world's wealth, they can – almost at will – control the direction of development anywhere in the world.

Yet it is US capitalism, naturally, that determines the direction of American political power. Opposition to capitalism, and the distorted social relations it promotes, does exist in the US. This is so despite the 2004 presidential election, which so clearly illustrated the extent to which corporate interests could combine with the fears – greatly exacerbated by the horrors of 9/11 – of millions of Americans seeking refuge in literal interpretations of the Bible. Despite the undisputed fact that the Republicans, led by George Bush, won both the popular vote and also Republican majorities in both Houses of Congress, let us remember that only 40% of the electorate voted. The Bush campaign was brilliantly organised and succeeded in swaying the concerns of large numbers of evangelical Christians away from such mundane economic issues as employment, medical care, etc., onto issues of personal sexual lifestyles, abortion, etc.

To add to all of this, it has to be realised that both the Republican Party and the Democratic Party serve the interests of US capitalism and its powerful global influence. In other words, it is reasonable to suppose that many of the 60% who did not vote felt that it would make scant difference to their real needs. Part of the reason for this is that the media are almost exclusively owned by the very same corporate interests. There is virtually no outlet for alternative political voices. The vast majority even of educated Americans are not aware that there are alternative approaches.

It therefore seems obvious that, as a first step, we must support American groups who are denied access to media outlets for their views. They need a much more open forum so that, instead of reacting on a reflex of fear and xenophobia to international issues, they have a better opportunity to discuss and debate their interests in such issues as healthcare and job security, both in the US media and globally. We need to be much more proactive in making our media open to them. We have much to learn from the US 'Silent Majority', and this author is constantly horrified at the way in which Americans are lampooned in the UK and EU as 'mindless rednecks' on the basis of the way that only 51% of 40% of them (20.4%) voted!

Therefore, the basis of any progress towards solutions rests on much broader levels of communications between US citizens and those of the rest of the world, so far outside of the total control of Fox News, the Rupert Murdoch media empire, etc. We cannot neglect to notice that even first world governments outside the US are increasingly having their media brought under the same kind of control by business interests. So far, we have tended to sell our souls rather cheaply. All of these issues need to be discussed much more forcefully within small communities and between communities worldwide. The means for doing so are increasingly available because of advances in computer technology. We are all affected and 'health issues' are only symptomatic of the wider problem.

The advent and rapid international deployment of access to the Internet are of immense positive value here. We have never previously in human history had such potential for global communication – and it will increase. One obvious reason that the masses of exploited third world people had reacted so passively in the past is that they were simply not aware of how disadvantaged they were comparatively. Now – even with only one email outlet in an entire village – levels of such ignorance and helplessness are vanishing. The potential of a 'political internet' holds immense promise. It contextualises much that we will now discuss about global health issues per se.

Targets set vs targets measurable

It is most instructive to read over the list of 38 targets set by WHO in 1985 in aiming for the objective of Health for All (HFA) 2000. Indeed, 22 of the targets were aimed for earlier than 2000 (1990 or 1995). However, on reading them, the question arose in this author's mind as to how one would know whether or not a target had been achieved. There did not appear to be a generally acceptable measurable benchmark to establish this. *See* Appendix H.

For instance, Target 1 (WHO, 1986) reads:

> *By the year 2000, the actual differences in health status between countries and between groups within countries should be reduced by at least 25 percent, by improving the level of health of disadvantaged nations and groups.*
>
> *This target could be achieved if the basic prerequisite for health were provided for all: if the risks related to lifestyle were reduced: if the health aspects of living and working conditions were improved; and if good primary health care were made accessible to all.*

The first paragraph introduces a precise mathematical figure (25%), but how on earth would we measure it? The second paragraph states what would have to occur for us to be in a position to know whether or not the target had been achieved. Basically, it points to the hardly irrefutable fact that we would know if the problems were already solved.

An international role for Health Impact Assessment

WHO's comments are certainly true and certainly praiseworthy. If the reader looks through all of them in Appendix H, he/she will see that some targets do not contain an empirically measurable objective, e.g. Targets 2, 3, 5 and several others.

To set measurable targets, we have to have international agreement on what is being measured and how. A step in the right direction is Health Impact Assessments (HIAs), as mentioned in Chapter 6. In that account we saw that HIAs have been, and are being, successfully applied in the first world, largely over local projects, such as construction jobs, etc. We need, as a matter of some urgency, to make HIAs part of the international agenda as quickly as possible. This is strongly suggested by several contributors, e.g. O'Keefe and Scott-Samuel (2002). As that article states in one of its conclusions: 'Health impact assessments can and should aim to provide tools that can capture the most deep-seated, systematic and global economic and environmental crimes in which humankind is complicit.'

For instance, all that has been said in earlier chapters about SAPs or about 'vertical', as opposed to 'horizontal', planning needs consideration. Both of these methods of approach protect the first world, but often bring about ecological damage in the third world of such a scale as to undermine health to a grotesque degree.

Setting up the framework for such international HIAs would require a much more radical approach than G8 or WTO summits can possibly provide. In fact, in this author's view, the matter cannot be based on arguments of relative costs to the governments involved. It is an essential and therefore has to be done without financial preconditions. Once we establish, through international meetings of the health experts, what must be done, we can then sit down and work out what participating nations need to contribute financially. The banks and corporations become 'service purveyors', but they cannot call the shots or determine ahead of time what might be in it for their first world stockholders. Consider what has been done already.

International Association for Impact Assessment and HuIA

The IAIA was established in 1980 to coordinate the efforts of researchers, practitioners and various users of HIAs in different parts of the world and therefore often finds itself advising on third world health issues.

It seeks to:

1 develop approaches and practices for comprehensive and integrated HIA; it thus does not confine itself to individual projects in various countries, but to take into account their total community impact
2 improve assessment techniques for wide practical application
3 promote public understanding and involvement in what they are doing and in setting targets
4 share their findings and publications.

IAIA identifies itself as the leading global authority in the use of HIA for decision-making regarding policies and programmes. It believes the assessment of the environmental, social, economic, cultural and health implications of government or international proposals to be a critical contribution to sustainable development. Consult http://iaia.org. This site was updated 30 July 2004.

An even more effective initiative for trying to anticipate what the health impact of some international trading or commercial proposal will be is considered by Human Impact Assessment in States (HuIA). It includes *both* Health Impact Assessment *and* Social Impact Assessment. The two, of course, are often inextricable. HuIA was initiated in Finland and famously applied in the elaboration of the Finnish Healthy Cities Network. Started in 1993, HuIA has recently been developing strategic prediction tools for global use in sustainable health. Consult http:/www.stakes.fi/sva/huia/huianstates.htm.

This seems a very tall order, but unless we set HIA criteria, as established by health experts and in consultation with the recipient communities, we are lost. The gap between rich and poor is still widening with respect to such human rights as health, education, access to pure water, etc. – basically 'human dignity' – and that is because we are treating the problems as ones that have to be solved in the context of business and corporate interests. Of course, many people (usually those in no danger of personal environmental threats to their own dignity) refer to the 'business model' as 'realistic'. Altruism, by that measure, is more often than not 'unrealistic'. But if we allow ourselves to live with that view of reality, we are guaranteeing more wars, more environmental disasters and an early end to our existence.

That is why the author called the serious and systematic application of HIA globally to trade and all other international transactions as 'radical'. In my view it need not involve major revolutionary upheavals and large-scale war. As explained in the rest of this chapter, we should be able to avoid that. There just needs to be a major revolutionary upheaval in our thought processes, an enterprise eminently worth pursuing to prolong civilised values and the pleasures of life.

The politics/health interface

An international focus on Health Assessment is as much a community enterprise as a clinical one. There is plenty of scope for lay organisation around the issues 'from below'. For instance, the People's Health Assembly is about to launch its first Global Health Watch Report in Ecuador in July 2005 – as an alternative to the World Health Report produced by WHO. Even that respected body has become, in some ways, too closely involved with the purposes of global capitalism for comfort. They even went so far as, for instance, to have their 2000 report edited by the chief economist of the World Bank!

Again, the whole asylum issue in the US and other first world areas (along with 'illegal' immigration) combines corporate global interests with those of community health. Banks in the US are anxious to process Mexican remittances, now that the World Bank has discovered that such remittances are running at just above US$90 billion, accounting for more than Foreign Debt Investment. President Bush in 2003 had to offer amnesty arrangements to 'illegals' who were sponsored by employers – state sanctioning of unprotected sweatshop labour. Indeed, in O'Keefe and Scott-Samuel's book (2002) they place much expectation on the voices of migrant communities in the first world as a potential part of the community action required.

A conspectus of possible strategies

So far in this book we have considered major problems which militate against a favourable environment for the maintenance of health in the third world. We have also considered a number of individual cases – both in terms of the problems and in terms of possible solutions. Now let us consider the vital issue of possible general approaches to remediation. Health promotion philosophies must underlie our endeavours if health is to be sustainable.

Health promotion has a well-established presence in first world thought and practice. But, for health promotion anywhere to be effective long-term, it cannot remain sequestered only in certain areas of the globe. On the other hand, the third world really is where the majority of the world's people live and we have seen that solutions that work in the first world are not likely to be easily applicable in the third. Therefore, what this boils down to is that health promotion never will become global unless we can elaborate strategies by overcoming the specific problems that prevent its development in the third world. This would constitute an important role for the 'political internet' referred to above.

It goes without saying that the third world is not in any sense a monolithic unity. It speaks with many voices, often mutually acrimonious, in many languages and in perseverance of incompatible agendas. For that reason a prerequisite to any solution is the transcendence of national interests and a shared focus on global interest as a priority. As an intermediate step it would seem, as well, that 'unions' or 'federations' of large clusters of the third world nations with agreed compatible economic interests will have to come into being. It has been tried before, e.g. Nasser's dream of a United Arab Republic or Nkrumah's hope for an Organisation of African Unity. How else to achieve even temporary trading equality with the European Union or the United States? One can, of course, consider really radical proposals, such as Christian Aid's Jubilee 2000 idea of unilaterally abolishing debts owed by third world nations to first world banks. But in the long term, we surely must think in much broader terms of bringing about global relationship changes.

Very broadly speaking, it might be useful to regard such global strategies as being either 'red' or 'green'. 'Red', of course, refers to a collectivist, community-centred ethic and can loosely be said to accommodate socialist models of positive human enhancement and cooperation. 'Green' refers to a concern for making sure that due regard is paid to the importance of our environment – both geographically and spiritually. In this we are speaking of the holy grail of sustainable development.

Both approaches are radical – and must be so – because they require significant changes, not only in governmental organisation, but in production and distribution processes as well. These changes, while affecting virtually every nation, would cause the greatest dislocation in the first world nations. However, it is not as though there is a choice. At best, the present system of third world exploitation can only be of relatively short-term benefit to the first world. It would not be too long before these inequities reflected themselves in job insecurity among first world people. Possibly, the bankers wouldn't worry – patriotic loyalty rarely transcends greed! – but that state of affairs would not long survive widespread unemployment in the West.

Some strategies cannot realistically be regarded as predominantly 'red' or 'green', but encompass both. For instance, we can say with certainty that two fundamental problems are common to most of the others; these are: unsustainability and inequity. These are not simple issues of wealth or of privation, but of who is consuming what and at what cost to others.

Unsustainability

Our planet, Earth, its atmosphere and all of the life forms on it can potentially re-uptake about 13.5 billion tons of carbon dioxide per year. But this uptake is not equally distributed among the countries of the world. If it were, then each person on earth would be permitted to discharge about 2.3 tonnes of carbon dioxide a year. But consider the reality: each US resident disposes of roughly 20 tonnes, a German about 11 tonnes and a Japanese nearly 9 tonnes. Although the discrepancies thus referred to are great, they are as nothing if we compare the northern hemisphere with the southern hemisphere! For instance, a resident of the Indian subcontinent gets rid of 0.8 tonnes, a Chinese person not quite 2 tonnes and a Brazilian 1.5 tonnes. Is this inequity sustainable? Well, if we all disposed of carbon dioxide at the rate, say, that the Japanese do, we would need an ecosystem 10 times the size of planet Earth's to process it each year. What this rather graphic analogy correctly suggests is that we are building up a processing deficit for carbon dioxide year on year and that clearly this can only continue for some finite time. Figure 14.1 illustrates the situation in historical terms (Sachs *et al.*, 1998).

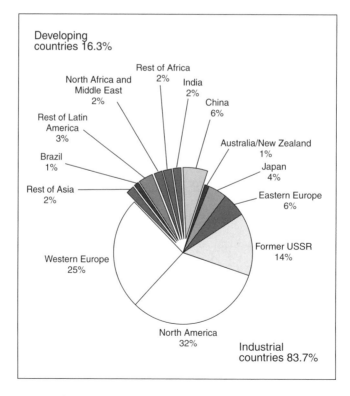

Figure 14.1: Regional contributions to global atmospheric increases in carbon dioxide, 1980–1988.

The problems of comparative measures

This whole phenomenon can be viewed as a resource problem relating to differential environmental degradation over the globe, or as a problem of social class
inequity. It does not easily lend itself to considerations of 'average' consumption of
one nation, compared to another, because the greatest discrepancies in consumption are often found within the poorest nations. On the other hand high GNP per
capita doesn't necessarily lead to greater equality. If we were to measure the
outcomes in terms of how much more money the richest 20% of a nation's
population has than its poorest 20%, we get the following ratios as of 1985 (World
Bank, 1997):

* India   5:1
* Indonesia   5:1
* Bangladesh   4:1
* Great Britain   6:1
* Australia   6:1.

Thus, using that criterion, Bangladesh would have to be regarded as a 'more equal'
society than Great Britain!

As mentioned elsewhere in this book, data produced by the IMF and the World
Bank about such issues are frequently called into question, a common accusation
being that such figures often reflect an ideological agenda. But even using such
figures, it is evident that there has been a massive shift towards greater inequality
since 1985, when the figures given above were cited.

No country is so egalitarian in this respect that the richest 20% consume less than
twice what the poorest 20% do, but the ratios can be enormous. Brazil is, in terms of
its resources, a phenomenally wealthy country, but the ratio there is 32:1! There is
some hope that matters will improve there under its present administration.

If we intend to analyse the discrepancy in terms of different countries or regions,
we notice that the discrepancy is growing, not diminishing. This, then, not only
suggests non-sustainability, but a decreasing timeframe to which to avert global
disaster. In 1965 the richest 20% of the world's population used up about 70% of all
income worldwide. By 1995 it was closer to 85% (UNCTAD, 1996).

Figure 14.2 (see overleaf) reflects this trend much more clearly.

Consider China. That country has had to report that 2004 saw its first increase in
poverty since 1978 (Watts, 2004). The report suggests that to show a rise in poverty
so soon after the market-oriented reforms of 1978 effectively annuls the country's
claims to be a socialist society. There is a sustained and growing gap between the
urban rich and rural poor, with a huge differential gap now in the health status of its
citizens. One in 11 rural residents now have to subsist on about 15 US *cents* a day.
During the 1990s, 6 million people a year were being lifted above the poverty line
(US$1.00 per day). But by 2002, this had dropped to less than 2 million.

Lin Yueqil of the Social Studies Institute of China was quoted as saying (*The
Guardian*, 2004):

> The economy is growing as fast as ever, but the quality of the growth is declining. It is
> less efficient in alleviating poverty so we are seeing a rising gap between the top and
> the bottom income groups.

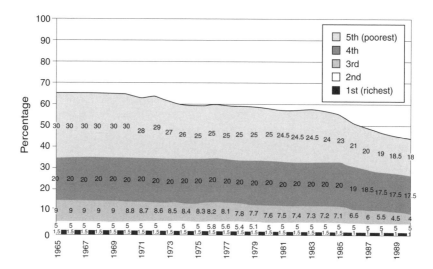

Figure 14.2: Cumulative share of world income by percentage of global population.

Corruption has also greatly increased with the rise of privatisation of services and the decline in emphasis on community values. The National Audit Association reported (2004) that 'about ten percent of the £2.96 billion put into government poverty elimination has been embezzled' (£1 = US$1.75 approximately).

Only a few months ago (June 2004), China hosted a global poverty alleviation conference during which it won praise from the World Bank, the British government and others for lifting 400 million out of destitution in the past 25 years.

But the crisis of inequality is growing apace. The Chinese Academy of Social Science reported that the average urban incomes were 3.1 times higher than those in the countryside. That makes it equivalent to the situation in Zimbabwe. When the cost of health and education are taken into account, the Chinese Academy branded the gap in the standard of living between urban and rural dwellers as the worst in the world.

Specifics of food supply and health

Any consideration of health promotion has to take account of diet. But diet is not, primarily, a matter of ethnic or cultural factors. In fact, all of these (probably) were determined ages ago in terms of relative food availability! This would vary according to such issues as existing soil quality and climatic conditions which, in turn, would give rise to differences of wealth.

For example, cereals are consumed approximately at the same rate over all the population, but that is not true of meat. Livestock production in much of Africa is restricted by infection by Trypanosome parasites. Going further down the food chain, we find that Cuba finds it difficult to produce enough milk to independently sustain its social policy of making a daily drink of milk available to every schoolchild up to the age of 14. Why is this so? Because alfalfa does not grow well in Cuban soil and the milk cattle must consume alfalfa as about 40% of their grazing intake.

If we look at health promotion indices in the non-dietetic context, the in-equalities persist, but often to the detriment of the first world. For instance, the richest 20% commandeer 90% of private cars and it could be argued that they thus are constrained to absorb more lead (or other unhealthy by-products) through respiration than do the poorest 20%. Such a view can be countered by the fact that poor people in narrow slum streets, and with access to fewer parks, are compelled to absorb the pollution produced by the car exhausts of the rich.

Varying health promotion parameters

Within any country, even a wealthy one, access to health promotion both indi-vidually and at the community level varies considerably. Clearly, if global health promotion is destined to be meaningfully addressed, action has to be taken within the regions and nations as well as transnationally. Sometimes such variations are based on the social marginalisation of certain identifiable subgroups within a population. Racism has obvious impacts on health promotion. For instance, in Germany under 50% of German nationals, compared with resident foreigners, live in poverty. The same sort of statistics prevail with respect to black and white people in the United States. This is clearly shown in Table 14.1, derived from the 1998 report of the United Nations Development Programme (UNDP, 1998).

Germany is a particularly interesting country to compare with the US, for in Germany a migrant to the country finds it extraordinarily difficult to gain citizen-ship. Even grandchildren of migrants, who no longer speak the language of their grandparents, and who never lived anywhere but in Germany, usually cannot gain German citizenship. In the US, on the other hand, foreign migrants can easily become citizens (only five years of residency is required) and many who do so take great pride in classifying themselves as 'American'. But if one examines the US population on black/white racialist lines, the figures compare with the German ones for foreigners/citizens.

Table 14.1: Social marginalisation: poverty in subgroups (families with children, 1980s)

	Average poverty rate	Those who escaped	Poor for three years or more
	(% of total in group)	(% of A)	(% of total in group)
Germany	A	B	C
Nationals	7	27	1
Foreigners	18	20	4
United States	A	B	C
White	15	17	10
Black	49	8	42

But the impact of this sort of thing on the third world is by no means trivial and likewise would need to be addressed in the context of internal politics before any rearrangement of international trade could make an impact. Consider India, for example, where the caste system still prevails sufficiently for it to differentially impact on intergroup health promotion. *See* Table 14.2, also derived from the same UNDP (1998) source as Table 14.1. In Table 14.2, 'scheduled caste' people from the states of Bihar and Orissa are compared with 'lower caste' people.

Table 14.2: Exit times from poverty status in rural households in India (two states compared)

	Household expenditures as % of national poverty-line for 1960–1990	Exit time in years
BIHAR STATE		
Scheduled caste	64	30
Lower caste	94	10
ORISSA STATE		
Scheduled caste	76	10
Lower caste	94	2

Is capitalism actually an option?

The opening comments in this chapter suggest the pivotal importance of this question. Much of the health data already discussed in this book suggests that the sort of radical change required in the first world in order to expedite global health promotion must of necessity be inimical to capitalism. How true is this? The question will be considered in greater detail later on in this chapter, but it is worthwhile now to see how it ties in with sustainability arguments.

There is first of all the old, but simplistic equation, that if every Chinese person were given a refrigerator, the impact on the environment would – under present technology – be disastrous. However, it is equally difficult to imagine the world remaining stable for long if the system prevailed by which some countries were compelled to remain poor in order to protect the world from the impact of unsustainable growth! Consideration of such problems by socially conscious people in the first world is often associated with the adoption of what are perceived as more environmentally friendly lifestyles and an ethical commitment to reducing consumption to far below what one's actual wealth might sustain.

But it has long been realised that levels of individual consumption in the first world rise and fall, even to the extent of causing changes in the economic cycles, without any associated or predictable change in third world economic well-being. When considering levels of production, many people seem to believe that there is a fixed supply of goods for the world's people, rendering direct the connection between one person's over-consumption and another's deprivation. But the relationship, of course, is much more complex than that.

For one thing, individual actions – especially along different lines or with different emphases – in some senses resemble quantum mechanics in that the slight variations are masked by the direction of the system as a whole. Even conscientious green consumerism is disappointing in its impact if practised by individuals outside of a wider and more coordinated political context. For a person from the first world to engage in the enterprise of green consumerism in an attempt to reduce negative effects on the environment takes no account of how retailing works. If environmentally friendly goods are not widely and easily available on the market, why would people go out of their way to purchase – at some inconvenience and at a higher price – a product which they could have obtained more easily and more cheaply if they had not been aware of the environmental argument (or chose to ignore it)?

Our 'democratic' freedom under Western capitalism does allow us to act as individuals, even to the extent of making it possible and legal for individuals to shop in an environmentally friendly fashion. But for this to be organised and directed so as to actually have a noticeable and planned impact would require such mass mobilisation and counter-cultural propaganda that it would probably have to be subversive in order to keep the democratic forces from effectively defending themselves against it. Without that, almost any realistic increase, say, in car usage in the third world would make less of a negative environmental impact than would even a small percentage reduction imposed politically and through legislation in the Western countries bring about in terms of a globally positive environmental impact.

In fact, the example of the internal combustion engine points to a crucial general consideration. This is that environmental destruction is caused less by actual consumption than by how specific consumables are produced. As Lisa Macdonald (1998) points out, 20 kilometres is the same in Sydney or in Punjab, but the difference is great indeed if the Punjabi travels it by bicycle while the Australian does it by car! Obviously wealth and consumption are not the same thing. The sort of improvement that urgently needs to be brought about involves a different view of what wealth is. If wealth were widely conceived as being understood in terms of an individual feeling enhanced through the exercise of the social good, it would be possible for wealth to be far more general than it can be at present.

There is no question that we are not merely discussing a 'feel-good' factor here, but are concerned with materially raising the eating and living standards of great masses of poor people up to a level consistent with operational definitions of community health. We can do this simply because even present-day technology can already deliver the products to make it possible. Altering the way in which these are distributed would make virtually no further negative environmental impact. Indeed, by eliminating the need for such wasteful practices as widespread deforestation, over-fishing, soil degradation and the like, the sum environmental impact would doubtless be positive over time.

This is where the political theories need to come in. In 1976, a seminal book was written by Barry Commoner (*The Poverty of the Planet*), basing much of his analysis on a critique of US capitalism. From 1945 to 1970, US per capita consumption rose 6% while per capita pollution rose by 700% or more! Suppose that US consumption standards could be achieved for the great majority in the third world, but at only a fraction of the environmental cost that it had entailed in the United States. That would certainly be possible, but it would be resisted by people and governments that were tied into the classical market-forces model.

Thus we are faced with a more basic task – altering people's mindset on a very broad scale. But, again, we really do not have any realistic option. Looking at it optimistically, that is the path we will follow – because there is no other – and the broad realisation of this by the world's people will bring it about without protracted revolutionary conflict. A more pessimistic view would see it coming about, but only through direct revolutionary confrontation and protracted upheaval – which itself might well be environmentally disastrous. But the most pessimistic view of all would be that these changes will not come about and the planet will gradually become a write-off, along with all of its inhabitants.

The optimistic view as a solution

How can the profit motive be replaced by a concept of wealth that is measured in terms of satisfaction of actual human needs? Surely large business corporations will use their power over governments to legitimise the continued production of destructive products. A fixation on short-term profit-making strategies would leave out any consideration of sustainability. What such a consideration implies is that environmentally sustainable methods really are inimical to capitalism.

This was extraordinarily exemplified late in 2004 by the work of Dr Alexandra Farrow, Course Leader of the MSc Programme in Health Promotion at Brunel University, and the enormous impact it has had on the media in the UK and elsewhere. At the purely epidemiological level, Farrow and her colleagues found that both air fresheners and aerosols contain dangerous chemical agents that impact deleteriously on human health – especially on mothers and babies and on the elderly. But the capitalist corporate interests promoting them are most anxious that this not become widely enough known to have a negative impact on sales.

Many university research projects – under the present ideology of privatisation – are funded by such large corporations. But they would obviously be wary of supporting research like Farrow's. This illustrates a number of things, but not least the power that capitalism (largely US capitalism) wields in controlling the direction of scientific research. Many honest scientists are placed in the invidious position of having to choose research topics favourable to international capitalist interests or to risk losing their university posts. The pressure to attract substantial research funding from private sources is currently driving staffing policies in many universities.

This also draws governments into covert complicity with the same capitalist interests. We have already, in preceding chapters, examined this with respect to the tobacco trade, etc. Farrow's research on air fresheners and aerosols suggests clearly that first world governments are actively promoting the uptake of aerosols in Eastern Europe and some of the poorer Central and Latin American countries in order to compensate for the growing awareness of the health risks by people in the US and elsewhere in the first world.

Many otherwise educated people, especially in the first world, have been conditioned to think that such a proposition is psychologically impossible. References are frequently made to 'human nature', as though that were a constant rather than a variable! But, of course, had such been the case, we would never have evolved as we have. Then again, reference is often made to the 'marketplace' – a figurative concept that supposedly determines what our social and political arrangements must be to meet 'needs' dictated by 'people's will'. In this, there is much putting of carts before horses, but the argument is obviously compelling nevertheless.

Let us take transport, for instance. Various convincing arguments based on environmental considerations, reduction in traffic congestion and the like, have been put forward in favour of increased government expenditure on public transport and a proportional withdrawal of its expenditures in facilitating private transport. Arguments against it are based on the sense of 'control' one has over one's movement in the private car as opposed to having to structure one's activities around public transport timetables. But in any big city today, the increasing frequency of huge grid-locked traffic jams, and the sheer tension engendered by driving defensively for, say, an hour before starting one's real work each day, is seriously eroding the appeal of the 'control' argument. By and large there is very little empirical reason for believing that people really care about *how* it is done, but *whether* they get from A to B comfortably, reliably and on time. Public transport, if it is even handled only moderately well, removes serious stresses from the lives of city dwellers. There is no worry that the car might be vandalised while one is at work. And, indeed, the element of personal control does not have to be lost. In Germany, for instance, car ownership is more widespread than it is in Britain, but use of private cars in urban areas and during the weekdays is far less. Basically Germans prefer to use public transport in town and private transport for weekend jaunts.

However, the issue cannot be addressed purely at the individual level. Considerable political leadership is required to render public transport a realistic alternative before, say, Londoners will become like Berliners in sufficient numbers to make a difference. At present a test of preferences is not realistic because public transport systems in much of the first world are deliberately run in such a way as to make them non-competitive with private vehicles. The oil industry, to name just one, is able to exert immense pressure on local and national governments to organise their transport spending in such a way as to enhance the private sector.

In his book, Commoner (1976) quotes from a 1974 report to a US Senate subcommittee which detailed the planned destruction of electronically powered rail transport in 45 US cities. The principal actors in this assault on public transport were three: General Motors, Standard Oil and the Firestone Tire Company. General Motors bought up the targeted railway companies, dismantled the tracks, substituted General Motors buses, and then sold the companies to private buyers. People's choices did not get a look in. Similar attacks on the public sector are now commonplace in Eastern Europe, where former communist regimes are being initiated into market forces (Athanasiou, 1996).

Pre-political Greening

The foregoing may easily strike the reader as a counsel of despair, but that is because we have focused on the link between the well nigh universal urge to be recognised as working for a social good that transcends consumerism and the role of constitutional democratic government. Together with attempts to revamp our social responses, we can consider various organised, but 'pre-political', green initiatives. In Britain, to begin with a negative critique of 'Uncle Tony', and the operational Toryism of the Labour Party, is to impose a crippling sense of defeatism. (Tony Blair, Leader of the British Labour Party, renamed 'New Labour', swept to a landslide victory in the national elections of 1997.) But, as the German Greens have shown, we must avoid seeing electoral politics as the first objective.

In fact, the German Greens discovered, to their cost and ours, that the green agenda, which matured during the 1960s in bedrooms, cafés and factory canteens, lost its vibrancy and much of its advocacy potential once it became respectable enough to enter government as a party. The road to victory often lies outside parliament. Consider the temporary victories gained by Greenpeace against Shell or the victories of grass-roots movements against the Multilateral Agreement on Investment. The international power of corporate capital is probably subject to more opposition or actions outside parliament than within it.

Ultimately, of course, particular democratic governments will be forced to accept responsibility, by a better-educated and informed public, for their lack of response to electoral prompting. It is their acquiescence, if not direct corruption, that has opened up the world's resources (primarily the third world's resources) to exploitation by their own transnationals. In this there is considerable scope for optimism, because the knowledge that their supposed representatives in parliament are succumbing to corporate pressures will increasingly lead the people to seek out other sources of power to challenge that. This should provide an opportunity and the time for Greens and Reds alike to establish a presence in the popular mind, a chance for a more hopeful alternative. It is a truism that any party attempting to gain power on a platform of environmental responsibility and of social equity will need to have established dependable roots in the social consciousness.

Can Green political power survive bureaucracy?

It has been said that Reds tend to be so preoccupied with organisation and reliable chains of command that their very ideological purity drives them into tightly controlled little splinter groups. If anything, the Greens face the opposite problem. They recognise the importance of grass-roots inspiration, but seem to have trouble organising it into a hierarchical structure without killing the spirit of the enterprise. As one well-known Dutch Green explained to me: 'our philosophical agenda requires us to aim at both social equity and environmental sustainability simultaneously. But at the individual level we can only take on the environment!'

However, this really is a false dichotomy if reduced to operational terms. The two goals are philosophically symbiotic – you can't have one without the other. This is because the most environmentally friendly way of providing for human need is for everyone to have equal access to what is produced. With respect to access to health, this has been well established by Richard Wilkinson (1996). Over two decades he made a longitudinal study of variations in people's health – where incomes have moved towards equality, the incidence of disease has dropped, while life expectancy has risen. Moreover, by multivariate analysis, he was able to show that these changes were independent of economic growth, better healthcare or even the movement of individual people out of absolute poverty. As Wilkinson rather starkly put it: 'There are too few people in absolute poverty in any of the first world nations for their death rates to have a significant influence on the statistics!'

Wilkinson (1996) points out that since the early 1970s, Japan has moved up from about the 60th percentile with respect to both life expectancy and income distribution to the top in both. Now Japan boasts the highest recorded life expectancy

(83 years for women, 80 for men) and also the most egalitarian income distribution in the world. Conversely, while British income distribution worsened drastically throughout the 1980s, producing the most glaring inequalities since 1885, British life expectancy figures also dropped. Since 1985, mortality rates for both sexes and between the ages of 16 and 45 years have steadily risen. Again, multivariate analysis allowed Wilkinson to remove AIDS deaths as a variable and yet the relationship still persisted.

What this means is that in Britain people are dying at an earlier age than they need, not because they don't have enough to survive on, but because the distribution of resources is inequitable. How this can be is a more difficult question to answer. If one has enough money to buy sufficient food, fuel, shelter, etc., to stay alive when there is not much variation in incomes, why should this prove harder if many others suddenly become wealthier? Wilkinson (1996) argues that it is a matter of social psychology. This would suggest the validity of my comment earlier in this chapter, that people cannot function optimally as individuals. They need approval, and the feeling that they are valued, to relate effectively to the larger community. Being low on income levels obviously devalues a person, decreases his/her sense of social meaning (and hence their meaning as a person), and can lead to a collapse of self-esteem. It is well known, of course, that this has a deleterious effect on health. That is a real clinical fact – not a supposition. Such people die of clinically diagnosed pathologies, but a psychologically depressed state renders anyone less able to resist such illnesses.

On this basis, Wilkinson (1996) argues that once an adequate level of national productivity has been attained, the most effective way of enhancing public health is not necessarily to produce more, but to aim for equalisation of incomes. In his words: 'This might be expected to improve the quality of life for everyone by improving the social fabric and simultaneously slowing the pace of environmental degradation.'

Such findings lead to strong empirical support to the primary thesis of this chapter that, not only is there a feasible basis for Reds and Greens to pool their objectives, but convincing evidence that they cannot act effectively in isolation from one another. Social justice, equity and respect for the integrity of the environment is the only policy by which global health promotion can become a reality. It is practical, not visionary, and probably our only choice.

Organising for transnational government

Throughout this whole book, we have made many references to the fact that major obstacles to global equity hinge on the fact that the highest level of action, as opposed to judgement, rests with individual governments. Thus, the UN, and its various agencies, can pass recommendations and even resolutions, as to what should be done, but the degree to which these can be made operational depend on national interests, not international ones.

Thus, various Secretaries General of the UN have had the experience of calling for peacekeeping troops to prevent conflict in various seriously disrupted areas, only to find that individual governments decide that it is not in their interest to contribute. In such cases the UN can do nothing.

A most ghastly recent example of this involved Rwanda and Burundi and the wholesale slaughter (later categorised as 'genocide') of the Tutsi people by some of the Hutu in 1994–95. Of course, there is a long history behind it all which it is not this book's remit to discuss, but the pivotal thing was that the UN appeared impotent to act. It claimed that lack of cooperation from other African countries was to blame, and in 1995 abandoned any attempt at sending in a peacekeeping force.

The idea of a peacekeeping force is that the troops are from uninvolved countries whose job is – as far as possible – to keep the opposing sides from direct conflict. That, of course, is much more difficult to do than many people appreciate. For one thing, it requires that all of the elements concerned defer to UN mandates. Troops in such a force must have their first loyalty to the UN and not to their own national government. But, if such an enterprise is to really work, it cannot be up to individual states to decide whether or not they wish to participate. The UN has to be able to move quickly – before a genocide really gets off the ground – to call on troops and move them in.

That was the original idea of the Canadian Prime Minister, Lester B Pearson, who received the Nobel Peace Prize in 1967 for his work in establishing the UN peace-keeping force to bring the Suez crisis to an end.

Of course, the Hutu–Tutsi crisis never was resolved and has led to warfare since, not only in Burundi and Rwanda, but in Zaire and the Democratic Republic of the Congo. The present situation in Sudan and Darfur could be contained and mediated by a UN peacekeeping force except for two problems:

- Almost all of the national governments approached to contribute forces to such a force declined to do so.
- The Sudan government will not agree to have such a force within the country.

If the UN has no transnational authority, it is powerless to address either of these problems.

A very topical example, of course, is provided by the Israeli–Palestinian impasse. Palestine has repeatedly called for an international peacekeeping force, to which it would agree to accede. But Israel has declared that it would not allow such a force into either Israeli or Palestinian territory.

While the matter of transnational authority cannot be set up, even the pre-conditions for equity cannot be met. The health and human dignity of millions of people is thus the price. It is to provoke widespread thought about such issues among as many people as possible that this book has been written.

For, as Percy Bysshe Shelley (1792–1822) observed in his epic satirical poem, *The Mask of Anarchy*:

> *Rise like lions after slumber.*
> *In unvanquished number,*
> *Shake your chains to earth like dew*
> *Which in sleep has fallen on you –*
> *Ye are many – they are few.*

Most of us, by far, really do want to reverse the present brutal inequities and to live in the security which only global justice and peace can guarantee. To do so, however, we need to make our voices heard and our votes count.

References

Athanasiou T (1996) *Divided Planet*. Little, Brown and Co., New York.

Commoner B (1976) *The Poverty of the Planet*. Alfred Knopf, New York.

Farrow A, Taylor H, Northstone K, Golding J and The Alspac Team (2004) Symptoms of mothers and infants related to total volatile organic compounds in household products. *Archives of Environmental Health*. **58(10)**: 633–41.

The Guardian (2004) China admits first rise in poverty since 1978. 20 July, p.4.

Macdonald L (1998) Malign design. *New Internationalist*. November. **307**: 122–31.

National Audit Office (2004) *Ten Faces of 2004's Economy*. www.vos.com.cn/enroot/2005/01/07_2494.htm

O'Keefe E and Scott-Samuel A (2002) Human rights and wrongs: could Health Impact Assessment help? *Journal of Law, Medicine and Ethics*. **30**: 734–8, by the American Society of Law, Medicine and Ethics.

Sachs W, Loske R and Linz M (1998) *Greening the North*. Zed Books, London, p.37.

UNCTAD (United Nations Conference on Trade and Development) (1996) *Trade and Development Report*. Georgetown University Press, Washington, DC.

UNDP (United Nations Development Programme) (1998) *Human Development Report*. United Development Programme Offices, Geneva, p.38.

Watts J (2004) China admits first rise in poverty since 1978. *The Guardian*, International News, 20 July, p.11.

Wilkinson R (1996) *Unhealthy Societies: the affliction of inequality*. Routledge, London.

World Bank (1997) *World Development Report*. World Bank, Washington, DC, pp iii–v.

World Health Organization (1986) Thirty Eight Targets: Health for all 2000. WHO, Geneva.

Appendix A

The regression line explained

Suppose you plant a seed of a Hohunk[1] plant that grows as follows: at 0 days (when it has just been planted) it has no height (mm), but at the end of Day 1, it is 1 mm high, at the end of Day 2, it is 2.4 mm high – as shown in Table A1.1.

A1.1: Growth of one Hohunk plant over first 10 days of life

Age (days)	Height (mm)
0	0
1	1.0
2	2.4
3	2.6
4	4.0
5	4.2
6	6.8
7	7.2
8	8.0
9	8.7
10	10.3

If you then graph it, you will get a graph like that in Figure A1.1. On that graph you will notice that I have superimposed a straight line. Your Hohunk plant is not growing exactly linearly (the same increase every day) but over 10 days it does balance out – with 0.6 mm too little on Day 2 but 0.6 mm above the 'line' on Day 3, etc. This might easily suggest to you that Hohunk plants generally grow linearly, for the first 10 days at least, but that minor physiological variations led to slight deviations on the daily basis.

The line I have drawn is the line of 'best fit' and it happens to be a straight line. We call it the 'regression line' because it is the line that most accurately describes the data. The word 'regression' means going back to an average or normal state of affairs.

Not only in medical statistics, but in all statistics, a regression line allows us to predict what the measure might be if we pick a value not in the data. For instance, on the assumption that my regression line is correct, we could ascertain how high

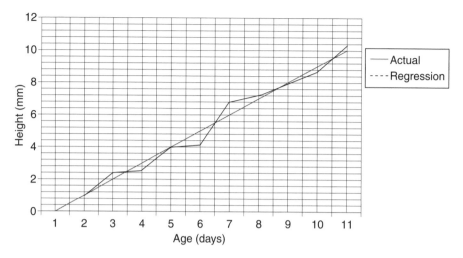

Figure A1.1:   Growth of one Hohunk plant over first 10 days of life.

your Hohunk plant might be after, say, 7.5 days. Looking along the Age axis of the graph, we can put a dot halfway between 7 and 8. From this dot, we then draw a perpendicular line straight up until it meets the regression line. Its length should read as 75 mm on the graph.

Estimating a value *between* two given measures in this way is called *interpolation* in statistics. Even better is *extrapolation*.

If we have some other horticultural information that Hohunk will continue to grow at this rate, we could make *predictions beyond* our data, rather than merely *within* it. This is called extrapolation.

Of course, regression lines are used not only when the data is linear, but even if it is *curvilinear*. To do so we have to work out an algebraic equation that will fit that curve. But with linear regression, things are much easier. All we need to know is the *gradient* (or *slope*) of the line. By that we mean how high the line rises (or how far it drops, if it is a negative slope) per unit distance from left to right along the horizontal. In the case of the Hohunk plant, the slope is positive (it rises as we move from left to right) and it goes up 10 mm for each one day. So its slope is +10.

Its equation is given by:

$$y = mx$$

where 'm' is the slope value.

So $y = 10x$ is the equation for it, where y is the height in mm and x is the Hohunk's age in days.

Of course, in real medical statistics, we are examining thousands of data and the regression line involves looking at the data and then calculating what line would be such that the sum of the vertical distances of the actual measures from it would be as small as possible. Since the distances above the line are positive and the distances below the line are negative, we simplify things by squaring each of them. That makes them all *positive* because, if you remember, a negative number times a negative number gives a positive product. So we find the line such that the *sum* of the squares of all the vertical distances is as small as possible. This is called the Least Sum of

Squares or LSS. From the LSS, we can work out what the slope of our regression line would have to be. And we definitely know at least one pair of values through which it passes – say, how high the Hohunk is on Day 6 – and thus we have the equation.

If the reader now goes back to Figure 1.1, the argument will be easier to follow.

Note

1   Entirely mythical plant for demonstration purposes only.

The compound interest formula explained

Most readers will have heard of 'interest' on money borrowed, and realised that it is an extra amount that is paid back to the borrower over and above the amount borrowed. But many people think of that extra amount as being trivial when, in fact and over time, it can become even greater than the amount borrowed (called the principal). To make sense of this, it must be explained that there are, broadly speaking, two types of interest – simple interest and compound interest. No financial institution uses simple interest but it would work as follows if they did. You want to invest £1000 over 10 years. Suppose your banker gives 10% per annum simple interest. Ten per cent of £1000 is £100, so you would earn £100 extra each year for 10 years. That is, in 10 years you would have £2000. So if you were borrowing instead of investing you would have to pay back over 10 years £2000 – i.e. £200 a year. You realise, of course, that you only borrowed £1000 and yet paid back £2000. However, for the convenience of having a £1000 lump sum when you need it, it might well be worth your while paying £200 a year for the privilege for 10 years.

Compound interest is much more ferocious than simple interest. In compound interest, you calculate the interest each year. Thus, if you were to invest £1000 at 10% interest compounded annually, your original principal (P) of £1000 is worth £1100 at the end of year one. At the end of year two, it is another 10% of £1100 – not of £1000. So your interest at the end of year two is £110. Your investment is now £1100 + £110 = £1210. At the end of year three, you add another £121 (i.e. 10% of £1210), so at the end of year three, your investment is £1210 + £121 = £1331.

Watch how it grows:

- Amount invested: £1000
- End of Year One: £1100
- End of Year Two: £1210
- End of Year Three: £1331
- End of Year Four: £1464.10
- End of Year Five: £1610.51
- End of Year Six: £1771.56
- End of Year Seven: £1948.82
- End of Year Eight: £2143.70
- End of Year Nine: £2358.07
- End of Year Ten: £2593.88

Thus, if you had borrowed £1000 at 10% compound interest over 10 years, you would end up paying £1593.88 extra for the privilege.

In general terms, suppose you invest P (the principal) at r% interest per annum for three years.

At the end of year one, your investment is worth:

$$P + \frac{r}{100} \times P$$

$$P\left(1 + \frac{r}{100}\right)$$

At the end of year two, your investment is worth:

$$P\left(1 + \frac{r}{100}\right) + \frac{rp}{100}\left(\frac{1+r}{100}\right)$$

$$= \left(1\frac{r}{100}\right)\left(P + P \times \frac{r}{100}\right)$$

$$= P\left(1 + \frac{r}{100}\right)^2$$

At the end of year three, your investment is worth:

$$P\left(1 + \frac{r}{100}\right)^3$$

You can see, therefore, that if you invested for m years, your investment would be worth:

$$= P\left(1 + \frac{r}{100}\right)^m$$

That is, the total amount (A) of your investment, is given by:

$$P\left(1 + \frac{r}{100}\right)^m$$

Most people borrow some money, say, for a car or a mortgage. The less financially informed reader might find it instructive to calculate his/her 'A' on one of his/her own loans!

Protecting breastfeeding from unethical marketing

The first step on the road towards health nutrition is protecting, supporting and promoting breastfeeding. A key vehicle for that effort is the International Code of Marketing of Breast-Milk Substitutes. Adopted by the World Health Assembly in 1981, it calls on all countries to regulate marketing of breast-milk substitutes to prevent breastfeeding from being undermined.

How countries enforce the Code

The International Code of Marketing of Breast-Milk Substitutes aims to promote infant nutrition by protecting breastfeeding from inappropriate marketing of infant formula and other breast-milk substitutions. It is a minimum standard, enforceable through 'national legislation, regulations or other suitable measures'. Only countries that have adopted legally enforceable measures implementing the Code in its entirety are listed in Category 1. Just 16 countries fall into this category – a disappointing showing considering that the Code is a minimum standard.

Countries in Category 2 have enacted only some of the Code's provisions. For example, the member states of the European Union, based on an EU Directive, have adopted legislation that is weaker than the Code. It provided that legislation only apply to infant formulas (and not to the wider category of breast-milk substitutes, bottles and teats) and that advertising be allowed in baby care and scientific publications.

Category 3 includes countries that have developed voluntary agreements with manufacturers providing no means of enforcement. In Australia this approach has proved reasonably successful. But the widespread violations reported in South Africa and Thailand show the shakiness of such arrangements. Also in Category 3 are countries that have drafted measures or are still examining how best to implement the Code. Many are from Central and Eastern Europe and the Commonwealth of Independent States, where the distribution of breast-milk substitutes was formerly centrally controlled.

Appendix D

Nutrition league table

Only 16 countries had achieved full compliance with the Code by 2000, meaning that they have adopted appropriate laws aimed at enforcing it.

Sub-Saharan Africa		Middle East and North Africa		Central Asia		East and South Asia and the Pacific		Americas		Europe	
Level of compliance		Level of compliance		Level of compliance		Level of compliance		Level of compliance		Level of compliance	
Burkina Faso	1	Iran	1	Armenia	3	India	1	Brazil	1	Austria	2
Cameroon	1	Lebanon	1	Georgia	3	Nepal	1	Costa Rica	1	Belgium	2
Madagascar	1	Algeria	2	Kazakhstan	3	Philippines	1	Dominican Republic	1	Denmark	2
Tanzania	1	Israel	2	Azerbaijan	n/d	Sri Lanka	1	Guatemala	1	Finland	2
Benin	2	Saudi Arabia	2	Kyrgyzstan	n/d	Bangladesh	2	Panama	1	France	2
Congo DR	2	Tunisia	2	Tajikistan	n/d	China	2	Peru	1	Germany	2
Ethiopia	2	Turkey	2	Turkmenistan	n/d	Indonesia	2	Canada	1	Greece	2
Guinea	2	U. Arab Emirates	2	Uzbekistan	n/d	Japan	2	Chile	2	Hungary	2
Guinea-Bissau	2	Yemen	2			Lao Republic	2	Columbia	2	Ireland	2
Mozambique	2	Egypt	2			Mongolia	2	Cuba	2	Italy	2
Nigeria	2	Iraq	3			Papua New Guinea	2	Mexico	2	Netherlands	2
Senegal	2	Jordan	3			Vietnam	2	Argentina	3	Norway	2
Angola	3	Kuwait	3			Australia	3	Bolivia	3	Portugal	2
Botswana	3	Libya	3			Bhutan	3	Ecuador	3	Spain	2
Burundi	3	Morocco	3			Cambodia	3	El Salvador	3	United Kingdom	2
Congo	3	Oman	3			South Korea	3	Haiti	3	Albania	3

Continued

Sub-Saharan Africa	Middle East and North Africa	Central Asia	East and South Asia and the Pacific	Americas	Europe
Level of compliance	Level of compliance	Level of compliance	Level of compliance	Level of compliance	Level of compliance
Côte d'Ivoire 3	Sudan 3		Malaysia 3	Honduras 3	Belarus 3
Eritrea 3	Syria 3		Myanmar 3	Jamaica 3	Czech Republic 3
Gabon 3			New Zealand 3	Nicaragua 3	Latvia 3
Gambia 3			Pakistan 3	Paraguay 3	Lithuania 3
Ghana 3			Singapore 3	Trinidad/ Tobago 3	Poland 3
Kenya 3			Thailand 3	Uruguay 3	Russian Federation 3
Lesotho 3			North Korea n/d	Venezuela 3	Slovakia 3
Malawi 3				USA 4	Sweden 3
Mali 3					

Key: n/d = no data

Peru's Letter of Intent, 5 May 1998

The following item is a Letter of Intent of the government of Peru, which describes the policies that Peru intends to implement in the context of its request for financial support from the IMF. The document, which is the property of Peru, is being made available on the IMF website by agreement with the member as a service to users of the IFM website.

Lima, Peru
5 May 1998

Mr Michel Camdessus
Managing Director
International Monetary Fund
Washington, DC 20431

Dear Mr Camdessus,

1 This letter describes the economic policies of the government of Peru for 1998. Real GDP grew by 7.4 percent in 1997, reflecting sharp increases in investment of the private sector and exports. Inflation was reduced from 11.8 percent in 1996 to 6.5 percent, its lowest level in 25 years, and the external current account deficit narrowed substantially, from 5.9 percent of GDP in 1996 to 5.2 percent in 1997. The net international reserves of the central reserve bank increased by about US$1.6 billion, with gross reserves exceeding the equivalent of 12 months of imports of goods and nonfactor services by year-end. As in previous years, all performance criteria were observed in 1997.

2 The government's program aims at continuing to build the conditions for sustained output growth, with reduced poverty, low inflation and external viability. The program hinges importantly on continued fiscal and monetary discipline and a deepening of structural reforms. The government will continue to make efforts to improve the efficiency and export competitiveness of the economy, and increase the efficiency and equity of public expenditure in health, education, the provision of justice and poverty alleviation programs.

3 Strong and sustained economic growth is essential for improving the living conditions of the population. Since 1993, real GDP has grown by 42 percent, or at an average of 7.3 percent per year; GDP per capita has increased by an average of over 5 percent per year. In 1998 the economy is being adversely affected by *El Niño*, which has required the government to undertake a vast effort of preventive measures, containment of damage, emergency relief, and reconstructive work and by the decline in prices of minerals in the international

markets. In these circumstances, the program for 1998 aims at achieving a rate of real GDP growth of 4 to 5 percent, with inflation in the range of 7.5 to 9 percent, with a downward trend in the second half of the year. The program also aims at a further strengthening of the net international reserve position of the central reserve bank, and an external current account deficit not exceeding 5.9 percent of GDP. It is envisaged that the external current account deficit will decline significantly in 1999, and a further reduction is projected over the medium term.

4   Total investment is projected to increase from 24.6 percent of GDP in 1997 to 24.7 percent in 1998 reflecting continued private investment in the mining, communications and energy sectors, as well as by the reconstructive effort being undertaken in the aftermath of *El Niño*. Investment in 1998 will also benefit from the measures adopted by the government to improve competitiveness, such as the reduction in tariff rates and the lowering of several other tax rates implemented in 1997. Following a significant increase in 1997, domestic savings are projected to decline slightly in 1998, reflecting the consequences of *El Niño* and the decline in the international prices of minerals.

5   The government of Peru places high priority on fiscal consolidation. In the period 1996–97, the overall deficit of the combined public sector, excluding privatisation proceeds, will remain at 1.7 percent of GDP. The fiscal targets of the program will be monitored on the basis of the quarterly ceilings on the net domestic financing of the combined public sector, as presented in the attached table.

6   Current revenue of the central government in terms of GDP is projected to increase from 14 percent of GDP in 1997 to 14.1 percent in 1998, despite the full-year impact of tax rate reductions implemented in 1997. To achieve this level of revenue, tax administration efforts will be further stepped up. Central government current expenditure will continue to be kept strictly under control, taking into account the necessary spending associated with *El Niño*. Wage policy will remain prudent and consistent with the objectives of the program.

7   Efforts to broaden the tax base and reduce tax evasion are being intensified in 1998. In particular, efforts are being made to diminish the gap between the number of registered and actual taxpayers and between tax amount declared and paid. Since October 1997, notices are being sent to registered taxpayers who have not filed their tax returns as well as to those taxpayers whose payments are below the amounts filed, asking them to regularise amounts due. The tax arrears regularisation program will continue to be implemented and the enhanced monitoring programs that currently apply to large taxpayers will be extended to medium and small taxpayers. In June 1998 the tax administration agency SUNAT will also start collecting information on personal wealth of large taxpayers and this information will be cross-checked with that on tax payments. In the value-added tax area, the system of cross-checking the tax returns of large companies with those of their suppliers will be broadened to include information on purchases made by public sector entities, and two half-yearly audits for the 1997 tax returns will be carried out. To reduce tax evasion further, SUNAT will continue the practice of integral audits in sectors of the economy where tax evasion is high, and strengthen its enforcement capacity,

including through exchange information arrangements with risk assessment bureaus, as well as giving publicity to cases of tax non-compliance. During 1998, SUNAT will develop a collection system for social security and pension contributions on behalf of the Social Security Institute (IPSS) and the National Pension Bureau (ONP), which is expected to become operational in 1999 and which will permit reductions in the collection costs of SUNAT, IPSS and ONP.

8 The implementation of an integrated expenditure information management system (SIAF) is at an advanced stage. Since mid-1997, spending units have started registering their payment operations with the SIAF, reaching 80 percent of all units by March 1998, with the remaining units expected to be included by year end. Starting with the 1997 budget, the government introduced reforms in the budget formulation and execution processes and in the registry system of public treasury operation, with technical assistance from the Fund. Concurrently, a new functional classification of the budget structure was introduced and centralised information on treasury operations will be available later this year. Treasury cash management will continue to be improved in close coordination with the Banco de la Nacion and the central reserve bank.

9 The central reserve bank will continue to promote the objective of reducing inflation. With this purpose, the central reserve bank will continue to keep developments in the money market under close review, and if needed it will be ready to tighten its monetary policy. In this context, it will continue to ensure that its rediscount window remains a source of liquidity of last resort. To monitor the monetary program, which assumes a growth in the monetary base consistent with money demand, quarterly targets on the net international reserves and ceilings on the net domestic assets of the central reserve bank have been established, as presented in the attached table. In 1998 the central bank has started a modernisation program of the payment system in order to introduce a real time gross settlement system with limited and collateralised intra-day credit.

10 The government will continue to pursue a flexible exchange rate policy and central bank interventions will be aimed at smoothing out temporary fluctuations in the exchange rate. The central reserve bank will monitor developments in the exchange market closely and if circumstances were to suggest the need for a further improvement in external competitiveness, the government will be ready to strengthen its fiscal position.

11 The government believes that the prudential ratios of financial intermediaries should continue to be strengthened. To that effect, in 1997 the Superintendency of Banks and Insurance (SBS) issued new regulations for the classification of bank borrowers and provisioning requirements, introduced a generic provision equivalent to 0.2 percent of performing loans and established a timetable for a progressive increase in this provision to 1 percent by June 2000. To strengthen provisions, the SBS also removed the deduction for collateral while adjusting the provisioning requirements for collateralised loans. New norms for consolidated supervision became operational in March 1998, and recently issued SBS regulations aimed at preventing money laundering will become effective on 1 July 1998. In order to foster a new culture in the administration of risks by banks and to introduce capital requirements weighted by market risk as mandated in the banking law, the SBS will introduce before the end of June

1998 new prudential regulations for market risks, which will become fully operational by end of 1998. Also, in March 1998 the coverage of its risk assessment unit was broadened, with the inclusion of information on loans of less than S/. 13,000.

12 The program for 1998 is fully financed, and the government of Peru intends to continue to treat the extended arrangement as precautionary. Peru's balance of payments has strengthened substantially in recent years, in part because of the agreements signed in 1996 and 1997 and official and commercial creditors which have helped further put the Peruvian economy on the path of fiscal solvency and external viability. The government will continue to pay close attention to debt-management policy, and the program for 1998 includes limits on the contracting or the outstanding short-term debt of the non-financial public sector, as presented in the attached table. The government of Peru has been taking steps to normalise relations with the few foreign creditors with whom small payments arrears remain, and intends to service its debt to all other creditors punctually.

13 The government of Peru will continue implementing its privatisation program, which is projected to generate US$0.7 billion in receipts to the treasury in 1998. The government intends to privatise enterprises in the energy sector, and to continue the sale of the assets of the mining complexes Centromin and Mineroperu. It also intends to sell the insurance and cement companies. To promote private ownership and investment in the agricultural sector, in 1997 the government sold 12 700 hectares of large plots of irrigated public land in the coastal region and in 1998 it intends to sell an additional 24 000 hectares. In 1998 the government will continue its program of contracting new areas for petroleum exploration and exploitation rights with the private sector; 36 such projects were in operation by the end of 1997 and the number is expected to rise to about 50 by the end of 1998.

14 In December 1996 the government enacted new legislation setting up the Commission for the Promotion of Private Concessions (Promcepri), a public agency in charge of evaluating and awarding concessions to the private sector for the provision of public services and infrastructure. The areas covered by the concessions include the production and distribution of electricity, petroleum processing and distribution, the construction and operation of tourism facilities, forestry management, highways, railways, sea- and airports, and telecommunication licenses. In 1997 and early 1998, the government granted several concessions for electricity generation and transmission projects, and the construction of an electricity transmission line in the southern region of the country. During the remainder of the year, the government plans to finalise concessions for at least two major road projects, a cellular telephone band outside Lima, and for the management of some seaports, airports and the use of railways. Earlier this year the specialised regulatory agency for energy, OSINERG, became operational and the government established a specialised regulatory agency, OSITRAN, to supervise compliance with concession contracts in public transportation infrastructure.

15 During 1998 the government will continue implementing the reform of the pension system initiated in 1993. In December 1997 the ONP issued pension bonds (*bonos de reconocimiento*) with a face value of S/. 687 million to some 36 900 former contributors of the public pension system who transferred to the

private system. By the end of 1998 an additional S/. 700 million in pension bonds will be issued to 40 000 former contributors. Last year, the government established the Consolidated Pension Reserve Fund, an autonomous fund with earmarked resources, to meet public pension obligations falling due over the medium and long term. Part of the 1998 privatisation proceeds will be placed in an investment fund, the yield of which will be earmarked to improve pensions. To promote portfolio diversification of private pension fund investments, the government will continue to broaden the range of instruments in which these funds can invest.

16 The government will seek to complement its efforts in the education and health sectors by facilitating private investment in these areas. In 1997 the government issued a new law allowing private companies to provide health services (EPS) within the social security system and the Superintendency of Health Services Providers, the regulatory body for the EPS, was established. During the first semester of 1998, the government will issue all necessary regulations for EPS to start operations.

17 The government has been improving the regulatory framework to encourage private sector investment in agriculture and fishing. To improve the definition and enforceability of property rights in land ownership, the government will continue implementing its land titling program and intends to issue 160 000 new land titles in urban areas and 200 000 new land titles in rural areas in 1998. In 1998 the government will continue improving regulations and supervision systems aimed at ensuring the long-term sustainability of the fishing industry and the preservation of fish species.

18 The government remains firmly committed to open trade, capital and exchange regimes. In April 1997 the government reduced the import tariff rates to strengthen Peru's integration in the world economy and enhance its external competitiveness. At the same time, a 5% temporary import surcharge was introduced on certain agricultural and agro-industrial products. In 1998 Peru will join the Asia Pacific Economic Cooperation Forum (APEC).

19 The main priority of the government program is to reduce poverty and to create equal opportunity among all Peruvians. Already, significant improvement has been achieved: the share of the population living in extreme poverty has been reduced from 24.2 percent in 1991 to 18.7 percent in 1996 and access to basic services has increased significantly, with the availability of drinking water and electricity in rural households having increased by 26 percent and 14 percent, respectively, between 1994 and 1996. To further reduce poverty as well as develop Peru's human capital, the government will continue to devote an increasing proportion of the budget to social spending, health and education particularly. Efforts also will be made to improve access and quality of health and education services, particularly outside Lima. To achieve this goal, the share of educational resources devoted to primary education will be increased, coordination among spending agencies in the social sectors will be strengthened and the targeting of poverty alleviation programs will continue to be improved.

20 The government believes that the policies described in this letter are adequate to achieve the objectives of the economic program, and will take any further measures that may become appropriate for this purpose. The government of Peru and the Fund will consult periodically, in accordance with the policies on such consultations, as specified in our letter of 4 June 1996. A midterm review

with the Fund will be completed prior to 30 November 1998, to assess progress under the program, including in the area of structural reforms. The performance criteria of the program are presented in the attached table.

Sincerely yours,

Jorge Camet
Minister of Economy and Finance

German Suarez, President
Central Reserve Bank of Peru

Peru: Quantitative performance criteria, 1998				
	31 March indicative	*30 June*	*30 Sept*	*31 Dec*
Cumulative changes from 1 January 1998 *(In millions of new soles)*				
Net domestic financing of the combined public sector (*see* footnotes: 1, 2, 3, 4)	-265	-635	-922	-615
Net domestic assets of the central reserve bank (*see* footnotes: 1, 2, 3, 4)	-8	704	-22	-353
(In millions of US dollars)				
Net international reserves of the central reserve bank (*see* footnotes: 1, 2, 3, 4)	-75	-330	-63	256
Contracting or guaranteeing of nonconcessional external public debt with maturity of at least one year	10	300	700	900
Of which: 1–12 year maturity	100	200	250	300
Short-term net external debt of the non-financial public sector	50	50	50	50
End-of-period stocks *(In millions of US dollars)*				
External payments arrears of the public sector	0	0	0	0

Notes

1 The limits on the net domestic financing of the combined public sector and the net domestic assets of the central reserve bank will be adjusted downward and the target for the net international reserves will be adjusted upward, to the extent that actual external disbursements to the non-financial public sector net of payments of principal and interest exceed US$432 million at end-June, US$544 million at end-September, and US$815 million at end-December. These amounts will be deposited in a treasury account at the central reserve bank.

2 The limits on the net domestic financing of the combined public sector and the net domestic assets of the central reserve bank will be adjusted upward, and the target for the net international reserves will be adjusted downward as follows: a) by any amount in excess of US$16 million used to finance debt- and debt-service reduction operations, or to prepay external debt, including equity swaps in the privatisation process; and b) by up to a maximum of US$238 million if actual cumulative project loan disbursements to the non-financial public sector are below US$229 million by end-June, US$400 million by end-September, and US$574 million by end-December. The adjustments specified in this footnote will only apply to the extent that actual external disbursements to the non-financial public sector net of payments of principal and interest do not exceed the amounts specified in the program.

3 For the purpose of the program, the foreign currency deposit of the Consolidated Pension Reserve Fund (FCR) or any other funds managed by the ONP held at the central reserve bank will be treated as foreign reserve liabilities. The deposits of the FCR or any other funds managed by the ONP will not be classified as part of the combined public sector and hence the limits on the net domestic financing of the combined public sector will be adjusted upward by the amounts of any combined public sector withdrawal used to increase these funds. Also, the limits on the net domestic assets of the central reserve bank will be adjusted upward and the targets for the net international reserves will be adjusted downward by any amount of combined public sector deposits withdrawal from the central reserve bank to increase these funds.

4 The limits on the net domestic assets of the central reserve bank will be adjusted downward, and the target for the net international reserves will be adjusted upward, to the extent that actual privatisation receipts exceed the assumed amounts of US$91 million by end-June, US$389 million by end-September, and US$653 million by end-December. These amounts in excess will be deposited in a treasury account at the central reserve bank. In the event of a shortfall in privatisation receipts exceed the assumed amounts, the limits on the net domestic assets of the central reserve bank will be adjusted upward, and the target for the net international reserves will be adjusted downward, up to a maximum adjustment of US$480 million by end-December. In the event that actual privatisation receipts are below US$180 million by end-December, the limits on the net domestic financing of the combined public sector will be adjusted downward by the amount of the shortfall, and this will imply a corresponding improvement in the position of the public treasury with the central reserve bank.

http://www.imf.org/external/np/loi/050598.htm as at 19 July 2000

A New Framework and Guidelines Enshrining A Fundamental Human Right to the Highest Attainable Standard of Health

United Nations

General
E/C. 12/2000/,
CESCR General
Comment 14
4 July 2000

Original: English

The right to the highest attainable standard of health:
04/07/2000. E/C. 12/2000/04, CESCR General comment 14.
(General Comments)

COMMITTEE ON ECONOMIC, SOCIAL
AND CULTURAL RIGHTS
Twenty-second session
Geneva, 25 April–12 May 2000
Agenda item 3

UNEDITED VERSION
SUBSTANTIVE ISSUES ARISING IN THE IMPLEMENTATION OF THE
INTERNATIONAL COVENANT ON ECONOMIC, SOCIAL AND CULTURAL RIGHTS

General Comment No. 14 (2000)

The right to the highest attainable standard of health (article 12 of the International
Covenant on Economic, Social and Cultural rights)

1 Health is a fundamental human right indispensable for the exercise of other
human rights. Every human being is entitled to the enjoyment of the highest
attainable standard of health conducive to living a life in dignity. The realisation
of the right to health may be pursued by numerous, complementary approaches,
such as the formulation of health policies, or the implementation of health programmes developed by the World Health Organization (WHO), or the adoption

of specific legal instruments. Moreover, the right to health includes certain components which are legally enforceable.[1]

2 The human right to health is recognised in numerous international instruments. Article 25 (1) of the Universal Declaration of Human Rights affirms: 'Everyone has the right to a standard of living adequate for the health of himself and his family, including food, clothing, housing and medical care and necessary social services.' The International Covenant on Economic, Social and Cultural Rights provides the most comprehensive article on the right to health in international human rights law. According to article 12 (1) of the Covenant, States parties recognise 'the right of everyone to the enjoyment of the highest attainable standard of physical and mental health', while article 12 (2) enumerates, by way of illustration, a number of 'steps to be taken by the States parties [...] to achieve the full realisation of this right'. Additionally, the right to health is recognised, *inter alia*, in article 5 (e) (iv) of the International Convention on the Elimination of All Forms of Racial Discrimination of 1965, in articles 11 (1) (f) and 12 of the Convention on the Elimination of All Forms of Discrimination Against Women of 1979 and in article 24 of the Convention on the Rights of the Child of 1989. Several regional human rights instruments also recognise the right to health, such as the European Social Charter of 1961 as revised (article 11), the African Charter on Human and People's Rights of 1981 (article 16) and the Additional Protocol to the American Convention on Human Rights in the Area of Economic, Social and Cultural Rights of 1988 (article 10). Similarly, the right to health has been proclaimed by the Commission on Human Rights,[2] as well as in the Vienna Declaration and Programme of Action of 1993 and other international instruments.[3]

3 The right to health is closely related to and dependent upon the realisation of other human rights as contained in the International Bill of Rights, including the right to food, housing, work, education, human dignity, life, non-discrimination, equality, the prohibition against torture, privacy, access to information and the freedoms of association, assembly and movement. These and other rights and freedoms address integral components of the right to health.

4 In drafting article 12 of the Covenant, the General Assembly's Third Committee did not adopt the definition of health contained in the preamble to the Constitution of WHO which conceptualises health as 'a state of complete physical, mental and social well-being and not merely the absence of disease or infirmity'. However, the reference in article 12 (1) of the Covenant to 'the highest attainable standard of physical and mental health' is not confined to the right to healthcare. On the contrary, the drafting history and the express wording of article 12 (2) acknowledge that the right to health embraces a wide range of social-economic factors that promote conditions whereby people can lead a healthy life, and extends to the underlying determinants of health, such as food and nutrition, housing, access to safe and potable water and sanitation, safe and healthy working conditions, and a healthy environment.

5 The Committee is aware that, for millions of people throughout the world, the full enjoyment of the right to health still remains a distant goal. Moreover, in many cases, especially for those living in poverty, this goal is becoming increasingly remote. The Committee recognises the formidable structural and other obstacles that result from international and other factors beyond the

control of States, and impeding the full realisation of article 12 in many States parties.

6　With a view to assisting States parties' implementation of the Covenant and the fulfilment of their reporting obligations, this General Comment focuses on the normative content of article 12 (Part I), States parties' obligations (Part II), violations (Part III), and implementation at the national level (Part IV), while Part V deals with the obligations of actors other than States parties. The General Comment is based on the Committee's experience in examining States parties' reports over many years.

I. NORMATIVE CONTENT OF ARTICLE 12

7　Article 12 (1) provides a definition of the right to health, while article 12 (2) enumerates illustrative, non-exhaustive examples of States parties' obligations.

8　The right to health is not to be understood as a right to be *healthy*. The right to health contains both freedoms and entitlements. Freedoms include the right to control one's health and body, including sexual and reproductive freedom, and the right to be free from interference, such as the right to be free from torture, non-consensual medical treatment and experimentation. By contrast, the entitlements include the right to a system of health protection, which provides equality of opportunity for people to enjoy the highest attainable level of health.

9　The notion of 'the highest attainable standard of health' in article 12 (1) takes into account both the individual's biological and socio-economic preconditions and a State's available resources. There are a number of aspects which cannot be addressed solely within the relationship between States and individuals, in particular, good health cannot be ensured by a State, nor can States provide protection against every possible cause of human ill health. Thus, genetic factors, individual susceptibility to ill health and the adoption of unhealthy or risky lifestyles may play an important role with respect to an individual's health. Consequently, the right to health must be understood as a right to the enjoyment of a variety of facilities, goods, services and conditions necessary for the realisation of the highest attainable standard of health.

10　Since the adoption of the two UN Covenants in 1966 the world health situation has changed dramatically and the notion of health has undergone substantial changes and has also widened in scope. More determinants of health are being taken into consideration, such as resource distribution and gender differences. A wider definition of health also takes into account such socially related concerns as violence and armed conflict.[4] Moreover, formerly unknown diseases, such as Human Immunodeficiency Virus and Acquired Immunodeficiency Syndrome (HIV/AIDS), and others that have become more widespread, such as cancer, as well as the rapid growth of the world population, have created new obstacles for the realisation of the right to health which need to be taken into account when interpreting article 12.

11　The Committee interprets the right to health, as defined in article 12 (1), as an inclusive right extending not only to timely and appropriate healthcare but also to the underlying determinants of health, such as access to safe and potable water and adequate sanitation, an adequate supply of safe food, nutrition and housing, healthy occupational and environmental conditions, and access to health-related education and information, including on sexual and reproductive health. A further important aspect is the participation of the population in all health-related decision-making at the community, national and international levels.

12 The right to health in all its forms and at all levels contains the following interrelated and essential terms, the precise application of which will depend on the conditions prevailing in a particular State party:

(1) *Availability* – functioning public health and healthcare facilities, goods and services, as well as programmes, have to be available in sufficient quantity within the State party. The precise nature of the facilities, goods and services will vary according to numerous factors, including the State party's development level. They will include, however, the underlying determinants of health, such as safe and potable drinking water and sanitation facilities, hospitals, clinics and other health-related buildings, trained medical and professional personnel receiving domestically competitive salaries, and essential drugs, as defined by WHO's Action Programme on Essential Drugs.[5]

(2) *Accessibility* – health facilities, goods and services[6] have to be accessible to everyone without discrimination, within the jurisdiction of the State party. Accessibility has four overlapping dimensions:

(i) Non-discrimination – health facilities, goods and services must be accessible to all, especially the most vulnerable or marginalised sections of the population, in law and fact, without discrimination on any of the prohibited grounds.[7]

(ii) Physical accessibility – health facilities, goods and services must be within safe physical reach for all parts of the population, especially for vulnerable or marginalised groups, such as ethnic minorities and indigenous populations, women, children, adolescents, older persons, persons with disabilities, and persons with HIV/AIDS. Accessibility also implies that medical services and underlying determinants of health, such as safe and potable water and adequate sanitary facilities, are within safe physical reach, including in rural areas. Accessibility further includes adequate access to buildings for persons with disabilities.

(iii) Economic accessibility (affordability) – health facilities, goods and services must be affordable for all. Payment for healthcare services, as well as services related to the underlying determinants of health, have to be based on the principle of equity ensuring that these services, whether privately or publicly provided, are affordable for all, including socially disadvantaged groups. Equity demands that poorer households should not be disproportionately burdened with health expenses as compared to richer households.

(iv) Information accessibility – accessibility includes the right to seek, receive and impart information and ideas[8] concerning health issues. However, accessibility of information should not impair the right to have personal health data treated with confidentiality.

(3) *Ethics* – All health facilities, goods and services must be respectful of medical ethics and culturally appropriate, i.e. respectful of the culture of individuals, minorities, peoples and communities, sensitive to gender and life-cycle

requirements, as well as being designed to respect confidentiality and improve the health status of those concerned.

(4) *Quality* – As well as being culturally acceptable, health facilities, goods and services must also be scientifically and medically appropriate and of good quality. This requires, *inter alia*, skilled medical personnel, scientifically approved and unexpired drugs and hospital equipment, safe and potable water, and adequate sanitation.

13 The non-exhaustive catalogue of examples in article 12 (2) provides guidance in defining the action to be taken by States. It gives specific generic examples of measures arising from the broad definition of the right to health contained in paragraph 1, thereby illustrating the content of that right, as exemplified in the following paragraphs.[9]

Article 12 (2) a: The right to maternal, child and reproductive health

14 'The provision for the reduction of the stillbirth-rate and of infant mortality and for the healthy development of the child' (art. 12 (2) a)[10] may be understood as requiring measures to improve child and maternal health, sexual and reproductive health services, including access to family planning, pre- and postnatal care,[11] emergency obstetric services and access to information, as well as to resources necessary to act on that information.[12]

Article 12 (2) b: The right to healthy natural and workplace environments

15 'The improvement of all aspects of environmental and industrial hygiene' (art. 12 (2) b) includes, *inter alia*, preventive measures in respect of occupational accidents and diseases; the requirement to ensure an adequate supply of safe and potable water and basic sanitation; the prevention and reduction of the population's exposure to harmful substances such as radiation and harmful chemicals or other detrimental environmental conditions that directly or indirectly impact upon human health.[13] Furthermore, industrial hygiene refers to the minimisation of, so far as is reasonably practicable, the causes of health hazards inherent in the working environment.[14] Article 12 (2) (b) also embraces adequate housing and safe and hygienic working conditions, an adequate supply of food and proper nutrition, and discourages the abuse of alcohol, and the use of tobacco, drugs and other harmful substances.

Article 12 (2) c: The right to prevention, treatment and control of diseases

16 'The prevention, treatment and control of epidemic, endemic, occupational and other diseases' (art. 12 (2) c) requires the establishment of prevention and education programmes for behaviour-related health concerns such as sexually transmitted diseases, in particular HIV/AIDS, and those adversely affecting sexual and reproductive health, and the promotion of social determinants of good health, such as environmental safety, education, economic development and gender equity. The right to treatment includes the creation of a system of urgent medical care in cases of accidents, epidemics and similar health hazards,

and the provision of disaster relief and humanitarian assistance in emergency situations. The control of diseases refers to States' individual and joint efforts to, *inter alia*, make available relevant technologies, using and improving epidemiological surveillance and data collection on a disaggregated basis, the implementation or enhancement of immunisation programmes and other strategies of infectious disease control.

Article 12 (2) d: The right to health facilities, goods and services[15]

17 'The creation of conditions which would assure to all medical service and medical attention in the event of sickness' (art. 12 (2) d), both physical and mental, includes the provision of equal and timely access to basic preventive, curative, rehabilitative, health services and health education; regular screening programmes; appropriate treatment of prevalent diseases, illnesses, injuries and disabilities, preferably at community level; the provision of essential drugs; and appropriate mental health treatment and care. A further important aspect is the improvement and furtherance of participation of the population in the provision of preventive and curative health services, such as the organisation of the health sector, the insurance system and, in particular, participation in political decisions relating to the right to health taken at both the community and national levels.

Article 12: Special topics of broad application

Non-discrimination and equal treatment

18 By virtue of articles 2 (2) and 3, the Covenant proscribes any discrimination in access to healthcare and underlying determinants of health, as well as to means and entitlements for their procurement, on the grounds of race, colour, sex, language, religion, political or other opinion, national or social origin, property, birth, physical or mental disability, health status (including HIV/AIDS), sexual orientation and civil, political, social or other status, which has the intention or effect of nullifying or impairing the equal enjoyment or exercise of the right to health. The Committee stresses that many measures, such as most strategies and programmes designed to eliminate health-related discrimination, can be pursued with minimum resource implications through the adoption, modification or abrogation of legislation or the dissemination of information. The Committee recalls General Comment No. 3, paragraph 12, which states that even in times of severe resource limitations, the vulnerable or marginalised members of society must be protected by the adoption of relatively low-cost programmes.

19 With respect to the right to health, equality of access to healthcare and health services has to be emphasised. States have a special obligation to provide those who do not have sufficient means with the necessary health insurance and healthcare facilities, and to prevent any discrimination on internationally prohibited grounds in the provision of healthcare and health services, especially with respect to the core obligations of the right to health.[16] Inappropriate health resource allocation can lead to discrimination that may not be overt. For example, investments should not disproportionately favour expensive curative health services which are often accessible only to a small, privileged fraction of the

population, rather than primary and preventive healthcare benefiting a far larger part of the population.

Gender perspective

20 The Committee recommends that States integrate a gender perspective in their health-related policies, planning, programmes and research in order to promote better health for both women and men. A gender-based approach recognises that biological and socio-cultural factors play a significant role in influencing the health of men and women. The disaggregation of health and socio-economic data according to sex is essential for identifying and remedying inequalities in health.

Women and the right to health

21 To eliminate discrimination against women, there is a need to develop and implement a comprehensive national strategy for promoting women's right to health throughout their life span. Such a strategy should include interventions aimed at the prevention and treatment of diseases affecting women, as well as policies to provide access to a full range of high quality and affordable health-care, including sexual and reproductive services. A major goal should be reducing women's health risks, particularly lowering rates of maternal mortality and protecting women from domestic violence. The realisation of women's right to health requires the removal of all barriers interfering with access to health services, education and information, including in the area of sexual and repro-ductive health. It is also important to undertake preventive, promotive and remedial action to shield women from the impact of harmful traditional cultural practices and norms that deny full reproductive rights to women.

Children and adolescents

22 Article 12 (2) a outlines the need to take measures to reduce infant mortality and promote the healthy development of infants and children. Subsequent international human rights instruments recognise that children and adolescents have the right to the enjoyment of the highest standard of health and access to facilities for the treatment of illness.[17] The convention of the Rights of the Child directs States to ensure access to essential health services for the child and his or her family, including pre- and postnatal care for mothers. The Convention links these goals with ensuring access to child-friendly information about preventive and health-promoting behaviour and support to families and communities in implementing these practices. Implementation of the principle of non-discrimination requires that girls, as well as boys, have equal access to adequate nutrition, safe environments, and physical as well as mental health services. There is a need to adopt effective and appropriate measures to abolish harmful traditional practices affecting the health of children, particularly girls, including early marriage, female genital mutilation, preferential feeding and care of male children.[18] Children with disabilities should be given the opportunity to enjoy a fulfilling and decent life and to participate within their community.

23 States parties should provide a safe and supportive environment for adolescents, that ensures the opportunity to participate in decisions affecting their health, to build life-skills, to acquire appropriate information, to receive counselling, and to negotiate the health-behaviour choices they make. The realisation of the right to health of adolescents is dependent on the development of youth-friendly healthcare, which respects confidentiality and privacy, and includes appropriate sexual and reproductive health services.

24 In all policies and programmes aimed at guaranteeing the right to health of children and adolescents their best interests shall be a primary consideration.

Older persons

25 With regard to the realisation of the right to health of older persons, the Committee, in accordance with paragraph 34 and 35 of General Comment No. 6 (1995), reaffirms the importance of an integrated approach, combining elements of preventive, curative and rehabilitative health treatment. Such measures should be based on periodical check-ups for both sexes; physical as well as psychological rehabilitative measures aimed at maintaining the functionality and autonomy of older persons; and attention and care for chronically and terminally ill persons, sparing them avoidable pain and enabling them to die with dignity.

Persons with disabilities

26 The Committee reaffirms paragraph 34 of its General Comment No. 5, which addresses the issue of persons with disabilities in the context of the right to physical and mental health. Moreover, the Committee stresses the need to ensure that not only the public health sector but also private providers of health services and facilities comply with the principle of non-discrimination in relation to persons with disabilities.

Indigenous peoples

27 In the light of emerging international law and practice and the recent measures taken by States in relation to indigenous peoples,[19] the Committee deems it useful to identify elements that would help to define indigenous peoples' right to health in order to better enable States with indigenous peoples to implement the provisions contained in Article 12 of the Covenant. The Committee considers that indigenous peoples have the right to specific measures to improve their access to health services and care. These health services should be culturally appropriate, taking into account traditional preventive care, healing practices and medicines. States should provide resources for indigenous peoples to design, deliver and control such services so that they may enjoy the highest attainable standard of physical and mental health. The vital medicinal plants, animals and minerals necessary to the full enjoyment of health of indigenous peoples should also be protected. The Committee notes that, in indigenous communities, the health of the individual is often linked to the health of the society as a whole and has a collective dimension. In this respect, that Committee considers that development-related activities that lead to the displacement of indigenous

peoples against their will from their traditional territories and environment, denying them their sources of nutrition and breaking their symbiotic relationship with their lands, has a deleterious effect on their health.

Limitations

28 Issues of public health are sometimes used by States as grounds for limiting the exercise of other fundamental rights. The Committee wishes to emphasise that the Covenant's limitation clause, article 4, is primarily intended to protect the rights of individuals rather than to permit the imposition of limitations by States. Consequently a State party which, for example, restricts the movement of, or incarcerates, persons with transmissible diseases such as HIV/AIDS, refuses to allow doctors to treat persons believed to be opposed to a government, or fails to provide immunisation against the community's major infectious diseases, on grounds such as national security or the preservation of public order, has the burden of justifying such serious measures in relation to each of the elements identified in article 4. Such restrictions must be in accordance with the law, including international human rights standards, compatible with the nature of the rights protected by the Covenant, in the interest of legitimate aims pursued, and strictly necessary for the promotion of the general welfare in a democratic society.

29 In line with article 5 (1), such limitations must be proportional, i.e. the least restrictive alternative must be adopted where several types of limitations are available. Even where such limitations on grounds of protecting public health are basically permitted, they should be of limited duration and subject to review.

II. STATES PARTIES' OBLIGATION

General legal obligations

30 While the Covenant provides for progressive realisation and acknowledges the constraints due to the limits of available resources, it also imposes on States parties various obligations which are of immediate effect. States parties have immediate obligations in relation to the right to health, such as the guarantee that the right will be exercised without discrimination of any kind (article 2 (2)) and the obligation to take steps (article 2 (1)) towards the full realisation of article 12. Such steps must be deliberate, concrete and targeted towards the full realisation of the right to health.[20]

31 The progressive realisation of the right to health over a period of time should not be interpreted as depriving States parties' obligations of all meaningful content. Rather, progressive realisation means that States parties have a specific and continuing obligation to move as expeditiously and effectively as possible towards the full realisation of article 12.[21]

32 As with all other rights in the Covenant, there is a strong presumption that retrogressive measures taken in relation to the right to health are impermissible. If any deliberately retrogressive measures are taken, the State party has the burden of proving that they have been introduced after the most careful

consideration of all alternatives and that they are duly justified by reference to the totality of the rights provided for in the Covenant in the context of the full use of the State party's maximum available resources.[22]

33 The right to health, like all human rights, imposes three types or levels of obligations on States parties: the obligations to *respect*, *protect* and *fulfil*. In turn, the obligation to fulfil contains obligations to facilitate, provide and promote.[23] The obligation to *respect* requires States to refrain from interfering directly or indirectly with the enjoyment of the right to health. The obligation to *protect* requires States to take measures that prevent third parties from interfering with article 12 guarantees. Finally, the obligation to *fulfil* requires States to adopt appropriate legislative, administrative, budgetary, judicial, promotional and other measures towards the full realisation of the right to health.

Specific legal obligations

34 In particular, States are under the obligation to respect the right to health by, *inter alia*, refraining from denying or limiting equal access for all persons, including prisoners or detainees, minorities, asylum seekers and illegal immigrants, to preventive, curative and palliative health services; abstaining from enforcing discriminatory practices as a state policy; and abstaining from imposing discriminatory practices related to women's health status and needs. Furthermore, obligations to respect include a State's obligation to refrain from prohibiting or impeding traditional preventive care, healing practices and medicines, from marketing unsafe drugs and from applying coercive medical treatments, unless on an exceptional basis for the treatment of mental illness or the prevention and control of communicable diseases. Such exceptional cases should be subject to specific and restrictive conditions, respecting best practices and applicable international standards, including the UN Principles for the Protection of Persons with Mental Illness and the improvement of Mental Health Care.[24] In addition, States should refrain from limiting access to contraceptives and other means of maintaining sexual and reproductive health, from censoring, withholding or intentionally misrepresenting health-related information, including sexual education and information, as well as from preventing people's participation in health-related matters. States should also refrain from unlawfully polluting air, water and soil, e.g. through industrial waste from State-owned facilities, from using or testing nuclear, biological or chemical weapons if such testing results in the release of substances harmful to human health, and from limiting access to health services as a punitive measure, e.g. during armed conflicts in violation of international humanitarian law.

35 Obligations to *protect* include, *inter alia*, the duties of States to adopt legislation or to take other measures ensuring equal access to healthcare and health-related services provided by third parties; to ensure that privatisation of the health sector does not constitute a threat to the availability, accessibility, acceptability and quality of health facilities, goods and services; to control the marketing of medical equipment and medicines by third parties; and to ensure that medical practitioners and other health professionals meet appropriate standards of education, skill and ethical codes of conduct. States are also obliged to ensure that harmful social or traditional practices do not interfere with access to pre- and postnatal care and family-planning; to prevent third parties from coercing

women to undergo traditional practices, e.g. female genital mutilation; and to take measures to protect all vulnerable or marginalised groups of society, in particular women, children, adolescents and older persons, in the light of gender-based expressions of violence. States should also ensure that third parties do not limit people's access to health-related information and services.

36 The obligation to *fulfil* requires States parties, *inter alia*, to give sufficient recognition to the right to health in the national political and legal systems, preferably by way of legislative implementation, and to adopt a national health policy with a detailed plan for realising the right to health. States must ensure provision of healthcare, including immunisation programmes against the major infectious diseases, and ensure equal access for all to the underlying determinants of housing and living conditions. Public health infrastructures should provide for sexual and reproductive health services, including safe motherhood, particularly in rural areas. States have to ensure the appropriate training of doctors and other medical personnel, the provision of a sufficient number of hospitals, clinics and other health-related facilities, and the promotion and support of the establishment of institutions providing counselling and mental health services, with due regard to equitable distribution throughout the country. Further obligations include the provision of a public, private or mixed health insurance system which is affordable for all, the promotion of medical research and health education, as well as information campaigns, in particular with respect to HIV/AIDS, sexual and reproductive health, traditional practices, domestic violence, the abuse of alcohol, and the use of cigarettes, drugs and other harmful substances. States are also required to adopt measures against environmental and occupational health hazards and against any other threat as demonstrated by epidemiological data. For this purpose they should formulate and implement national policies aimed at reducing and eliminating pollution of air, water and soil, including pollution by heavy metals such as lead from gasoline. Furthermore, States parties are required to formulate, implement and periodically review a coherent national policy on occupational accidents and diseases, by minimising risks, as well as to provide a coherent national policy on occupational safety and health services.[25]

37 The obligation to *fulfil* (facilitate) requires States, *inter alia*, to take positive measures that enable and assist individuals and communities to enjoy the right to health. States parties are also obliged to *fulfil* (provide) a specific right contained in the Covenant when an individual or group is unable, for reasons beyond their control, to realise that right themselves by the means at their disposal. The obligation to *fulfil* (promote) the right to health requires States to undertake actions that create, maintain and restore the health of the population. Such obligations include:

(1) Fostering recognition of factors favouring positive health results, e.g. research and provision of information;

(2) Ensuring that health services are culturally appropriate and that healthcare staff are trained to recognise and respond to the specific needs of vulnerable or marginalised groups;

(3) Ensuring that the State meets its obligation in the dissemination of appropriate information relating to healthy lifestyles and nutrition, harmful traditional practices and the availability of services;

(4) Supporting people in making informed choices about their health.

International obligations

38 In its General Comment No. 3, the Committee drew attention to the obligation of all States parties to take steps, individually and through international assistance and cooperation, especially economic and technical towards the full realisation of the rights recognised in the Covenant, such as the right to health. In the spirit of article 56 of the Charter of the United Nations, the specific provisions of the Covenant (article 12, 2 (1), 22 and 23) and the Alma Ata Declaration on Primary Health Care, States parties should recognise the essential role of international cooperation and comply with their commitment to take joint and separate action to achieve the full realisation of the right to health. In this regard, States parties are referred to the Declaration of Alma Ata which proclaims that 'the existing gross inequality in the health status of the people particularly between developed and developing countries as well as within countries is politically, socially and economically unacceptable and is, therefore, of common concern to all countries'.[26]

39 To comply with their international obligations in relation to article 12, States parties have to respect the enjoyment of the right to health in other countries, and to prevent third parties from violating the right in other countries, if they are able to influence these third parties by way of legal or political means, in accordance with the Charter of the United Nations and applicable international law. Depending on the availability of resources, States should facilitate access to essential health facilities, goods and services in other countries, wherever possible and provide the necessary aid when required.[27] States parties should ensure that the right to health is given due attention in international agreements and, to that end, should consider the development of further legal instruments. In relation to the conclusion of other international agreements, States parties should take steps to ensure that these instruments do not adversely impact upon the right to health. Similarly, States parties have an obligation to ensure that their actions as members of international organisations take due account of the right to health. Accordingly, States parties which are members of international financial institutions, notably the International Monetary Fund, the World Bank, and regional development banks, should pay greater attention to the protection of the right to health in influencing the lending policies, credit agreements and international measures of these institutions.

40 States parties have a joint and individual responsibility, in accordance with the Charter of the United Nations and relevant resolutions of the UN General Assembly and of the World Health Assembly, to cooperate in providing disaster relief and humanitarian assistance in times of emergency, including assistance to refugees and internally displaced persons. Each State should contribute to this task to the maximum of its capacities. Priority in the provision of international medical aid, distribution and management of resources, such as safe and potable water, food and medical supplies, and financial aid should be given to the most vulnerable or marginalised groups of the population. Moreover, given that some diseases are easily transmissible beyond the frontiers of a State, there is a collective responsibility on the international community to address this problem. The economically developed States parties have a special responsibility and interest to assist the poorer developing States in this regard.

41 States parties should refrain at all times from imposing embargoes or similar measures restricting the supply of another State with adequate medicines and medical equipment. Restrictions on such goods should never be used as an instrument of political and economic pressure. In this regard, the Committee recalls its position, stated in General Comment No. 8, on the relationship between economic sanctions and respect for economic, social and cultural rights.

42 While only States are parties to the Covenant and thus ultimately accountable for compliance with it, all members of society – individuals, including health professionals, families, local communities, inter-governmental and non-governmental organisations, civil society organisations, as well as the private business sector – have responsibilities regarding the realisation of the right to health. State parties should therefore provide for an environment which facilitates the discharge of these responsibilities.

Core obligations

43 In General Comment No. 3, the Committee confirms that States parties have a core obligation to ensure the satisfaction of, at the very least, minimum essential levels of each of the rights enunciated in the Covenant, including essential primary healthcare. Read in conjunction with more contemporary instruments, such as the Programme of Action of the International Conference on Population and Development,[28] the Declaration of Alma Ata[29] provides compelling guidance on the core obligations arising from article 12. Accordingly, in the Committee's view, this core includes at least the following obligations:
    (1) To ensure the right of access to health facilities, goods and services on a non-discriminatory basis, especially for vulnerable or marginalised groups;
    (2) To ensure access to the minimum essential food which is sufficient, nutritionally adequate and safe, to ensure freedom from hunger to everyone;
    (3) To ensure access to basic shelter, housing and sanitation, and an adequate supply of safe and potable water;
    (4) To provide essential drugs, as from time to time defined by WHO's Action Programme on Essential Drugs;
    (5) To ensure equitable distribution of all health facilities, goods and services;
    (6) To adopt and implement a national public health strategy and plan of action, on the basis of epidemiological evidence, addressing the health concerns of the whole population; the strategy and plan of action shall be devised, and periodically reviewed, on the basis of a participatory and transparent process; they shall include methods, such as the right to health indicators and benchmarks, by which progress can be closely monitored; the process by which the strategy and plan of action is devised, as well as their content, shall give particular attention to all vulnerable or marginalised groups.

44 The Committee also confirms that obligations of comparable priority include the following:
    (1) To ensure reproductive, maternal (prenatal as well as postnatal) and child healthcare;
    (2) To provide immunisation against the community's major infectious diseases;
    (3) To take measures to prevent, treat and control epidemic and endemic diseases;

(4) To provide education and access to information concerning the main health problems in the community, including methods of preventing and controlling them;

(5) To provide appropriate training for health personnel, including education on health and human rights.

45 For the avoidance of any doubt, the Committee wishes to emphasise that it is particularly incumbent on States parties and other actors who are in a position to assist others, to provide 'international assistance and cooperation, especially economic and technical'[30] which enable developing countries to fulfil their core and other obligations indicated in paragraphs 43 and 44 above.

III. VIOLATIONS

46 When the normative content of article 12 (Part I) is applied to the obligations of States parties (Part II), a dynamic process is set in motion which facilitates identification of violations of the right to health. The following paragraphs provide illustrations of violations of article 12.

47 In determining which actions or omissions amount to a violation of the right to health, it is important to distinguish the inability from the unwillingness of a State party to comply with its obligations under article 12. This follows from article 12 (1) which speaks of the highest attainable standard of health, as well as from article 2 (1) of the Covenant, which obliges each State party to take the necessary steps to the maximum of its available resources. A State which is unwilling to use the maximum of its available resources for the realisation of the right to health is in violation of its obligations under article 12. If resource constraints render it impossible for a State to comply fully with its Covenant obligations, it has the burden of justifying that every effort has nevertheless been made to use all available resources at its disposal in order to satisfy, as a matter of priority, the obligations as outlined above. It should be stressed, however, that a State party cannot, under any circumstances whatsoever, justify its non-compliance with the core obligations set out in paragraph 43 above which are non-negotiable.

48 Violations of the right to health can occur through the direct action of States or other entities insufficiently regulated by the States. The adoption of any retrogressive measures incompatible with the core obligations under the right to health, as outlined in paragraph 43 above, constitutes a violation of the right to health. Violations through *acts of commission* include the formal repeal or suspension of legislation necessary for the continued enjoyment of the right to health or the adoption of legislation of policies which are manifestly incompatible with pre-existing domestic or international legal obligations in relation to the right to health.

49 Violations of the right to health can also occur through the omission or failure of States to take necessary measures arising from legal obligations. Violations through *acts of omission* include the failure to take appropriate steps towards the full realisation of everyone's right to the enjoyment of the highest attainable standard of physical and mental health, the failure to have a national policy on occupational safety and health as well as occupational health services, and the failure to enforce relevant laws.

Violations of the obligation to respect

50 Violations of the obligation to respect are those state actions, policies or laws that contravene the standards set out in article 12 of the Covenant and are likely to result in bodily harm, unnecessary morbidity and preventable mortality. Examples include the denial of access to health facilities, goods and services to particular individuals or groups as a result of *de jure* or *de facto* discrimination; the deliberate withholding or misrepresentation of information vital to health protection or treatment; the suspension of legislation or the adoption of laws or policies that interfere with the enjoyment of any of the components of the right to health; and the failure of the State to take into account its legal obligations regarding the right to health when entering into bilateral or multi-lateral agreements with other States, international organisations and other entities, such as multinational corporations.

Violations of the obligation to protect

51 Violations of the obligation to protect follow from the failure of a State to take all necessary measures to safeguard persons within their jurisdiction from in-fringements of the right to health by third parties. This category includes such omissions as the failure to regulate the activities of individuals, groups or corporations so as to prevent them from violating the right to health of others; the failure to protect consumers and workers from practices detrimental to health, e.g. by employers and manufacturers of medicines or food; the failure to discourage production, marketing, and consumption of tobacco, narcotics and other harmful substances; the failure to protect women against violence or to prosecute perpetrators; the failure to discourage the continued observance of harmful traditional medical or cultural practices; and the failure to enact or enforce laws to prevent the pollution of water, air and soil by extractive and manufacturing industries.

Violations of the obligation to fulfil

52 Violations of the obligation to fulfil occur through the failure of States parties to take all necessary steps to ensure the realisation of the right to health. Examples include the failure to adopt or implement a national health policy designed to ensure the right to health for everyone; insufficient expenditure or mis-allocation of public resources which results in the non-enjoyment of the right to health by individuals or groups, particularly the vulnerable or marginalised; the failure to monitor the realisation of the right to health at the national level, for example, by identifying right to health indicators and benchmarks; the failure to take measures to reduce the inequitable distribution of health facilities, goods and services; the failure to adopt a gender-sensitive approach to health; and the failure to reduce infant and maternal mortality rates.

IV. IMPLEMENTATION AT THE NATIONAL LEVEL

Framework legislation

53 The most appropriate feasible measures to implement the right to health will vary significantly from one State to another. Every State has a margin of discretion in assessing which measures are most suitable to meet its specific circumstances. The Covenant, however, clearly imposes a duty on each State to take whatever steps are necessary to ensure that everyone has access to health facilities, goods and services so that they can enjoy, as soon as possible, the highest attainable standard of physical and mental health. This requires the adoption of a national strategy to ensure the enjoyment of the right to health to all, based on human rights principles which define the objectives of that strategy, and the formulation of policies and corresponding rights to health indicators and benchmarks. The national health strategy should also identify the resources available to attain defined objectives, as well as the most cost-effective way of using those resources.

54 The formulation and implementation of national health strategies and plans of action should respect, *inter alia*, the principles of non-discrimination and people's participation. In particular, the right of individuals and groups to participate in decision-making processes, which may affect their development, must be an integral component of any policy, programme or strategy developed to discharge governmental obligations under article 12. Promoting health must involve effective community action in setting priorities, making decisions, planning, implementing and evaluating strategies to achieve better health. Effective provision of health services can only be assured if people's participation is secured by States.

55 The national health strategy and plan of action should also be based on the principles of accountability, transparency and independence of the judiciary since good governance is essential to the effective implementation of all human rights, including the realisation of the right to the health. In order to create a favourable climate for the realisation of the right, States parties should take appropriate steps to ensure that the private business sector and civil society are aware of, and consider the importance of, the right to health in pursuing their activities.

56 States should consider the adoption of a framework law to operationalise their right to health national strategy. The framework law should establish national mechanisms for monitoring the implementation of national health strategies and plans of action. It should include provisions on the targets to be achieved and the timeframe for their achievement; the means by which right to health benchmarks could be achieved; the intended collaboration with civil society, including health experts, the private sector and international organisations; institutional responsibility for the implementation of the right to health national strategy and plan of action; and possible recourse procedures. In monitoring progress towards the realisation of the right to health, States parties should identify the factors and difficulties affecting implementation of their obligations.

Right to health indicators and benchmarks

57 National health strategies should identify appropriate right to health indicators and benchmarks. The indicators should be designed to monitor, at the national and international levels, the State party's obligations under article 12. States may obtain guidance on appropriate right to health indicators, which should address different aspects of the right to health, from the ongoing work of WHO and UNICEF in this field. Right to health indicators require disaggregation on the prohibited grounds of discrimination.

58 Having identified appropriate right to health indicators. State parties are invited to set appropriate national benchmarks in relation to each indicator. During the periodic reporting procedure the Committee will engage in a process of scoping with the State party. Scoping involves the joint consideration by the State party and the Committee of the indicators and national benchmarks which will then provide the targets to be achieved during the next reporting period. In the following five years, the State party will use these national benchmarks to help monitor its implementation of article 12. Thereafter, in the subsequent reporting process, the State party and the Committee will consider whether or not the benchmarks have been achieved, and the reasons for any difficulties that may have been encountered.

Remedies and accountability

59 Any person or group who is a victim of a violation of the right to health should have access to effective judicial or other appropriate remedies at both national and international levels.[31] All victims of such violations should be entitled to adequate reparation, which may take the form of restitution, compensation, satisfaction or guarantees of non-repetition. National ombudsmen, human rights commissions, consumer forums, patients' rights associations or similar institutions should address violations of the right to health.

60 The incorporation in the domestic legal order of international instruments recognising the right to health can significantly enhance the scope and effectiveness of remedial measures and should be encouraged in all cases.[32] Incorporation enables courts to adjudicate violations of the right to health, or at least its core obligations, by direct reference to the Covenant.

61 Judges and members of the legal profession should be encouraged by States parties to pay greater attention to violations of the right to health in the exercise of their functions.

62 States parties should respect, protect, facilitate and promote the work of human rights advocates and other members of civil society with a view to assisting vulnerable or marginalised groups in the realisation of their right to health.

V. OBLIGATIONS OF ACTORS OTHER THAN STATES PARTIES

63 The role of the United Nations agencies and programmes, and in particular the key function assigned to WHO in realising the right to health at the international, regional and country levels, is of particular importance, as is the

function of UNICEF in relation to the right to health of children. When formulating and implementing their right to health national strategies, States parties should avail themselves of WHO's technical assistance and cooperation. Further, when preparing their reports, States parties should utilise the extensive information and advisory services of WHO as regards data collection, disaggregation, and the development of right to health indicators and benchmarks.

64 Moreover, coordinated efforts for the realisation of the right to health should be maintained to enhance the interaction among all the actors concerned, including the various components of civil society. In conformity with articles 22 and 23 of the Covenant, WHO, ILO, UNDP, UNICEF, UNFPA, the World Bank, regional development banks, the International Monetary Fund, WTO and other relevant bodies within the UN system, should cooperate effectively with States parties, building on their respective expertise, in relation to the implementation of the right to health at national levels, with due respect to their individual mandates. In particular, the international financial institutions, notably the World Bank and IMF, should pay greater attention to the protection of the right to health in their lending policies, credit agreements, and structural adjustment programmes. When examining the reports of States parties, and their ability to meet the obligations under article 12, the Committee will consider the effects of the assistance provided by all other actors. The adoption of a human rights-based approach by United Nations specialised agencies, programmes and bodies will greatly facilitate implementation of the right to health. In the course of its examination of States parties' reports, the Committee will also consider the role of health professional associations and other NGOs in relation to the States' obligations under article 12.

65 The role of WHO, the Office of the United Nations High Commissioner for Refugees (UNHCR), the International Committee of the Red Cross/Red Crescent and UNICEF, as well as non-governmental organisations and national medical associations, is of particular importance in relation to disaster relief and humanitarian assistance in times of emergencies, including assistance to refugees and internally displaced persons. Priority in the provision of international medical aid, distribution and management of resources, such as safe and potable water, food and medical supplies, and financial aid should be given to the most vulnerable or marginalised groups of the population.

Adopted 11 May 2000

Explanatory Notes

1   For example, the principle of non-discrimination in relation to health facilities, goods and services is legally enforceable in numerous national jurisdictions.
2   CHR Res. 1989/11.
3   The Principles for the Protection of Persons with Mental Illness and the Improvement of Mental Health Care adopted by the UN General Assembly in 1991 (UN GA Res. 46/119) and the Committee's General Comment No. 5 on persons with disabilities apply to persons with mental illness; the International Conference on Population and Development held at Cairo in 1994, as well as the Beijing Declaration and Programme of Action of 1995 contain definitions of reproductive health and women's health, respectively.

4   Common article 3 of the Geneva Conventions (1949); Additional Protocol I (1977): Protection of Victims of International Armed Conflicts, art. 75 (2) (a); Additional Protocol II (1977): Protection of Victims of Non-International Armed Conflicts, art. 4 (a).

5   Cf. WHO Model List of Essential Drugs, revised December 1999, WHO Drug Information Vol. 13, No. 4, 1999.

6   Unless expressly provided otherwise, any reference in this General Comment to health facilities, goods and services includes the underlying determinants of health outlined in paras. 11 and 12 (1) above.

7   *See infra*, paras. 18 and 19.

8   *See* Art. 19 (2) ICCPR. This General Comment gives particular emphasis to access to information because of the special importance of this issue in relation to health.

9   In the literature and practice concerning the right to health, three levels of healthcare are frequently referred to: *Primary healthcare* typically deals with common and relatively minor illnesses and is provided by health professionals and/or generally trained doctors working within the community at relatively low cost; *secondary healthcare* is provided in centres, usually hospitals, and typically deals with relatively common minor or serious illnesses that cannot be managed at community level, using specialty trained health professionals and doctors, special equipment, and sometimes in-patient care at comparatively higher cost; *tertiary healthcare* is provided in relatively few centres, typically deals with small numbers of minor or serious illnesses requiring specialty trained health professionals and doctors and special equipment, and is often relatively expensive.

10 Since forms of primary, secondary and tertiary healthcare frequently overlap and often interact, the use of this typology does not always provide sufficient distinguishing criteria to be helpful for assessing which levels of healthcare States parties must provide, and is therefore of limited assistance in relation to the normative understanding of article 12.

11 According to WHO, the reduction of the stillbirth-rate is not commonly used any more; today, infant and under-five mortality rates are measured instead.

12 *Prenatal* denotes existing or occurring before birth; *perinatal* refers to the period shortly before and after birth (in medical statistics the period begins with the completion of 28 weeks of gestation and is variously defined as ending one to four weeks after birth); *neonatal*, by contrast, covers the period pertaining to the first four weeks after birth; while *postnatal* denotes occurrence after birth. In this General Comment, the more generic terms pre- and postnatal are exclusively employed.

13 Reproductive health means that women and men have the freedom to decide if and when to reproduce and the right to be informed and to have access to safe, effective, affordable and acceptable methods of family planning of their choice as well as the right of access to appropriate healthcare services that will, for example, enable women to go safely through pregnancy and childbirth.

14 The Committee takes note, in this regard, of Principle I of the Stockholm Declaration of 1972 which states: 'Man has the fundamental right to freedom, equality and adequate conditions of life, in an environment of a quality that permits a life in dignity and well-being', as well of recent developments in international law, including UNGA Res. 45/94 on the Need to Ensure a Healthy Environment for the Well-Being of Individuals; Principle 1 of the Rio Declaration; and regional human rights instruments such as art. 10 of the San Salvador Protocol to the American Convention on Human Rights.

15 ILO Convention 155, art. 4 (2).

16 *See* para. 12 (2) and footnote 8 above.

17 For core obligations, *see infra*, paras. 43 and 44.

18 Art. 24 (1) CRC.

19 Cf. World Health Assembly Resolution on maternal and child health and family planning: traditional practices harmful to the health of women and children, WHA 47/10, 1994.

20 Recent emerging international norms relevant to indigenous peoples include the ILO Convention No. 169 concerning Indigenous and Tribal Peoples in Independent Countries

(1989); arts. 29 (c) and (d), 30 of the Convention on the Rights of the Child (1989); art. 8 (j) of the United Nations Convention on Biological Diversity (1992), recommending that States respect, preserve and maintain knowledge, innovation and practices of indigenous communities; Agenda 21 of the World Conference on Environment and Development (1992), in particular chapter 26; and para. 20 of the Vienna Declaration and Programme of Action (1993), stating that States should take concerted, positive steps to ensure respect for all human rights of indigenous peoples on the basis of non-discrimination. *See also* preamble and art. 3 of the UN Framework Convention on Climate Change (1992); and art. 10 (2) (e) of the UN Convention to Combat Desertification in Countries Experiencing Serious Drought and/or Desertification, Particularly in Africa (1994). During the last years an increasing number of States have changed their constitution and introduced legislation recognising specific rights of indigenous peoples.

21 *See* General Comment No. 13, para. 43.

22 *See* General Comment No. 3, para. 9; General Comment No. 13, para. 44.

23 *See* General Comment No. 3, para 9; General Comment No. 13, para. 45.

24 According to General Comments Nos. 12 and 13, the obligation to fulfil incorporates an obligation to *facilitate* and an obligation to *provide*. In the present General Comment, the obligation to fulfil also incorporates an obligation to *promote* because of the critical importance of health promotion in the work of WHO and elsewhere.

25 UNGA Res. 46/119 (1991).

26 Elements of such a policy are the identification, determination, authorisation and control of dangerous materials, equipment, substances, agents and work processes; the provision of health information to workers, and the provision, if needed, of adequate protective clothing and equipment; the enforcement of laws and regulations through adequate inspection; the requirement of notification of occupational accidents and diseases, the conduct of inquiries into serious accidents and diseases, and the production of annual statistics; the protection of workers and their representatives from disciplinary measures for actions properly taken by them in conformity with such a policy; and the provision of occupational health services with essentially preventive functions. *See* ILO Occupational Safety and Health Convention, 1981 (No. 155) and Occupational Health Services Convention, 1985 (No. 161).

27 Article II, Declaration of Alma Ata, Report of the International Conference on Primary Health Care, Alma Ata, 6–12 September 1978, in: World Health Organisation, Health for All Series, No. 1, WHO, Geneva 1978.

28 *See* para. 45, below.

29 Report of the International Conference on Population and Development, Chapters VII and VIII, Cairo, 5–13 September 1994, A/CONF.171/13/Rev.1, Annex.

30 Based on the Declaration of Alma Ata adopted by the International Conference on Primary Health Care jointly sponsored by WHO and UNICEF in 1978, *see supra*, principle XX.

31 Covenant, art. 2 (1).

32 Regardless of whether groups as such can seek remedies as distinct holders of rights, States parties are bound by both the collective and individual dimensions of art. 12. Collective rights are critical in the field of health; modern public health policy relies heavily on prevention and promotion which are approaches primarily directed to groups.

33 *See* General Comment No. 2, para. 9.

http://www.unhchr.ch/tbs/doc.nsf/MasterFrameView/
40d009901358b0e2c1256915005090be?Opendocument as at 19 July 2000

State of the IBFAN Code country by country

Status of the Code

Asia	1 Law	2 Many provisions law	3 Policy or voluntary measure	4 Few provisions law	5 Some provisions voluntary or guidelines	6 Measure drafted, awaiting final approval	7 Being studied	8 No action	9 No information
Afghanistan					●	●			
Bahrain	●								
Bangladesh		●							
Bhutan			●		●				
Brunei				●					
Cambodia					●	●			
China		●							
Hong Kong SAR, China				●	●				
Macao SAR, China			●						
India	●								
Indonesia		●							
Iraq					●				
Israel				●					
Japan			●	●					
Jordan						●			
Kazakhstan							●		
Korea, Dem.P.R. of									●
Korea, Republic of				●					
Kuwait		●							
Kyrgyzstan						●			
Laos		●							
Lebanon	●								
Malaysia			●	●					
Maldives				●					
Mongolia			●						
Myanmar						●			
Nepal	●								
Oman		●							
Pakistan		●							
Palestinian Authority						●			
Philippines	●								
Qatar				●					
Saudi Arabia				●					
Singapore[2]					●				
Sri Lanka	●								
Syria[1]						●			
Taiwan[2]			●	●					
Tajikistan						●			
Thailand				●					
Timor Leste					●				
Turkmenistan						●			
United Arab Emirates				●	●				
Uzbekistan						●			
Vietnam		●							
Yemen	●								
Oceania	**1**	**2**	**3**	**4**	**5**	**6**	**7**	**8**	**9**
Australia			●	●					
Cook Islands			●						

Status of the Code

Africa	1 Law	2 Many provisions law	3 Policy or voluntary measure	4 Few provisions law	5 Some provisions voluntary or guidelines	6 Measure drafted, awaiting final approval	7 Being studied	8 No action	9 No information
Algeria[1]			●						
Angola					●				
Benin	●								
Botswana			●		●				
Burkina Faso	●								
Burundi					●				
Cameroon	●								
Cape Verde	●								
Central African Rep.					●				
Chad							●		
Congo, Dem. Rep. of				●					
Côte d'Ivoire					●				
Djibouti		●							
Egypt			●						
Equatorial Guinea									●
Eritrea							●		
Ethiopia			●		●				
Gabon				●	●				
Gambia					●				
Ghana	●								
Guinea				●	●				
Guinea-Bissau				●					
Kenya		●			●				
Lesotho					●				
Liberia									●
Libya[1]			●						
Madagascar	●								
Malawi					●				
Mali							●		
Mauritania							●		
Mauritius					●				
Morocco				●	●				
Mozambique				●	●				
Namibia					●				
Niger		●							
Nigeria		●							
Rwanda							●		
São Tomé & Principe			●		●				
Senegal		●							
Seychelles		●							
Sierra Leone					●				
Somalia					●			●	
South Africa			●		●				
Sudan				●					
Swaziland			●				●		
Tanzania	●								
Togo							●		
Tunisia		●							

Status of the Code	Law	Many provisions law	Policy or voluntary measure	Few provisions law	Some provisions voluntary or guidelines	Measure drafted, awaiting final approval	Being studied	No action	No information
Fiji							•		
Kiribati					•	•			
Marshall Islands							•		
Micronesia					•				
New Zealand²			•						
Palau							•		
Papua New Guinea		•					•		
Tuvalu									•
Vanuatu					•				
Samoa					•				
Americas	**1**	**2**	**3**	**4**	**5**	**6**	**7**	**8**	**9**
Antigua & Barbuda								•	
Argentina	•								
Bahamas					•				
Barbados			•						
Belize							•		
Bolivia			•			•			
Brazil	•								
Canada				•					
Chile			•	•					
Colombia		•							
Costa Rica	•								
Cuba¹				•					
Dominica			•						
Dominican Republic	•								
Ecuador			•	•					
El Salvador							•		
Grenada			•						
Guatemala	•								
Guyana			•						
Haiti							•		
Honduras					•	•			
Jamaica			•						
Mexico		•							
Nicaragua		•							
Panama	•								
Paraguay				•					
Peru	•								
St Kitts & Nevis								•	
St Lucia					•				
St Vincent					•				
Surinam								•	
Trinidad & Tobago			•	•					
United States								•	
Uruguay	•								
Venezuela²					•	•			

Status of the Code	Law	Many provisions law	Policy or voluntary measure	Few provisions law	Some provisions voluntary or guidelines	Measure drafted, awaiting final approval	Being studied	No action	No information
Uganda	•								
Zambia			•				•		
Zimbabwe	•								
Europe	**1**	**2**	**3**	**4**	**5**	**6**	**7**	**8**	**9**
Albania	•								
Armenia				•					
*Austria		•							
*Belgium		•							
*Bosnia & Herzegovina			•	•			•		
Bulgaria							•		
Croatia							•		
**Cyprus						•	•		
**Czech Republic							•		
*Denmark		•							
**Estonia				•					
*Finland		•							
*France		•							
Georgia	•								
*Germany		•							
*Greece		•							
**Hungary				•					
Iceland								•	
*Ireland		•							
*Italy		•							
**Latvia							•		
Liechtenstein									•
**Lithuania								•	
*Luxembourg		•							
Macedonia			•						
**Malta								•	
Moldova								•	
Monaco								•	
*Netherlands		•							
Norway		•							
**Poland							•		
*Portugal		•							
Romania								•	
Russian Federation								•	
Serbia & Montenegro									•
**Slovakia								•	
**Slovenia									•
*Spain		•							
*Sweden			•						
Switzerland²						•	•		
Turkey			•				•		
Ukraine								•	
*United Kingdom		•							

WHO HFA (2000) Targets for Equity in Health

1   *Reducing the differences*
    By the year 2000, the actual differences in health status between countries and between groups within countries should be reduced by at least 25 per cent by improving the level of health of disadvantaged nations and groups.

    This target could be achieved if the basic prerequisites for health were provided for all; if the risks related to lifestyles were reduced; if the health aspects of living and working conditions were improved; and if good primary healthcare was made accessible to all.

2   *Developing health potential*
    By the year 2000, people should have the basic opportunity to develop and use their health potential to live socially and economically fulfilling lives.

    This target could be achieved if health policies in member states gave a framework for developing, implementing and monitoring programmes that provide the environmental conditions, social support and services required to develop and use each person's health potential.

3   *Better opportunities for the disabled*
    By the year 2000, disabled persons should have the physical, social and economic opportunities that allow at least for a socially and economically fulfilling and mentally creative life.

    This target could be achieved if societies developed positive attitudes towards the disabled and set up programmes aimed at providing appropriate physical, social and economic opportunities for them to develop their capacities to lead a healthy life.

4   *Reducing disease and disability*
    By the year 2000, the average number of years that people live free from major disease and disability should be increased by at least 10 per cent.

    This target could be achieved if, for instance, comprehensive programmes aimed at primary prevention of accidents and violence, cardiovascular disease, lifestyle-related cancers, occupational diseases, psychiatric disorders, alcoholism and drug abuse were developed, and adequate curative and rehabilitative services provided to all; if current knowledge regarding infectious diseases prevention were systematically applied; if genetic counselling services were made more generally available; if research were intensified with regard to disabling neurological and musculoskeletal disorders; and if preventive measures in oral health were effectively implemented.

5   *Elimination of specific diseases*
By the year 2000, there should be no indigenous measles, poliomyelitis, neonatal tetanus, congenital rubella, diphtheria, congenital syphilis or indigenous malaria in the region.
   This target could be achieved through a well-organised primary healthcare system ensuring effective epidemiological surveillance, vaccination coverage, malaria control measures, education on the risks of syphilis, screening and, when necessary, treatment of expectant mothers.

6   *Life expectancy at birth*
By the year 2000, life expectancy at birth in the region should be at least 75 years.
   This target could be achieved if, by the year 2000, no country or group within a country had a life expectancy of less than 65 years; if countries that reached this level in 1980 had a life expectancy of more than 75 years; and if all countries had reduced by at least 25 per cent the differences in life expectancy among geographical areas and socioeconomic groups and between the sexes.

7   *Infant mortality*
By the year 2000, infant mortality in the region should be less than 20 per 1000 live births.
   This target could be achieved if, by the year 2000, no country or group within a country had an infant mortality rate of more than 40 per 1000 live births; if countries with a rate below this level in 1980 had a rate below 15 per 1000; and if all countries attempted to reduce significantly the differences among geographical areas and socioeconomic groups.

8   *Maternal mortality*
By the year 2000, maternal mortality in the region should be less than 15 per 100 000 live births.
   This target could be achieved if, by the year 2000, no country or group within a country had a maternal mortality rate of more than 25 per 100 000 live births; if countries with a rate already below 25 in 1980 had a rate below 10; and if all countries had reduced significant differences among geographical areas and socioeconomic groups.

9   *Diseases of the circulation*
By the year 2000, mortality in the region from diseases of the circulatory system in people under 64 should be reduced by at least 15 per cent.
   This target could be achieved by a combination of preventive and treatment methods that would reverse the trend in countries where ischaemic heart disease mortality is increasing or stable, and accelerate in countries where the mortality is decreasing, thereby contributing to the current decline in cerebrovascular mortality in all countries.

10   *Cancer*
By the year 2000, mortality in the region from cancer in people under 65 should be reduced by at least 15 per cent.
   This target could be achieved if tobacco-related cancers were reduced as a result of a major decrease in smoking and cervical cancer following the establishment of screening programmes; and if current methods in early diagnosis,

treatment and rehabilitation were applied in an appropriate way to all cancer patients.

11 *Accidents*

By the year 2000, deaths from accidents in the region should be reduced by at least 25 per cent through an intensified effort to reduce traffic, home and occupational accidents.

This target could be achieved if, by the year 2000, no country had a mortality rate from road traffic accidents of more than 20 per 100 000; if countries below that level reduced it to less than 15; if all countries reduced the differences between the sexes, and age and socioeconomic groups; furthermore, if the occupational accident mortality in the region were lowered by at least 50 per cent; and if the mortality from home accidents were significantly reduced.

12 *Suicide*

By the year 2000, the current rising trends in suicides and attempted suicides in the region should be reversed.

This target could be achieved if improvements were made with regard to societal factors that put a strain on the individual, such as unemployment and social isolation; if the individual's ability to cope with life events were strengthened by education and social support; and if the health and social service personnel were better trained to deal with people at high risk.

13 *Healthy public policy*

By 1990, national policies in all member states should ensure that legislative, administrative and economic mechanisms provide broad intersectoral support and resources for the promotion of healthy lifestyles and ensure effective participation of the people at all levels of such policy-making.

The attainment of this target could be significantly supported by strategic health planning at cabinet level, to cover broad intersectoral issues that affect lifestyle and health, the periodic assessment of existing policies in their relationship to health, and the establishment of effective machinery for public involvement in policy planning and development.

14 *Social support systems*

By 1990, all member states should have specific programmes which enhance the major roles of the family and other social groups in developing and supporting healthy lifestyles.

The attainment of this target could be significantly supported by establishing close intersectoral links between health and social welfare programmes, primarily at the local level, and by securing funds for projects that enhance joint community action.

15 *Knowledge and motivation for healthy behaviour*

By 1990, educational programmes in all member states should enhance the knowledge, motivation and skills of people to acquire and maintain health.

The attainment of this target could be significantly supported by ensuring an adequate and effective infrastructure and funding for health education programmes at all levels.

16 *Positive health behaviour*
By 1995, in all member states, there should be significant increases in positive health behaviour, such as balanced nutrition, non-smoking, appropriate physical activity and good stress management.

This could be achieved if clear targets in these areas were set in each member state, e.g. a minimum of 80 per cent of the population as non-smokers and a 50 per cent reduction in national tobacco consumption, and if steps were taken by WHO and other international organisations to promote cooperation in health promotion activities throughout the region in order to make a wider impact on basic health values.

17 *Health-damaging behaviour*
By 1995, in all member states, there should be significant decreases in health-damaging behaviour, such as overuse of alcohol and pharmaceutical products; use of elicit drugs and dangerous chemical substances; and dangerous driving and violent social behaviour.

The attainment of this target could be significantly supported by developing integrated programmes aimed at reducing the consumption of alcohol and other harmful substances by at least 24 per cent by the year 2000.

18 *Multisectoral policies*
By 1990, member states should have multisectoral politics that effectively protect the environment from health hazards, ensure community awareness and involvement, and support international efforts to curb such hazards affecting more than one country.

The achievement of this target will require the acceptance by all governments that well-coordinated multisectoral efforts are needed at central, regional and local levels, to ensure that human health considerations are regarded as essential prerequisites for industrial and other forms of socioeconomic development, including the introduction of new technologies; the introduction of mechanisms to increase community awareness and involvement in environmental issues with potential implications for human health; and the development of international arrangements for effective control of transfrontier environmental health hazards.

19 *Monitoring and control mechanisms*
By 1990, all member states should have adequate machinery for the monitoring, assessment and control of environmental hazards which pose a threat to human health, including potentially toxic chemicals, radiation, harmful consumer goods and biological agents.

The achievement of this target will require the establishment of well-coordinated monitoring programmes with clearly defined objectives; the development of methodologies and health criteria for the assessment of data in relation to control procedures; the investment of adequate levels of funding for control measures and their introduction and maintenance; and the training and utilisation of sufficient numbers of competent personnel for all aspects of environmental health protection.

20 *Control of water pollution*
By 1990, all people of the region should have adequate supplies of safe drinking water, and by the year 1995 pollution of rivers, lakes and seas should no longer pose a threat to human health.

The achievement of this target will require, in the less developed countries of the region, the investment of higher levels of funding for the construction and maintenance of drinking water supply facilities, with the appropriate mobilisation of international and bilateral assistance to reinforce national endeavours, and with the training and utilisation of adequate numbers of competent personnel; and in all countries of the region, the introduction of effective legislative, administrative and technical measures for the surveillance and control of pollution of surface water and groundwater, in order to comply with criteria to safeguard public health.

21 *Control of air pollution*

By 1995, all people of the region should be effectively protected against recognised health risks from air pollution.

The achievement of this target will require the introduction of effective legislative, administrative and technical measures for the surveillance and control of both outdoor and indoor air pollution, in order to comply with criteria to safeguard human health.

22 *Food safety*

By 1990, all member states should have significantly reduced health risks from food contamination and implemented measures to protect consumers from harmful additives.

The achievement of this target will require the introduction of effective legislative, administrative and technical measures for the surveillance and control of food contamination at all stages of production, distribution, storage, sale and use; and the implementation of measures to control the use of harmful food additives.

23 *Control of hazardous wastes*

By 1995, all member states should have eliminated major known health risks associated with the disposal of hazardous wastes.

The achievement of this target will require the introduction of effective legislative, administrative and technical measures for the surveillance and control of hazardous wastes; and the introduction of effective measures to eliminate health risks due to previously dumped wastes.

24 *Human settlements and housing*

By the year 2000, all people of the region should have a better opportunity of living in houses and settlements which provide a healthy and safe environment.

The achievement of this target will require the acceleration of programmes of housing construction and improvement; the development of international health criteria for housing, space, heating, lighting, disposal of wastes, noise control and safety, while taking into account the special needs of groups such as young families, the elderly and the disabled; legislative, administrative and technical measures to comply with such criteria; the improvement of community planning in order to enhance health and well-being by improving traffic safety, providing open spaces and recreational areas, and the facilitating of human interaction, etc; and the equipment of all dwellings with proper sanitation facilities and the provision of sewers and an adequate public cleansing and wastes collection and disposal system in all human settlements of sufficient size.

25 *Working environment*
By 1995, people of the region should be effectively protected against work-related health risks.

The achievement of this target will require the introduction of appropriate occupational health services to cover the needs of all workers; the development of health criteria for the protection of workers against biological, chemical and physical hazards; the implementation of technical and educational measures to reduce work-related risk factors; and the safeguarding of especially vulnerable groups of workers.

26 *A system based on primary healthcare*
By 1990, all member states, through effective community representation, should have developed healthcare systems that are based on primary health-care and supported by secondary and tertiary care as outlined at the Alma Ata Conference.

This could be achieved by clear statements from the highest national author-ities and political leaders of all levels of authority in the health field, backed by effective legislation, regulations and plans, making primary healthcare the hub of the healthcare system, with secondary and tertiary levels in a supporting role and only carrying out those diagnostic and therapeutic functions that are too specialised to be carried out at the primary healthcare level; the establishment of effective ways and means of bringing consumer needs and interests to bear on the planning and delivery of primary healthcare; and free discussion with all groups of health personnel, supported by appropriate modifications of health manpower policies and programmes, to obtain their full commitment and support for carrying out this policy in their daily work. Such developments should take due account of the constitutional provisions of each member state.

27 *Rational and preferential distribution of resources*
By 1990, in all member states, the infrastructures of the delivery systems should be organised so that resources are distributed according to need, and that services ensure physical and economic accessibility and cultural accept-ability to the population.

This could be achieved by a combination of planned development and a wide range of carefully designed incentives to direct the necessary healthcare resources to the primary healthcare services, in order to ensure that the distribution of the services and the care they provide correspond to the needs of the population; and by similarly gradually readjusting hospital resources, wherever necessary, to form a system whereby secondary and tertiary care resources are distributed in a regionalised system according to needs.

28 *Content of primary healthcare*
By 1990, the primary healthcare system of all member states should provide a wide range of health-promotive, curative, rehabilitative and supportive services to meet the basic health needs of the population and give special attention to high-risk, vulnerable and underserved individuals and groups.

This could be achieved by establishing clear policies in all member states with a description of the full range of services that the primary healthcare system should provide, based on the principle that most preventive, diagnostic, thera-peutic and care services and activities could be provided outside hospitals and

other institutional settings; modifying basic and continuing education programmes for health personnel to ensure their active support for this development; and reviewing planning, referral and incentive systems to ensure that
they support these policies.

29 *Providers of primary health care*
**By 1990, in all member states, primary healthcare systems should be based on
cooperation and teamwork between healthcare personnel, individuals, families
and community groups.**

This could be achieved by policies in the countries that clearly define the role
that different categories of health and social personnel should play in healthcare; basic, specialist and continuing education programmes for health personnel that provide insight, motivation and skill in interprofessional teamwork and
in cooperation with individual families, groups and communities; and health
education programmes that provide a realistic picture of what services can be
expected from health professionals and give help in developing lay care skills.

30 *Coordination of community resources*
**By 1990, all member states should have mechanisms by which the services
provided by all sectors relating to health are coordinated at the community
level in a primary healthcare system.**

This could be achieved by recognising the responsibility of the primary healthcare sector to determine what matters require special attention, change and
reorientation, and to coordinate efforts in those directions; in each local community, where representatives of the community itself, and health and other
sectors can make joint analyses of local health plans and determine what contributions each sector should make to improving the health of the community.
Such mechanisms should, of course, be developed with due regard to the
various constitutional provisions of each member state.

31 *Ensuring quality of care*
**By 1990, all member states should have built effective mechanisms for
ensuring quality of patient care within their healthcare systems.**

This could be achieved by establishing methods and procedures for systematically monitoring the quality of care given to patients and making assessment
and regulation a permanent component of health professionals' regular activities; and providing all health personnel with training in quality assurance.

32 *Research strategies*
**Before 1990, all member states should have formulated research strategies to
stimulate investigations which improve the application and expansion of
knowledge needed to support their health for all developments.**

This target can be achieved if member states establish machinery to ensure the
effective application of new knowledge in the development of health policies
and programmes; determine what gaps there are in the knowledge needed to
support the strategy of health for all and set research priorities accordingly;
ensure a balanced representation of all academic disciplines relevant to health
and of providers and users of health services as well as health policy-makers, in
the planning and coordinating of research for health for all and make the
research community an active contributor to the development of health for all;
stimulate relevant multidisciplinary research; and allocate sufficient resources

to conduct the research needed, giving preference to aspects that have not received the support they deserve.

33 *Policies for health for all*

Before 1990, all member states should ensure that their health policies and strategies are in line with health for all principles and that their legislation and regulations make their implementation effective in all sectors of society.

This could be achieved if all countries were to make a systematic review of their health policies and health legislation in the light of the regional health for all strategy and targets, and to develop health for all strategies and targets and amend or extend their health legislation accordingly, taking due account of the specific legal, political and structural conditions in each member state.

34 *Planning and resource allocation*

Before 1990, member states should have managerial processes for health development geared to the attainment of health for all, actively involving communities and all sectors relevant to health and, accordingly, ensuring preferential allocation of resources to health development priorities.

Such a process should cover the systematic planning, monitoring and evaluation of health for all activities, with due regard to the specific legal, political and structural characteristics of each country.

35 *Health information systems*

Before 1990, member states should have health information systems capable of supporting their national strategies for health for all.

Such information systems should provide support for the planning, monitoring and evaluation of health development and services, the assessment of national, regional and global progress towards health for all and the dissemination of relevant scientific information; and steps should be taken to make health information easily accessible to the public.

36 *Planning, education and use of health personnel*

Before 1990, in all member states, the planning, training and use of health personnel should be in accordance with health for all policies, with emphasis on the primary healthcare approach.

This can be achieved if all countries analyse their needs for the different categories of health manpower required to implement their policies of health for all, adopt suitable health manpower policies, and decide on the numbers and educational qualifications required for each category of personnel.

37 *Education of personnel in other sectors*

Before 1990, in all member states, education should provide personnel in sectors related to health with adequate information on the country's health for all policies and programmes and their practical application to their own sectors.

This could be achieved if public policy stressed that health protection was also a key concern for sectors other than health, and training programmes for the personnel in such sectors stressed the reasons for actively supporting health for all activities.

38 *Appropriate health technology*

Before 1990, all member states should have established a formal mechanism for the systematic assessment of the appropriate use of health technologies and of their effectiveness, efficiency, safety and acceptability, as well as reflecting national health policies and economic restraints.

This could be done if governments adopted a clear policy for the systematic and comprehensive assessment of all new technical devices designed for use in the health field, to be carried out in a manner suited to the characteristics of their countries; and if an international system for the exchange of information on this subject were set up.

Index